Trials of Life

Oritsesemisan Megbele

chipmunkapublishing
the mental health publisher

Published by
Chipmunkapublishing
United Kingdom

http://www.chipmunkapublishing.com

Copyright © 2015 Oritsesemisan Megbele

ISBN   978-1-78382-229-4

Book Description

The books have been written by a diagnosed paranoid schizophrenic written with zeal for self actualisation and a test to awareness of our inner self, consciousness and may be sum up what this world we dwell in view of pain or suffering. What he feels are the issues related to his mental health and much more such as his beliefs paradigms of what brought suffering into the world. Are the gods or deities to be blamed because of suffering should he blame God for allowing suffering in the world?

He has partly written the books based on consistency and inconsistency of a child born premature. What sensitive, mysterious or enigmatic repercussions of being a premature child the consequence of its relation to science of medicine, modern-day technology, and ways of life from different perspectives.

His books implies effigies of what dense molecular structures could stamina, equal, or have the same interplay to the molecular structure as, that of superman a crucifix or juju? Implying I am superman might mean as Orunmila I had picked something up from planet Krypton and divested myself of my powers as Orunmila or to refine myself more based on trials of life. The author is a child born in the UK during the Biafra war in Nigeria he and his immediate elder brother with their mother left the UK for Nigeria by sea just after he was born.

If any love is right if ever two stars was crossed, if ever the touch was right if ever there was love and it is right while relationships we have seems not to fad, it was you and that person you coup and get along with because, we are now at a time when the rain is trickling down the window screen.

The book accounts for his early childhood experience, family upbringing, background, culture, politics and family history how he became unwell, hospitalised and diagnosed with paranoid schizophrenia detailed with episodes of his life trials.

His books are a continuation of more than four series. He gives account of people he has the notion are the reincarnation of late members of his family in the UK. His hopes for the future, how hearing voices have been part of his everyday life and his own account of the illness schizophrenia. If you should read his other books titled memories of a schizophrenia, paradigm of my schizophrenia and the worth of our experience all based on family history which encapsulate modern ways of living, his perceptions of mental illness and life such as what are the basis for being in this world his readers are left to the strong and powerful paradigms on which the authors books have been written. He also gives account about his care, working life and the people around him. Haven written his books he hope his cares, family and friends might understand his thoughts, emotions, about life in general and what he is going through under an illness of paranoid schizophrenia.

About The Author

I lost my mother just after I took resident at my number 13 Gorman road block of flats. Within this period my father Chief (Dr) Frank Anirejuoritse Megbele the Agbueju of Warri Kingdom was on a visit to the United Kingdom with his new and fourth wife Mrs. Tsainomi Ayo Megbele.

After my mothers' death I received a massage from my father in Nigeria through Mrs. Comfort Iyinboh from Delta state I should not travel to Nigeria for my mothers' funeral.

No reason was given why I should not be in Nigeria for my mother's funeral at Ibadan in Oyo state I became distress. I called my immediate elder brother Mr. Omagbemi Oluwagbenga Megbele when I heard my father was about to pay his second visit to the UK after our arrival back into the UK just after mother's death; I told him I would not let my father enter my council flat.

On my father's visit to my flat with my brother Mr. Omagbemi, I did not let my father into my flat after which I began feeling unusual, feelings of insecurity. I found myself wandering with long walks but not confused as to where, I was going. It was as if I was carrying great rituals of (Etutu or Ebo) into heaven. Etutu or Ebo in Yuroba means sacrifices to solve problems or suffering. We all know what sacrifice is the giving up or foregoing of some valued thing for the sake of something of greater value or having a more pressing claim. The most complex form of sacrifice one can give is change. Most of us are yet to realize that the spiritual realm like the physical one requires some sort of giving in order to receive.

After the incident at my blocks of flat, about three or four months later without seeing my brother he visited me with a lady friend Ms. Nwamaka now Mrs. Nwamaka Megbele, it was my first time of seeing her and I never knew they were coming; I was not sure of myself of what was going on around me or what was wrong with me.

The same thing happened on this their visit to my flat I would not let my brother and his lady friend into my flat.

One morning as I was walking down to the Woolwich Spray street job centre after my early morning job at the club by Woolwich New Road a police vehicle with two police officers pulled up just by me without asking any question pulled me into their vehicle and drove off.

They took me to the Greenwich hospital at Vanbrugh Hill; after a few discussions with the receptionist, they took me into its mental health ward. This was in 1995 where I was diagnosed as a paranoid schizophrenic.

I find it difficult believing am going through what I was going through at the time, in spite of it, I did not believe I still had the strength to coup and recap with my every thoughts and feelings which were always sober.

Then I began writing about thing that has happened to me from my childhood as a schizophrenic with premature birth.

I feel fortunate having the opportunity to come out with these epilogues of my life regardless of my illness if I do not come out with it, nobody would know or tell. Have you ever in your life thought of whatever you deed or went through when you were a kid that wasn't right and wasn't your fault?

Have you ever thought in your life you had to pay the price for a wrong that was not your fault when you reminiscence? If it's all gone wrong for you, it's about time you sit down and tell I told myself one afternoon, it's all up to me at least I would know if it had been my fault or if, they weren't mine.

I find myself talking to myself in my sleep and when am awake from my sleep, I hear voices telling me to do things to herm myself, make myself inferior or adhere to what they tell me to do. Each day I find myself going through different stages without knowing if they are mental health issues or not, I find myself feeling depressed with less control of myself are they as a result of my schizophrenia which, I do not wholly accept I believe what is left of me and my appearance is myself residual self image comprising of my digital self. Any one walking along the street, would take me like any other individual walking in our street in London while at the same time I long for people to realise that I have been scotched nevertheless, I pose myself to live as any other normal person would.

I consider I have to reform my digital self so that no one would notice the inconsistencies attached to my mental illness, I have programmed my physically and spiritually to up-hold myself against the beast that rules and exist within me.

My mind and soul seek to live within my very body because it suits my purpose. It's for a reality having an assurance to completely divest myself with nothing left of me, but just my residual self image, could this be why I am a paranoid schizophrenic?.

The illness has an attribute of making a sufferer live a life of abnormalities such as being senseless to the right applicable things or attitude that are customary when, they are required to be applied in once daily life, they way you view the world its people and its environment. It is often initiated by other people in certain aspects of the illness this can be ascertained by feeling their presence, aura, and mirage or through hearing their voices in such case try to understand the spirit level in which they present or portray themselves.

A dreadful feeling if you care to outlive the illness is you live in fear you cannot control yourself only if you are well-disposed to yourself and to others, having feelings for the safety of your life or wellbeing having such temperament is a good start if one is to outlive or capable of managing with the illness the most dreadful part is that as much as you try the situation are always seems uncertain for the rest of once life.

Bibliography

This whole writing of mine over many periods of my illness; brought about a father and son poem which was read by me on father's day 15th Of June 2008 at Saint Michael and all Angels Church Woolwich just by Frances street SE18
It reads and titled perhaps we'll never understand each other..........

Perhaps we'll never understand each other
Loving doesn't mean that we agree
If that were so, then I would say, why bother?
But there are things I know I'll never see
I'm sure your heart knows what I don't yet know;
The pain of loving a reluctant son;
The anger, coming fast, and building slow
Of being helpless to control someone
You want only that I grow up right,
But you know what right is, and I still don't.
I have to learn to wield my inner light,
And if I follow yours, well, then I won't.
I'm sorry for the anger in the air;
Though we fight, my love is always there.

What is a true relationship between a father and son? I began to contemplate. Who among a father and a son relationship is more obliged?

From an appointment on the 10th of February 2009, I know through Dr Hughes, he is a member of the medical organization called balance bipolar. Before the appointment, I had already written documents about my life and experience as a diagnosed paranoid schizophrenia Dr. Robert Hughes gave me addresses of web sites relating to bipolar.

When I surf the internet about bipolar spectrum and related sits on schizophrenia I could not help but ask myself am I really a schizophrenic? Several times I have posted or handed word processed documents about my writings to Dr Hughes including other associates of his at the Ferryview health centre.

The organization in 1990 came up with the Bipolar Spectrum Diagnostic Scale of patients with mental health issues. The scale was developed by Dr Roland Pies with his permission included on the website. I was interested on exploring if it could rather be I am not suffering from schizophrenia or rather suffering from bipolar spectrum diagnostic scale or if my so called illness was just a general effect of several life inconsistencies such as my being born premature, or as a result a broken relationship within both my parents?

In their opinion, they interpreted individuals, who experience manic depression could take ten years, getting correct diagnosis. Bipolar disorder is said to be a psychiatrist diagnosis describing categories of mood disorders, which invariably, could be defined by the presences of one or more episodes of abnormalities in a person's life.

One thought that came to my mind because of my condition of birth and most of the things I have gone and pulled through was, am I something of a superhuman.

I was at the Charlton disability resource centre 16 Sandpit Place, Erwood Road SE7 8HE to see Mr. Daniel, Mr. Dilip and Mr. Paul Clayton working at its I.T. section every Tuesday and Wednesdays of the week, to surf the internet, improve my I.T. skills. I photocopied a questioner based on the Bipolar Spectrum Diagnostic Scale of Manic depression.

At the time I went through the bipolar questioners Dr Hughes gave me, I began considering if I have been suffering from manic depression or suffering from paranoid schizophrenia. I suffer from mood swing and other symptoms. My observations is people suffering from bipolar are impressionist but are not good at it while schizophrenias display outgoing characteristics' I am outgoing, good at taking details the more I see myself as a schizophrenia not a bipolar.

At Greenwich hospital in 1995, my doctors, psychiatrist and care workers at the time of my admission, did not discuss with me what my illness was about! Within 1995 and 2009 other drugs had been manufactured for the cure of mental illness and depression. Just like Quetiapine Seroquel tablets which I am now on; of which I prefer minimal dosage because my metabolism is very sensitive.

This was the real reason I had an appointment with Dr Hughes on this very day the 10th of February 2009, because, Dr. Chatterjee my psychiatrist suggest, I go for higher dosage with my continual treatment through medication I often feel my molecular system and structure are revitalized through medication.

I often felt my mood going through lots of changes, energy level shifts drastically from time to time radiating with the sun, which takes place every so often. My energy level are never low, if they become low I am moved to surmounts my energy again and revive myself.

I never feel lack of energy, I dread nothing, but hope nothing dreadful would occur to me with bipolar sufferers they usually become agitated not accompanied with vocal but with impression one can easily read their moods because they ascribe it to their feelings. One of the weak points with mental health problems is that families, doctors and cares never notice you for what you are they generally do have their own inclinations they never take note of how patients try to outlive the illness in their own terms.

If my thoughts and deeds are not as good, as other people feel it should be, if they are aware of my condition, why should I always receive negative impressions? People who give me impression of my illness should not make me feel bias or I will feel repressed. Would it help me to resuscitate myself in all goodness out of my reverie especially during relapse?

I never feel helpless; my ability to function at work is not socially impaired except if I am confronted with anything about my job from another person with deliberate intention to out-do or distract me. I have low days without reason some times, or with consideration on certain impending matters that could make me feel low, with normal moods in between mood swing.

I hardly have high moods I neither suffer from feeling irrational or irritation. I could be on edge not to other people but to myself, which leaves me very thoughtful as I try at each stage to be at ease within myself.

Through the internet on bipolar web site; I came about screening questioners initially developed for use by clinicians, which are also used by many individuals as the starting point for discussing health care plane.

Their intention was its use will lead to accurate diagnosis earlier than might otherwise be the case, with a scale said to be applicable to the entire spectrum of Bipolar disorder.

Based on my assessment, the bipolar spectrum diagnosis scale was intended as a substitute for professional opinion and advice. Being a schizophrenia I want to shear my experience with other people and those who care for me based on what I had word processed on; in relation to my illness before Dr Robert Hughes introduced me to the questioners and Bipolar web-site.

In my opinion the second phase after diagnosed schizophrenia is manic or chronic depression. As far back from when I was diagnosed as schizophrenia, I seem to be doing fine, but as time went by, with the worlds event, and predicaments which I was faced with e.g. disappointments, I became more depressed and unsettled.

As I read through the Bipolar spectrum diagnosis scale in its web site; it all sort of fit in to my experiences each day with my illness, though the intention of the diagnosis scale is based on hope it will lead to accurate diagnosis. Several years after being diagnosed as a paranoid schizophrenia the Bipolar spectrum diagnosis scale relates in certain ways on what I have been going through or wants me to be I had to pull myself out of the reverie by continued writing.

Some of the symptoms I suffer from are:
I often notice my mood and energy level change drastically

from time to time.

I experience at certain times, my mood and energy level is low or high.

During low phases of my illness, I tend to feel lack of energy, a need to stay in bed lying down or get extra sleep. Little or no motivation to do things I need to do such as doing my house chaos going to the gym, parties or cinema are out of the question.

I do often put on weight especially when am on certain medication or I eat too much an example of such medication is Olanzapine which I have been on since the month of March 2009, My Olanzapine had then been reduced to 10 milligram in the month of May from 15 milligram.

During low phase of my illness I feel blue, sometimes sad or depressed.

During low phases of my illness, I could feel hopeless or helpless having something to do or a job in short; thinking of such prospects is good resuscitation for out coming of such dilemmas.

But not in my ability to function at work or my socially interaction impaired working or having something to do keeps me preoccupied which take my mind, thoughts, feelings out of predicaments of my illness or what goes on around me especially if they do not interest me or are setbacks.

Typically these low phases could last for two weeks or for a month sometimes, they may last only for a few days. I could experience periods of normal mood in between mood swing, during which my mood and energy levels feels right, with my ability to function like any normal individual who are not disturbed.

I do notice marked shift or switch; in the way I feel sometimes, going through phase I should talk to myself aloud which really disturbed me or people are inside me who can be identified talking to me this really did disturbed me as well. They can confuse my thoughts or bulge into my thoughts as if there is a voodoo act they want to posses not only my soul but also my physical nature.

My energy level dose increases above normal or decrease for me to get things done, which a normal person or most other paranoid schizophrenia would not be able to do.

During certain phase of my illness, I feel as if, I have too much energy or feel hyper for example having feelings that I brought they sun shine with me from Africa to the UK, the streets light and candles lights at church radiate all around me creating a sense of vigour around me and within my every movement. At each phase, we are talking about a lot self control here!

I could take note of too many activities at one time though I might not be involved. I spend money on things I shouldn't have bought or have no use for I could all of a sudden change my mind. I am no talkative as I used to be when I was young; I am an outgoing sort of person. I do not feel outgoing sexually this does not mean I am gay I could be expressive.

My behaviour does not seem strange or annoying to other people. I have not frequently gone into conflict with co-workers or have had any problem with the police involved. I could have been an alcoholic at certain times and a chain smoker, but I do not take non-prescribed drugs cocaine, marijuana or ecstasy etc never had I taken any of such drugs. If I do, the easier my life and soul could be taken over by people who enforce voodoo or juju.

Apart from the above; I sometimes lose interest and pleasure in doing things which interest me when am feeling down, depressed and helpless, I could have too much sleep while some times I could find it difficult having a good night sleep.

Sometimes I find it difficult reading e.g. news papers, watching television, up-grading my computer skills reading or practicing on my computer at certain points I could suffer from feelings I have been let down on all aspect of my life. Worry thoughts go through my mind, I hardly feel cheerful. I get feeling something is churning in my stomach, which could result to my having less interest or feeling good about things I do or the food I eat.

I do not frequently have thought of harming myself but it occurs in my mind to do so when I suffer from relapses during very depressed relapse. A sufferer might fall deeper into such temperaments with emotions affected. In my case my relapse are not drug related it has to do with my moods, feelings, thoughts and how I coup. I get sudden feelings of panic, which makes me restless moods of being tensed and wound-up then I coil into a shell like a snail.

The effect of my panic attack are stimulating myself up in cases of fear of uncertainties, if things should go wrong it's a good sign because it makes me respond to endeavours we all have its feeling inside our subconscious in an event of something especially if it is something we favour. It could be the reveres.

Each day I find it difficult enjoying things I love to do for example word processing. I frequently have feelings that am in an awful situation about my life, with a sense of insecurity.

Being mentally healthy does not mean one could not suffer from mental illness. Mental illness is another terminology for low emotional health or wellbeing. We all have time in our lives when we feel down, stressed out or frightened going through invigorating period or mood sometimes make us feel the same way. For some people, such feelings pass by, I mean they overcome it. For other people, it develops into a more serious problem. It could happen to any one of us.

Each individual is different you may be able to overcome a setback, while some other people may not be able to overcome their set back. With some of us, through such setbacks our mental health might not always stay the same, difficult it would become in overcoming such setbacks or disappointment if our lives had been filled with too many inconsistencies especially at that very particular time.

Some of which weighs down on our lives, stereotyping could be involved or we have become imbalance in our perception. Planet earth is not the same as it was 50,100 or a billion years ago. We live in an ever changing world. Mental illness in any given community signifies intolerance, the failure or downfall of that community.

I published this book with some help from Mr. Paul Clayton, Mr. Daniel and Mr. Dilip who were my assistants at the GDRC centre. Question always pop-up in my mind such as what really is the meaning of mental illness. I do not believe we know what they are really about, what we know is always left in a closet door issues involve are delicate and concerns everybody within the community though there are treatment and medication, more still need to be done by the science of medicine, each community as a whole need to come out with sure awareness and cure for the illness.

Everyone has heard of the word schizophrenics, it has become a part of our daily lives within any community all over the world most people do not know what it is, or what courses the illness and what could be done for sufferers some nation have done much while some have done nothing.

People have different ideas about the illness. One example of such opinion is that schizophrenic means suffering from personality disorder why so; we all suffer from personality disorder of course there are degrees to different types of personality disorder. Mental illness, is a mask other people would differentiate they are not wearing the mask to dignify themselves such people are indifferent to people suffering from mental illness.

A person likely suffer from personality disorder because probably their lives have been distorted by
What! By other people making you what you are, their environmental, social and economic, ways of livelihood, background, race, tradition or culture. Personality differs in wide arrays of environment humans have difficulties deciding what is real or not real this, is one reason why we exist. Diagnosis of mental illness which is just a fraction of human context deals with terminologies relating to humans.

For some of us, existence is like having dreams, elucidations and dilemma which, progress into anxiety why? Because we are living in this always changing world our ways of life changes every decade strange things happen. Could the illness be as a result to perceptive mind of a sufferer?

For example If I wake up one morning to see my GP tell him or her I have been going on astral travelling in my sleep, I see myself coming out of my body floating above my body and I fly by night when am asleep I would be told, to go and see a psychiatrist. It would be termed as personality disorder. If you say you travel at night during your sleep as superman or you feel you are superman you are likely to be referred to the nearest hospital mental health home treatment team yet we dwell in a planet where we are yet to see its real view.

I might just be sleeping on my bed it becomes as if am in another world each day seems like something new and different from the one gone by. Rarely can some sufferer put it into any full meaning or assimilation what are such affects on them coupled that most schizophrenics are unable to put into meaning what causes them to suffer from paranoia's related to schizophrenia or how the illness really evolves. Then I for example begin to experience strange things.

Sufferers should be treated and cared for with the outmost care and tenderness, giving them an assurance that help is at hand, we are yet to know, what the illness, its effects, symptoms and treatment is, or which is a right treatment for a patients speedy recovery within different ethnic background. I came to a conclusion that the bipolar spectrum feet into my experiences mind you, the bipolar spectrum was only based on speculations.

Some schizophrenia could come out with outburst, or aggression unexpectedly this should not be the case. Though some sufferers are resilient enough through their own developed method to outlive the illness. Such are the delicate once. There should be put on less frustration and in other to reduce anger, or the patients becomes aggression, anxiety or depression or annoyed depending on the situation might become confused. If help is not at hand at such a stage to put them in a positive mental attitude and reassurance things might go wrong. Anger, frustration and aggression means the patient have collapse on the hands of their family or cares.

It is not only a medical illness; sufferers should be reassert to keep taking their medication with periodic assessment on the effect of their medication. Some patients show positive sings but are unable to outlive the illness. Some of us suffer from medication fever, which I do suffer from. The cause or what is really the illness schizophrenia is yet to be known it is revealing each day that the illness is deadly it eats into people's lives, soul and wellbeing.

If the illness is well known about? It would likely be the patient who has the knowledge to know more about the illness in some ways that reaches the core on how it affects them put it into meaning in their own way relate it to their lives and in respect to how the illness affects them and what it is doing to them. If this could be done they suffer less but often the most depressed once should be under care before they go into negative stages of hallucination.

Not all patients are able to do this not being able to do so, some of us, could become apprehensive this, is a good sign because, the patient could welcome and accept treatments and advice. Nobody has his or her full mental faculty. I have used the word (Phrenic) to infer; 'several levels' because I wonder why bipolar is measured on a scale.

A mental disorder or mental illness apparently is a psychological or behavioural pattern generally associated with subjective distress or disability that occurs in an individual, and which is not a part of normal development or culture Could this be true?

The recognition and understanding of mental health conditions has changed over time and across cultures, and there are still variations in the definition, assessment, and classification of mental disorders, although standard guideline criteria are widely accepted.

A few mental disorders are diagnosed based on harm to others base the subject's on perception, mood and distress. Any means of confronting the subject should not initiate aggression. Over a third of people in most countries report meeting criteria for the major categories of being harmful at some point in their lives.

The effect of being a schizophrenic is strong and strange. I suffer strange emotions in relation to everything. I seem to live in two different worlds or even three.

Better if the effect is not as if, your whole world is about to hit the rock not all mental health sufferers are the same. Some of us behave normally. If the concept of bipolar was a reality, it was arrived at philosophically and psychiatrically before hand, before the effects are now being experience in the lives of patients all over the world.

It is believed schizophrenics are a violent, dangerous or come very too often with outburst which occurs when frustrated or angry regardless of such symptoms' some of us are quiet, timid and fearful at times. Uncertainty leading to insecurity or just one little misshape in a person's life could trigger the illness such when a person is dehumanised.

Some people who are not schizophrenia do also have violent outbursts when they are frustrated or angry which gives me the idea there are degrees of being phrenic. Majority of schizophrenics are prone to be attacked on the street for no reason by other people.

The UK with its structure of civilisation with a multi-cultured race from e all over the globe, result into multi-complex ways of people doing things, living and conglomerating easily in some part of the world may not be difficult, in some other part it's the opposite.

Personality disorder could be either true or false if it is being imposed it is true, if it is imposed by the sufferer themselves it is false. In either case, they may be happy with it or rejects it. If it is being imposed on a sufferer it is left in the hands of psychologist or an exorcist, or the Church who could deliberate on such imposed personality disorder.

Any sufferer is likely to be provoked, attacked by friends or families or people they do not know, this could happen within sufferers themselves. Schizophrenia is now a major mental illness all over the world. Looking at it from perspective the illness affects every aspect of a sufferer's life.

Something important to me in my life, I would not kiss goodbye as I reminiscent each day is my reality. Regardless if I am now residing in the UK certain things still affects my everyday life and expectations as they were whilst, I was in Africa. Most sufferer are sensitive individual which is one reason why they are schizo, schizo in my own terms means 'effects'.

The illness always cause problems for sufferers in their everyday life going through different stages of the illness with defaults, their thinking, thoughts may be jumble, unclear and not precise, not all sufferers reach these stage, it is a positive signs of recovery rather than collapsing at certain unexpected phase depress mood, anxiety, frustration might weakens a sufferers defence, isolation, wondering about without knowing what to do or where to turn. Wondering about dose not only mean walking about, the mind, soul thoughts and feelings could suffer from the same effect.

Some of them for example may think of going to the gym, leisure, day care activity as an option coming out of the reverie of the illness, because they are often depress, such activity might not interest some of them. This is likely to be a critical point in the life of some people who are about to suffer from mental illness.

Cares should be more careful at this stage if the patient is agitated or seems confused, what the cares need do is work a little bit harder for the sufferer or patient succumbing to therapy, such symptom I do have when going through a phase of relapse I feel I should be helped and encouraged to come out with my feelings.

Some sufferers would shy from anything that could make life worthwhile. They would seem rather perplexed. If those around them i.e. family, friends, or cares are not rapid enough to pull the patient out of such reverie the patients care at these early stages might not be productive.

Other attempt to revive the patient can be to take up sport, reading, writing, and knitting, prepare meals e.g. baking bread or listen to music. Some of these could take a patients mind off drinking, smoking or taking drugs; even if it's for a short period of time. Not all schizophrenia displays the same degree of symptoms of interest or anxiety.

After the initial stage, if a patient is not recovering they go through several relapse which comes with lack of concentration, thinking quickly or clearly and feeling sulky. Their symptoms might become worse, if they are left frustrated or something bad happens during such stage.

This could begin to result to personality disorder it could be resolved if the sufferer is alleviated from anything that is bordering them or causes the disorder. Infarct, at that stage, they could have a job and be very good at their job because it would have added as a therapy.

Conversation with other people family or neighbours could be troublesome at times e.g. because of family problem a sufferer may be preoccupied with their own thoughts, while feelings of frustration could set in. Have any one ever asked what could the reason for sufferers becoming frustrated? Our cars do not go into these in details on our care planes they only attribute it to benefit, housing, immigration needs.

Frustration is a mental health problem it has to do with all aspects of our lives, our environment or the level at which each individual can coup. It could likely be because they still care for their thoughts, feelings and needs or whatever they cannot do but wish they could do. This is a good sign which could lead to positive recovery.

It is of paramount importance at such early stage opportunities are given to a patients to reconcile. I don't know how I do mine, it just comes to me, or maybe it's because I feel am blessed, or that I am not really human on earth. It comes a time when some schizophrenia sufferer cannot care for themselves; they become carefree, helpless and neglect themselves even further this is where advice or therapy comes in. I feel most mental health sufferers do more harm to themselves than to others e.g. suicide but not frequently murder while some of them could feel differently.

5th April 2010 the first TV advert in view of tackling issues of suicide was to be aired during commercial breaks in Scotland. About two people a day in Scotland take their own life which continues to be a leading cause of death in young people.

Those behind the campaign were of the opinion the target audience for the government backed up advert were within men aged between 18 and 44 years. I was really reassured about the news on television hearing the public health minister Shona Robison say helping people break the silence surrounding suicide is very vital within our communities.

We know of some symptoms that come into mind when we talk about schizophrenia i.e. not sleeping or eating well, cannot wash the clothes, difficulties at the bathroom, ironing, cleaning, eating the right meal, visiting relatives, phoning friends and families in the UK and abroad, finance is another matter. It's so sad when schizophrenia sufferers go through such phase, if help is not at hand or something have not been down about it, it makes them feel frustrated I can understand frustration is something we all go through in this case, there is an illness involved

With early diagnosis, treatment and care, sufferers might suffer minimal effect it was what occurred in my own case. At the early stage while cares would invariably; detect when to move on, to the next stage of their patients' treatment. If not handled properly something might go wrong. Such as go out with group friends taking drugs then feeling suicidal. At this point, psychiatrists, cares and social care workers, might not be able to handle a mental health patient impulse.

They might attack cares and social worker's. It is always surprising, it is at such stages, psychiatrist, cares and social worker show concern when something have drastically gone wrong.

I hear voices; I hallucinate, have unusual beliefs of what have been done to me in the past or about things that have gone wrong in the past and present. I look into the future with anxiety; my strongest strength is I can go through frustration because I have realities about myself based on things and experience I have gone through some of which are for my own adjudication.

No matter how am frustrated I always feel I have a strongest link, create avenues in continued resilience towards confronting my life and my illness. In 2009, I was 43 years of age all I have left, is what life has to offer in outliving my illness before I unleash this evil spells I fight with my existence or to hold back in this, I hope the last phase of my existence.

I cannot say I know how my illness has developed could it had been because expectations had fall short which has made me heartfelt I feel scotched or is it, this force around me to over look the dark side and not let it take over me.

If Sufferers go through stages of manipulation, it leads to frustration or it raises questions. It is most common with people with certain morals at their teens not based on self will, who seek reasons to have been a simple minded individual and innocent. In my case my life has been filled with me playing great roll in all aspect of my life with a weak point of not being a go getter. There are founded concepts to outlive mental illness it most have been founded from when they were young existence is based on trials of life. Lots of things are said about people with mental health issues could it be said their lives are not symbolic?

Symbolic interaction is a sociological theory that places emphasis on <u>micro-scale</u> <u>social interaction</u> to provide subjective meaning in human behaviour, the social process and <u>pragmatism</u>.

This is useful in solving complex social problems. People act toward things based on the meaning those things have for them; and these meanings are derived from social interaction and modified through interpretation. Human beings are best understood in relation to their environment. 'These meanings are handled in, and modified through, an interpretative process used by the person in dealing with the things he/she encounters.'

Thus, human interaction is mediated by the use of symbols and signification, by interpretation, or by ascertaining the meaning of one another's actions thus connotes emphases on symbols, negotiated meaning, and social construction of society.

Symbolism is the practice of representing things by symbols, or of investing things with a symbolic meaning or character. A <u>symbol</u> is an object, action, or idea that represents something other than itself.

I have lived complex lives relating to many different people. In my own case it becomes eminent to neutralise myself into position's of consultation of theories instead of hypotheses. I would described the illness as no different a scenario after a phase when someone goes through after a war in which the things you love were lost, in which you see yourself in a dream; you find yourself faced with bitter emotions except but for a star shinning above your head your only hope, is to reach out for that star to either see through it or hold it in your hand in which there is light and there is darkness such is the only way I would describe the phenomenon.

The illness is coursed when some people with moral capability choose to do things morally, philosophical or physically right, but things went wrong. Why and how are there countless ways witchcraft, voodoo, juju, modern day frustrations in our ways of live we still sell our lives to the devil for a price if you have lived a good moral life, you can nearly outlive the illness the illness, is like an Omen.

Especially when surfer's no longer have no real capability, motivation to choose willingly to undertake or not to take action which comes in various ways in their mind and attitude about their lives. In most cases, they might have taken actions already which they might have regretted or lucky enough to have avoided. In whichever case, they become unwell; if over powered by the real fullness of the source of the illness I quote 'the sours of their illnesses'.

This is not farfetched when it is possible for an individual to take over another person's soul, mind and body e.g. a sufferers becomes overpowered by the real fullness of the source that could later in a person life, cause mental health.

It could have been caused through lack of working as a team in a family or within an environment with too much empowerment which lack respect for individuality, within friends, community or working environment. This is why in the 21st century our homes, community and working environment are nothing else but institutions.

When you look at all the disadvantages of a business or a working environment, if the disadvantages outweighs its advantage, expectation could fall short for some people they become depress, take up drinking, become an alcoholic or take up smoking and later in life take heard drugs leading to suicide more so if they grow-up from an unstable family or environment.

What then is the illness schizophrenia? It is about something that you want, but you cannot have or you are compelled by nature or is it a trial of life. It could be because of something all men and women of power want which you also seek which is one factor that is actually spinning planet earth around; it is customary people would do anything for money, you could be wealthy today or you could have been running a business if it all go bust you friends would desert you in some cases if you suffer from mental illness, your family may desert you depending on your family background.

You could be lucky enough on how the illness affect's you if you are realistic because then one can be resilient to coup probably accept the consequences of the illness or disappointment as a trials of life. Mental illness are caused by varied factors more than because of the lost of a love one, it could be because of hat, greed, disappointments; it could be because you are special it could also be what our sub-consciousness want it to be in other to bring the best out of us or it may be to you and me asking questions about relates issues and experiences if they are religious or philosophical.

In the 1980 Africa, Jamaica, India, Barbados, Caribbean and India children born in the UK were given open doors to come back into the UK as to improvise intervention on immigration. What have been given to such no longer children but adults from their parental native land coming back into the UK is to ascertain through our experience e.g. how with our African parental background we could blend into the British community as Britain move closer into EU relationship.

Other reason is for the British relationship with for example West Africa nations should become stronger, productive in relationship and better understanding of each other. As some of these UK born children from other countries come into the UK, they improvised, assimilating themselves into new ways of life, they have to re-adjust and improvise for what they have or something they lack in life.

While African British children who have lived in the UK all their lives, immune from what their parental native land is all about. Because of this, I decided to write and tell my life story as part of my mental illness. I am not only from two different cultures in Nigeria; I was bread in Africa for 22 years and have now, spent 22 years in the UK.

In my case among many others in the same shoe like me as African born British, life is full of expectation especially when you have to live Africa for the UK as a British citizen. It's a time to start readjusting to a new life; Britain is not the same place as one would find in Africa.

One thing is for sure is planet earth subsuming? Surrogacy, cloning of humans, being gay, a lesbian, transsexual, genetic illness, climate change, solar energy, mental illness and organic food. There are lots of questions and answered to be asked in vast arrays one cannot but contemplate if planet earth subsuming!

If I need readjust, what would be the comparison of amplitude with those who come into the UK as asylum seeker merging the relationship of other nations and Britain? Opportunities are always for grabs it's quite a distinguishing trait of all humans. With those born African British who have lived all their lives in the UK I want to cheer my experiences and undertaking's with you all we have lots of thinking and assimilation to undertake.

It is inevitable that history is always repeating itself and being abused coupled that it is common for history to repeat itself; blessed are those who choose to undergo their trials of life and pray not for ease that their way should be whatever they want out of life those who are the go getters would do it for them. Blessed also are every individual who keep themselves intact for the sake of improving humanity, to renounce all evil. It's what every woman child should want to accomplish.

It is by choice for one to assimilating once self into humanity. I have arrived into a stage of self individuality of human impulse. If as Superman I never chose to divest myself, I would have become nothing else, but an astro, or a hydroid or a human without muscular co-ordination. I rather have chosen to divest myself under trials of life. In relation to my present life as an African for the goodwill of Africa that there would be no recurrence of primitive characteristics that were not present in distance ancestors but in the present once.

At certain days and time, if I walk certain distance; it seems as if, I have been walking about two miles as if, the walk have no end these occur mostly during sunshine and during when the moon is on the sky I am like a shadow at such times when walking on the street.

At such time I experience feeling of weightlessness', floating into the air, with a feeling I am assimilating into the air with a sensation of just being a spirit and a soul with no muscular but just my physics.

Having such experiences I am assimilating myself within a

body comprising of my soul, spirit within a body with form and recognition of my body impulse for example it is a common sight finding schizophrenia haggard, on tattered clothes or hasn't had a bath for three days I might be well clothed and have had my bath each day at certain times, I might moved to do or feel the same way. I try each day in my meditation to understand the world behind the spiritual and the human soul. Sometimes to my understanding its nothing but void, a thin air into space, where there are bubbles of balls with different colours bouncing against each other all around me.

These experiences often occur more on sunny days and towards the evenings. After such experience I usually feel powerful, not has superman sort of able to lift up a car. I feel complete, revitalized with spiritual strength and awareness, with no general body weakening. If am not on earth to face reality, I am here to reside in certain respect of preconditions. Everything of ancient history always catches my fancy. They seems to draw me closer, it could be a slab, sculpture or a relics.

I feel a need to be in Great Britain is to ask question on what are the reality of being an Africa and being African British at the same time being part of the European nation, my obligations to my parents and the obligations my parents owe me should reconcile this also applied to my brothers and sisters, relatives and friends.

If my background and family had caused any incoherencies of which other people were displeased, they are my parents and relatives, I could in time do justice to the obligation they owed any one that was never fulfilled or they were displeased about and the once I owe them. I would not let it be done for me because, they are my family. It could be just anybody because of personal grudge, with some people outside my family.

Conflicts within families should be avoided so we can sort out indifferences. As it says in the Holy Bible children would bear the sins of their fathers and forefathers if so, why should family relationship continue to deepen this has become wide spread within Africans within the UK why should we continue putting ourselves in a state of derisory?

If this is the case, two brothers need not be in conflicts, or one brother dominating the other one. Because in effect, they are suppose to pioneer obligations that entwines them as brothers within their family in other to lighten the burden of the community in which they reside.

Not just anybody should come into their family and do it for them they would usurp a family member infarct probably the whole family why should they have been children to their parents in the first place? Lot of Africans come into the UK for all sorts of reason let us make our stay or visits worthwhile.

Throughout my upbringing, I have been initiated into a nation and background, in which I am influenced by other people within or outside my own family who predominantly seek to be domineering over each other which is constantly becoming unavoidable within relationships it triggers conflicts and mental illness depending on the circumstances.

With reasons I feel people should not observe my residing in the UK as a sugar coated topping in my hands I am faced with confronting myself, my background and my identity. Writing this book, is not taking liberty, one has to be wise, collaborative and not be an avoider in other to reset many of life's incoherence's. I live an isolated life, socially withdrawn, I prefer other people get to know me better but how without imposing on others? It is human nature to be very sceptical. It is not conflicting with me because, I am as open hearted as a Seagull bird not all mental health sufferers are scatterbrains.

I feel sensitive living among the Europeans and that I originate from Africa. Infarct for me, it is an accomplishment, an accomplishment which irrevocably is justified if I adhere to principles, realities and trials of life.

After Superman would have circle the universe to undo the cause of his reversing the cause of nature, which Miss. Julie my co-worker at Iceland frozen food plc Lewisham was aware of. I would describe her as someone who had in several past lives through reincarnation lived as a country girl in America. She always wear tights, she is one person who felt something strange about me that I could be Superman, she at one time referred to me as the man on the moon she is one person who made me realise that as it is in heaven so it is on earth.

Superman had to later in his existence, bow before the gods of nature, for him to divest himself from his rob, and strength, to be like any other human being.

Superman's has been reincarnating through several different lives as one of the pillars of the universe, become man to strife with humanity. For someone like my co-worker Miss. Julie it was not something to go unnoticed because she as well, had lived several lives through repeated trials of reincarnation, just as anyone would undergo trials in freemasons when duly and thoroughly called upon.

Every human must before the clock and cycle of Superman is completed reincarnate through several life cycles for what, they hope would be their last reincarnation. By going through repeated trials of life, to become like the son of man to dwell with the body which have taken its defined form with which, to dwell with for all eternity?

Without pain or sorrow, to become like angels living in define spiritual form, I have been soul searching for many centuries. Do not take those mental health sufferers who you see on the street dirty with tattered clothing as all jokes and antisocial behaviours there are devils in them fighting them for something they have by nature.

Our lives all over the world are filled with all sorts of stereotyping partly of our own making I feel my existence had been set to undergo extrication from life in body to a defined spiritual form. I like the body with which I am at the moment dwelling with on earth. There is nothing more enjoyable than the exhilarating feeling I get from the sun shine above on my dark skin and the feel of water on my body.

These are part of my precondition of being quit different from what I experience the next day or a week later. Within a system I had to assimilate myself into, it's like two broken coins or a slab that fit together perfectly.

The conditions of being in Africa and Europe have been conducive to me, though with its unique differences has fulfilled my purpose perfectly well. Just as I want the spirit so also I want and have chosen my present body. The condition in Africa was conducive but because of further preconditions, I have to come back to the UK.

Great Britain my place of birth, it is more favourable for anyone to pass away in his or her birth place because it is the place their star first fell. On the other hand it has relevance to once existence for example you have a mission. It does not make me an English man even if it does? I will still be an African.

Britain operates what Africa find difficult to operate for many who are truly Africans it's their origins, the condition would always sooth them with which, they have been preconditioned to survive as Africans nevertheless they should change to precondition to change that suits them.

I have been looking forward to this, I hope would be my last reincarnation to have originated from Africa as a testimony, to examine its relevance's within an African and European community background.

The African body is not as brittle as the Europeans through being black African I could refine myself into the abysmal I mean the underworld or the empty holes beneath the African earth crust; which is still obscure as part of our existence, for me to assimilate myself into its system, to indefinitely be a part of me because I want to extricate myself from my Krypton memory and crystal.

Good water supplies is not common in Africa, so is sanitation, clean streets, fit for dwelling housing, in retrospect here I am in the UK with all such amenities available for my own use if it is for the moment I live to apply myself to its goodwill . Africa and the UK as allies I would always appreciate Africa would always develop under their umbrella.

I grow up in Africa until the age of 22 years; my father slaughtered a sheep for me on my 21st birthday. Within a year and some months later I had to leave West Africa for Great Britain. My 21st birthday fell on the 27th of July 1987.

It was time in my life changes had to take place I would at that time want to take a wife of my own before coming to the UK I felt lifeless a general body weakening but did not felt symptoms of fainting or frazzle.

How have I been dwelling in Africa? E.g. having my bath each morning and at night, where water is scares; without the tapes running 24 hours a day sometimes water had to be fetched, I lived within step mothers brothers and sisters.

I have experienced what it is like in the UK for one to have a bath with cold water during a sunny day in the South East of England. Many Africans would have been residing in the UK for years without knowing what it is like to have a bath with cold water which is customary in Africa. For me the experience was exhilarating very soon, every homes would be supplied with water meter, to account and pay for the amount of water we use in our homes each day.

I pay for my gas and electricity through card and key. As developed and rewarding as Great Britain could be, the whole result and effect it has on me, is to read my genetic makeup at the same time, enhance my spent force which is truly me but am only slightly aware of.

Everything at certain times, are bound to go into extinction when their purpose has been fulfilled this is why we go through series of evolution and extinction through reincarnation.

Everything about this earth of ours its awesome to fathom or explain what have we been doing? We have been laying palm leaves on the ground after which, it all depends on what you and I have been doing in relation to death after life.

I was never born to be unwell mainly the sun, water and food is all my body needs for my survival. It was the first time at the age of 42 years I first realise moment I have out lived my youth or consider my age to detail, my diet changes constantly, I go through different emotional state but my nature remains sublime everything little epilogues of my life, leads to substantiate for another epilogue of my past and what lies before me. The first thing I was told, when I was taken unwell at the Greenwich hospital was that, I was going to be put on medication for life and it had to do with mental illness. At first, I felt devastated which as time went by, I accepted I needed to be on my medication.

I hear good and bad voices of people I know and of those I do not know impressions as well. Voices of my relatives, friends and voices of people I am not familiar with. They might be far away or close by. Since my mother death, I have been hearing her voice speaking to me, cautioning, guarding or directing me of things, I should do and things I should not do, of places I should go and places I should not go with the same tone of voice I use to know her as my earthly mother now her voices comes in the tone of voice with much clarity of a young white race English girl I saw who I have the notion is the reincarnation of my late mother.

Such as time to do things like e.g. wake up from my sleep, clean my flat, when to wash my cloths, and what kind of food to prepare she is one person, I hold dear to my heart or may be because I chose her and she chose me from the beginning in a mother and child relationship.

When I look into the mirror to have my shaving I see the face of my father, sometimes, my facial expression changing to different members of my family this, is what I call my own experience of personality disorder and arachnophobia the expressions' of hat, love, commands, indifference or to replicate me there could be signs of being possess which I overcome through my own belief and spirituality.

I do get impressions e.g. from almost everything in my flat, the thing I buy and make use of, e.g. currencies I withdraw from the bank always reflect thoughts. Sometimes, I buy things I do not really need or have no use for some I have use for yet am imposed on to move them out of my flat it could relate to paranormal.

I have been hearing voices of my father before and after his death in 2004 before this time, I experience my father was inside me, i.e. soul, mind, temperaments, speaking to me in some case trying to control me. I told Dr Oliver at Queen Elizabeth mental health home treatment team of the voice I hear from my father and other people being adamant, domineering, and possessive, towards me. This does happen at certain times of the day.

I am on medication; I do experience going into relapse, with distorted hallucination about myself, my life, my existence, human nature, my environment and the world in general, e.g. the earth, and creatures on earth. I do have feelings I am known to all creatures.

Sometimes it's as if I could see through below the earth abyss, the dead and holy departed are with me, they seem to portray that they love me, showing concern for me but there is nothing they can do to help me I should accept the consequences as my life's trial and also that the Devil seek to possess my life. It is when I have such experience I feel secure or insecure. If I tell other people about my experience, the more they feel something terrible is wrong with me.

Sometimes I feel the sun radiating all over me, different colours radiating all over me especially my forehead, I feel am a sours of the sun and moon, the sun shines for me and shins because of me, telepathic messages come to me. During such feelings I feel very powerful, with spiritual forces all around me. If people could be telepathic is hearing voices an illness?

Telepathy is the direct transference of thought or feelings from one person to another person without using the normal five physical senses of sight, hearing, touch, taste and smell. It is the ability to communicate on another level rather than using speech you communicate well using only the power of your mind.

This is the way other species communicate with each other. It has been proved in numerous studies that animals communicate among themselves using telepathy, sometimes over great distances.

Today more and more people around the world are opening their minds and rediscovering this wonderful natural ability. The experience makes me feel good, apart from being depressed with distorted thoughts filled with dread or arachnophobia at the initial stage of my hearing voices of which, I have overcome most of. The furniture's in my flat move into different shapes, take different forms, as if the furniture's in my flat are trying to express messages to me.

Creating feeling of one kind or another e.g. shaking and vibrating, or taking form into another object with a glowing sensation on top of my head, at certain times I am unable to figure out the impression. I hear voices attached to the objects as if they are speaking or sending impression to me. If it comes to my mind to say a prayer it's as if the whole skies and pillars hear me.

As I was word processing on the morning 8th of July 2007 my door bell wrong, it was a lady by name Ms Shimon in her early twenties, who wanted to shear news of the Bible with me; we had conversation about what are the sources of evil. Shimon opened her bible and read from it Psalm of King David chapter 37 verses 10 'A little while, and the wicked will be no more, though you look for them, they will be not be found. But the meek will inherit the land and enjoy great peace'.

Before Ms Shipman left, she asked me if it was ok for her to call at my flat on another occasion. I said its fine. She was on my door step several times. I asked her what she thinks about people hearing voices, could it be distinguished from good or evil as to what schizophrenics' illness is.

We discuses about evil being out of control
- I asked her what is the source of all evil and how

could it be exposed and how far it has filled the whole earth.

- How our lives, heart and soul is safe guarded against evil.
- She talked of Satan's evil influence; I told Ms Shimon evil have had its share in every life it should be over with by now or why should our eyes each day be filled with tears?
- I told her how I felt; the beauty of Israel was being thrown down from Heaven to earth?
- How could one feel if another person hides his or her ears to their grief?
- Signs of manhood i.e. circumcision and heavens views on it, and what makes a Christian look up to God and the Heavens we are likely to be less conscious of while on earth?
- From scroll to codex how the bible became a book.
- Unfading records of endurance, limitations can come in many forms and in different degree example many have become impaired in their disability to communicate, they still cherish fond memories of heavens love and under-served kindness.
- Are the elderly ones a blessing to the young ones?
- Family influence.
- Influence on fellow worshipers.
- All such issues have one or two relationship and something to do with psychological inherent traits I asked her are there reason why people suffer from the illness of schizophrenia, manic or chronic depression it helps if you are religious, cautious, resilient it would depict if you could be regarded as a good schizophrenia or a bad schizophrenia.

Never had I gone into personal, family matter in conversation with Ms Nwamaka Megbele my brothers' wife she, never told me she was studying caring and mental health. Completing her studies close to this period, in May 2007 I become seriously unwell for several months I had to go back to work as time went by, I could no longer work I had to be put under Queen Elizabeth mental health home treatment team.

I considered our family relationship with some details and concern of which I told the home treatment team. Some of them were the some care workers whose care, I was under in 1995 at the Greenwich hospital.

My sister-in-law never goes into any conversation with me concerning herself, her relatives or friends; I can count the number of times we have spoken to each other even if the situation poised asking question because I have no intention of going into conflict with her for some reason for example everyone is entitled to their own private space I had to write my books. After I had come out under Queen Elizabeth home treatment team, my brother, his wife, and children were in my flat. They had not spent up to three minutes with me; she wanted to, in the presence of their children which no mention or questions had been asked since 1995 within me, my father, brother and his wife, that we should discus about my illness! It was a festive season and I had not seen her since 2004 I told her we should not talk about my illness whilst the children were present.

Taking matters lightly without us going into any further discussion about my illness in the presence of their children, my sister in law accompany me to my mental health appointment at Queen Elizabeth home treatment team. At the hospital with me, she and Dr Niangua started with her recent accomplishments with her studies again! I asked myself; this was after Dr. Niangua who was one of the psychiatrists I saw during that period at Queen Elizabeth mental health home treatment team who, took over my care from Dr Oliver.

My sister in law picked me up from my flat in their car when she accompanied me to Queen Elizabeth home treatment team prior to this within the week my brother accompanied me to Ferryview mental health centre with Mr. Engi as my care who after I was discharged from hospital in 1995 is one of the cares who came to my flat to administer me Depixol injection. My brother came to my flat towards the evening by bus or train we parted at the Ferryview mental health centre while he went to catch a train at Woolwich Arsenal, while I went to Riverside housing office in Woolwich to sort out my problem of an overpayment of housing benefit which I told my brother on our way out of Ferryview mental health centre.

UK, Saturday 23 Aug 2004 Hospitals Told To End 'Unfair' Parking Charges. The Government tells hospital trusts to give free or cheap parking to the relatives of chronically ill patients. Hospitals are told to give free or cheap parking to the relatives of chronically ill patients. Health Secretary Jeremy Hunt said new guidelines for English hospitals have been created in order to end the stress of 'unfair' charges.

Patients with disabilities, those who have frequent appointments and members of staff working shifts will also benefit from the changes, Mr Hunt said. The guidelines states hospital trust should waive fines when overstay is beyond the control of the driver, for instance if treatment takes longer than planned. Mr Hunt last month admitted he was concerned about parking fees being charged at some hospitals after being pressed by backbenchers to end 'rip-off' costs. The guidance sets out for the first time that hospital trusts are responsible for the actions of any private firms they use to run parking facilities.

It also calls on hospitals to look at introducing pay on exit systems so those visiting only pay for the time they have used. Mr Hunt said: 'Patients and families shouldn't have to deal with the added stress of unfair parking charges. 'These clear ground rules set out our expectations, and will help the public hold the NHS to account for unfair charges or practices.' Shadow health minister Andrew Gwynne said: 'The Tory-led Government scrapped Labour's plans to phase out car parking charges for patients and Jeremy Hunt needs to take responsibility for the fact that, since then, one in four hospitals have increased parking fees. 'Any action to ease the burden of car parking charges on patients and their visitors is welcome. When people go to hospital, the last thing they want to worry about is parking fees.'

When I and my sister in law got to Queen Elizabeth hospital she dropped me by the entrance of the home treatment team said she was going to park her car while she was looking for a parking space if she can't park within the parking lot by its entrance. As she went about this, I went in to the reception desk and introduced myself then she came in later. By the time my appointment was over I and my sister in law had to cross the road to a visitors parking area I was aware for the first time since I entered Queen Elizabeth hospital. One reason given to why I was brought into Greenwich hospital in 1995 was that I crossed the road in a way that put me at risk. Right from the time I was hospitalised at the Greenwich hospital in 1995 I had continually asked myself why didn't the police officer entered its psychiatrist GD ward and introduced themselves or give reasons why I was being hospitalized regardless if they had done so at the hospital at a reception below before we went to GD ward. The police officer left me at its entrance with Mr. Akim a care who took me over from them.

My brother Omagbemi Network through working for London Underground also known as The Tube he came to my flat with public transport on the day he accompanied me to my appointment at the Ferryview mental health centre with Mr. Engi as my care for the day. The Underground is a rapid transit system serving a large part of Greater London and some parts of Buckinghamshire, Hertfordshire and Essex in England. It is the oldest underground railway in the world, the first section of which opened in 1863 on what are now the Circle & Hammersmith & City lines and part of the Metropolitan line.

In 1890 it became the first to operate electric trains. The whole network is commonly referred to by Londoners and in official publicity as the Tube, although the term originally applied only to the deep-level bored lines, along which run trains of smaller and more circular cross-section, to distinguish them from the sub-surface 'cut and cover' lines that were built first. I have been living in Woolwich before the Ferryview health centre was built it was a bear piece of land it most have been so, for a very long time because of its condition before the health centre was built below it runs a railway line.

No matter how Africans, Jamaican, Barbados, Trinidad's might want very much to be in Europe by having their stay in the UK, I have been taken to Africa like a shell, lived there and have perspective of what it is like being an African, which stills dwell with me as an individual, this have to do with African parental attitudes towards their children which at the end of the day adds less or nothing to the up- bringing of their children while the wives, children or close relatives, could be found of manipulating each other.

In African Culture or juju somebody going into phase like mine suffering from schizophrenia is regarded as if; it is because I have done something bad in life to incur such suffering. The same way it is looked at in Africa if someone is impotent or could not have a wife or children, or my coming into this earth through premature birth. If such presumption is attached to culture why do Africans and Jamaicans not stop such practice of juju and voodoo through invoking predicaments?

This is not always true, infarct we go through such phase in life because life on earth, is a trial. If some people think it is the case, what have they got to say about some people who could will other people to do things they could possibly not imagine that they could do? Just because they are being use by someone else through means of forces with which, they just want to control other people, with juju, voodoo or witchcraft.

I would not allow myself to be used by my brothers, uncles' aunts, elder brothers and sisters this is what I feel is the course of conflicts, schizophrenia, social contrast lack of integration, within culture and environmental discipline, deteriorating ways of social interaction and social abuse. The effects could be social collapse cares should be watchful dealing with the care of schizophrenic it should not relate to social outcast their illness and its effect are not of their own inclination.

Cares should be collaborative; considerate the illness could makes sufferers less conceptual of whatever could be happening around them, they could possibly find life less appealing become less assertive or dependant.

Residing in England it should all be a matter of everybody doing their own thing as it is best for them to do. But the most important thing, is do not get on somebody else's way. Life in the UK could be based individuality this why synergy have work well for them and should be based on respect for each other except when things get terribly wrong for example the issues that compels me to write this book. Because Britain has a structured system in different perspectives for its citizens to live their lives as they choose freely without being biased by other people could such an encounter make one feel bilious?

The British welfare system has been well set in place; all that could be most welcome in receipt from the next person is how you are getting on! Or how is life treating you, so easily can we then reach out in union of friendship peacefully, working practice are enforced amicably there are huge piles of work for different people to do and not enforce yourself on others then we can enjoy the beauty of what we do, the world we live in and find peace within ourselves.

Welfare is very important for which reason, everybody loves Europe but can the British and American feed the whole world or the entire of Africa nations? It is not good to be too dependent.

I cannot have spent 22 years of my life in Nigeria, a witness of considerable development that has taken place now in the UK the education I am receiving from Africans here in the UK bewilders me to say a kind of benediction of my own. We have experiment on free education, roads and bridges are a common sight in Nigeria, car assemblies, Pfizer, Jonson and Jo pharmaceutical, more and more houses have been built, hotels, clubs, there are internet services, mobile phones satellite view on television is available.

All sort of Nigeria's food product we can easily get hold of within the UK from Asian food stores which are Nigerian Products brought into the UK it cannot be all that bad in Nigeria the nation has to change for the better it's about understanding each other.

At the early stage, within two step mother's and lots of young girl friends of my father later had, my only sister from my mother's side Miss. Oritsegbubemi Megbele now Mrs. Oritsegbubemi Ajagunla who fought her way in life to be responsible for herself before she got married was of concern to my father, just as he was concerned about me since, I was my mother's last child for him among four children. It surprises me how people change. My father changed over the recent years after he dished my mother, then began with only concern for himself what more would one expect under a polygamous home.

At this time my father was part of the reformed Ogboni fraternity in Nigeria. His mother was also a member of the cult, my sister Oritsegbubemi was chosen to succeed our grandmother from our fathers' side in the cult complications within the family did not allow this to happen.

Jealousy from both her step mothers our father would not allow our step mothers into the cult, because, he felt, they will be on his way, when he wants to show his own self importance indulgence, credibility or his authority not to be overridden within his family.

Spiritually, philosophically, I and my grandmother from my father's side chose each other within a vendetta. She died just after I was born in the UK my father had to travel to Africa in Nigeria for her funeral. We must have manoeuvred each other forth and back to earth to co-exist as witness or call it a testimony.

She was part of Krypton and had lived several pervious lives in Europe. She is something I could call a handmaiden of Angel Michael. I have really been doing a lot of searching since I came back to the UK I discovered my grandmother Mrs. Awoma Akinlami from my father's side of our family had reincarnation into the UK just at the same time, my parent moved back to Africa..

Whilst I was born in the UK on the 27th of July 1966, my father lost his mother in Nigeria without his presence in the UK when I was born. There was a switch within me and his mother. She was of mixed race in Nigeria but reincarnated into the UK as an Irish and English decent. I met her in

1989 as a co –worker at Iceland frozen food plc Lewisham she was known as Miss. Michelle Cook I was two years older than her who, I have the notion is the reincarnation of my fathers mother.

Immediately I was born I, my immediate elder brother Mr. Omagbemi Megbele and our mother returned to Nigeria. Back from our adventure in Africa I observed Miss. Michelle Cook as an individual, as I worked with her at Iceland frozen food store Lewisham; I was a fellow student of hers; at Lewisham collage she left the school before I become a student.

I could have befriended her but my father became too involved I felt he was looking into it too privately. If my father was aware of this, having lived under my father I would have guessed what my father's philosophy behind it would be.

Miss. Michelle Cook had set of hands and palms in size similar to my mother. I felt if she was my late father's mother she took sides with my mother after her rebirth regarding our family affairs because the situation in our family changed just after she died. My father took another wife from his mother's origin. Her name is Mrs. Cordelia Megbele.

Most of what my step mother Mrs. Cordelia Megbele told we children when we were young about our late grandmother was to hypo-personal herself e.g. she knew our fathers mother very well before she died, she was very much liked by our late grandmother, Cordelia told us she was proper Itsekiri with our father and his mother from Mid-Western Nigeria.

We the first children of our father to our mother Barrister Oritseweyinmi, Mrs. Oritsegbubemi Ajagunla, Mr. Omagbemi and myself Mr. Oritsesemisan Bamidele Megbele, were half Itsekiri and half Yoruba's from Western Nigeria. Others were half Itsekiri and half Kalabari from Eastern Nigeria, Mrs. Cordelia told us our fathers' mother Mrs. Awoma Akinlami wanted her to marry our father which took place just immediately after my father buried his mother which was not up to a year when, I was born which meant how my father's relationship blossomed before we three I, my immediate elder brother and our mother arrived back home from the UK to Nigeria.

Why should Cordelia Megbele tell us children stories, of such nature? We should be one big happy family as I grew up, I realise all children really need both parents. By the time my mother took me and Mr. Omagbemi back to Nigeria from the UK, our parents had separated I would not have been more than a year old.

I had feelings for Miss. Michelle Cook; I had already considered remaining a celibate at that time of my life I was 23 years going to 24 years of age and she would have been 21 years going to 22 years. Most of my father visit to the UK during these periods was to personalised himself with the issues which was all my own doing to have met with and identify the reincarnated of my late grandmother.

My father took me out to visit friends around Lewisham and the Lewisham shopping centre making it all public flair of his own. African children, who take to their parents in looks, considerations, and aptitude, are too often used, by their parents.

My father a cult member, a freemason, recently became a chieftaincy title holder, did not back off from me and Miss. Michelle Cook's relationship. Dose any universal law imply I and Miss. Michelle Cook should not be together? Life is choice.

Opinion holds it my father should have been long died before I met with Miss. Michelle Cook. As a cult member, a successful business man, a freemason, my father bribed his way into chieftaincy to prolong his life.

If what, he wanted was to prolong his life, he should have literary, backed off from me and Miss. Michelle Cook affairs, if my father had looked at it from his business perspective, My father, could had found more things to consider him wiser, such as come to the conclusion we were both working for him. Life is choice, and I and Miss. Michelle Cook have made our own choice to be together it did not necessary mean, as lovers, but as friends.

It is human nature to twist things around which sometimes hinder other people's interest and progress it is not my course of action to be of such wimp.

We choose our own family on earth before we are born. I know my father too well, it's a competitive world we live in, competition need not be found within family members, or parents and family member would find it difficult, welcoming or appreciated every step they make in some case, one is more likely to be used by friends of their relatives they are meant to work as a team.

No reality is too far for any humans to attain, in some cases, it might not be the way we want things to be. My relationship with Miss Loraine O'Connor makes it clearer am always in search of anything realistic, by coincidence if my conscience approve of it. It might not be as I want it to be to some extent it naturally serves a purpose such, is one of the prerequisite that determines if one wants to live a good life failure is not a misgiving it makes us more assertive.

Miss. Michelle Cook ones asked me 'Mr Semi Only if, we could make this world one big happy family or, is there anything wrong with two people being together if, they choose to be together? My reply was no!

There is nothing wrong I replied. It might be because some people could be found of choosing their own way in life and make choices for other people rather than let predicaments create the choice that we make why do we have common sense? The road to heaven chosen for an individual, should be the part, they should follow. Mind you in relation to these words of mine, there are obstacles in this planet of ours, where there is love, greed and hat.

This is one reason, why it is wrong to tell lies. She said but there are no lies when it comes to falling in love. I said well! Most people have to fall in love, to make other people happy. But this is not the case with both of us, I am sorry!

My father is too much involved. Her face become ashen few minutes later, she come back from Littlewoods and offered me sweets that was, when I realised she knew who she was to me! Michelle had tested me children grow up before they become adults I latter realised she did and said those words subconsciously while I was subconsciously subjugated to react the way I did.

I asked Michelle one afternoon at work, if she would like to be a nurse it was a question that came from my sub-conscious mind or probably in years to come, I would be unwell., to my surprise seeing Michelle two years later just by Spray Street Woolwich job centre in 1993, she told me sub-consciously she heard of my mother's death, she was a student studying nursing or nursery. Then it strikes me she had always been the red haired head next to mine and a crucifix or could it have been the coral bead on my chest when I paid homage to the Olu of Warri that made me resilient in life trials.

I was happy to hear her tell me about her nursing or nursery career prospect in my mind I thought, my mother did study nursing in London whilst I was born, she could mean something to me some day in another perspectives or to someone else.

The same notion I have about Miss. Michelle Cook being the reincarnation of my grandmother from my father's side the same feeling, I had when I encountered Miss Joan Keeble Ms Janet Clarks first daughter as being the reincarnation of my grandmother from, my mother's side, tradition and custom holds it am not suppose to tell her age neither of those of my lat father or my mother. My late mother's birthday falls on the month of May. Because of Miss. Michelle Cook and Miss Joan Keeble, I asked Mr Harry Gordon Slade what century was black and white photography invented. They both still have resemblance to their past.

The history of underline photography has roots in remote antiquity with the discovery of the principle of the underline camera obscura and the observation that some substances are visibly altered by exposure to light. As far as is known, nobody thought of bringing these two phenomena together to capture camera images in permanent form until around 1800, when Thomas Wedgwood made the first reliably documented although unsuccessful attempt. In the mid-1820s, Nicéphore Niépce succeeded, but several days of exposure in the camera were required and the earliest results were very crude. Niépce's associate Louis Daguerre went on to develop the daguerreotype process, the first publicly announced photographic process, which required only minutes of exposure in the camera and produced clear, finely detailed results. It was commercially introduced in 1839, a date generally accepted as the birth year of practical photography. The coining of the word 'Photography' has been attributed in 1839 to Sir John Herschel.

Since childhood, I had always observed pictures of myself and the rest of my family. The photographs I saw of my grandmother from my mother's side, was on black and white pictures. Miss. Joan Keeble, though she is white in origin, shorter in height compared with body build, looks very similar with those of my grandmother from my mother side from the pictures I had seen of her in Nigeria.

Just after I moved into my flat, after a while I began working at the Woolwich Gala club within months I took short evening course in business planning and management at the University of Greenwich.

2004 my father died at Ibadan, buried in Delta state of Nigeria. I have this notion he reincarnated into the UK through Mrs. Mary Rodney a Ghanaian and a co-worker of mine at the Woolwich Gala Bingo club gave birth to him.

Mrs. Mary Rodney has good resemblance to Miss. Michelle Cook in looks, body build, status and height the only difference was colour. My resemblance to both ladies is acute but not in height. It takes a lot to stress out such phenomenon it is as if, we have known each other in a past life and we are seeing, through each other's eyes. It was as if something had happened in Ghana that concerns three of us in a past life and probably had something to do with Great Britain and it had to do with our past life. Mrs. Mary Rodney husband to my surprise in height, body build and facial resemblance looks very much to that of Mr Calvin Sudelu who I have the notion is the reincarnation of my grandfather from my father's side of my family Known as Mr. Goldpine.

Probably to control my late father's destiny it came to me as a perspective Mrs. Mary Rodney wanted my father, before he become Michelle's son since the early 19th century. To have him back in this 21st century, Mary had to leave Ghana for the UK. It could be the reason why I was born in the UK lived part of my life in Africa and came back to the UK.

In 2002 my father was in the UK handing back to me the coral bead he had given to me during his chieftaincy titled with which, I had paid homage to the making of a king Godwin Toju Emiko the Atuwase of Warri during the making of his first Coronation anniversary Ogiame Atuwatse the second the Olu of Warri conferred on my father a chieftaincy title on the 12th of November 1988 as the Agbueju of Warri Kingdom.

Two years later, Mrs. Mary Rodney began working at the club within one year and few months, she gave birth to a boy who, I have the notion is the reincarnation of my late father.

My father gave me back the coral bead, insinuating himself and the coral bead, to be born in the UK with it while it was in my possession.   I was the one who gave him, the opportunity so he would understand how I felt regardless if our friendship did not continue as it was, while I was young lad.

Most of the Children born in the UK from African decent are people who are our lost parents and relatives from Africa who reincarnate into the UK.

From my youth, I would do anything for my father which had always been the case until his death. It was too late for him, to have handed it back to me for it having any significance or implication to my life, rather through it, it has implication for him to reincarnate. At this time my schizophrenia illness has taken over me my mind and body was taken over, by my father.

There are far greater things than money or power one could have. Such as simple wisdom and understanding though you have to sheer some few tears, wisdom and understanding do not come easily because there are barriers, I would applaud to experience anything realistic about life, so I gave him the opportunity. For me, it left an anthropological proof about life, a reality of who I am on earth as an individual.

This experience and observation had not been easy for me to go through; I hope my father, enjoys all the good things he hopes to enjoy being born in the UK in his new reincarnation. It's certain we all can pave our way for ourselves either for good or for bad in relations to what pleases us because we have freewill. I do not in any way feel bad about it or I would lack understanding or become less resilient to life trials; moreover, my father had honoured me in Africa initiating me as an apprenticeship member of freemason.

As at 18th march 1999, I have obtained EA degree in freemason. I have divested myself after I have undergone repeated trials with approbation, and a wiliness at all times to undergo examination when properly called upon.

On one side of my mind jumbled with thoughts I said to myself thanks to the heavens, grace and all might to the existence of God. I hope my chore would all be over after this life of mine. And that my trials would all have been over for the last time with no more reincarnation to undergo. Brother Mr. Godwin .U. Newe is our secretary and my father as RWM in Warri Highland Lodge Delta state before his death in 2004.

I have this feeling my father used the coral beads in relation to culture in extracting almost all the Nigerian currencies and notable Nigerians Naira of Motalar, Arisekola, M.K.O Abiola, Jakunde, Nnamdi Azikiwe , Ojukwu and Olunloyo from my life including the gari, pounded yam, grand rice, shaky, cow tongue and goat meat. I have recently grown thinner with lost weight before he handed back the coral bead to me.

Having worked at several stores for Iceland frozen food company plc, and at the Woolwich Gala club as a cleaner my looks and physical statues are still very much intact for this reason I began having the notion I am a boy as lovely as a tree.

I perceive the episodes as a miracle about my life it was too good to be missed my father after my mother's death showed no signs that he knew and he could have no excuse for saying he did not know because he wasn't in London when I was born as a premature birth growing up in Africa not after all those long journeys I took with him in his Mercedes-Benz with him from Port Harcourt to Warri, from Warri Delta state to Lagos and Oyo state; is like a storm breaker. And it was better for me, as I was not aware of all the facts at the early stage of my life. My late father would had been more than successful than he was if he had motivated himself to such respects he was someone I had high hopes for I was never shy expressing my hopes for him but he was a man who lived his life on his own terms based on the way he conducted himself it poised problems not only for him but also for members of his family. Members of his family who love him or show concerns about him are always left wearied.

There are several business men in Africa I mean wealthy men like late M.K.O Abiola started his business by first selling firewood at the age of nine years, He later founded a band at age fifteen where he would perform at various ceremonies in exchange of food, he started his professional life as bank clerk with Barclays Bank plc in Ibadan among many of his life achievements. My father started his career as a linesman in Nigerian ports authority before he came to the UK with my mother.

He worked in a poultry firm, and as a postman my mother studied nursing back to Nigeria she worked for a pharmaceutical company as far as I knew and worked for a motor assembly plant. My father worked in clearing and forwarding and as a stevedore managing director. In Nigeria I did not usually go unwell, have feet or was a problem to my parents and I made attempt to join the army and I was partly here and there were all these issues have concern all I knew was that I was running errands. I see myself as a miracle because I survived my stay in Nigeria. I travelled from Port Harcourt in a Nigerian Okada airliner to Lagos on my father's errand three weeks later he went to Lagos through the same process. I have not counted times I have travelled alone or with my father in his car within Port Harcourt and Delta state, from Lagos to Oyo and from Ibadan to Ife. On several occasions I went to Port Harcourt from Ibadan to visit my father at Port Harcourt, I had to travel through my mother's company cars drivers through different drivers running company errands from Oyo state to Aba in Abia state. The driver stops at Aba which was his destination I had to, travel through local drivers from Aba to Port Harcourt in Rivers state to visit my father at Port Harcourt township.

Aba is a city and a big trading centre in Abia State, south eastern Nigeria, located on the Aba River. Aba was established by the Igbo People of Nigeria as a market town and then later a military post was placed there by the British colonial administration in 1901. The city became a collecting point for agricultural products following the British made railway running through it to Port Harcourt. Aba is a major urban settlement and commercial centre in a region that is surrounded by small villages and towns. The indigenous people of Aba are the Ngwa. Aba is well known for its craftsmen. As of 2004 Aba had an estimated population of 1,020,900. Yet I have been in Britain for the past 20 years I have not been able to visit Scotland it is a place I would like to visit because of its features. I look forward to visiting Scotland someday rails; airplanes can go there it would be a memorable visit for me and probably to visit America.

No wealthy man or women in Nigeria always like to carry worried or troubled effect near their body; there must be something about you before they make close interaction with their children friends and relatives. It has a lot in saying how parent bring up their children in Africa there are cultures involved in how parents, family members and relatives interact I do not want to divulge in it could be observe with questions asked why are family relationships in West Africa not always happy within themselves.

Experiment it if you like take two children from the same family or within a polygamous background let them live in a different setting and observe how the children behave in time, involve their parent and observe one or both children. One would in their first encounter display symptoms of withdrawal. Children who show symptoms of withdrawal in presence of their parents around other people are children who know their parents for what they are like and they are often the once, who show concern for their parents.

Immediately, my father reincarnated the coral bead had fulfilled its purpose for him, I had known what he wanted before he handed it back to me, I later felt probably after handing it back to me, it would bring a new meaning into my life. Giving it to a member of my family or selling the coral bead could result to my being used all over again.

I wait for the once I could walk with under the rain, who will make me feel fine and less heartfelt about life. Whoever said love is blind, I hope had not excluded the troubles, pain and heartache associated with love to have come about such a saying.

African parents know how to adjudicate for their children for their personal reasons and heartbeat, coupled that they sell their children into mental and spiritual slavery. Their children find it difficult to realise the concepts of individuality such as having a life of their own.

This was partly why, for some personal reason I had not endeavoured to travel out of the UK since I came back.

I often have feelings I am a miracle, I guess one can say everyone and everything we have around us is a miracle. I will not let my disability, be on my way as a stumbling block. Going through all these, I felt happier because, I am facing my reality.

The reality of knowing my last earthly father the way I did draw me closer to my universal goal. My father owed me, my mother and the rest of his family's obligations, but left us all, always whimpering for him, he did not fulfill is won obligations, except to himself.

A reality of purpose in life I really want to get hold of everybody wants to get hold of it and as humans we are found of making too many mistakes. It depends on how other people apply themselves to you, their perception of you and your own perception of them. I know my father very well, as for my mother, I know her too well. Looking into the pros and corns of good and bad about life, leaves me disillusion, but high in spirit because I feel, I know why I am here.

Could my general practitioner, psychiatrist, and care workers see the trouble with me, my family background drove me insecure, left me unhappy, alone and isolated. Without close ties or consideration for each other for which reason I seek happiness within myself. It's difficult but within the UK it's bearable because, you could live your life dependent on yourself and what are the implications of once conscience there is freedom of expression.

The act polygamy has come a long way, what I see about marriages really beguiles me; polygamy would leave one shaky without being able to bubble. I chose to be a celibate

The UK, Americans and develop world did not just come all this way with such things like civilisation, benefit, hospital care, education and social care with easy pixy. Mind you, there is always an assessor of every situation and interventions; moreover we are all here on earth to access ourselves. I cannot wish for any other thing, than this!

I met Mary and her husband Mr Rodney at Powis street in Woolwich not far from where I live and their son who I have the notion is the reincarnation of my late father she was pregnant before I stopped working at the Woolwich Gala club. Looking at him in his pushchair, steering at me, with one of his leg making involuntary movement I had the feeling he recognised me; he looks very much still in resemblance to my father. It wasn't a surprise because, I, Michelle Cook and Mrs. Mary Rodney have close facial resemblance.

I was thoughtful about the environment I met them, I remembered Miss. Michelle Cook, before, she worked for Iceland frozen food plc was a staff of McDonald's who lived at Peckham.

2007 in the month of May I began to emaciate, losing so much weight with general body weakening; I realised for some reason I have to slow down from work because of my condition of health.

I considered it thoughtful of me, over the years; to have achieved some qualifications and certificates to go into an office job. Mr. Dotun Sobowale who has resemblance to my uncle Mr. Tamitayo Akinlami, considered offering me a job at the Day care disability centre in Charlton as his secretary.

Mr. Dotun Sobowale has three daughters he also had been a student at the University of Greenwich in the 1970's.

Children should let their parents speak for them, but not brothers, or sisters speaking for them in a family they customary make the situation their won cup of tea. It depends on the situation in cases of resolving conflict in a family, resolving conflicts in a polygamous family in Africa always turn out to be, a total disaster. It deepens relationship. When we go to other parts of the world, we still deepen our relationship into conflicts to show off rather than beating on the dark side, we should be starting with new endeavours, spirit level that cerate's harmony.

Children like me under the European Union; our lives are taking new turns that needs to be put in perspectives and by the look of it, we are no different to ourselves in the UK as we are to ourselves in Africa. Blessed are those who wait, who see reason to face reality.

The more, I felt I would meet an opposite sex more amicable to me. If such over the years does not occur. I still have the grace to wait. Coming into the UK, some of us do not care to wait within months there is a pregnancy on the way they way they imply their relationship it gives me a sense of paranoia not out ruled within my parents in the 1960's when I was born that we are found of downgrading ourselves.

This was years ago how could it be the something 43 years later why repeat history on a dark level I could be British by birth I have lived here for 23 years let's see if I still have pride for my native land in Africa life is a trial. Lots of people are suffering now in the UK inconsistencies' are taking place in our social and economics who would take the blame of retrograde?

The more I will wait for Mr Sola Awe my mother's last child and step brother, becoming a family man before I consider going into a relationship because of psychological reason if people tie knots it is left for you and I to untie the knot not when, it may lead to further inconsistencies some of which are not made by some of the participants by choice such as if I do not wish to be a celibate any more. Everything has laws and effects, human existences are prone to preconditions which at certain incident one could be pressed to be an avoider only reasons can be diverted into reality.

Am 12 years older than Mr Sola Awe, I was 41 years of age in July 2007, my wisdom tooth was to be extracted what a happy birthday indeed! When I was taken unwell in 1995 diagnosed as a paranoid schizophrenia I spent my birth day in hospital all my life most distressing things which comes up in my life takes place during my birth day yet it never puts me down from being resilient to move forward.

A single mother and her male friend died in a car accident, I asked if, there was a child in the car when the accident occurred, I was told she had a son but he was not in the car. I said thanks heaven her child was not in the car. It is left for the father and son to make up, what they think of her as a wife and a mother.

At Saint Mary's church 5th August 2007, the service held by Reverend Jean Griffiths, Preaching, did say some things about death when it has taken its toil there should be time to forget the pain, headaches and to start anew.

This whole episode of my life during the year, reminded me of my days as a born again Christian in Deeper life Christian ministry, at Ibadan Oyo state whilst at secondary school. 'One of the hymns we sang on this Sunday was Jesus shall rein where're the sun dose his successive journey's run'

A lot could be realised with one being a celibate i.e. self awareness, simple mindedness and patience can lead to solutions to conflicts, disagreements, misunderstandings, most important insolvent, copping with illness, disability, disappointment rather than self wimp if you are self wimped, you can hardly outlive mental illness it's a way of differentiating sufferers.

This I told Mr. Dotun Sobowale also known as Mr. Dax Sobowale we both attends the same church at Saints Mary's Magdalene Woolwich. I can't just believe it I told him. With a birth condition later in life suffering from psychiatrist illness, from humanistic point of view of synergy and psychology, should I be keeping a job?

As a premature child at birth and growing up I keep myself serine and coup very well with aggravation not physical but emotional nevertheless I do feel better when I am active very active.

What could be the requisite for stopping conflicts, unwarranted action within people who have no reason but to justify their own wimps? I believe in good purpose, respect for individuality. Most people are very well known for carrying out sacrileges within which at certain points, nothing is ever left behind but homage for other people to live with or outlive.

One of my thoughts about Miss. Michelle Cook was Michelle two wrongs cannot make a right; let me seat by your side, if I weren't meant to be your partner. Before my birth and after your death, we both represented a two sided coin. Whatever, we have tried to build, something real and true to seal our love or relationship appeal or probably our existence, it is not all sex that matters in all relationships, it is the after mount of the relationship and whatever, it represents for good cause.

In achieving such relationship as ours, we try and tried each day, months and years with our lives, because of something we both have, a seal for our salvation no one can take away from us. We would always belong to each other never the less it is customary on earth for other people to make us what we are.

As we read meaning into our lives, so do others around us read meanings into our lives and endeavours some of them can help us through our lives perils, is how we get to know people around us. For which reason I ask Miss. Michelle Cook do most people feel free to do, as they wish, with their own personal opinions of making choices?

Reincarnation dose open avenues to correct mistakes or incoherence's in a past or present life, in this case, she was suppose to be my wife, but I was her grandson before she died and reincarnated again probably she holds the key to something I want out of life. Hereditary does not always have to do with wealth.

Miss. Michelle Cook in some ways knew I respected and appraise her, because it could have came from her sub-consciousness or spirituality that led me to where she was working at Iceland Frozen and at Lewisham collage. She most had wanted something of a change in her past life.

I have been doing lots of sacrifices and compromise, to be with her, I am ready to climb the highest mountain, to compromise on what we have been truly trying to build. I had to hold on to Miss. Michelle Cook my reincarnated grandmother from my fathers' side from Nigeria. With an ironic involvement Michelle was one time an Ogboni fraternity member before she reincarnated into Europe from within a white race. This time, she held the greatest of all seal of my Krypton memory or a seal to the Ogboni fraternity.

We were sown to each other before time was created, it was

a situation, we were faced with either we had faults of our own or, we wanted to solve a fault.

Every human being dies, but there are some individuals, who will not die when, they are supposed to die apart from using the science of medicine, they would fight teeth and nail, when they are about to die with juju, voodoo, witchcraft, talisman. It is during such a time in a person life when things dose happen unexpectedly or go wrong all of a sudden within the family.

The whole episode I suffer under my family background at certain times, never send shrill through my body veins and mind but consideration but they ought to.

It is possible for some people to use means to prolong their lives, of which side effect through its effect dose occur. It could affect other people's lives especially those who are close to them. One or two of the parties involved would have to suffer lose, or to withhold a proceeding. If I had my own fault and Michelle had her own faults, it would have been some faults in our past lives or our family affairs is in antagonise with our past life just as what lies before us in this present life.

For example in reality we might have become close friends not only so but partners. Not everybody believe in reincarnation, If my father had died when he should be dead, it becomes practically possible for me and Michelle to have a relationship then in the Ogboni cult proceedings people would say, there are justifications, the person who should be dead might hold back secrets to justifying himself in other arenas that suits him but not in our own interest. There is a mystery involved the book of the dead takes life while the book of the living gives life. I and Miss. Michelle Cook were working for a food chain store.

Since my father became a chief, he should stay put and reside in Africa for the rest of his life, or he should have given me the coral bead to bring with me, into the UK before, he could set his feet on Europe again. The coral bead was part of his mother's closet. The oracle had instructed me on what to do. In relation to the scenario it is what should be that I and Michelle should just be friends. The reasons are philosophical, recently documentation was on television with Michael Palin in African where native witch doctor and juju and un-natural witchcraft are in practice the documentary was facial what lies behind such practices in Africa, are awesome.

The NHS have been putting such seniors into perspectives, at one point of my treatment I was cared for by a Dr. Gbadamosi a psychiatrist at the Ferryview mental health centre from Yoruba origin, I have come across some of my cares from within different culture who have traditional tribal marks on them that depicts their origin. Could science in this modern day taken interest in African, Jamaican, Barbados juju, voodoos and witchcraft? Yes, it has. Britain is a country which assimilation all culture into its country considering the huge impact of science of medicine, technology and engineering have on different culture and our ways of life, religion, beliefs and interaction amidst different kinds of assimilation.

If my father wanted to imply he is aware that Miss. Michelle Cook was the reincarnation of his mother, before I came back into the UK, he had made certain implications so had his step brother Mr. Temitayo Akinlami.

My father Chef Dr Frank Anirejuoritse Megbele the Agbuaju of Warri Delta state Nigeria did endeavoured telling me who I was, when I was initiated into freemason, with him presiding as the grand patron immediately my father had just become a chief. But he would not give me back the coral bead since it was taken out of his mother's closet. When I mean Closet for example the moment the coral bead was handed back to me, it is in my closet sort of representing my position within my family in relation to every members of his family including those who are no longer with us.

He became a chief in 1988, his business was getting along fine, He had always in his past take trips into the UK on visit's, I thought it was to paint old, new and open pictures. She could likely be the only person who could hold back or in the right perspectives based on what he had been practising considering I had been in Africa for years lapping, now with Michelle and myself in the UK lapping, I and Miss. Michelle Cook had to combine our strength.

Coming across Miss. Michelle Cook in the UK in 1989, it took no time, before I realised who Michelle was infarct I had been working in other stores of Iceland before I met with her. She was all in resemblance to my grandmother except in height, hair colour facially the look alike was cute, she once offered me sweets, and I took it from her! I need strength coming in terms with my experienced I need all the courage and I could get. It was all part of body language of understanding within us. Standing next to me, Michelle gives me a feeling physically she was me from my breastplate to my stomach.

By this time, we were close friends; it never crossed my mind of having sexual involvement with Michelle I just liked her. Cross each other's heart, we would do anything for each other. If some people had not poked-nose into our relationship, instead of being avoiders, we both came to the conclusion we would use the conflict for the better with compromise and collaboration. Since Miss. Michelle Cook holds one seal of my Krypton I might not have thought about having the pepper soup ingredients Cordelia Megbele gave me but I did the phenomena was strange and awesome in my notion brought about the reincarnation of my grandfather from my father's side of our family. Yet ye I am in 2015 still drinking alcohol, smoking and on medication it might all be out of my own choices.

True love can be born to each other because we were sworn to each other, before we were born and in our past life. Sometimes you and I could do less depending on not the scenarios but the conditions that lies ahead; we were within proximity of reality and good intention. Since I came back into the UK, I am still piecing it all into reality it has been quite an experience.

Most of us only venture into this world to set ourselves free, Michelle understood this scenario about me, it is inevitable if she was one time my earthly grandmother. I was not only a jowl in my family; I would be to her a pendulum or a barometer, Michelle had done well for me in the first place at Lewisham collage and the second time at Iceland frozen food chain store plc.

Some people raise up families, yet they do not know, what it is to raise a family. What I mean is that, they cannot face their responsibility or they have them because of what they can receive. Subconsciously all children know why, they are within the family they are born into, it's all in the meaning of getting together to be more than friends or to know each other very well. I believe in synergy that it holds a very huge meaning to human existence yet we go through unending conflict.

We all have mission to complete as we undergo our trials of life Michelle at the time I knew her was the only female child to both her parents at the time I was working with her among other children her parents had. I guess the reason for this, is that she needed to be educated, live another life of trial, pay a price or give explanation to all the Megbele's she had given birth to in her past life as Awoma while I endeavoured to loosen the chains around me.

All schizophrenics are said to suffer some unusual behaviours, odd speech, ideas, aggressiveness, outburst or in-cooperative behaviours, it needs thorough explanation. Schizophrenia illness always occurs within people close to when something in their life is about to end it could be brought about by a bitter lose disappointment or you feel things should have been different. The effects are i.e. seizure, relapse, disappointment or unpredictable bitterness about life.

In Africa we hardly treat each other rightly we are very segregated right from our grassroots', I have always grown up, hoping for other people, to treat me right as much as I want to treat them right. Most people go into another people's country, wanting to be treated right. 21st August 2014 immigration in the UK has increased drastically.

Charity begins at home? Africa should at this stage, be a

protocol within us in Africa and Jamaican's, Caribbean's, Trinidad's treating each other right, there are too much of conflict and antagonism. If this goes on for another several years, I would want to send out a message that we are just going into other peoples countries to yearn for whatever they have, which could be termed as greed which leads to obscurities in the way we live our lives for example in the UK. We long for what is right but we cannot initiate right, justice, love, and peace instead we initiate hate, misunderstanding and, conflicts within ourselves.

We are no longer isolated from the rest of the world; no part of the world should be isolated from the rest of the world. In the case of Africa, Jamaica, Barbados, Caribbean and some parts of Asia something fell down from the sky, The Western hemispheres paved another avenue, by moving us from Africa to Jamaica, Caribbean, Trinidad, because, we were scotched from the skies.

We Africans for no reason like to suffer in soul, body, and mind; If only we could no longer be like children at nursery school, the quite pupils during school terms are not found to be playful; they hardly speak to other people and their play mates. They are meant to be observers which, they could be very good at...

During the end of school terms, such children are found to be in doors with their parents at homes, they are hardly found coming out to play with their nursery mates. About time for nursery term to begin, this is when they might go out of their homes playing with their friends, peeping, observing their fellow school mates, for awhile just about when another school term is about to begin. This should be a time when such children are completing their home work or revision this, is what I want us to be.

At such school terms they could spend longer hours outside with their school mates, when they really get to know their school mates and environment better. It could be done with some attitudes, which should not be observed with the wrong impression about such children as being too playful or what makes a bird fly? Its Purpose.

As a schizophrenic sufferer, I am undergoing a trial of my own choice because of certain life inherent incoherencies through various life cycles at the same time, I wonder when this whole world would become one big happy family just as Miss. Michelle Cook had said.

It is the glory and God unveiling himself that initiates humans to do the right things, to repent instead of to sin this are what has been greeting the world moving from one stage of our existence to another. It depends if we are happy with it. Of course we should be happy with it, becomes, we have choice because God have made man far too sufficient.

Such is the characteristic of schizophrenias, their attitude depict a suffering with implications, that they might be completing their life trials on earth, if not, their next phase of life which, could be of drastic concurrence or structured with ingrained and determined actions they cannot come in terms with.

With such concurrences about their life they display inherent traits if coupled with unprecedented events or procedures; mental health issues depict our community as a state of the art in relevance to its failures.

They also depict the world as a state of the art with its inconsistencies. The same situation applies to love, parentage, they subsume in relevance with life incoherencies such as cloning, surrogacy, being gay, lesbian, transsexual or a situation where our relationship is now a dating sight which makes me sigh!

Nevertheless there is nothing happening in the world, that does not happen for reasons, good or bad, as far those of us, who have kept our faithfulness, with our wings intact to fly away free and stay away from the rubbles of the earth that are unholy, with no way to shield our selves, while we divest ourselves from evil and inconsistencies. It is not all cases of mental illness that has to do with drugs, aggressive behaviours some of them are cause by some ingrained fault of life inherences and not by our own doing.

Would the world subsume, life and all things on earth have their purpose, it is filled with too many unsolved mysteries. It is evil in the world that would subsume, that is why we have, confirmation and baptism at church as we eat the bread of life and the drink the blood of life.

Just as the Arabs as Islam wash their hands and legs before prayers so should we all, wash our hands, mind, body and soul out of sin and evil. In heaven, we would only dwell in spiritual form. These are part of my hallucinations that my illness is a trial of life, also that I am a slave to righteousness as other people are slaves of unrighteousness.

We can all know ourselves as we once were before the universe was created, because God and the Heaven had made human and all things sufficient. Yet not everybody believes in the existence of God. It is therefore left for each individual in their own way and by choice to become wise and realistic based on what; they are confronted with in life which is my explanation of existence.

It is about time those who have been true to their existence, having kept their wings intact before creation, put on their dancing shoes for taking off. Our lives should not all be dreams that never comes true, it should not be, because in reality each day, our lives are ruled by chance or coincidence; we should become aware we belong to the Heavens, know what it feels like to have been once part of the Heavens, before we are actually there when our chore are all over.

By this time, one would have conquered death we have thousand of incoherencies that depicts these in our lives based on realisation, e.g. death itself, illness, pain, broken hearth, suffering e.tc. Only on earth do we humans come across the good, the bad and the ugly.

Our lives are always a state of the art life itself stands on a scale, the earth is on hobbits. All evil people know themselves for what they are; just as the good know themselves but in pain. It is customary for each of us to know if we are good or bad, we have choice.

God have made man sufficient in a world where there is beauty, ugliness and death, who else, need judge you or me? In a world of existence in which not only I but numerous people could suffer from mental illness, one can be impotent or be a transsexual what do we think we would be, when we die? Our religious leaders hardly know or depict heaven for me, tell me one thing about heaven what then, is this great religion about heaven we hardly know most of them do not know.

If one is good, knowing it of once self in trials of life, self sacrifices are made, it is customary for one to be shaken, heartfelt or incapable of standing firm to remain good natured. Such scenarios at times could make us feel life is not fear to us!

All things have a singular and plural meaning to our existence in this universe of ours; we go through various lives blind folded filled with incoherencies. With each individual learning lesson to ascertain, explicate and invariably become masters of their soul, mind and body if this is basic? Could mental illness be all that bad? No not if our existence on earth is a trial of life while there are a million inconsistencies.

For example it is my choice to be a celibate, I am living up to my own expectations in view of reality, people; especially from my fellow Africans who find these about me as unprecedented. With an illness, personal care, hygiene, concern for my children to be, self scarifies is what I should put forward to pay my tights. I do not have to be a Christian, Islam, pagan or native doctor to understand my life expectations.

It does not mean am living up to the expectation of the Western hemisphere being a celibate, it is a matter of choice, with me using my common sense in relation to my ethnic origin, family background, scenarios in my life, what I feel is right without my being judgmental, all am asking for is my freedom!

I and my brother initiation as a freemason were based on a mode to be celibate if we have the intuition or willingness to be a celibate, realising its implications in our life trials.

My initiation paved another avenue for me to remain firm in my trials of life, if it had occurred to me to change my mind. It was a matter of choice within me, my fellow brethrens in freemason, with the presence of my father and my immediate elder brother Mr. Omagbemi.

Earth itself is a state of the art involving the good the bad and the ugly. The world we live in is no game mostly those who want to be masters are aware of this. Being good, might be observe as living a life filled with dreams. Everything has its reality our dreams, our hallucination or our consciences even the thoughts in our minds.

What stops anyone, if they are good, to carrying on being good, being truthful and just, to themselves and to other people? While on earth, it is the reality about our existence that really matters and the reality of being good is your head is always bowed down rather than lifting your head high. For once head to be this way means there are certain things you do not approve of or certain occurrence has taken place in your life making you feel this way. Other people might choose otherwise depending on our intentions in life

Trying at all time as much as possibly to be good would be fear to our conscience and God our creator. It is an irony that being good dose not means you get attention or become stronger or successful. It goes deeper into testing your credibility of being good or being who you are.

Regardless of life inherent in-concurrences our soul, mind and body should seek to entwine with whatever source we feel, have initiated us into this world. If the source is discovered initiating us to be constantly good and we feel fine about it at all times, it would be like a weddings in our heats i.e. till death do us part, while other people may consider you as weak.

No matter the circumstances if with our life having vast

differences with singular, plurals and adverbs attached to every situation we find ourselves in, it could become difficult proving our credibility to pull through so much of life difficulties, such as conflicts, illness, failure or natural disasters.

Of which, our lives could naturally become drained of happiness, various illnesses such as schizophrenia, depression, feeling suicidal or sudden death. Other people learn lessons from what we are. We all depend on each other's lives, to ascertain reality, and what our existence is all about or what it is worth. Such are the principles that underline our world where there is suffering. It is the soul and mind that is suffering.

My happiness about being a freemason was that my initiation was pronounced with the gong thou architect of the universe.

26th March 2009, once again Astronauts have taken stunning photos of a heavenly eye watching over the earth from outer space, believed to be the eyes of God or the heaven I hope, I had the feeling they will discover the several pillars that holds the universe this will be when they will see the eyes more clearly. The universe is a system going round its hobbits it has already been programmed with whatever would be as a result of every experience we encounter. It would be a battle until the content of the cup is empty.

It is all about life's trial since time begins between me and Miss Michelle who is anyone to judge us, just as things began getting better within both of us as time went by. It's our life to hold each other; heaven holds the joy of our lives, praise to the heavens for giving us both, the strength to continue undergoing our trials. If love is what you give, love is what you would get.

Heaven has made it possible for both of us and many others to live our lives without controversies as two people with a mission. Putting smile on our face, regardless of the unusual experiences we under go in life. I thank all woman child for their smiling face coupled with the things we have to go through in life.

Britain could be a sugar coated topping for most of us, yet we still have questions to ask about where are we heading to, with all that is happening day in day out without an anthological proof that God exist, we are left to make wise decisions' through our existence on earth because it is the only way we could get closer in discovering ourselves and our creator..

I observe all good intention serves good purpose, so dose all evil intentions serves evil purposes then it is no irony we can only learn right from evil; then who dear says God allows evil in this world? For some people they take on to life like a bull. We would all have, our cheer of good and bad times in life whether we like it or not. Our existence should be based on depicting wisdom against any of life inconsistency. One way among many others of observing it, is through mental illness.

Wherever I have been before if I receive a protocol I would go back to the place and give it a kiss once again especially if there could be one or two lost memories and make my presence more realistic as you read on, you would become aware that I know a lot of people in past life I can hardly keep count of them. Just as in the DVD Johnny English staring Rowan Atkinson. (I know you; you will come back and dig your grave again. I have a very shy personality.

The situation could be considered with an example of smoking; we all know smoking is not good to our health. Let's consider from a perspective of a celibate and a smoker with children, who among the two is more considerate not having children about when they smoke?

With a celibate more consideration have been given to a child yet unborn, than a parent having children and then smoking when their children are around considering they might not be in good health. The same applies in a home using ship port pan for frying chips rather than using a microwaves with children around it is more dangerous using frying chip pot then why not use a microwave?

Two friends of opposite sex divorce met and became friends they both had two teenagers of the opposite sex. At the same time the relationship within the two divorcees began to peak; the same thing occurred within the two teenagers. Within both parents and children who should be compelled to make a sacrifices their parents or the children?

These are some philosophical common sense placate of reasoning which calls for results when implying some psychological constructive criticism about consideration, i.e. I prefer having a light up when I want to smoke only when am in doors in my flat and not when I am outside, within the midst of other people.

The Africa I went to years ago, have changed a lot, as a child in Africa growing up I did not go there to play. I was born with a birth condition which was favourable for me in many ways to reside in Africa at that particular time. While the petroleum wells might be getting dry.

Premature children are less likely to over react over irrationalities; they are like a pendulum or a barometer in an environment they are akin to. If I had spent all my life in the UK with my birth condition I might not have survived.

I was born four months premature; as I discovered recently children born four months premature do survive. Thanks to medical science, for making it possible, four months babies born premature can now survive in the 21st century, I may have tails to tell! Yet, Test tub babies, sperm donor's babies, cloned and children with surrogate parents their time will come; they would have more than tails to tell!

From my personal point of view, regarding Miss. Lydia Omagbuse Megbele my niece, Mr. Omagbemi Megbele my immediate elder brother's daughter, with condition of birth as a suzerain in connection to my being born premature in the 1960's what or how could it have reflected my niece genuflected through her birth as a suzerain. What is it that could have been between, me and my brother who were both born in the same hospital in Islington in the district of Tollington in London? My National Health Service card issued by the Inner London Executive Council with NHS number KTFBT 129 was issued under the name of Dr. B. Anderson 8545; 143 Blackstock Road who administered me international certificate of vaccination of Smallpox our dwelling at the time is 101 Plimsoll Road N.4. Islington my register of birth is Beatrice H. Stockbridge.

Children such as I and my niece Miss Lydia Megbele with protocols of condition of birth are probably because of some life inherent traits through in-concurrences i.e. nature, family background, environment, or life style this time, for my niece, it was in 1995, when I was taken ill as a paranoid schizophrenics at Greenwich hospital.

To confirm peculiar reason based on reality within a particular family relationship, when there could be unpredictable incoherencies by nature within a family. Could scenario have been attached to my family relationship when I was born?

For what reasons, do such incoherence's do occur, It calls for an awareness of realisation that the earth, and the Universe have pillars, laws, which puts everything that happens on earth in place and check, e.g. our iniquities, our motives, the things we should do and not do some of which leads to the occurrence of e catastrophes which are all part of our trials of life and endeavours. If we are moving towards civilisation the first thing appropriate to do, would be, to do away with conflicts.

The nature we see awesome effects whilst on earth naturally should compel each of us to do almost everything we are confronted with right in plausible manners or be on our guard. It becomes more evident that it is the wicked mind, with true and deliberate intentions to be wicked that makes our existence fall short of purpose and reality. We live in a complicated world, only time will tell!

With my condition of premature birth, consider the situation how we handle, and spend currencies in Africa, our market place, the roads, the nature of our homes and after rubbing body all over African in such scenarios' coming back to reside in the UK was for me, to have a better chance to live longer. Was this an implementation of juju or witchcraft? No it is a condition.

A child born premature to an African parent in the mid 1960 when television took its advent in Nigeria, sign a business contract to the parent the father has an office safe; he owns a briefcase there are all types of children born with illnesses within a child compared if they are male or female suffering from epilepsy, jaundice, premature birth, dyslexia, rickets which one of them would account or withstand currency in a briefcase or in a safe if born with a strength or force taken from something of superman krypton?

The child's father was a freemason, a lodge member the mother was a nurse the child was sworn into life with an insignia considering in the UK, America and in Europe before the father or mother of the child were born currency had always been served to the general public through a counter in a bank or in post office.

Saturday the 23 rd of August 2008, I woke up restless, for two days, I have not had a meal, because, I couldn't eat. I decided to have a walk outside. As I was going down Rectory Place in Woolwich, I met Mr. Dotun Sobowale on the way he lives at Rectory Place, just by Kingsman Street. Mr. Dotun had been helping me a lot, keeping in touch with me and my psychiatrist appointments at the Ferryview mental health centre at John Wilson Street and have over the years been very concerned about my health.

As I was passing by Rectory place, Mr. Dotun was inside his car, he called me as I was walking by. I told him how I felt this Saturday morning, he was of the opinion that I have regular walks; it could make me feel better health wise.
With my naturally coyly hair, and Pony tail, Mr. Dotun commented, that I look much better than when we met earlier.

I and my niece Miss. Lydia Omagbuse Megbele are now involved in the 21st century studies of cybernetics, a branch of science in which, electrons and mechanical system are studied and compared to biological system. Who say I have not been lucky that I have not yet had my driving license.

I have been more than lucky for my sake or for anyone else I later in life, suffer from this paranoia that I cannot stand or face the tremor of having an accident or injuring someone through an accident. In my own case in the early 1970's at Port-Harcourt I was knocked down by a bicycle when I and Omagbemi were walking down to primary school I was hurt and bleeding through my nose.

Entering the 21st century, solar energy is coming to effect, very soon all over the Western hemisphere, whilst I was in Africa under so intense sunshine I felt better. White race British, always travelling regularly to places like Jamaica, the Caribbean and Barbados to bask on sunshine what good, would the British cold weather had been to me, if I had remained in the UK since my birth for me whilst in Africa, the pillars of Africa where light enough for my survival until I was drenched.
Then, there were less dumping of toxic waste water shortage, overcrowding and too much noise, bribery and corruption which made my head buzz. In Africa I enjoyed the rain and sunshine it was good on my skin which made me felt energetic.

All those years in Africa the effect of thunderstorm never occurred to me or how I had been surviving with the effect until I was told at the age of 18 years by my mother that I was born premature the thunderstorm was always cantered right on top of my head so what makes me so different? Global warming is just around the corner in the Western hemisphere which, I am now part of. Nature is beauty it could be kind to some of us only if, we know how to implement ourselves within it.

One of my purposes in life is to hold, the statues of Zeus above my head with the sun above it, while the earth hold me down. By this time, I would be like any other human being, to possess one of the most beautiful of all women from the heritage of Zeus. By which towards the end of time my Krypton seal and strength as Superman would hold down many intolerable genetic diseases and caters trophies.

Orisia was her name she was not only beautiful, she was charismatic with great mysteries, power and authority who hopes to bring peaces at sea. She traded mysteries and power with an African priest by name Orunmila who, I consider as myself; this where during ancient eras. There are white and black witchcraft, sorcery, and magic, myth for good or for evil among mankind some individual wanted powers that has to do with mysteries or to unfold mysteries.

Orunmila's heritage was so filled with conflicts; Orisia had suggestion to refine the situation. Orunmila was a priest with good intentions. This was a case which did implied being good those not mean you get attention, good only gets attention when thing have gone wrong.

She told him it was foreseen in her own origin strife was about to come that would split nations the gods and the underworld. In which case, both of them had to combine their strength. It wasn't going to be easy but is worth endeavouring.

Orunmila and Orisia have been friends long before time both of whom have been living various reincarnated lives to this present 21st century. They were both man and woman among many others from life after death to reincarnate once more where in all scenarios both of them were found to be always powerful and resilient. Could it be for some reason why people of their origin moved towards Celestial and Aladura worship in Nigeria?

It is natural for some people with power to ask their inner selves why power won't leave them alone. This is why in my opinion; life on earth is to divest ourselves why do we have dreadlocks. Adam and Eve were better off in the Garden of Eden; they would have been better-off to dwell within heaven and the Garden of Eden? Why should man been created, placed in the Garden of Eden then driven out of the Garden of Eden why should it be so? Rather to live a life with pain toils and conflict.

One of the reasons I have written this book is to obtain the views of my doctors, psychiatrist and philosophers, physiologists, scientist, and sociologist to address the issues contained in this book I seem to be living three lives at the same time; we could be the only humans in the universe each individual has to undergo procedures before it could result to developments of the human mind, soul, body, and their environment and towards eternal life. Coupled with life incoherencies and concurrences to be put in right perspectives; why do we exist in a world, where there is beauty, ugliness and death.

Within my life in Africa and Europe, I have undergone philosophical, physiological, and sociological and psychiatrist change through nature which are yet to be observed and put thoroughly into perspectives by scholars? It would be an important step that the studies might probably confirm that life on earth is a school. That it is when some people get fed up with life that they suffer from mental illness or either because something unexplained had happened or cannot just leave them alone. Existence could be torn apart based on what is reality or what is unrealistic

The Western hemisphere, believe in science, technology, and developments. They apply it in almost very thing they do, through interaction and associating with other nations bear it in mind they also did practice witchcraft, magic and sorcery during ancient times. An irony is that interaction among black race because of such issue like slavery could have brought about love and respect within themselves, we should have been able to create stronger ties within each other, no wonder, we are still in a hollow, and we should be one big happy family.

At this stage in the 21st century we have everything, other nations could look up to us for such as great expectation for ourselves and the rest of the world we are in disposition now to sum up courage use our recourses to our own advantage, make our livelihoods better to meet present and future demands to make ourselves more happy. No more basking in ill-gotten wealth cutting and reaping each other off. Statues and self importance mean more to us than developing our nation it is time we stop making excuses it does not seems our future holds room for excuses anymore

The same thing applies to Jamaicans, Caribbean's, Barbados, Trinidad's, Indians and West Indies. Could it be we love going through pain in body, mind, soul, heartaches and augments' because we care less for each other we would rather want to use the next person predicament to appraise ourselves in action and deeds. From what, I have experience in Africa we are the same thing here in Europe.

Suffering from a disability in my opinion is for a sufferer becoming wiser under natures inconveniences, the experience really matters to some people with disabilities it is not all of them who cry each day asking God why should we suffer.

If after your life on earth with suffering or disability all of a sudden you find yourself in heaven tomorrow would it not be for the ample or the little grace you received for being in heaven, if anyone seeks to go against God, the more you will be ready to sign your allegiance to God for not wanting to come back to what your disability used to be before?

In many cases people know of their sufferings with little knowledge of why they suffer or why suffering is attached to their existence nobody likes suffering then, if you have and you see people suffer why not help them out rather than imply why should God not come down and take their suffering away if he is God we are his people and we are suffering?.

It is the good minded once amongst us who would be of the opinion that life is not all that unfair to them because they have disability or they are suffering! Heaven bless them. In Africa, some people have no disabilities, yet their condition of suffering is far worse in body, soul, and mind and in spirit than with having disabilities. Yet, each nation in Africa has got a government.

The NHS, doctors, physiologist, psychiatrist, philosophers, sociologist and religion groups, should try speaking to some of us, to really ascertain how we feel about the world, our communities and about our disabilities. All science wants to do is acclaim that science is better than believing in God science is knowledge and knowledge is God this, would be unfair to humanity.

What is this issue about my being a celibate? It's not a big deal; it is part precaution to some life incoherent, inconsistent and concurrences I do not want to hold on to. Much could be attached to putting celibacy in the lamplights, but considering:

A woman or a man could be so disable that sex is not an issue in their personal lives.
More complicated it is about gay clergies getting lawfully married at church. Every church is a place of Gods sanctuary devoted to God, our mind and our spirituality. I am not judgmental gay or lesbian priests rather, I am doing three things:

Queries on why disabilities dose occur what are the true meaning of cloning and surrogacy.
Vice, homosexuals, lesbians, which might have happened, that through such practices, has led to transsexuals in both male and females.

The churches all over the world are querying doctors, businesses, our environmentalists, our homes and personal lives.

Today, many people are of the opinions, that the church is also now a profitable business, which is true calling for moral consideration of what is happening in our world of today. This is a good thing to observe.

Why should a priest be gay or a lesbian while some of them are happily married or celibates'? So that we all should be more observant and true so at the end of the day, it would not be a matter of, you where there on earth, where you blind! When another apocalypse dose took over the earth they are meant to be guardians then, you should look up to yourself spiritually.

They might be in the process of telling the whole world

something is wrong with our family lives more than the politician can do or the science of medicine can do.

This reminds me of Reverend April Keech once a Vicar of Saint John's church Lewisham. As a dedicated member of the church, for years whilst she was the vicar I was not only a member of the church but also a member of the church's choir, I observe Reverend April Keech as a dedicated, spiritually gifted, strong, powerful vicar. Everything she does and says, puts everything in a right perspectives, so did other members of the congregation at Saint John Lewisham. She is one I would describe as having a close resemblance to my mother Mr. Joy Tomori Abeni Faneye Megbele I met her after my mother's death a striking feature I encountered in the young girl I saw at Iceland Frozen food plc Woolwich who, I have the notion is the reincarnation of my late mother has a slight resemblance to Reverend April Keech.

One Sunday in 2004, she told us that God gave her a call that she should move on. In my opinion why, after you have put so much efforts in this church for years making it strong with members of the congregation continuing to worship in good faith! Our efforts on our trials of life can be upheld by religion in this our modern day ways of life the theme should be perception of ultimate spiritual reality. Such is life, it does have implications in our everyday ways of living things happen to redress them in our lives.
More and more children are being born with different medical conditions. The future is yet to tell if each part of the world is playing their part under a universal certainty from the wish of the heavens or of God the architect of the universe.

We live in a world where things happen within people that are not supposed to happen that is when we raise our eyebrows or pay attention to our inner self based on what is going on than reality creeps in.

14th December 2007 I had began to inrush on how I would have my manuscripts published. I was only on income support and disability living allowance as my only income, I had to pay back Greenwich housing council over £900.00 to pay towards an overpayment of housing benefit thanks heaven they did not put down all the overpayment as recoverable after I made a plea at least I know what landlords do in Nigeria when tenants do not pay their rent.

When things like these happen it is common for mental health sufferers to feel they are being intimidated by the organisations involved, I have undergone worse sonorous in Africa under a polygamous home where children can't speak to their parents openly for school materials at certain times children have to make a plea or beg. Step mother are there to see their own children get better of whatever you need if your own mother or father is not around within their polygamous home.

This book have been written in other to initiate changes, it is not only common in Africa, rather than reacting, you are compel into taking every situation at other peoples stride probably, with heartfelt feelings, situation one is not compelled to be obliged with. In developed parts of the world, if you are keen you could go on lightly un-scotched because you are free not to do as you please but to do whatever, you feel is right or suits you.

People admit it is because, they are civilised it is not that there is no poverty. To my understanding the full meaning of civilisation has it full potentials when the entire or 99 percent of its population residing in the community are happy, in high understanding and exhilaration.

Within some people from multi-cultural race from all over the world residing in the UK, I put it through to Ms Sally Bryden Head of Strategic Development for Oxleas NHS that the UK is structured for which reasons it brings out the best of its citizens. Yes structured yet in some ways for some people to personalise themselves within its structure, or why do I choose to work with an illness while on the job, someone else wants to hypo-emphasis his or her own charisma with my condition.

Hypothetically Africans, Jamaicans, Caribbean's, Barbados, and Trinidad where all once part of Africans I cannot believe in this century we could reside in Europe and attend to ourselves with indifference.

Some people suggest in the UK all multi-culture groups should have and run their own schools, some say they should have their own film industries and medical practice. It would only result to more segregation and stigma. Infarct some members of our community e.g. schizophrenia's have been attached with stigma and victimisation for the rest of their lives. They all cannot be that bad.

Some people suggest Africans children in the UK should feed on African dishes; all this is happening in our very eyes yet; the community is silent about it. Some English says if you are born in the UK, you are English while in some part of Europe African are observed in their communities as alien's all under the nose of civilisation.

Victim support is a national charity giving free and confidential help to victims of crime, witnesses, their family, friends and anyone else affected across England and Wales. They also speak out as a national voice for victims and witnesses and campaign for change.

They are not a government agency or part of the police and you don't have to report a crime to the police to get their help. They can be contacted at any time after a crime has happened, whether it was yesterday, last week or several years ago and they have offices throughout England and Wales and we run the Witness Service in every criminal court

Europe still has a long way to go through its self actualisation process in view of our new shape of civilisation process. On letting Ms. Karen Dadby at victim support know I was writing a book, not about what was going on at victim support I was told to withdraw as she told me so, I heard a voice saying but if, I do really know what was going on I should write about my own experience. The content of my writing then, had nothing to do with victim support at the time of my volunteering, and then I decided to include what I felt as my experience through my volunteering.

I sent my word processed document which had nothing to do with my volunteering to Ms. Karen Dadby my co-ordinator at victim support London implying that here in the UK certain experience could be the same as it could be in Africa or entwine. Two of my co-volunteers Mr Jay has resemblance to my half brother Mr. Sola Awe his girl friend Miss Say had resemblance to both I and Miss Loraine O'Connor.

I felt, we were there because we all had something in common and the situation had already been mapped out by victim support that we meet. I felt, they were of the opinion I should go and have a mate and have children before my brother Mr. Sola Awe follows. As the notion occurred to me I felt it was good for us to meet and shear our family and background experiences. May be they were just concerned! With my condition of birth if I should have a molar tooth extracted who, would inherit it? Few months after my experience my step brother Mr Sola Awe paid a visited to the UK from Nigeria and visited me in London which made my experience and the notions I had seems practicably real and I had no idea he was coming to visit me. To make me understand he had a perception of what had taken place because he used a terminology of words that I felt it was the spoon that was bending but it was I that was bending.

Mr Sola Awe should speak for himself he did through his visit news travel fast these days, I felt they should be more concerned to know more about my ups and downs may be, they would then understand why I chose to be a celibate and I have mental health issues. I looked at both Mr. Jay and Miss. Say and wished them all the best in their relationship. They are both lovers and were at university we were told to bring in memorabilia they brought those of their parents and family members. I would have brought a picture of my late mother but I brought a picture of Miss Loraine O'Connor as my memorabilia. Other applicants came from varied work of life ethnicity, background and race such as housing, security staff others were students and single parents.

We are all living in an ever changing world we are not aware we have reached the age of perception. I wrote to Ms. Karen Dadby and Charles victim support told them little about me and Mr Sola Awe. Victim support is now a state of the art, you go there to meet people who are replicas of other people you are probably involved with such as what you do actions that you might take, may also affect them you sit down together at victim support and you discus and it determines if you would play a good role with victim support if you are accepted. Ms. Karen Dadby, Mr Charles, Derek, Angela, Sue, and many other would be volunteers were replicas and of people I know. Victim support is now a forum for hearing indifferences, giving support to each other.

We have immigrants who come in from Africa personalising with the lives of Africans who are born in the UK. They should rather make good reasoning for the better of how we UK born Africans feel because to some of us we feel biased we have no African background to return to I guess it might have been the same way I made some people feel when I came back to the UK. Children from African backgrounds born in the UK if they have lived all their lives here or came back from their native land should check on themselves more of us are being driven into mental illness and social exclusion. We try each day to adjust to other ethnic groups which are divers in race from all over the world, culture creeds and opinions and its not easy for us to manoeuvre our ways through them. Britain is a country that changes very too often one could be taken by surprise it is not easy for children born in the UK who have lived outside Britain from their youth. They usually need to adjust moreover we came from diverse background and upbringing arrayed with conflict or prejudice from our parental native land before making Europe our dwelling place where culture, heritage, working practice, social life are also divers and more sophisticated it takes time to adjust if one is really here to live sensibly. Our parents and leader within our developing countries need to do something based on what is going on out there in our native land for us to look back home to and really upon it would improve our livelihood here in Europe. They also having children here in the UK, should understand the situation most of whom are not looking forward going back to their native land children born here have the livelihood they need such as food, shelter and clothing, education, school meals, including their native diet if they choose to feed on them, good roads for crossing and motor way, leisure activities with wide arrays of initiatives in a more sophisticated level they also need to understand themselves and what is going on in the land of their root while they tend to hassle about their children for what? They are in good hands. Voices I hear from my mother in her new reincarnation are my child has prepared Jolof rice, my son ate Egusi when I go to the African market I hear her voices saying do not buy the goat head I mean she encourages me in lots of ways it's as if she is discussing with are age groups she speaks English I hear the interpretation of her words in Yoruba which gives this assurance she was destined to have been my mother the whole experience is like a miracle. In her new reincarnation she has resemblance to Miss. Joan Keeble facially their body build is almost similar. I do not hear voices from Miss. Joan Keeble only impression of understanding whenever we meet. Most times we meet, there is something bordering me.

They do not fetch water on their heads distance away from their home, tap water are running with good central heating, they do not wash their clothing's or those of their parent cloth by hand or polish their parents shoes by hand as I use to do in Nigeria whilst living with my parents. It takes time, energy, effort and consideration to put forward what Britain has got to offer they should be acknowledged for their great effort. While we hardly show feelings we care for ourselves I mean within ourselves it's the conflicts back home that rules us.

Teachers 'Giving Food Handouts to Poor Pupils' thousands of pupils on the poverty line are missing out on breakfast and lunch because they cannot afford to eat, a report claims. Teachers are helping hungry school children with food handouts and money to buy lunch, a survey revealed thousands of pupils on the poverty line are missing out on breakfast and even lunch because they cannot afford to eat, ultimately affecting their concentration and performance in class. According to the study by The Children's Society, more than half of the UK's teachers are seeing hungry pupils at school. Almost three in four of those questioned said they have seen youngsters coming into school with no lunch and no way to pay for one. A teacher said, 'I can't see why I can't put my hand in my pocket just to help them out for that time.' The survey, conducted with the Association of Teachers and Lecturers (ATL) and the National Union of Teachers (NUT), reveals that two-thirds (66%) of school staff say that teachers are providing pupils with food or money for meals if they turn up for lessons hungry. Highlighting just how tough it was for some pupils on the poverty line who cannot afford to eat, one tutor said in the report: 'Myself and many teachers in other schools feed children with bread or crackers in the morning from their own budget.'

'They lose their concentration and make poor behaviour choices in class. It's compounded if they have not had breakfast and lunch.' The government says it is committed to providing free school meals for those that need them the most, but campaigners say proposed benefit changes next year may see some losing out.

Matthew Reed, chief executive of The Children's Society, said: 'Something is going badly wrong when teachers themselves had to feed children. When the Universal Credit starts next year it must make free school meals available to all children living in poverty.' Which the government would do all they can to provide in the UK which is constructive but what about other constructive ideas because of the recent GCSE result and the universal credit, what about other constructive ideas about student having to obtain student loans and university tuition fees they are complaining about the turnout of events during the recent years they have the right and the authorities would listen that is living with people who care.

Gratitude, thankfulness, gratefulness, or appreciation is a feeling or attitude in acknowledgment of a benefit that one has received or will receive. The experience of gratitude has historically been a focus of several world religions, and has been considered extensively by moral philosophers such as Adam Smith. The systematic study of gratitude within psychology only began around the year 2000, possibly because psychology has traditionally been focused more on understanding distress rather than understanding positive emotions. However, with the advent of the positive psychology movement, gratitude has become a mainstream focus of psychological research. The study of gratitude within psychology has focused on the understanding of the short term experience of the emotion of gratitude state gratitude, individual differences in how frequently people feel gratitude trait gratitude, and the relationship between these two aspects. This is something I want to experience in Britain existence is choice we should make ends meet by being realistic am not being prejudice to anyone or any race the future which lies before us determines our predisposition.

A third of the teachers questioned also said they felt the size of the school meal offered was small or inadequate.

On the same day it was on the news as children's charity used advert to remind people that child abuse remains a widespread problem. This is using caution, understanding and checks informing the public on what is going on in our communities no good parent would see their children hungry and off to school or unable to provide school meals no country provides for its young and old age than the United Kingdom children have their lives and future in their hands in the UK while people go through all sorts of problems and tremors around the world the UK is going through a phase at the moment only reason, emphasis, appreciation and insight of the situation on its pros and corns can elaborate on and not just one sided because right now the world is observing each other.

What is going on Britain and America today are ideologies to make each child gain access to their future and destiny other countries need them and the world is changing fast while we consider it the age of reasoning. Children these days are adults before they are grownups' and they are being treated so by parents and organisations who understand this about their children or youngsters because they want the best out of them'.

It is not right to come into this world then tomorrow you say you have everything and later say, you are not ready to give but take now is the time to have something and really know having that thing is really worth having. There are beliefs; creed and justification to becoming rich, wealthy, wise or prudent. If so, one can be authenticated.

Destiny or fate is a predetermined course of events. It may be conceived as a predetermined future, whether in general or of an individual. It is a concept based on the belief that there is a fixed natural order to the cosmos. Although often used interchangeably, the words 'fate' and 'destiny' have distinct connotations.

Traditional usage defines fate as a power or agency that predetermines and orders the course of events. Fate defines events as ordered or 'inevitable' and unavoidable. Classical and European mythology features three goddesses dispensing fate, known as Moirai in Greek mythology, as Parcae in Roman mythology, and as Norns in Norse mythology. They determine the events of the world through the mystic spinning of threads that represent individual human fates.

Destiny is used with regard to the finality of events as they have worked themselves out; and to that same sense of 'destination', projected into the future to become the flow of events as they will work themselves out.

In other words, 'fate' relates to events of the future and present of an individual and in cases in literature unalterable, whereas 'destiny' relates to the probable future. Fate implies no choice, but with destiny the entity participates in achieving an outcome that is directly related to itself. Participation happens wilfully.

The point is are we, ready to go through a thorough and defined destiny for the better or do we choose going through traumatic destiny? We need not wait until it becomes a crisis situation before something is done.

Some of us are more heartfelt about what is going on in Africa than most people think. Why should they want to speak for us in the UK when all they bring to us are our dashed dreams of our parental background which leaves us disillusioned? The predisposition with which we have viewed the Europeans' from within our parental native land and here in Europe are quite different from the way they would view them. We are on a level for bargain of acceptance few months of their coming here they know the system better than we do while we are observed as weak or rather it is our portrayal on the level of acceptance which makes us weak coupled that there are other race involved with whom we have to create or be in harmony with their presence in too large numbers makes us fragmented from our reality. We want to feel accepted they want to be accepted within us who, would feel the pinch and biased of the inconsistency going on within our native land such scenario does not concern only African born in the UK who have lived their lives at home and within Europe other countries face the same problem especially under developed countries. While they mostly continually make us suffer from default, segregation and general weakness of facing our realities because we are often being laid backward. It's not all Europeans' hearts that are open to immigrants Britain is always trying to help our situation here and back home. My parent giving birth to me in Europe, taking me back to Africa to raise me up is a good initiative it should not go to waste. Why dose education in Britain seems to be no long free?

Most people who come to the UK are from poor background bear it in mind there are level of poverty in developed world at least most of them can still raise their head high moving to higher levels of life.

I have this notion when I took the student loan for my university degree course I took the money from my employer who, I was working under the money I took is my inheritance to gain when working for another employer working for that employer I have to pay part of it towards my student loan which means working for my new employer if I should go back to work after my recent relapse the money becomes more my inheritance including the work I would be carrying out and knowledge gained money do not grow on trees.

Business men and women starts businesses from the scratch it grows becoming probably a multinational business over the years young graduates after leaving university are sort to work in such businesses making lots of capital of their own in some cases after few years becoming chief executives of the company or board of directors naturally, they have taken over. Lots of businesses which started from scratch becoming large cooperate business lose out to them while the market is thriving through other nationals that are not only efforts put in by the graduates this over the years have been hitting business men and women heard coupled they are often faced with competition, social, environmental, economic and government commitments and regulations. Am not surprised student loan was introduced the British government do not come out with such significance as to what the real issues are giving everybody the chance to think and reason it out for themselves especially those who would do the right thing. And one thing about such issues is that they are too decent coming out with it in the open too drastically out of being civil.

Ambivalence is a state of having simultaneous, conflicting feelings toward a person or thing stated another way; ambivalence is the experience of having thoughts and/or emotions of both positive and negative valence toward someone or something. A common example of ambivalence is the feeling of both love and hate for a person. The term also refers to situations where 'mixed feelings' of a more general sort are experienced, or where a person experiences uncertainty or indecisiveness concerning something. The expressions 'cold feet'and 'sitting on the fence' are often used to describe the feeling of ambivalence.

Ambivalence is experienced as psychologically unpleasant when the positive and negative aspects of a subject are both present in a person's mind at the same time. This state can lead to avoidance or procrastination, or to deliberate attempts to resolve the ambivalence. When the situation does not require a decision to be made, people experience less discomfort even when feeling ambivalent.

In psychoanalysis, the concept of ambivalence (introduced by Bleuler in 1911) refers to an underlying emotional attitude in which the co-existing contradictory impulses (usually love and hate) derive from a common source and are thus held to be interdependent. Moreover, when the term is used in this psychoanalytic sense, it would not usually be expected that the person embodying ambivalence would actually feel both of the two contradictory emotions as such. With the exception of cases of obsessional neurosis, one or other of the conflicting sides is usually repressed. Thus, for example, an analysand's love for his father might be quite consciously experienced and openly expressed while his 'hate' for the same object might be heavily repressed and only indirectly expressed, and thus only revealed in analysis. A drug addict may feel ambivalently about their drug of choice; they know that the drug has a destructive effect on their lives (socially, financially, medically, and otherwise), while simultaneously seeking and using it.

Another relevant distinction is that whereas the psychoanalytic notion of 'ambivalence' sees it as engendered by all neurotic conflict, a person's everyday 'mixed feelings' may easily be based on a quite realistic assessment of the imperfect nature of the thing being considered.

Those who have become graduates under the student loan scheme are now more after their rights and privileges as gradates in all areas of work now is the time to consider feelings of ambivalence such as having worked for over 20 years once working and social life looks grim imagine what would happen in Britain.

Because of such an event, I know of someone who is unwell and had studied under the student loan scheme at university who, had used some of his disability living allowance and Employment and Support Allowance to pay back his student loan at least he is facing the reality money do not grow on trees.

There should be peace among us only then, can we face realities being realistic is the greatest strength to face culture, religion, history and our development if we do not try, it can't happen.

With the concept of harmony dose the saying really goes if you travel somewhere, do as they do as much as you try, you would still be who, you are. You are still customary obliged to do as they do to make ends meet.

Approach-avoidance conflicts as elements of stress were first introduced by psychologist Kurt Lewin, one of the founders of modern social psychology. Approach-avoidance conflicts occur when there is one goal or event that has both positive and negative effects or characteristics that make the goal appealing and unappealing simultaneously. For example, marriage is a momentous decision/goal/event that has both positive and negative aspects. The positive aspects, or approach portion, of marriage are togetherness, sharing memories, and companionship; however, there are negative aspects, or avoidance portions, including money issues, arguments, and mortgages. The negative effects influence the decision maker to avoid the goal or event, while the positive effects influence the decision maker to want to approach or proceed with the goal or event.

The influence of the negative and positive aspects creates a conflict because the decision maker either has to proceed with the goal or event or not partake in the goal or event at all. To continue with the example of marriage, a person might approach proposing to a partner with excitement because of the positive aspects of marriage: having a life-long companion, sharing financial responsibilities. On the other hand, he or she might avoid proposing due to the negative aspects of marriage: arguments, money issues, joint decision making.

The approach side of this type of conflict is easy to start toward the goal, but as the goal is approached the negative factors increase in strength which causes indecision. If there are competing feelings to a goal, the stronger of the two will triumph. For instance, if a woman was thinking of starting a business she would be faced with positive and negative aspects. Before actually starting the business, the woman would be excited about the prospects of success for the new business and she would encounter (approach) the positive aspects first: she would attract investors, create interest in her upcoming ideas and it would be a new challenge. However, as she drew closer to actually launching the business, the negative aspects would become more apparent; the woman would acknowledge that it would require much effort, time, and energy from other aspects of her life. The increase in strength of these negative aspects (avoidance) would cause her to avoid the conflict or goal of starting the new business, which might result in indecision.

In England everybody have their right and privileges protected to certain extent I hope after publishing this book I would carry out a survey on Africans, who have lived all their lives in Europe and those born in the UK who have lived part of their lives in Africa. You could be born in the UK, lived all your life here or, you have lived part of your life within your parental background, your background is always still part and parcel of our lives we are mostly taken by what is happening in our native land the news we received makes us unsettled or unhappy the situation calls for consensus decision-making and conflict resolution.

Conflict resolution is conceptualized as the methods and processes involved in facilitating the peaceful ending of conflict. Often, committed group members attempt to resolve group conflicts by actively communicating information about their conflicting motives or ideologies to the rest of the group (e.g., intentions; reasons for holding certain beliefs), and by engaging in collective negotiation. Ultimately, a wide range of methods and procedures for addressing conflict exist, including but not limited to, negotiation, mediation, diplomacy, and creative peace building.

The term conflict resolution may also be used interchangeably with dispute resolution, where arbitration and litigation processes are critically involved. Furthermore, the concept of conflict resolution can be thought to encompass the use of nonviolent resistance measures by conflicted parties in an attempt to promote effective resolution

When personal conflict leads to frustration and loss of efficiency, counselling may prove to be a helpful antidote this was what I felt victim support tried to achieve through we some intelligent resourceful applicants. Although few organizations can afford the luxury of having professional counsellors on the staff, given some training, support groups may be able to perform this function.

Nondirective counselling or listening with understanding or sometimes the simple process of being able to vent one's feelings that is, to express them to a concerned and understanding listener, is enough to relieve frustration and make it possible for the frustrated individual to advance to a problem-solving frame of mind, better able to cope with a personal difficulty that is affecting his work adversely. The nondirective approach is one effective way for support groups to deal with frustrated subordinates and co-workers.

There is other more direct and more diagnostic ways that might be used in appropriate circumstances. The great strength of the nondirective approach however, lies in its simplicity, its effectiveness, and the fact that it deliberately avoids the counsellor's diagnosing and interpreting emotional problems which would call for special psychological training. Listening to with sympathy and understanding, calling on others who might narrowly be involved may sooth the problem, and is a widely used approach for helping people to cope with problems that interfere with their effectiveness in life.

It is not as common as it use to be in the past for some well to do African parent sending their children to Europe for University education, after their studies they usually go back to Africa to do as their parents say because it draws them towards wealth or prestige. During their education in Europe such undergraduate look for money coming from their parents in anxiety, at certain times depression set into their endeavours, while at the same time studying they had work part-time.

I wonder why they go back to Africa after their education without having dreams for the development of their native mother land they usually become authoritarians. Most of such Africans do nothing but accumulate wealth. When I mean wealth I mean money; money is not wealth, I mean tangible wealth. They might have been stereo-typed to be self centred yet they are better off developing their native land which they do nothing about how can such ice be broken within third world nations? Could the once coming into Europe in the 21st century do any better?

As a UK born citizen in this 21st century, I have to pay tuition fees, take student loan on conditions I should not be on any state benefits. I have to pay for my council flat, buy my books; I should have had a family of my own. My parents and background have already played its part in my life before I came back to the UK with my experience it is difficult to be realistic.

My late mother worked for R.T Briscoe pharmaceutical while we were living at Lagos and Leyland motors limited Ibadan Oyo state. I depicted myself in Nigeria as man of steal. I told my psychiatrist about my feelings about all creatures in my neighbourhood are my best friend's cats, dogs, rats, tootle – dove or pigeons, the Raven, Black-bird, butterflies, insect and the seagull bird makes me suffer from hallucination. Not only this, I also have the intuition that I was once Orunmila.

My benefit office implied that because of my disability as schizophrenics, I would not have been able to word process letter posted to them with regards to my claim for benefits. I was taken aback it was as a result of my birth inherent threat things like computers interest me.

Putting it into perspectives it was later after becoming graduate most elites began using computers most of them had to go on short courses in computing. With the use of computing in every working place and at our homes, everyone including third world countries is interested in computing. Almost every individual are now interested in computing.

I am writing this book because it is my entitlement for being British, probably it could be the reason why I am born as a British subject have lived part of my life in Africa in my youth with a next phase of my life in Britain.

I told Dr. Banjac my psychiatrist about my being upset and a painful congestion in my chest. He gave me a note to report to Endoscopy department at Queen Elizabeth hospital to see Dr. Saxena for gastroenterology on March 19th 2007. My consultant gastroenterology was Dr Alistair McNair. Going through it I realised I had gone through an ordeal because instead of having the test through an anaesthetics, I had it without anaesthetics.

Coming back in doors I felt traumatised, depressed, and uncomfortable. I had to report to the Ferryview health centre Dr Tran put me on Mirtazapin my usual antidepressant just for some time.

At one point I did usually suffer from dizzy spells I developed swaying, feeling giddy and symptoms of weightlessness I lost more weight considerably immediately after my gastroenterology test.

I had to continue working because I needed something to keep me preoccupied or I become restless, Dr Banjac told me I should stay off work for some time. My suffering was so intense at one point I had to go personally to the hospital by dialling 999 for an ambulance because of the utmost intensity of the pain.

At the hospital when the ambulance got there I was taken in for examination which took some time. Then I began to feel better but because of my dizzy spells with sawing and feeling giddy, I was then taken to the psychiatrist ward they put me on prescribed Omeprazole 10mg capsules.

After some time rather than being admitted I told them I did not want to be admitted they should call me a taxi to take me back to my flat can you imagine my taxi ride was free of charge courtesy of Queen Elizabeth Hospital. With the care and attention I received if I were in Nigeria within people I do not know or have not met with before could I receive such an attention and care?

Afterwards the side effects of my medication after some days was putting on weight with big appetite, feeling sick, and dizziness, feeling faint, and having difficulty sleeping. I could not complete the dosage of my medication before running to Dr. Sami Rached at the Ferryview health centre because of the side effects namely depression, confusion, loss of memory, and difficulty in breathing, mood swing such as irritation, abnormal spasm, and skin rashes.

At one time I do usually suffer from dizzy spells every day, this symptom became worse, and I developed swaying, feeling giddy and symptoms of weightlessness. I began having eating problem with losing weight.

Then I began having pains all over I was directed at the health centre to the hospital, blood test was carried out Co-codamol forte tablets was given to me at the hospital. I had taken it to some length before reading the leaflet information. I realised I was suffering from almost all its side effects.

I had to see the GP again this time it was Dr. Sami Rached again. I complained of dizzy spells; I become worried about my health. On the 9th of May 2007, he prescribed 14 Zopiclone tablets 7.5MG one to be taken daily. To my surprise, one of the side effects was dizzy spells but it worked my dizzy spell became minimal.

Then it was time for my next appointment to see my psychiatrist I had to see Dr. Sobowale instead of Dr. Banjac who was said to be on leave. It was on the 14th-May 2007 I told him how worried I was about my dizzy spells which had at this time had taken me off work with sick note. It had become so unbearable that I was at the point of quieting my job at the Woolwich Gala Bingo club I began filling benefit claim forms with hearth felt feeling that I might never be able to go back to work again.

Dr. Sobowale Prescribed 14 Clonazepam rivotril tablets intended for me to sleep well at night. To my surprise the unwanted effects are feeling drowsy or tired, muscular weakening, dizziness, light-headedness, floppiness' when walking, bad co-ordination and unsteadiness when walking.

Why tablets for the treatment of epilepsy I asked myself? All I wanted it for was to help me through my sleepless nights. I complain at some length that I was being given treatment that had side effects of my complaint. How would I get better was my concern? Two of my GP Dr Andrew and S. Duvall would not prescribe any thing for me rather they advice I stop taking these medication. This was within 14th and 27th May 2007.

I had to book another appointment with Dr. Sobowale advice me if my symptom of dizzy spells continues I should go to the hospital to see a neurologist the illness might not be of mental illness. I asked Ms Barbara the receptionist at the mental health centre if she could confirm from Dr. Sobowale if it was a pathologist or neurologist I should go and see at Queen Elizabeth hospital, because I had forgotten if, he had mentioned pathologist or neurologist I was not given a note. What I could have done is look it up in a dictionary it did occur to me to do this.

I was shaking all over, I had become so worried to the point; of being confuse as well. Since they could not attend to me immediately, I thought in my mind was this not one of the reasons why new GP pathways are being established within different Boroughs in the UK? I had to see a GP again immediately I had to book an appointment. On getting there, my appointment had to be for the next day I said it should be on the same day, or else I would go straight to the hospital. I went back into my flat and took all the medication I was on and went straight for the hospital.

Because I had not been sent to the hospital through my GP or psychiatrist, I had to go through outpatient appointment. Showing the consultant the medications I was on after, I told him how I felt; he looked through my prescribed medications. The word that came out of his mouth was so you feel you have not been given anything for your dizzy spells. I said yes. He prescribed Betahistine 8mg tablets of which I should take two to three a day after meals on taking Betahistine to the second day I felt at the initial stage of taking the medication convulsion run through my whole body system on the third day, I began to feel better.

I have been working for the past 13 years after my diagnose as a schizophrenics staying off benefit except on housing benefit I even had to pay for my prescriptions, eye test and glasses at certain times not that I had the income but to empower myself. I wanted to live and get on with life as any other normal person would have wanted to regardless of my illness. One thing about some people, who come into the UK as citizens, is that we do not always care to know about how the system works for example what benefits we are entitled to, we do not dwell on such issues.

I wonder why patients should be segregated because they have mental health issues. It is the lowest way one can demoralised another person while we are suffering mentally. Or is it schizophrenics who customary break into people's home and steal their properties and commit crimes in our community such are some of the ways in which, we are being stigmatised.

I was present at safer neighbourhood panel meeting held in 2007 with the Mayor of Woolwich Chancellor John Fahy as chair. The motion was about bad activities in some blocks of flats while some people were of the opinion it was partly because there are too many schizophrenics as occupants in some particular blocks of flat. The Borough housing council and housing association are working hand in hand with each other if the community felt anti-social behaviours are been caused by schizophrenics in our communities.

It surprises me immediately it was mentioned because in my blocks of flat at Gorman road, two out five of us suffer from mental health problem. The question is why do landlords see it appropriate to put large number of mentally ill people in the some particular blocks of flats if it is resulting to problems such as anti social behaviours to put social fault on them I suppose.

My opinion at the meeting was that, It should be given thoughtful consideration the NHS should have words with the Greenwich council, because it does not improve our quality of life and not all mentally ill patients are the same., it does not improve our Borough's moral quality. It leaves room for us to view each other with suspicion. With each one of us trying to deduct who is the devil in disguise in our neighbourhood who else would the blame fall to? This does not in any way put us in a situation where we live our lives in harmony moreover during my treatment and my hour of need in 2007, I felt, I was being stigmatized by certain people.

Other members of the Woolwich safer neighbourhood panel were Nigel Levitt sergeant of the metropolitan police, Leonie Wilson PCSO metropolitan police, Jane Gilbert project manager of homeless project and victim support Greenwich, Richard Whitbread crime prevention designs adviser metropolitan police.

Dale Olowofusi pastor in New Wine Church, Cheryl Keen neighbourhood investment co-ordinator L&Q, Val Knight DCNO Greenwich Council, Eve McKinley DCMFG Derek Cheeseman TA, Julie Gray resident association King Henry's wharf, Helen Ives resident association King Henry's Wharf, Laura Buggy resident association King Henry's Wharf, Ray Ringwood TSO Greenwich Council Derek Cheeseman Office and Mark Riordan operation manager youth offending services.

Caroline Forrester housing officer for Spindle Close, Ernie Trendell intelligence analyst Metropolitan police, Barbara Barwick councillor Greenwich Council, Adam cater station manager Woolwich fire station, Bob Newland parking support manager Greenwich Council and Mickey Jules youth project manager Greenwich YMCA.

Others were Phil Lovelock ASB park and open space Greenwich Council, Lawrence Hayes manager Len Clifton House, Walati Singh community safety and hate crime Greenwich Council, Stephen Scoulding crime prevention officer MPS, Terry Hales Councillor Greenwich Council and last but not the least Jay Lowman for Greenwich Council ASBO team.

My anxious feelings at certain times is anxiety, nervousness, worried, I panicked and was afraid. I was feeling that things around me were strange, unreal, and foggy. I felt detached from all part of my body with sudden unexpected panic spells, apprehension, and sense of impending doom, feeling tense, stressed, and uptight and on edge if there is benefit system, why should I feel this way?

My anxious thoughts are if I should have difficulty concentrating, fainting I would be at the verge of losing control, fear of fainting or passing out, fear of physical illness and fear of being alone, isolated and abandoned.

At that time of the year, there were talk of more like the Ferryview health centre to be established where rather than going to the hospital one can visit partway clinic run by GP's to lessen congestion in our hospitals.

I had been put on Trifluoperazine tablets as my usual medication for my mental illness since 2002 till 2007 I have had no distrust whatsoever towards my community health services, having under gone thorough observation of the above medication and the effects it has on me, I then looked at the side effects of Trifluoperazine tablets (Stelazine).

It says that before I take the medication asked if was on

sleeping tablets, pain killers, medication which reduce white blood cell I remembered Dr Sobowale checked if I was becoming anaemic.

Unwanted effects of Stelazine tablets are experiencing weakness, drowsiness, restlessness, difficulty in sleeping, dry mouth which was better off at this stage but far more worse when I was put on Olanzapine 10mg, blurred vision, I now use contact lenses, muscular weakening, over eating, faintness on standing up suddenly, skin rashes, increasing sensitivity to the sun. I read the effects of my stelazine medication for the first time which I had been taking for the past five years.

If I had not suffered from any of the symptoms I was having which in details I sent to the department of health and pension on two white papers hand written with my hand shaking because I was too unwell to word process, I would not had sent them.

I would give an advice to present would be medical students starting from now to another ten years time, the medical association, would need to form a faculty of medicine for research on side effects of all medication. It would only be a beginning for progress but would lead to the surest method in curing many illness and diseases and to do away with their side effects, establishing a stable NHS trust, accuracy in prescribing the right prescriptions.

The development should be based on correcting the side effects of most prescription. The science of medicine has come a long way, it is time to digress and examine various medications compared with the recent once being used by our medical services before it goes into privatisation if, it would.

Having said all these, this is a riddle. What are spectra, spectrum, prism, a seal, a meniscus, crystal or a kryptonium? Don't ask me what celibacy means at this stage it literally means I have got the key to something about my life.

In 1960 they very time coloured televisions became popular in some homes in Africa. My birth condition and experience provides me the understanding that I was born from reliable science. Such condition of birth might embarrass an African family but it was for my own sake being what I am; Superman.

There are certain things that are quite difficult to explain for the sake of simplicity with a well known riddle what is stronger than the lion and what is sweeter than horny?

- I am the last child both my parents had with each other.

- My father was a general manager of stevedoring, clearing and forwarding company.
- Of loading among other consumer's good, pipes for drilling petroleum and offshore service towing.
- I and my immediate elder brother Mr. Omagbemi Oluwagbenga Megbele in the 1960; s with our mother we went back to Nigeria from the UK by sea, after our mother qualified as a nurse.
- I worked for my father's company in Nigeria.
- I and my immediate elder brother Mr. Omagbemi come back to the UK in 1989.
- I see myself as a seismograph.
- I immediately took employment at the royal festival hall at Waterloo.
- I worked for extra staff on several jobs block making factory, B&Q at this time in Nigeria my father was building his second house with all the money he had, I wonder why he waited so long, before he completed building his house?
- I took full time employment with Iceland frozen Food plc I worked at several stores.
- I had worked at Woolwich Gala Club as a deputy cleaning supervisor under Initial cleaning services.
- I am a celibate.

I am aware that over 96 metals have been discovered which exist in physics all that is left of me now is my residual self image as part of the matrix since it is a partway that would lead to reality about my existence because of something I want accomplish which is to divest myself!

There is ample reason for me working with Ms Janet Clark and her family; her colour of skin and hair is no different from the soil of the land when it was bear before, my father built a house on it. I hardly approach Janet while at work except, it is absolutely necessary.

I cannot accept the whole idea as stereotyping or mental illness because; I have to use my own initiatives very too often. I do frequently suffer from dizzy spells, feeling shaky and unsteady; I have to keep my body running just like the Doctors have advised me to, having regular walks exercise or bus ride. The terminology I would use is that I had been going through process with experiences that are varied rather than doing exercise I kept a part time job through which I realise positive initiatives help in managing the illness schizophrenia.

Ms. Barbera tried to make my next appointment with Dr. Banjac sooner immediately he comes back from leave. Another two months is a long wait. After waiting for two months on meeting with Dr. Banjac he gave me one month's sick leave from work hopefully I would recover and go back to work. It's now 2015 I have not been able to go back to work.

Most schizophrenic feels our bad moods are as a result from factors beyond our control, we ask, how can we possibly be happy when we are viewed with stigma that contributes to one third of mental health suicidal case?

Our psychiatrists, cares and social workers should care much for our happiness as much as they care for our mental health issues. Do they usually consider these about us when we go out to see them on our outpatient appointments? I cannot be pulling face, at the same time they are pulling faces as well. And then we are let down feeling inferior, feeling perplex about the reality of seeing ourselves as unwell rather than getting out of our illness.

As you would observe from my writing as a schizophrenic, you may say that our sour temperament most have resulted from some events that had not been forgotten buried deep in our sub-consciousness or very heartfelt.

It is natural for some patient to have bad temperament when they are unwell. in most case the patient might have recently experience a disappointment or a whammy e.g. the shaky economy, the bad weather, taxes, traffic jams, the threat of nuclear war, misery, medication and there side effects, how can they coup with their illness, look after ourselves or acknowledge ourselves as to how our illness affects us.

We are not all that thoughtless people our illness are inevitable some if not all of us are very concern this, is the heart of civilisation nobody wants to go around wearing tattered clothing roaming our streets, not making hay while the sun shines, smoking, intake of hard drugs and substance, staying on benefit nobody is that senseless in a civilised part of the world so what is wrong? It is a social problem.

The truth about it is that our feelings undoubtedly are influence by external events from our past or present however, these theories could be based on the notion that our feelings are beyond our control. If we say, we cannot help they way we feel or other people make us feel, we become victims of misery that is if we care or have consideration for ourselves and the things people do around us. Apart from the help we receive from our carers. The most important issue is how to change the way we feel from a negative diagnosis to a positive diagnosis.

With my looking forward to a speedy recovery, I realise that my thoughts and attitudes both internal and external takes me through different phase of suffering from relapse which I go through every now and then. I learn to change the way I think, feel and behave in simple but revolutionary principle to help me change my life for example not looking down on myself or my illness.

I do this by trying to illustrate important relationship in writing about my feelings, my thoughts and my moods in the way I feel and react towards complicated matters that affects me, my environment, my care and my illness, at each word processing I do, I feel pleased with every outcome of my mood. Feeling less embarrassed but with fear in the back of my mind that my condition do not get worse.

In each stage, I calm myself down by inner initiatives e.g. putting my illness aside. I do not see anything wrong in people hearing voices it's what they do when they hear voices that should be of concern. There are good and bad people, I could hear good and bad voices, so could there be good and bad schizophrenics.

It is better to coup with the illness by not feeling inferior, most patient are not reassured at the initial stage of their illness or treatment. Ho! Some of us would say why do I have to suffer from mental illness? They become socially withdrawn and isolate themselves from family, friends and activities within the community. Those who have strong background could feel inferior, guilty for no particular reason. If nothing is not done to reassure the patient in such a stage, they become depressed even further into chronic or manic depression or, you could receive sudden unexpected outburst from them.

In some cases we have heard of patient hitting or slapping their care worker or social worker, or go into augment with their cares. I have witness such conflicts at job centres, benefit office and at the chemist. The reason for these could be that the patient feels insecure, anxious, and worried or that their care is inadequate. Somebody you are caring for thinks you are inadequate, it need not necessary be, it could be a sign that they have something to tell you that they have difficulty coming out with and you are not about to listen depending on the situation, you can get an outburst it's a natural human reaction. The English spoken centuries ago is different from the way it is spoken today most of which slangs have been added to slangs are a form of outburst.

If the care worker is a problem solver he or she should avoid conflict they should be of the habit of reassuring their patient regardless of conflict. I do not see anything wrong for a patient to respond positively or negatively at least a diagnosis can be reached, amends can be made, and you get to know your patient.

They should not be put under pressure or become emotional or the carer might be losing a customer or implication of being a care worker. It is the way, your patients see you as a carer are how they respond to you, your respond to their treatment is the basis on which you would be appreciated or that you are talented.

If more barriers are created the care would loos touch to see a patient recover? Of which, there could be resistance from the patient. The patient might snap out, out of bad mood on their cares or anybody around them.

Mental health team should come up with techniques practical and straight forward caring for patients such as therapy section outdoor activities e.g. sports where they could be watched closely under observation rather than for them, to be left with gangs who would introduce them into taking drugs. If this happens, they have found comfort somewhere else, while all you would have given them in the first place, would have been simple reassurance. Most of the recent activities were hustled up most of them, were initiated by the patients themselves it is left, for cares to make them user friendly.

Such cognitive behaviour therapy can change the way patients observe their cares and doctors which is very important in all stages of the patients treatment towards recovery and to change the concept of how the patient's illness is observed by they themselves. Nobody needs be told there are bridge between patients and cares in the NHS as of today because, there are bridges...

Patients should have their say on how they feel they could coup with their illness and how the NHS service can be improved to meet their needs as public users. The purpose should be on endeavours to reach out to patients based on assertive guide to speedy recovery, communicating what help are there that are available in the NHS to reassure patients that help is available.

If the NHS wants to break the bad mood and barriers within themselves and their patients with mental health problems, they must first of all understand the everyday type of negatives aspects and effects of their patients on how the illness affects them.

By now the NHS should have acquired more information calling for better treatment of psychiatrist illness its effect on patients in relation to good and bad moods, sadness, harmful thoughts, depression, loss and frustration resulting from unfulfilled expectations or disappointments. Such scenarios in a patient's life should be known and easily be detected!

Patients should be reassured enough to come out with how they feel because no one can know until they come out with it. Or it may come out as a chock and surprise a patient you have been caring for without the slightest idea they could commit suicide ends up committing suicide. What would you say as a care if such a thing should happens? They do happen in our communities, it's just that, we hardly hear about them.

Doctors and care workers should have been looking at ways through observation in which there should be more fulfilment, less frustration and more expectation on how patients could outlive their illness with less anxiety and panic attacks that could lead to self harm.

Awareness of my illness are sadness and depression relating to rejection, the death of a love one, the loss of a job, failure to achieve an important personal goal, anger, irritation, annoyance resentment feeling that someone is treating you unfairly or trying to take advantage of you.

With frustration in the lives of most patients if their lives is falling short of expectation it is; customary for them to insist that things should be different this is found in all case of schizophrenic. They sometimes feel the traffic is always slowing them down even when they are not in a hurry.

Anxiety, worry, fear, nervousness, and panic, at which period danger is always near or apprehension something bad is about to happen which was one way I felt in two recent visits to Queen Elizabeth hospital. For example at one point, I had to call for an ambulance, I was shaking all over with no strength in me on how to coup on my own indoors with sadness I had to get another sick note to be out of work for another two weeks.

At most times I do not feel any better no matter how I try. I thought of what my employer would say as I had been given another sick note again to be off work. My mind was going blank. The Ferryview health centre was closed, it was a bank holiday, treating patients should not all be about paper work, if this should have been the case, the field of medicine and science would not have come this far in its scientific attainment in this 21st century.

I began packing up the idea of going back to work, coupled with the recent outburst on the radio that those with disability are less active at woke. The workers union are concerned about people with disability working. Why don't they do their job and let others do their job yet, they complain about people with disability claiming benefits.

I think the idea is to frustrate people with disability; we also have a life to live as well just as they have their own life to live. While the government and benefit department want to close the gap within people with disability claiming incapacity benefit, I do not see any reason why people with disability should not be given the same opportunities as other people it could be another avenue getting to know and understand how the illness affects patient. It is not unheard of that some people just work in other to show off.

Why are they disgruntled about people with disability working, everyone have to contribute to the community people coming into the UK to seek their stay might welcome it because, it creates avenues for them to take over. Such people who are disgruntled about people with disability working are the once who keep two different jobs at the same time, going out each day to complicate one job with another job. If a person with disability wants to work, they should be allowed to work there is lots of competition in the job market today it's really unfair to people with disability.

Not everybody likes to live on state benefits such are the sorts of concern I had tried many times to raise about during my illness based on my achievements throughout the recent years of my illness after I was diagnosed as a paranoid schizophrenic. What do I get out of it; it's just as if I have been creating a hollow situation for myself. I had attended lots of interviews to get a full time job in vain as a result I began suffering from relapse.

I had been straining myself too far with physical work. It has been an extreme case of hopelessness and discouragement. Some people with disability are contesting about what they feel about work, that they should also be contributors to the community in which they live.

Something to be grateful about regardless of my illness is that I hardly feel inferior or inadequate; I don't compare myself with other people I believe in individuality, I feel I have talent am very creative or should I say very good with my hands e.g. I paint, I draw and I can word process. Such are the sort of things that could convolution mood swings attached to mental illness towards recovery. You can hand write then later touch typing your message through on your computer.

I changed my refrigerator, washing mashing for my laundry's with new once and did my shopping to last me for some time because I was going to have one of my wisdom toot extracted so that I can coup with the after affect and for ease and my comfort when I go through the ordeal for the first time. My shopping had eaten through my savings all I have to leave on was my SSP. Imagine what it is like, to be entitled with statutory sick pay with a private cleaning company.

I go through hearing voices; my hallucinations' are like seeing visions, people talking to me clapping their hands, objects in my flat shaping into and taking forms of other objects. I tried to relax and calm myself I never feel lurch with my word processing, while at other times. I feel macrocosm like a large complete system.

Polygamy in Africa creates demarcation, self centeredness and segregation within families and their relatives, less cohesion and neglect of family ties. The only thing that brings them together is when something absurd or a ceremony takes place apart from these, the environmental experience are always chaotic. While we would have stood by each other, making each other our private joy, rather we make our lives a misery why should this be the case?

It's not every individual in a world like ours who could be said of being capable to withstand an existence in a world, where there are conflicts, starvation, and disease with this earth each day going down with less moral values in the way we live our lives. The good thing about it is that it makes each individual reflect on existence that is, if you have a heath.

The influences of culture to individual personalities is difficult to pin down, it is not also easy through culture to face indifference among people in a societies. Better off, if at the end of each preludes of being part of a culture one should be left to view culture through perspective's rather than believing culture is frogs under water it should be based on values, values that are productive today it is accompanied by self wimp.

The British government was open to all views from all corners around the world. Right from 1986 many immigrants were allowed into the UK from all over Africa and around the world who were born in the UK who live outside the UK. I do not know how many of them were allowed into Britain, I was certainly one of them. I and my brother British passport was sought for us through the Oyo state Nigerian embassy at Ibadan by our late mother it was and was handed over to us at the British embassy at Lagos in the presence of both I and my brother and our father our mother was not present. We were given a British Passport with the intention that if we choose, we I could come into the UK as a British citizen.

I had the feeling I would not fit in within carrying out such delicate jobs in the UK like working for the NHS, Policing and fire brigade. Though I tried applying for such jobs on contemplating on it I decided such jobs are for the home-grown in the UK. At Lewisham collage in 1989, I took up BETEC in electronic engineering, government, politics and philosophy, rather than studying on any programme that had to do with Social care or the NHS.

I later began to realise that within the UK most people especially the young once from African background who have never lived anywhere else outside the UK are unaware of the ways most UK born Africans lived, their lives in Africa. Most people are hardly aware of how, our parents had initiated us within African culture, family history and background in e.g. Nigeria. Or how the environment affected us, our dreams and hopes based on our parental home land should develop into, as a better place. We need not necessary be like the Europeans' because we have, our own background.

I was not aware until later years whiles in Nigeria, my father do send me to buy him his medications from the local chemist, just as he had always sent me when I was younger to by him cigarettes. Though we had house helpers, my parent would not trust them to run such errands for him. They would not be comfortable sending house helpers to buy them e.g. medications, tooth brushes or cloths.

Parents use such customary errand to wedge favouritism within their polygamous home eyebrows are raised if they are not the once called to do the errand because you have been called or someone else had been called, to do the errand.

My mother did the same thing in her own way, but she made me understand what ever she does. She also gave me opportunities to understand and express my feelings on whatever she does, which did enabled me to keep an open mind, such deeds is common among all African culture and oracles also bear in mind that not all children of African background take to culture or tradition by asking questions.

To self search the implication of the true meaning of your culture and tradition one has to be open minded to understand the culture from which you emanate. In some cases, heredity is involved and at the same time one is prone to face situation in which you are being used. One is likely to go through incarcerated.

All culture in Africa has something to do with peculiar powers and characteristics for the purpose of culture and tradition which are customary. But the practice needs a good mind to wedge culture on, such children from childhood I would call an unblemished sheep being taken for a sacrifice.

Wherever Jujus is practiced, they do work and take effects, it could push someone into doing things out of the ordinary, or something out of life inherent traits mind you, Africa jujus are enact and governed by law of its rituals. The question is how did they come about having such powers or forces? There are many forces all over the world for good or for evil they are invoked or revoked.

Understanding of jujus is through revelation of certain implications about life inherent traits that gives rise to supernatural forces. If, there should be incarcerations involved with another party e.g. parents, relatives, or friends then; the result will not only be an the illness of paranoia it is also slavery under the hands of Native Witch doctors while it would be said of your, that your parents or relative practice juju.

Whatever could have gone into me to have told my father, he is not welcome into my flat, was for many reasons which did resulted into good outcome for me and some members of my family. I couldn't have done such a thing to hurt my father's feelings deliberately. I have walked into the UK with no other close relatives other than my father and immediate elder brother.

It could be juju that had been placed within me and my

father, by my step mothers or relatives, so that my father should see reason creating bond with them and their children. Which might have already been implanted in me before I left Nigeria for the UK? You see my father had just become a chief, and so were many other eminent families in Delta State of Nigeria.

I was always found of studying my father the first time my father visited the UK after my arrival I queried my father, told him I was living in an hostel for men through which, I was seeking accommodation for a flat this was in my brothers flat where my father was staying on his visit. This was a flat my brother recently moved into through a hostel in Clapham common. I had kept my passport and some of my belongings with my brother at his flat before I moved into Lancelot Andrews hostel in SE 1. The documents I took with me to the hostel where my birth certificate, my letter of entry into university of Port Harcourt were I was about to study geography before coming to the UK and pay slips as a staff from my employment at Iceland frozen food plc. The only time I had show my birth certificate as a document before I become diagnosed as schizophrenia was when I was enrolling as a student on a evening course at Lewisham collage where I studied BETEC in electronic engineering under Mr Seli though I had a British passport I only spent one year on the course paid my school fees since I was working at the time. The following year I study Government, politics and philosophy as a combined course under Mr M'Chaine It was during these period I transferred from Iceland Frozen food plc Camberwell to its Iceland Lewisham store where I worked with Miss. Michelle Cook I never realised until later I got the mystic, strength or courage to confront my father through Miss. Michelle Cook for blood is thicker than water. There are other collages in Southwark why did I choose Lewisham collage as I gathered from Michelle while working with her at Iceland frozen food store at Lewisham she was once a student at Lewisham collage worked at McDonald and was at that moment working for Iceland and she lived at Peckham. He had money he could have built a house for each, of his wives or the whole family to live in before he became a chief how dose his wives and children feel when two children of his first wife are in the UK people hear that you are coming to the UK for a visit but to hear you are coming to the UK to reside leaves them asking questions such as what about me, what about us. You would have lived in Africa, observe family relationship, its environment and culture, in other to understand what I am trying to postulate In view of my father's rituals one thing that might be of importance to him, is my birth certificate he was not present during my birth in the UK I was taken back to Nigeria by sea by my mother and my father's business in which, he is the general manager has to do with shipping.

I always take measure to respect tradition and culture towards my elder brothers and sister. I had made way for my brother Mr. Omagbemi to have had his own accommodation first before I have mine as tradition would permit since he is older than me on which he made move to insist. As it turned out, at the time he was seeking his accommodation, I was working my brother was not all too happy about this he always wants to come first. I was the one within me and my brother who wanted to be schooled by our father, always subtle I was towards my father.

I was always calm and reserved, it was out of respect I had for my father through which reason, he find course to lecture me with his actions as my father and to observe his deeds and reactions.

It is the right thing to do under a polygamous family with step brothers, sisters, wives uncle's aunties, countless distant relatives, and friend in which, it is customary to find yourself being used or influenced by the next person.

I have always come out outright no matter how the journey of my life had been difficult. In respect to all my actions and endeavours while in Nigeria was with disposition of tolerance. Though it hurts sometimes I take it all as part of my trials of life.

I meet with the right people at the right time and at the right place. My father knows me as someone who is always straight to the point; without losing face or my confidences as I under take my life trials.

My brother Mr. Omagbemi is too forward he wants to make himself peculiar with insights taken from his relatives to make him and his friends more peculiar in such scenarios as within polygamous relationship if parents do not lay the same emphasis within children things might go wrong parents also make mistakes one child may use their mistakes as go getters on which cause parents should not act with indifference.

It is one attributes associated with African parents because they always want something to go by with as parents or as head of a family the result is indignation one reason why we live with lack of respect for each other always in conflict

It could be tolerated to some extent by one member of a family while the parents are still alive if it goes deeper an inch it might not be tolerated when they are dead. Some member of a family would want to be peculiar among friends but not with family relatives as a result we log behind in our family relationship, create disrespect for family ties and frequent situation, friends would lobby family members. I have never seen anywhere in the world, where there is so much conflicts than in Africa its chaos we should not leave it this way because it darkens our future.

Since I become unwell it has been part of my illness to experience my brother Mr. Omagbemi is inside me, as if he is embedded within my soul and spirit through which I constantly hear his voice from within and outward. Sometimes I try shaking myself off the voices I hear from him the voice I hear, are words which seems to be domineering to control, or tell me what to do or insist some of the wrongs our father had done, are right.

One person could be found too domineering in a polygamy home it is natural, it is also natural for one to feel alienated within a family, you could be within twenty members of your family, and still feel as if, you were not there, because nobody takes notice of you, except when they want you to run an errand for them or to make a choice for you

In Asia it is recorded young girls are forced into marriages so are some girls and women forced into polygamy in Africa. They end up in the streets if their husband dies, ending up in the market place buying and selling in the open market place in the streets of Africa, with children behind their back, with flies and mosquitoes roaming around them, with no place to sleep, while the African government do nothing to help the situation. So, it goes for Africans caring less for each other how long would this go on for?

The government with the wealthy in Africa hardly involves any humanitarian concepts. With such eminent men once they die, their wealth is taken over or purpose of their business goes down the drain with relationship within family members go deeper into conflicts. Houses and wealth other people would take over for this reason they tend to show off with their wealth, wedge respect and control while they are alive for such obvious reason they lay too much emphasis on themselves to make their name stand out. The illness of schizophrenia dose results from difficult family issues,

I experience my brother Mr. Omagbemi inside me, trying to dominate me with the voices I hear from him I wake up some morning's with my face disfiguring, changing like my brothers face, with him making faces at me on my bathroom mirror, like an evil spirit chasing me all around everywhere I go. This was the same experience I had with my father just before and after his death. My Krypton strength was becoming a spent force it was leaving me and I was becoming drenched.

I summon myself up facing the scenario without being frighten, since am on my own with no one to turn to I find myself revoking them in all aspects when I hear their voices telling me to do things to herm myself. He talks inside me; he knows my every movement in respect to what am doing or about to do which I have not told him about with infarct my every move through the voices I hear from him and it's not only his voices I hear I do hear voices from lots of other people.

The same experience I have with other members of my family? I feel all that is left of me is nothing but a family seal of juju with which my father sealed his chieftaincy title.

On the day my father was conferred his chieftaincy title, as I bowed down to my father's origin way of culture, down on once knees and head to the ground with all together saying in a loud voice (Ogiame soooh) which is the word pronounced when obeisance to the king his made. I was filled with exhilaration found myself crying as I looked into the face of our king Godwin Toju Emiko the Atuwase of Warri the second, to my surprise, I found out there were also tears on his face.

Whilst the celebration was taking place in my father's residences and began to take its peak, with juju music, cultural dance, with the usual slaughtering of cows and preparation of meals for the celebration. I remembered drinking a lot and started once again to cry, it was good for me because my strength had become spent.

The oracle was consulted to find out why I was crying and praying uncontrollably on the ceremonial sward, it was revealed that I should be the one, who should be my father's predecessor of our family seal after my father. The oracle was not very pleased with my father. This might have been part of the reason why there was conflict within me and my father the oracle have missed some one out, who should have had his place within my father's cultural seal.

It was because I was more powerful than them but why so, is something for them, to discover themselves. It was part of the requisite I wanted to undergo at that time in my subconscious life; so that I would allow myself to be ingrained in culture and rituals, and let the custom of the culture and rituals take control of me. The spirit of the culture was sent into me to get hold of me.

My spirit and bones have been broken; afterwards all that was left of me is to brace myself up each day that my soul will rejoice once again, I would not allow myself to be put in a confused state of mind, deeds, and actions conditions have to change. Expression not impressions has to come from them that they could care.

The only thing I could do was to embrace myself in a new life in the UK were each day everything seems to change, I am braced with new amour for my tears are painful, my memories are painful, while as a celibate I hope and pray for all woman child, to forgive me, if it's a sin, for me to have made up my mind not to have children.

I have seen lots of schizophrenia sufferers in the UK, from the discussion I had with them, they seem to know what is wrong with them better than their psychiatrist in certain respect all they could do better, is come up with the terminology of the illness. In most case the patient could have opted out or do something about the illness before it becomes too late.

In most cases the right thing for one to do at the early stage of schizophrenia is to brass once self up and seek support, but not all of us are aware of the support available. For some of us, the illness just take over us too quickly before, we realise whatever is happening to us or all of a sudden, the next thing to our surprise, is that we find ourselves in a psychiatrist ward. That was how the symptoms of my diagnosed schizophrenia started, I mean I couldn't have known that it was something to do with mental illness all that came to mind, was that my seal had been broken.

If it gets to the point where the illness is eminent eating through the patient's life, at such a stage if doctors, cars and psychiatrists are not so helpful e.g. they do not discuss much with the patients on what the patients feels are the ingrained reason of the causes of their becoming a schizophrenic, manic or chronic depression.

At this level it could become a level for suicide or they come out, with outburst. There should be awareness patients do not neglect taking their medication, they should know what is particularly wrong with them and why they are on medication. I know these things because it happened to me, I never knew the medication or injections I was on, and they never cared to tell me. But as time went by each day I braced myself to know about my medications and the injections I was on.

Am always trying to look good, well dressed, well shaven, while within all odds such are the sort of things some schizophrenic find difficult to do, I feel the same way too, but I create the feeling inside me that they are the customary things I should do or, am neglecting my obligations to myself. And for the simple reason that I do not under estimate my abilities to still remain the boy as lovely as a tree most people can hardly tell my age.

From voices I hear as a schizophrenic, the first thing I do is to consider what the voices are telling me to do, if it is right I would do it. If it is not a right thing to do, I would not do it or reject the voices I hear which is not so easy at certain levels of the illness. Nevertheless in most cases, I would have done whatever the voices tells me to do, before I realise I have done what I shouldn't have done that the voices tells me to do.

One should always put once self in a position of doing the right things at all times. If you know it is not the right thing to be done, do think of something else appropriate such as, scone the person's voices you are hearing, you will become more confident in yourself as time goes by because, you would tend to ignore the voices.

If not your condition could became worse or sometimes it becomes so worse that you would have to be put into hospital. If as a patient you are admitted into hospital very too often you would become more depress, too dependent, you will see yourself as a failure and unable to care for yourself what I mean is that you become more unbalance. Infarct you will be at the mercy of the illness sort of, it has taken over you to a disposition you feel you can hardly help yourself. It is better not to be hospitalized except in extreme cases.

With my initiation as a freemasonry followed with the loud bang with the pronunciation of thou architect of the universe, which my father and other members had waited for so long as members of freemasons. My father was a little bit taken aback in the presence of other members probably because he was a patron. Since, he was my father he should have let his good and family friend Chief Meneafejuku also a patron and business man preside over the initiation at Warri Island lodge. So there I was not only a son to my father but also, his brother.

Chief Meneafejuku had been an adviser and patron to my father through many course of my father's success since my father's youth. Chief Maneafejuku was quit older than my father, very well known to my grandmother from my father's side; he was also an Ogboni member.

My father need not be uptight I know he had hoped for years as a Freemason to be greeted by the loud bang moreover, before my initiation, he had become a chief. It is not always possible to have both sides of a coin.

Why is it always difficult for Africans to hold one ideology; it is a problem to administer one ideology why are always the successful once in Africa always self centred. It is customary when such eminent Nigerians dies; they die with their wealth and business with the rest of their family confused, without knowing which way to turn to and in conflict as to who, should have the largest sheer of the deceased wealth. If you should have one or two step mothers in such a home, where would it leave you?

After my father's death, no one could come out with a sure way to restore, my father's business and wealth among his children except that we are popular with the name he had created for himself as a chief and a well known individual in Nigeria.

My father's business went down with him. Almost all shipping business particularly in Delta state are all now in the hands of other business men and probably partly in the hands of King Godwin Toju Emiko the Atuwase of Warri Delta state of Nigeria who conferred the chieftaincy title to my father.

Immediately I arrived in the UK, I was fund of going different places to get, to know my new environment. I took resident in quite a number of places with private landlords, in Peckham close to where Miss. Michelle Cook lived whilst we were co- workers at Iceland Frozen food plc. I also took resident in Camberwell, Old Kent road, and Borough high road SE1.

I go down to the Royal festival hall at Waterloo road where I had my first employment as a cleaner. On each weekend I go to sit and leisure by the sea side close to London Bridge.

Whilst living at Lancelot Andrew hostel close to Borough High Road, I often through bus rides came down to the Woolwich dockyard passing through Greenwich where once set a Port, old relics of ships and guns decorated the area.

Let me shed some insight on what I know about Greenwich If you really want to discover Greenwich, as a peculiar place where information goes out to millions of visitors coming to the Greenwich Maritime every year. A new £6 million cultural venue at the Old Royal Naval Collage opens to the public recently which unlocks the borough maritime history and acted as the starting point for understanding and appreciating one of the world's most heritage sites for international tourist attraction in London.

The centre has a micro-brewery depicting historical and modern beer's, a bar, cafe, restaurant as well as Greenwich council new tourist information centre. Discover Greenwich state of the art that tells the true stories of Maritime Greenwich and Old Royal Naval Collage with over 500 years of history from Henry VIII's Tudor Palace, Wren's Royal Hospital for Seamen and the Royal Naval Collage which is explored each year by many tourists from all over the world.

Amidst all these suddenly Woolwich a part of Greenwich finds its self with the vital commodity to the development of a thriving town centre MP Nick Raynsford hit the nail on the head when he said, having wider pavements, extra space at bus stops and more areas where members of the community, visitors and tourist can walk seems a small but obvious thing in its self. The difference in Woolwich at the moment is truly remarkable, while there are lot more to come such transformation over the next 12 month of the new Woolwich squares that would simply create a new Woolwich.

While Greenwich council is committing itself ensuring safety for its residents and well-lit streets that would reduce the fear of crime, completion of the phase two works paves the way for Greenwich council programme in regenerating Woolwich Squares as part of the Mayor's Great Spaces initiatives.

Pedestrians are benefiting from signal crossing at key junctions, raising entries at side roads making it easier for people using wheelchairs and buggies with new streets lightings as well as new longer bus shelters. This are with addition to the installation in 2008 of the super crossing on Plumstead Road, the planting of over 100 new trees with the installation of high quality street furniture's.

The completed facilities and work that has been going on at Woolwich Square is revolutionary. Regeneration of the town centre with the ongoing Woolwich centre that would offer access to a range of Greenwich council service in one convenient location which would include, a service centre dealing with all face-to-face council business, a major town library, a new office for 2,000 council staffs, a business centre for the council and its partners and the Greenwich Gallery striking public exhibition and meeting place with viewing gallery.
It would include development of new shops, hundreds of new homes with 35 per cent being affordable and an 8,000 square metre Tesco store. The store has a low-carbon design, a green roof with the use of solar panels and wind turbines. While the new DLR station carrying more than five million passengers since it was opened in January 2009 is another major part of Woolwich regeneration programme over the last ten years.

While the former Royal Arsenal site has now been transformed into a major new urban area featuring new homes, business, a river pier offering daily commuter services, the Firepower museum and Greenwich heritage Centre and CROSSRAIL the fast east-west link across

London is due opening a station in Woolwich Arsenal in 2017 complete with 2,500 homes, cinema, hotel, shops, restaurant, community facilities and offices with Woolwich Barracks a venue for the London 2012 Olympic and Paralympics Game.

I do pass by the Greenwich hospital on my way from Elephant and Castel to the Themes Barrier at the Greenwich training centre to study under Ms. Clare Eglin as principal, Mr. Paul computer and office skills, Mr. Robert White carpentry and joinery, Ms. Vicky Lawford and Ms. Tammy office skill, Mrs. Linda Ross as painter and decorating skills.

I became acquainted with Miss. Natalie Annette French, Miss. Sonia Malani, Mr Darren, Mr Robin, Mr Jimmy, and Mr Rodney; they ware all, like people I had known in a past life. But I never knew that one day; I would be residing in Woolwich or become a patient at the Greenwich hospital as a paranoid schizophrenia.

From Lancelot Andrews hostel South East through coordination of JART 26 Chapter Street SW1P 4ND London, I was provided with a council flat at number 13 Gorman roads block of flats Woolwich on the 24th of September 1991. My tenancy commenced on the 30th of September 1991. It's now the 11th of May 2009. I have been residing at the same blocks of flat for the past 18 years as a celibate having worked at the Woolwich Gala Club for 15 years.

My father had encouraged Omagbemi into shipping through correspondent courses within the UK and Nigeria whilst we were in Nigeria my brother was only bordered studying to attain the full qualification in shipping while we were in Nigeria.

As much as our father endeavoured to interest him about shipping my brother abounded the privilege. He could not spend time studying with too much friends. Yet when we came back into the UK he could not continue with his shipping course to attain his full qualification.

Though my father had a driver he encouraged my brother

Mr. Omagbemi to do some of the driving to and fro from Delta state to Port-Harcourt on business and when visiting the family at Warri. By now my brother would have become a shipping magnet in the shipping business within the UK and Nigeria, which would have been easy because he is an African British.

With just one wife a family could be faced with countless biased problems, while with a polygamous family it could be disaster. For example our stepmothers had the opinion their own children should be allowed to have the same privilege as we the eldest in the family had.

Such as studying shipping, drive the family car as well when they grow up! By the time, I and my brother was about to leave Nigeria for the UK, they were almost grown-ups. While in my case, when I was younger, I had to wash the cars, wash the plate and tidy the house especially the Kitchen after each cooking and after meals.

Polygamy is always one of the causes of conflicts and indifferences in every given social community and depending on the degree of relationship. Omagbemi was at boarding school at Port-Harcourt my eldest brother was taking his GCE general certificate of Education after secondary school while My sister was just about leaving secondary school this was in 1976.

Three days before, I would have my molars tooth extracted my brother Omagbemi and his wife visited me, with food , a whole tilapia fish not one but three tilapia fried fish with the fish bones still intact how am I going to eat such when am having tooth problem? Rice prepared in the traditional way (you know African Pam oil), while I had already developed loss of appetite to put food in my mouth. But why fish I asked myself or is that my brother was going on about the differences I had with my father it makes me meditate more on the true relationship within a father and his son if I feel certain aspects of my upbringing is not right I do not think there is anything wrong in it for me to come out load to have confronted my father.

My brother and his wife brought fish to me with the fish born still intact, considering am having tooth problems, his he out of his mind? In reality to me and my brothers relationship as two brothers from African background, my brother could mean don't talk to you father like that since how many years, had the incident occurred? Without indicating any set back within me and my father's relationship. Rather than getting rid of the food I managed eating the fish and rice under feelings based on superstition beliefs no wrong can befall me since, it was not by a deliberate intention and he never asked me if I was finding difficulty with food here in the UK.

He should not fight for our father or tell me what is right or wrong from the look of it, it made our father turn to him better for him! If my father knows what is right or wrong, he should have let us grow up with our mother in his house, he had never told anyone of us particularly why our mother had moved out of his family home if he had, he never told me if he had told any of us from our mothers children would be, to have raised sentiments towards his own favour we know what our parents are like.

My brother wants to speak for my father e.g. to be found more favourable to my father. This is why I do not associate myself with friends too easily. Am a loner and I like being a loner it's because of my background and experience. Yes no children from any African background speak to their parents that way. But if they do, they have gone over the moon all that would be left, is that consideration should be applied, it wasn't because, I was in the UK as a citizen.

I and my brother Omagbemi are of the same parent; we grew up within a polygamous home. Our relationship should not be as such, we should rather be found to blend within each other. If I should speak openly to my father because of something I was heartfelt about. He has no right to be prejudice against me; my step mothers, brothers and sister would do this better than him from knowing him as my brother what positive things had he in his own term initiated me to do?. I am not in any way implying he should take sides with me.

My step brothers and sisters would do me far worse apart from being prejudice against me. I did not kill my father all I did was cry out loud because something was wrong it was no time to pull a baby face. Other members of my family and my father can speak for themselves if not for a brother who my wrongs are always his righteousness such are what is akin to all polygamous homes.

I am not saying am right under African background a child is never in the right there parents are always right. My father can speak for himself, he had all the time and chance to speak.

My father never at anytime asked me why or what made me so heartfelt about during his visits to the UK. My father did not ask me, because he knew I was always watching him and he had always been the centre of my life. All African parents are the centre of their children's lives or where else, would they have three square meals a day?

It is customary whenever you notice people or have give them a second glance it means you care or you are interested in them or they mean something to you such is the way it went within me and my father among such African parents, you would always be their favourite. Not that they would pamper you, they would make you grow up the hard way while at the same time; you are their Mojo.

My father knew I loved him I always felt concern for him, what more can a child give, to their parents but there are always indifferent, moreover, I was the last child he had with my mother it would be customary for a child to feel this way. My father was aware of the intent of the oracles which weren't happy with him, because he did not do anything for me the rest of the family felt the same way, to be his predecessor or the intent was to gear him into its philosophy that they also have their own demands. So they summoned me up to confront my father on the things, he should have done.

Most prominent Nigerians know how to inquire into private lives including those of their children through spiritual churches and oracles of native doctors who would have the probability of knowing I would write this book but weren't certain. If my father would had gone to them, rather than keeping silent they would probably had informed him his son would do something outward towards his irrational nature.

As it always happens they would not have told him it would result to my writing this book or telling my father off when he visited my flat the inconclusive would have been rather than my father taking it from a son and father relationship depending on the magnitude of whatever he had been told by a celestial church or a native doctor might have driven him making his own inferences while I felt I might have been sold into a disclaimer at the same time, he wanted to make inference he was a chief.

If my brother Mr. Omagbemi had anything to say, he could have done so when our father was alive, in the presence of my father, just as I had spoken to my father when he was alive if not all, most people would understand.

After this experiences with my brother after I have had my molars tooth extracted. On their next visit after a year had passed. I told them, they should not bring food to me again to my flat. I came to a conclusion with so many computers, mobile phone in our hospitals, and the recent occurrences of hospital burgs, meals should not be brought into hospitals by relatives of patients when they are under hospital care.

My father ended up suffering from diabetic after several treatments in Delta state and Oyo state, he died at Ibadan close to my mother. I hope my relatives saw reason to believe my father on his last days on earth came to a conclusion from his son (ME) to die close to my mother. I was grateful on his part, to have made it so because one reason for being a parent is that, you should look up to your children as much as your children look up to you. We all make mistake, it is how you react after the mistake that makes a huge difference.

Polygamy reduces once morals and confidence it does not make any one feel high about their parents or background.

There are lots of advantages parents and children could enjoy without polygamy. A family is viewed in its realty as true to themselves, in their sense of creating bound and the support they generate within themselves as members of a family. Within polygamy, talking to some relatives of your family today in the UK or in Africa is like talking to strangers.

The atmosphere after my father's death was not sound with four wives with my mother dead just after which I was taken unwell as a schizophrenic. After my father's death, the three women in his life as wives were all scattered about in Nigeria! Who says I should not speak when I have not only the chance but also, the opportunity?

With nobody to look after the next person within the family, my father left little money in the bank. All that was left for the family was house to live in which cannot accommodate the whorl family, with wives at their old age, whom no other men would want to look at again twice. Coupled that with some women, they would still want to have sex or befriend a man. The wives cannot do both, so what have my father left behind? 90% of All African family's face such consecutive outcome each decade. It is about time such un-conceptualized inherited traits are done away with.

Who said I have done wrong to have quickly acted, it brought a new setting for my younger brothers and sisters, for them to be educated and my father showing some concern for my younger brothers and sisters almost all of them had gone through University education before my father's death.
As for the relationship within me and my brother Omagbemi I hope he and his wife Mrs. Nwamaka Megbele are not making an excuse that she is working for Oxleas NHS because of me! She had at one stage, told me that it is what I carry in my mind that was wrong with me. Could there be anything wrong for anyone to have his or her own moral values about life?

I was taken aback that Nwamaka held such an opinion of me. That it is what I carry in my mind that is wrong with me! What is it that I carry in my mind? What else could be the trouble if not that I care for my family? Blood is thicker than water.

My sister in law is now a case within two brothers after her first relationship with Mr. Calvin Sudelu's father who has never lived in harmony within their family with my brother taking her as his partner; she ought to know she now has cause to create harmony within two brothers. In any instant I and my brother had lived together with any of our parent we had not spent more than three years living in the same house with them as our parents. He always comes in or out when situation are rough for me until our father deliberately held him to himself. The only time I would say he felt the same way was while I moved in to live with him and my father at Port Harcourt after I had completed my secondary school education why should it be? I was told by someone else the dwelling my sister in law occupied along Lewisham Vale had been rented out to her or her partner by an Asian landlord while I could have experience or encountered something of my own experience whilst living in Nigeria that personally has to do with Mr. Calvin Sudelu's father or any member of their own relatives with whom I go out in parties, ceremonies or celebration with in the UK. I am not one who is against what other people do but if they see that I apply reason or common sense in what I do, they should appreciate it.

In the case of my brother Mr. Omagbemi as I watch him grow up in many ways except everything meets with his own favour he is not satisfied or uses the opportunity to define his own ways. His presence is hardly found within the rest of the family; but for the sake that he has a little brother from both parent in a polygamous home to knock on the head to portray his authority to get the attention of the others at any time he feels like which has over the years made me reserve and withdrawn towards him.

Everybody in this world wants recognition and are always power hungry. In my case, polygamy under my father made me self-restrained.

All these are happening in our family, it is his wife Nwamaka who is sane enough, to have found her way working in mental health.

In this world you do other people favours in return to your surprise you will find out that you are being ruined from behind I in particular could had taken the situation to a Babalawo and make juju of my own out of the scenarios to enhance myself or status. From what it involves back home I feel some of the participant would think from what it would have resulted to I would have been suffering from not only schizophrenia but madness from the effects though am in my council flat in London I know what is going on within my family in my native land. When are we all going to be one big happy family? She knows I suffer from mental illness before she took up her studies. Dose the scenario emerge that we are becoming one big happy family if she did not communicate with me of what her intentions where instead, it was left for my own brother to have informed me?

On the day of my father's chieftaincy ceremony at our dwelling at Warri Delta State after the knife had slit through the throat of the cow as it was being slaughtered my father suddenly said something in Yoruba in anger asking why Igbo men were doing the slaughtering of the cow I took notice of the knife used for its slaughter taking note whoever holds the knife after my experience on that day later occurred to me holds something of a significance to take from me or am faced with distraction and disintegration countless prayers have been said on my behalf I have always said prayers added to theirs that would make realities of my life become real inwardly, I know God is with me each time the blessing or prayers are stolen from me such feelings became different when I began having the inclination I am Orunmila .

This incident as part of my father's chieftaincy ceremony might be why he made several visits to the UK after my brother and his wife's wedding at a register in London. My father took the initiatives on his sons Omagbemi's behalf to be in his wife's Home Town within her relatives to carry out traditional wedding for them. One reason might be to get control of any omens of the knife which was used for the slaughtering of the cow for his chieftaincy title ceremony if I go any further than this in narrating the episodes; it might be counted I am hallucinating, paranoiac or suffering from psychoses.

I realised during the slaughtering of the cow the knife was resting more than higher above the cows' neck it was only the hand holding the knife I saw. When a cow is being slaughtered in a vacuity of the sea it blots out its omens in such a scenario only a sea goddess can intercede this occurring within Yoruba land or origin the knife rest below the cows, fowls or goats' neck with an 'Ase'- veneration.

Ase (or àṣẹ) is an African philosophical concept through which the Yoruba of Nigeria conceive the power to make things happen and produce change. It is given by Olodumare to everything - gods, ancestors, spirits, humans, animals, plants, rocks, rivers, and voiced words such as songs, prayers, praises, curses, or even everyday conversation. Existence, according to Yoruba thought, is dependent upon it. In addition to its sacred characteristics, ase also has important social ramifications, reflected in its translation as "power, authority, command." A person who, through training, experience, and initiation, learns how to use the essential life force of things to wilfully effect change is called an alaase. Rituals to invoke divine forces reflect this same concern for the autonomous ase of particular entities. The recognition of the uniqueness and autonomy of the ase of persons and gods is what structures society and its relationship with the other-world.

At certain points of my illness, I thought I was my sister in laws property she talks inside me since 2004 and 2015 I hear her voices all day long.

On 25th of February 2008 with middle rat disability living allowances I choose to buy my prescription worth over £40.00 getting them free from boot the chemist free makes me feel irrational I guess at this time, I was suffering from a sort of enigmas about my medication nothing his free in life. It's all part of a temperament I suffer from my illness as a paranoid schizophrenic in other to identify my spiritual self.

Whilst I was working at the Gala club buying my medications

makes me feel good even if I had to pay for my medications through my low income at certain time or I was experimenting on myself. It could have probably been due to some philosophy or psychological feelings of my own within me, in relation to my personality, my up-bringing, background and the way I felt towards my illness and my community the experience makes me strong and more myself.

It was something of a superstition intuition that it would make me recover from my illness, with the belief that if I do such things even if, it had to be at a loss; it would make me be myself and recover from my illness, in some ways a superstition that it would ward off the evil that had brought mental health illness into my life.

I born premature with my first nice from my brother Mr. Omagbemi was born a suzerain at Lewisham hospital the day next to my birthday in 1995. At this time I was hospitalized after my return in the UK with mental health issues and diagnosed as paranoid schizophrenia.

I have more than reasons for being a celibate.

Because of what had happened within my parents whilst they were in Nigeria, before I was born and after my parents came to the UK to have given birth to I and my brother. It now boils down to me due to some philosophical, sociological and psychological inherence to be celibate. I hope my observers, would see my point of view why I choose to be a celibate by choice.

Stereotyping could be involve I think rather than confronting it from the dark side, I am using the brighter perspective not only, to be in control but also, to call for awareness and change; to query if this world will ever be a better place?

I do not want to be hurt anymore; I cannot run from myself, because there is nowhere to hide. I have sheered my life with them, I hope they take me for what I am, because I will never change my colours or ask for too much. But with this quest inside me, that I do to run from myself I want to be me.

They see right through me, yet they break down each walls am leaning on to; without taking me for what I am, I struggle not to follow where they want me to follow but the parts destined for me by the grace of the heavens. They make me cry and whimper each day of my life. As I face each day of my life I find out, I do not want to be hurt anymore. With all these feelings inside me, I find myself running away from them which is for one reason why; I live an isolated life.

I know they can see through me, they know how hurt I am inside all I hope to do, is pull through some life inconsistencies it's something I cannot explain but needs to be revoked.

They have made me close my doors; build a barrier around myself though with my resilience I have other reasons apart from failing family commitments to face the rest of the world. I feel they have broken down everything I am holding on to. The only alternative for me is to unfold the mystery behind my existence.

Hearing voices makes me depress during the day, I have to come out aloud, finding time to write because   actions speaks louder than voice which could make a most lasting impression for the better.

2008 a lot of people come from third world countries into the UK to seek residence through asylum, for education or to have children. It would not stop me from my quest for the source of strength that would hold me firm. I am not in the UK to enjoy I am here for a purpose to break down barriers related to my background and upbringing.

A father gives a son a coral bead to bow to a king on his coronation as a chief within numerous cultural traditional occasions of rituals, not all his children bowed to the king except this very son probably holding to why his mother got married from that particular origin. Once he had used the coral bead to bow before the king, the coral bead is immediately in the traditional achieves belongs to the son; whatever goes wrong the gods and the oracle are not to blame because the coral bead now belongs to the son.

Could it be right if the father decides to use the son and coral bead for his own personal rituals? I see it as part of the norms and omens of our cultural and traditional heritage.

If my father would use me for his own personal rituals, he would have provided me with education this I would consent to as pleasant because he would have given me an opportunity to crave for my own dignity if not self restrain. He had made it clear before his death and after his death everything depends on him.

How would I manage with three step mothers in a home where my mother was never present? At certain points one can be confused to imply our existence is a ritual depending on lots of factors such as confusion, perception, what is or what are not realistic about our existence depends on individuality though other people contribute to what make you whatever you are at the end of the day, each individual take the blame for their conduct.

After having lived part of your life in a third world nation as other people whether asylum seekers, to seek a stay or as a immigrant a lot is at stake considering as British it could take you another ten years of your life to settle down with another ten years to understand the people around you another ten years making a deduction of what you think of the people around you in the UK among other things like work, the environment, its structure and fragmentation. There is no likelihood of thoughts of antisocial behaviours I mean you are British among these, you want to be educated, have a wife with children, buy a house and have friends considering you have to spend eight hours a day working.

For someone who, is an immigrant or an asylum seeker he takes ten years having his or her papers to stay whoa this is when they come alive they have had their papers to stay in Britain before this time, they have always been complaisant for example in all cleaning aspects of their work as a cleaner. Now they are about to become masters develop a no nonsense attitude they become no different from the kings or government officials in their native land and implement most incoherence's and concurrencies her in the UK as the situation is in their native land yet, they ask for change. Take a trip back to their native land the news spread out as if they have won a lottery jackpot. They are now better off; they are less caring for things and prospects they hope should have changed years ago before they came into the UK as immigrants or asylum seekers.

What do most people think of people who come into the UK for visits they do not only implement for the kings and dignitaries' as they would implement for themselves, they usually do it, as if they are the dignitaries themselves. Where does preferment leave me when it comes to my pride and joy?

One morning he was being driven by his drivers in his white Mercedes-Benz passing by our family house at G.R.A close to the Naval Base.

I noticed he saw me, as I waved at him in greeting and waved back at me in reply. As his Mercedes-Benz moved on I wished I could informed him I was going to the Delta state Naval base for the commandants' signature on my application form for entry into the Nigeria defence academy and make a plea Atuwase of Warri should be my referee, If I could come and see him for a reference letter to be attached on my application form into the Nigeria defence academy as well. How, I would have boil with excitement I would have a place in my entry as a Cadet.

Could the Olu of Warri by choice have really wanted me as a member of my family to hold his sword as a king and to stand by his side during traditional occasions? This is a most for all families in Delta state titles holders each household customary have a sword to be held by one of the bear's son.

I personally polished my father's sword made of gold with Brazzol for his swearing in as a chief. I personally went to my father's traditional shops to collect his chief wipes and fan with the inscription of his title inscribed on it.

In 2004 I went to Greenwich African shop in Blackheart and bought myself African culture whip and fan from a dealer in African culture I heard voices saying that they where Ghanaian made, with which I decorated my council flat why? I was making a choice on what was about to happen subconsciously.

This was just after my father's death what ever made me do so, was beyond my own personal initiatives which meant, I did not do it out of my own personal will something beyond my control made me. Wearing the coral beads he gave back to me on his last visit to the UK in 2001; I took pictures with them wearing my traditional clothing's related to both my parental background whatever did move me to do this was beyond my own will but I consented.

On the day my father was confirmed his chieftaincy title after the confirmation, I, my elder brother Barrister. Oritseweyinmi and is friend Mr Jide both graduates from university of Ife Oyo state in philosophy, went to pay obeisance to the King.

Paying obeisance to King Ogiame Atuwase the Olu of Warri, The crowds steered at me as if who is this young handsome man feet to be a chief, my elder brother and his friend as we three bowed, were greeted with loud cheers from all sides of the crowds at this time, I and my brother Mr. Omagbemi were about to leave Nigeria for the UK.

It was one of the issues I wanted to discuss with Mr Obi my co-volunteer at victim support Charlton that the king and the crowed and the oracle wanted me to be the next person in line of heredity. My brother Barrister Oritseweyinmi, my step mothers and their children, also wanted the position how do you go about achieving it in a place like Nigeria?
Our father had invested on my elder brother Barrister. Oritseweyinmi from my mother's side because of the amount of money he had spent on him becoming a graduate in Nigeria and a graduate of law at Buckingham university. The king is also a layer and presumably the first educated ruler of the Itsekiri kingdom of Warri.

My father did not invest on me while I felt as little as I could do investing on myself would yield significantly to my endeavours in life all I needed was a nudge. I was about to leave Nigeria for the UK. My military endeavours were my own personal endeavours to redress some family issues such as the conflict within my father and his brother, our family relationship because we are always quarrelling among ourselves.

One aspect of these issues is that Africa cannot progress if it is always a situation if one joins the army it is for the purpose of prestige, wealth, fame and authority. The same thing applies to being a graduate. Dose the development of a country and the true meaning and joy which emanate from the activities of culture, tradition or custom implies that, they should be at all cost become wealthy? No wonder Africa in retrospect is an inferno. Nobody cares for the next person if they do, they want you, to do something for them or they want to use you! Should the British invest in full towards my education in the UK?

By the time they reach such stages of having wealth, they hold a knife against anyone who would do them wrong or go against whatever they do or say which also means more business for the African Juju priests.

News about me and my brother leaving for the UK was kept secret from most people. With my father being conferred a chieftaincy titles, with his two sons about to leave Nigeria for the United Kingdom, would be too much for my father's enemies to take in too well and peacefully, or why should everything always have to happen for the better for my father?

At the time of my paying homage with the coral bead to the Olu of Warri all cooked up traditionally. Culture held the king as I steered at him, he wanted to say something, but the words would not come out of his mouth. Then I heard voices of the king saying 'do not give the coral bead back to your father' It was the only thing he possess within me and you.

Hearing these words form the king, before I came out of the

reverie, all of a sudden the king had to leave, with each family that have been conferred with chieftaincy title going back, to their resident for celebration. Outside, the crowds were about making move to leave after the occasion, my father made a move towards me for the coral bead. I shielded away from my father. I felt something had overcome my father infarct I knew I shielded away from him but it was not of my one doing voluntarily.

I and my father both come in for the ceremony in is Mercedes-Benz , rather than going back home with my father, his immediate younger brother from his father's side drove me home to my family resident.

Driving in into our resident, my father comes in from behind in his own Mercedes-Benz car, he made another move for the coral bead which was around my neck, never then did I know what he wanted it for. Considering the situation, he even called me and told me I should hand over the coral bead to him before undressing changing into new English clothes, I took the bead to my father handing it back to him, if he wanted it's so badly, let him have it! When things like these happen in a family the rest of the family pay ignorance to it or some of them would take bribe it is wrong I mean what dose a family stand for?

I was in front of our residence when the cow called 'malu' in Nigeria was brought in I took active part in the hiring of chair, tables, canopies arranging them outside and bringing in the drinks as part of the ceremonial activities. Nobody asked me if I was hungry or wanted something to eat throughout the day and the next day until in the evening the next day Cordelia offered me epuru.

A cloud came over me conditioning me to watch as the malu was about to be slaughtered it all occurred in a jiffy when it was brought in but I took it all in. I heard a voice saying a prayer ought to be said before the knife slit through the cows throat but it was made after the knife had cut through. It was on that day I realise precisely my eyes and ears become open. I heard voices coming within me and from the cow it said I should consider being a celibate because what it implies is very serious in view that it is a celebration I should accept it as it is. As it so happened it has been realised I am Orunmila as the knife slit through the throat of the cow at that point I heard myself say silently in alarm with my eyes wide open 'Orunmisila' meaning 'and my throat gush open' I guess somebody or some people want to travel a further distance or gain wealth. I remembered the phenomena come back to me when I was being initiated into Freemason. It was part of what conditioned me to say prayers on the ceremonial sward in our family home during the celebration after drinking so heavily for the first time in my life not bear but whisky, brandy, campari and gin when all the family had gathered and witness this a few gestures of rituals in words and actions was made and I felt I had to have some sleep and so I went to sleep it was almost midnight during my sleep from what I observed the next day that occurred during the night it all happened to me in my sleep. After the knife had cut through the cow a prayer was quickly said with poring of whisky on the cows gushing throat with blood I coming out of my reverie saw phenomena of images of some people in the form of mirage began to engulf the bleeding cow two of the people I later realised were of my sister in law Mrs. Edith Nwamaka Megbele and Mrs. Mary Rodney through the phenomena they seem to vow they would do something or they were compelled to do something. Working with Mrs. Mary Rodney at the Woolwich Gala club as cleaners Mary could not turn-up for work at some days especially when she became heavy with child she wanted me to do covers for her while she would pay me by cash with her name recorded as turning up for work I told her at some stage when I began experiencing general body weakening I would rather have it recorded on my pay slip. I do not know how to explain to my brother except from writing my books if Mr. Calvin Sudelu is really the reincarnation of our grandfather Mrs. Edith Nwamaka Megbele had already own her prize before he met her this does not in any way mean am against their being together.

Around the world, many people—perhaps the majority overall—accept a belief in reincarnation as part of their religion. Not many people in the West believe in it, though. In fact, many scoff at the very idea and regard it as nonsense.

How do I go further to explain this when people even cares view mental health problems as hallucination, paranoid or psychosis?

Since I arrived back into the UK, the coral bead stills hold a meaning within me and my father. After few years in the UK, I realise that some people do change, while some people would not change. In no way did my father went for the coral bead he had given to his other children as he came back for the coral bead he had given to me for the occasion around my neck.

He wanted it so he could raise his head higher above mine with my head below. This over rides my krypton crystal relationship. This was something; the Freemason would have known better off to have condition my father to initiate me into Freemason before hand in Nigeria before I come into the UK.

I wonder what most people think is the cause of my hallucinations, movements of furniture's in my flat, creating impressions or taking shapes into something else e.g. the shape of an eye, frame of humans making impression as if they are trying to tell me something, but they cannot speak, could it be it was through the coral bead.

I believe all humans and creatures do reincarnate, we are all prays to each others. It all depends on if one is of good nature, or bad nature. In some case if it's not the reincarnated person, it's another person coming into the world to up-hold the true intentions of another dead person, in which case he or she had been relieved of their journey after their trials of life.

I have tried getting my driving license through British school of motoring at Camberwell Green just by Peabody housing estates and with driving forces 16 Cambridge Green Eltham SE9 2AQ department of transport approved driving instructors.

I owned a rover vehicle registered KG Registration. With the hope I would get it on the road after attending driving lessons, in theory and practical test in other to attain my British driving license. For some reason of moving home, I could not attend on the right date for my driving test. This was before theory and practical test was introduced.

I had a Nigerian driving license. I tried taking several steps to get my UK driving license; I do not loos hope and faith too easily towards my endeavours. I am often too spiritually oriented for other peoples liking. I believe in reality with simplicity because I like facing facts. Each time I had tried to attain my driving licence, something always goes wrong preventing me from getting a driving licence in the UK

My father's first son Mr. Olu Megbele was not from my mother, my mother's first child a son for my father is Barrister Oritseweyinmi Megbele being the last child for my father with my mother what my father left within for me to consider in our relationship as father and son I would describe equivalent to Christ shouting in Calvary saying father, father why have thou for sake me. May be it was as a result that I too often look up to him.

I only find myself compelled to pay allegiance to my parents and to other people if only I am not obliged to carry out their wish if it would be harmful to me or someone else how are we compelled to do this in Africa are we living a healthy sociological life in Africa how are children compelled to behave, how do adults behave.

I have strength, capabilities beyond the reach of most humans yet I am in this world to divest myself, to become human how far could Africans understand or react over this they do.

The history of hospitals cares and manufacturing holds my sources of strength which inwardly comes to me from the sun and my medication which I take regularly. Within few years of my stay in the UK comes the use of solar energy and electric cars.

With my birth condition I have never suffered from any breathing problems, vomiting or seizures or feats in my life, which comes as relief to me and my GP's, with no illness of Aids, venereal deceases or sickle cell anaemia with an all clear from Queen Elizabeth hospital in late 2007. I have not become anaemic or suffer from tetanus.

Attending schools in Africa, Living with step mother, sisters, brothers, uncles, aunties, friends, working with my father's accountant as a clerk, Military speculations, Universities, Working in the UK in a cold store as sales assistant, B&Q store, cleaner, petrol station assistance, accommodations with private landlords and in hostels. I have had to sleep in hotels at crystal palace at certain times.

I do things in precision and sequences in certain respect before they unfold or before it gets hold on me I was once complemented by one of my fellow students from Spain Mr Albato at South Bank University that I do things in precision. I told him he should not over compliment me doing things in precision could be due to inherencies.

I hallucinate, visualise and perceive events before they happen but would not interfere. I live with grace of serenity attached to everything I do. I do suffer from harmonic the science of musical sound. The greatest request in all my prayers to the heaven even before I was born was for heaven to grant me peace.

My mind is always at work with racing thoughts; I have experience living for seven days without sleep, feeling relaxed, working and going out doing the shopping. Such experience at Ibadan Oyo state was me being without food for three days during lent; and after being baptized for the third time.

As much as I want to come out with my feelings for Africans, Jamaicans, Barbados, Trinidad's or West Indians with what I think of them. I find it difficult to come out open because we do not try to come too close to each other.

We are always too keen to get whatever we want if we care so much for our personal needs why not we all come together in unity to progress. It is about time we come of the reverie of slavery and its effect. It would do more harm if we continue to dwell on it; it has over the years not brought about any changes that would lead to collaboration within ourselves and the nations involved we all should be asking why?

In Africa, there is only two ways to describe the situation, of which you are either at the top or at the bottom, if you are at the bottom you will ask yourself many question, such as dose God exist, why do we have to suffer? It is because we never seem to reach deadlocks.

There is never a realisation if it pays to be evil and what are the consequences each day is right before our eyes. More than twelve people each day dies on the street of Lagos after being run down by a vehicle with no one, to pack their corpse and bury them, vehicle tyres crush them into thinly bits on the road without any second thoughts from passers-by. You are left each day, to suffer and wonder if there is God. If you are religious considering if you will go to heaven or not, you are left to suffer since you are going to heaven. I need not wonder why it is always only the poor who call and cry out to God is this what, the atheist consider to be the Gods delusion? Just take a look at those people and their suffering; they believe they have no life on earth but in heaven. They know better than the atheist that, though they may believe in God but the God they serve is not raining down honey into their lives. The big question now is what have the atheist got to offer that God had not offered to them? Life is a test of faith for all who wants salvation.

With suffering comes the reality to querying, where we are likely to be going or coming from. I hope in this my present life after previous life through reincarnations all around the world; I feel I am taking my last journey based on trials of life. At each stage of my reincarnation my strength is always being spent.

Britain is a country that allows people into its country with fewer barriers, such initiatives creates understanding with other nations, especially third world nations. Depending on the condition people come into the UK for. But when we arrive here, we want to look after other people while most of us come here because we want to be looked after.

It is always customary for us to do anything to be part of a defined structure of systems within the UK without consideration for being at the right places or work in the right environment.

Gone are the days of the archaeologist and the exorcist in Africa and all third world nations, we are now left with luxury goods imported from all over the world through technology, science and medicine all that needs to be corrected is greed and jealousy. Our lives are no longer clouded by the dark side that brought in the archaeologists partly because of science and technology.

If we are all trooping into Britain and America who among us will take an initiative to make Africa a better place , who among us is ready to take the brunt of making Africa our true home?

From what I have observed, we are yet to realise Britain and the rest of Europe is likely be the place where the archaeologist and exorcist would take its last chorus of omen. When are we going to stop being dependant?

The secret or the key to celibacy is that the individual has a secret or a key to creation or a secret of the universe e.g. the DVD Men in Black-one of the secret of the universe is tied around a lion's belt. If they perceive for any reason that the forces of evil is against the secrets they hold, by all odds they would not refrain from setting the balances right.

There are laws and rules to everything we do which could be confronted in relation to our entire existence for good or for evil. It's not in my nature to see bloodshed, violence or injustice this, is one reason why, I am in the UK where bloodshed is at a limit compared to if I should be residing in West Africa.

Immigrants given their stay in the UK do they change constructively? Regardless if the UK operates a welfare state, there is starvation in the UK as well. At the early 1990's, £35.00 income support, before the end of each week; claimants are waiting for the next income support payment coming through the post.

This same benefit amount is equivalent to what I earn working part time under initial cleaning services at the Woolwich Gala Club. As at 2008, income support had gone up with inflation to £60 a week at the same wages I am paid working at the same job. I am faced with paying £60 a week on my gas utility bills who say's the war in Iraq, Afghanistan and Al-Qaeda have not affecting everyone in the UK?

It was on BBC news computer disk holding incomes support disability living allowance, child benefits was lost through the post, how is the community going to function. It is about time we are creative towards our destiny conflict is inevitable but whoever they are carrying such acts if it is deliberate should be sympathetic towards those who have nothing to do with the ongoing conflicts for instant children, the needy and disable or a passers-by just going to work they have nothing to do, with the conflicts or misunderstanding.

For some Africans life in the UK is bliss, in flashy cars, and places they would be recognised even on the road, they seek recognition when most of us recognise them as people, who would do something about such issues. In my opinion, they seem without recognition of the difference in road condition of Africa compared with the road conditions in the UK.

I do feel like asking them it's good but what about the roads, houses and living condition in Africa? If the roads, and the ways of life and infrastructure please us in the UK it would be natural for us, to be filled with such an astronomical surge and temperament to better the road conditions and the ways of life in Africa. Immediately we are given our stay in the UK, we give-up our feelings or dreams of our native land too easily that; is if we have any left. If we go back on visits to Africa, we are usually filled with pride when we get there we boast about our lives in the UK. This is no longer necessary because, we now have mobile phones and satellite in Africa, we use solar energy.

If this is the way I feel, it is natural of me when for example an African in the UK flaunts a traffic regulations I feel embarrassed with an opinion, something should be done drastically about them, to mend their ways. Some of them go back to Africa, to boast, they have British driving license, they own a vehicle and they drive on the roads of Great Britain more important I hope they should want better traffic regulations conducive for the environment.

They immediately become driving instructors in Africa when they have only worked or drive for just one year in the UK for even less than a year if their feelings are not genuine they are making their way up the ladder to either gain contract or recognition. It is changes we want to see and the need to improve our quality of life and not a terminology of themselves. What I mean is that some of them go back to Africa demonstrating false self importance which never generates development.

In some ways, it is good because, it creates more awareness but, they are too filled with pride and self importance while the conditions are not getting any better they should be filled with great surge for developments.

Its carelessness when vehicle drivers flash rain water on predestines by the road when they are walking in the road, they should pay attention, to people walking on the road. We should not seem to loos our sensible human ideologies I might be implying this simply to free myself from myself.

Monday 01 December 2014 from Sky news source says England's Road Network to get £15bn Investment. The move is very much welcome as far as motorist take caution on the road when they see pedestrians, me or other people riding their bicycle on the road. It would mean that motorists are presumed to be at fault in civil actions after an accident with a cyclist or pedestrian, unless they can prove they were not to blame. It would also mean that cyclists would be presumed to be at fault for accidents involving pedestrians.

A tunnel at Stonehenge is among plans, to be included in the Autumn Statement, which Labour brands a 're-announcement'. More than 80 new road schemes have been unveiled as part of a £15bn Government drive on English motorway and trunk routes in the next five years. The schemes include a tunnel at the notorious bottleneck on the A303 at Stonehenge, as well as £1.5bn on extra lanes on some motorways. Improvements to M25 junctions, the A27 in Sussex, approaches to Liverpool and the A1 in the North East are also part of the Road Investment Strategy, which was revealed ahead of the Autumn Statement on Wednesday. Transport Secretary Patrick McLoughlin said the schemes were 'the biggest, boldest and most far-reaching roads programme for decades'.

The projects include:

:: South West - £2bn dual carriageway for entire A303 and A358, including a tunnel at Stonehenge.

:: North East - £290m dual carriageway on A1 to Ellingham.

:: North West and Yorkshire - M62 from Manchester to Leeds will have lanes increased, and increased capacity on trans-Pennine routes between Manchester and Sheffield.

:: North West - links to Port of Liverpool improved.

:: South East - £350m improvement to A27 to tackle congestion at Arundel, Worthing and Lewes.

:: East - £300m to put in dual carriageway sections on A47 and improved connections to A1 and A11.

:: London and South East - A third of junctions on M25 to be improved.

:: Midlands - Improvements to M42 east of Birmingham, and improved connections to Birmingham airport, National Exhibition Centre, Enterprise Zone and High Speed 2 interchange station.

There would also be £100m of funding to improve cycling provision at 200 key locations, and a £300m environmental fund to combat carbon emission and reduce noise pollution.

Mr. McLoughlin said: 'Roads are key to our nation's prosperity. For too long they have suffered from under-investment. 'Better roads allow us to travel freely, creating jobs and opportunities, benefiting hardworking families across the country.' Shadow transport secretary Michael Dugher said: 'This is just yet another re-announcement on promised road improvements. The Government has 'announced' plans for road investment at least three times since 2013 and no additional money has been announced.

'Ministers will be judged not on what they promise to deliver in the next Parliament, but on what they have actually delivered in this one - and the truth is barely a shovel has been used in anger on our nation's highways over the last four-and-a-half years.' There has also been an accusation that two-thirds of the improvements will come in Tory or Lib Dem areas.

However, Deputy Prime Minister Nick Clegg denied the locations had been selected for 'short-term political reasons' and pointed to plans across Labour strongholds in the Pennines. He told Sky News: 'You don't make these kinds of decisions based on a political map - you make them based on a map of the country. 'Many of these projects have been spoken about for years.' Motoring groups welcomed the proposals.

AA president Edmund King said: 'We can no longer ignore the inadequate resources going into the mainstay of the UK transport system - our roads - which carry 86% of passenger journeys and more than 90% of freight. 'At long last the Government has recognised that we need a long term coherent plan for our roads, with guaranteed funding, to end the stop-start mess experienced over the last few decades.'

Meanwhile, Mr Clegg reiterated a Government pledge not to increase fuel duty ahead of the Autumn Statement. 'We've been clear we're not going to put up fuel duty because we know filling up your car or van with fuel is one of the most expensive parts of a household budget,' he said.

This law will help make Britain's roads safer for cyclists by increasing the awareness and caution of motorists. It will say to motorists 'if you choose to use one ton of metal that can move at some speed to transport yourself, then you need to be extremely careful in every manoeuvre you take'.

I reckon I should be the Nigerian British console working for the Nigerian Embassy in the UK. Or why did I once embark for a place as military cadet for the Nigerian Defence Academy? Being British by birth does not mean I should extricate myself from African politics and affairs and its relation to other parts of the world.

What sort of a individuals could have a true vision of Africa on how it should be governed with credibility, why are there so much asylum seekers in the UK from third world countries is this a good or a bad sign for me as an African British residing in the UK?

Who could be said to be a better person to do the job of an ambassador within Africans and British relationship? I am an African born British no different from an African expatriate is this what could be said of me? It's about time some constructive measures and criticism are taken concerning these issues for a common goal to be reached. Or how do I fit in, in the UK as an African British, who had lived for several years in Africa. Within a multi-cultural nation it would be wrong to make people feel unwanted. Some inferences of mental illnesses are self made others are conferred on a sufferer by other people while others are social, environmental or the state of our planet.

Born in Britain having lived half of your life in Africa after being taken by some of the ways the British live their lives over here coming back into the UK after so many years, the British say, they as other nations have their own problems what disposition dose this put me? What I do not like about my background in relation to how things are over there and here is something I would say, is cynical yet, we are not in any way trying to change the situation especially about our lives and standard our reputations are low others are taking advantage of us which, is no body's fault but ours.

I have not yet been given my own freedom, yet much freedom has been given to many individuals from all works of life in the UK from all around the world. Freedom, for the sake that many of us might see reason by being realistic either in our Mercedes-Benz, flashy sports cars, houses or being British by birth. Such Africans are the once who seems to be getting on fine but the aptitudes are not right. It is in query with no ideology and too much dependent on others.

Look at them going to the moon, the planet mars, very soon, anyone who has the dosh, might take a trip to the moon, no more diesel vehicles but electricity cars. May be all we Africans and Asian want out of life is own houses here in the UK, or English ladies as wives, of which since its effects years ago have been the result of Jamaicans, Barbados, Trinidad's and West Indians through the creation of mixed race. We are still yet to create a strong bond through our relationship?

People from third world countries are given opportunities in the UK to have their stay, to be educated and to work. How do I feel about an African with tribal marks on his or her face should be my psychiatrist, care or social worker at Oxleas NHS Farryview mental health centre! In my knowledge it would only have had to do with an exceptional European lady who wants to give a testimony that she had once been a close friend with Orunmila an African deity.

She would be no one else than She who must be obeyed by Orunmila known to him as Orisia.

If I couldn't have had a wife in Nigeria before coming back into the UK, for some reason I felt, I should have been married in the UK before My immediate elder brother. For the sake of simplicity because of my birth condition, I felt I had to go in first, before my immediate elder brother comes in I have the feeling both of us should have been given birth to as twins.

At least I would have had the chance of expressing whatever my condition was before he gets married. Considering this would not take place as far as culture was concerned, which implies, that the eldest of the family, should always come first, with reason I preferred because of some inherent coherences to remain a celibate.

Why did my father waited for so long border me before building his house at Delta state Nigeria? This land my father owned was handed down to him through his late uncle and relative to his mother who was then the Ologbosere of Warri of Delta state.

Some children meet with different faiths with their parents labouring very hard with difficulties to raise their children up to attain University education in West Africa. They are later dependant on these children, who after same time would have children of their own to look after. The bottom end do raise one or two conflict e.g. Such as if their parents were not privileged to choose a wife for them, their children future relationship with their wife or husband could be met with conflicts with their parents.

Some parent because of such conflicts later could induce their children with juju to do as they wish e.g. As a parent they would claim, they had slaved to bring up the child up to where he or she is, or the parent could do juju's against the child if, the child would not do as their parent wish, Parents and children relationship in Africa are often found to undergo vicious circles in Africa.

Especially if privileges have been granted to a child through hereditary e.g. my father's uncle Ayeye Dudu once the Ologbosere of Warri of Delta state during my father's youth in Nigeria did actually gave opportunities and land to my father among many other relatives depicting them whilst, they are young to govern the family clan depending on the amount of wealth thy could have among them. My father became a chief in 1988 as the Agbueju of Warri Delta state Nigeria born in 1936 and died in 2004 at the age of 68 years. Its

The land my father inherited from his uncle had something to do with me before, I was born. It was the last place I placed my mantle before, I was born going further into Olumo Rock.

This uncle of my father had children of his own whom lands and the blessing of his title were conferred on before his death. But culture do not always work this way in Africa, it is the amount of wealth you come about with no matter how you got hold of the wealth, is what makes you whatever you can become in all communities in Africa.

Rather than my father becoming the Ologbosere of Warri the second highest rank and authority in the history of Delta state chieftaincy and traditional hierarchy after his late uncle. It was all an opportunity for my father to take but it fell short, we all welcomed his title because we needed someone from our clan to represent us or our voice would not be heard and that the title had been given to my father from his youth by his uncle, my father's mother was half English from an African mother not only that, it was also because my father's mother was related to this uncle of his.

With the implications of the British presence in Delta state through the Nigerian ports authorities my father was sure of making himself a wealthy business man my father had studied shipping in the UK.

All my father had to do on his arrival with my mother in the UK in the 1960's was to study shipping. Knowing what it would mean to him in Delta state where a shipping port recently stands. If you know the ways of Africans the rest episodes are nothing left but clichés if you know what I mean e.g. he shrug my mother off his life, since she was a Yoruba woman or why else were they not together any more immediately after, they both left the UK in the late 1960s.

My father just had to marry someone like Cordelia from the same origin of both his parents. Hoops the things we do that gets us, where ever we want to be in Nigeria e.g. wealth, fame, popularity some of them could be very embarrassing.

Mrs. Cordelia Megbele is my father's second wife after my mother throughout our youth Cordelia was always of the opinion that, until the day my father dies vowed, she would never leave my father for another woman it's how African women treat their men just to hold on to them. Though my father married another wife after Cordelia, both women had to live with my father as mates. Mrs. Cordelia did not leave my father as she vowed in spite of my father getting married to a fourth wife from the same origin as Cordelia and himself. Life is complicated enough in Africa, why make it more complicated with propagandas?

Cordelia's father was well known during the reign of my father's uncle as the Ologbosere of Warri, within few years my father went back from the UK to Nigeria for his mother's funeral, Crodelia had a daughter for him Miss. Anita Oritsewarami Megbele now known as Mrs. Oritsewarami Temile and later had engineer Arnold Ukunoritsemofe Megbele. When Cordelia had these two children for my father within Delta state in the early 1970's which was then Bendel state and part of Mid-Western Nigeria and Port Harcourt before we moved on to Lagos state Nigeria in the mid 1970's.

My father went after the next closets Nigeria ports authority From Delta state which was at Rivers state Port Harcourt with his family including Cordelia we moved from Delta state to reside at Port-Harcourt where our father got married to his third wife the daughter of an (Amayanabo) The word Amayanabo signifies a title in Rivers state held by Mr Al-well-brown father of Mrs. Aya Gogo Megbele from Kalabari origin in Rivers state. This was within two years of our moving to Port-Harcourt.

The Kalabari are a tribe of the Ijaw people living in the western Niger Delta region of Nigeria. The name Kalabari was derived from their ancestor Perebo Kalabari. The Kalabari, like most Nigerian coastline tribes, were wealthy as a result of their interactions with the Europeans.

Living at Port-Harcourt in the early 1970's Mrs. Aya Megbele's mother called Mata Al-well-brown there was no time, I would go and visit Mrs. Mata Al-well-brown she wouldn't offer me something to eat; Its all juju or candy as a bribe so that as a child and my father's favourite, I should move closer to her daughter in our father's home.

Mrs. Mata Al-well-brown usual welcomes me with greeting (the English man has arrived) while her daughter who was now my step mother Mrs. Aya Megbele stopped every member of my family from stroking my coyly hair.

Her usual words were that they should (leave his Oyinbo head alone) which means they should stop stroking or ruffling my English mans coyly hair alone (Oyinbo) in Pigeon English means English. Sometimes I wished she was with me at school to witness what young African girl my age group do to my coyly hair during my nursery and primary hours at school. Aya worked as a television news presenter at Rivers state Broadcasting cooperation. She was a sister to Miss Senaye Al-well-brown also a presenter.

Mrs. Aya Mebgele as far as I could remember when she

moved into my father's house, was always reserved. She was found of displaying manners towards we young children trying to bring us up with good manners, for example she showed interest in educating us on how to have our meals with knives and forks, how to set a table for breakfast, lunch and dinner. How we children should seat up and eat at a dining table. My father at that time was making lots of money working as a manager for a stevedoring owned by Mr. Ramalam and sons who are from the North of Nigeria.

All Aya Megbele wanted, was to use we children to gain control over her house-mates Mrs. Cordelia Megbele because Cordelia was not all that educated. At this time with all that was happening around me, I never knew I was born British infarct I become aware of it while residing with my mother at Ibadan Oyo state, while I was 17 years of age after completing secondary school.

Few years after Mrs. Aya Megbele moved into my father's house for some reason, I couldn't have been aware of its meaning to me at that time or that, it would have implication to my life in the near future was that prior-to when she met with my father she had, had her appendicitis taken off. What has that got to do with me I was only a young lad at the time it made no inference then.

Towards the time our father was to become a chief, she became a lodge member at Warri Island lodge with approval from my father. When my father become chief, about the time I was to leave Nigeria for the UK, she advised me that if by any chance, I should have my appendicitis taken off for any reason I should give consideration to celibacy.

The reason she gave was that having an appendicitis taken off has the same implication as a tattoo on once body.

I asked her what then was her opinion about children born in polygamous homes? She looked at me and smiled pronouncing my name (Osemisan) which is my name Oritsesemisan for short frequently used by members of my family when calling on me. She said to me you know something of what, you have been used for in this family before she answered my question which was; according to her polygamy is an exaggerated publicity and it is questionable. It's only my father in our family who calls me by my full name Oritsesemisan.

I never knew it would turn out the way it did later in my life because according to Mrs. Aya Megbele's interpretation of taking off an appendicitis is the peak and the end of a family tree with regards to African culture.

The issue had something to do with why I did not take my friendship with Miss Loraine O'Connor too strongly any longer after the year 2000 because it was close 1999 when I had my appendicitis taken off at the Greenwich hospital just before it was short down having my appendicitis taken off meant I am now wearing a Kilt; I mean a Kilt as in Freemason.

My mother left me in the care of Mrs. Cordelia Megbele while I was only a baby, I was about four years old when my father got married to Aya Megbele this was the time it could be said I started realising what was going on in my family. I was always a free spirit within the family everybody was my friend and I was a talkative. Until I began noticing things for example, there was no time I considered Cordelia and Aya Megbele as not being my mother's. It was mummy, mummy this and that.

I talk and play with everybody without realising at that time it was Cordelia who had made it turn out the way it was within Aya Megbele and the children in the house. For example my becoming more close to Aya Megbele than Cordelia. Or it could have been a grudge from Cordelia because she had been the one looking after us children in the family before Aya moved in.

Cordelia was of the opinion where did Aya came from anyway to have taken her man away from her since Aya Megbele had partially taken her place as a new wife to my father, Aya should start taking care of me and my mother's children according to Codelia, she had her own children to look after. But this same thing happened again on Aya's part after she had two children of her own in the family and in some sort of ways; our father began to be a different man from what she had expected.

I lived with these two women to realise as time went on, they only cared for themselves and their own children in respect to these, how do I view my father? The real view never occurred to me until several years faced with uneasiness about what was happening, two women in eagerness to please my father then later themselves, worried and tense moments that causes more anxiety.

This event in my family in the early 1970's meant little or nothing to me, I was only a young child Aya Megbele tried as much as she could, to be friendly with we children all I knew was that I liked her because, she was friendly she even played prank with we children one of which made all of us receive a good flogging from our father for the first time in our life one evening when he came back from work because I at the age of seven years I length how to smoke cigarettes it most have been Cordelia who had let the cat out of the bag!

Mrs. Aya Megbele's origin in Nigeria is much closer to that of my sister-in-law Nuwamaka Megbele. Both my step mothers had grown-up there when they were young within Nwamaka origin from Eastern Nigeria. Both women could speak and understand the language customary to Nwamaka's origin.

From what have happened so far in my family I wonder, why should I grow up accepting Cordelia Megbele speaking for Nwamaka's origin. It should rather be applicable for Mrs. Aya Megbele to do just that.

I blamed my conscience for leaving my mother at Ibadan after my secondary school education to reside with my father and the rest of the family, though I paid visit to my mother at Ibadan but I did not see her for a long time, before I left Nigeria for the UK. I felt, I should have at least paid her a visit before I left she was not at the airport to see me and my brother Mr. Omagbemi leave Nigeria for the UK.

There were certainly one or two things to learn from both my father's wives and form Mrs. Tsainomi Ayo Megbele whom my father got married to as his fourth wife after I had left Nigeria for the UK with Mrs. Aya Megbele probably forced to move out of the family home years before, my father's death in 2004.

All humans go through periodic reincarnation the process will continue to go on as long as there is continued sex, sex, sex. Many are called but few would be chosen. At each periodic stage, we either have omens or an epilogue of an era at each step we make.

What gives me the impression I knew my father before I was born to have become his child and that, I know him too well, just as he knows me very well. If I had become his child, within me and my father who dose the courtesy belongs to me or to him? In a father and son relationship since he is the father, I think he owes me the courtesy because, I have through birth been made to be dependent on him; if I was dependant on him at some stages of my life, a time comes when am no longer dependant on him because, I have a life of my own to live right from our youth each individual is compelled to live their lives in certain ways that applies to them that makes not only each individual but the world we live in unique you respect other people as you would want other people to respect you.

Some people are of the opinion it is because of whatever evil one has done in a past life induce them to suffer during another life in some ways, it is true but what if they do not want to carry on in line with their families abomination, while some within a family would want to live in line with their families abomination while some others would not want to because, they cannot change while others could change.

Existence on earth is always a state of the art and there are forces of nature. Why do the burden of the world bring more suffering on the once who seems to have chosen the Milky Way which is the least one could do because certain aspects of human existence could be very complicated at certain point, it could drive one insane that is, if they are aware of the situation; if they are aware of the situation, it means they care or there is something about the situation that beguiles them.

Could it be for the purpose to make us, search for our inner self as to who and what we are? We cannot see God whoever, and whatever God is, is all around us in our body, soul, mind, consciences and environment this does not mean we are all the time conscious of God. If the nature God is offensive in any way, to human existence, we would not have beauty as part of our existence. Yes beauty, beauty that each day crumbles dose it crumbles to reflect the presence of he, who has created the entire Universe or we as the occupants of planet earth?

You can be anybody rich or poor it does not stop you from being good or evil what I mean is in each other way we can be both, some of us are of the opinion the humiliating effect of the scenario is that individuals with good intentions and integrity attached to their lives, are the once who suffer and loos out the most.

In every community shedding blood makes poor mortar, for blood to be capable of serving the quest of evil purposes? It should be sweet, sweet enough to be used for juju's don't you know this yet I asked Miss Lorain on one of our discussion about African rituals her reply was that it was for such issues which makes us more perceptive.

I asked her how could being a Christen be relevant to my Africa background call it theology if you like she replied; she told me it was for me to find out or what else could have driven me to come from such a background? Our jujus, rituals, culture and tradition are too exploitative she said.

So you believe it has to change I asked her; yes she replied lots of things have to change and put in the right perspectives. I asked her since she is a Christian she should hope for me, to face my reality, it is another reason why am here in the UK and why Lorain had you lived part of your life in South Africa I wanted to ask her. At this point, I held back any other question in my mind the conversation on this topic should wait for awhile because, we were about to have dinner. During our dinner I contemplated on our discussion.

After our dinner, I said to Lorain let me tell you what I saw, what did you see she asked? there was a star shining so brightly above the sky, giving us hope and strength to grow, where all individuals with good intentions know the answers as long as love is in their heart, that there is a place for them above the star which gives them strength, hope and courage to tarry on with good intention in this troubled world of ours filled with too much trifle, pain and sorrows why else do the stars at night shine above the sky? What I wanted to deduct from her through our conversation was why are our lives filled with too much inconsistencies, our hopes are easily dashed.

This book is based on how I feel about life and existence based on revelations about my parents, relatives and my illness as a paranoid schizophrenic and how traumatised I am about many of life inconsistencies in which, I am compelled to be just an observer. I am not holding any grudge or trifles it is for a purpose of making a brighter tomorrow we need to change, not just change, but change for the better based on reality and purposes otherwise we have no future.

Are we aware of English man or women running for the post of Mayor, a member of parliament or a very wealthy individual come out openly about their personal life to an extent if they are gay, a lesbian, or a drug addict this, is not common all around the world.

One thing we know about Britain and its polices as a nation for sure is that, if any unpleasant thing goes on in our communities, there is always accountability for example consider the issues surrounding members of parliament expenses row.

If they are corrupt, hatful or spiteful would any other nation listen to them or take their advice, or involvement in the Middle East peace process, The row over President Mubarak of Egypt to hand over power as President.

They not only involve themselves as tourist within other nations without avoiding poorer nations. They are concerned for peace, in third world and developing nation and they act by showing they care. If other nations do the same, rather than involving themselves in conflict, we would be moving towards peace on earth.

The Europeans created the media and its technology with huge investments and labour even, in some of the most remote villages in Nigeria, they could watch television. Why don't they ignore other nations in crisis? It is good to join hands and heads knowing what goes on around planet earth or we would be ignorant of each other. For instant, it is the 21st century words went out, that in a certain part of the world, cannibalism is going on they would be considered as aliens from other planets.

Could there be any thing wrong with me coming out with some of life traits or trials which I am faced with? This is bound to happen, or we would live as a community where we hardly know each other yet within it, there are conflicts. 60% of Britain live their lives in isolation we hardly know each other but we could come out openly on how we feel about almost any issues affecting our livelihood. We could be confronted with problems yet we set them right. If it were in Nigeria for example nobody cares and you dear not come out openly to question any unpleasant happenings related to those in authority.

For some Africans in the UK such an outburst could injure their pride, this should not be the case because we African, then Jamaicans, Barbados, Trinidad etc have more than tails to come out with about ourselves and our purpose and predicaments in life because I hardly see anything good coming out of us in which case, the more we are just mere other peoples instruments. Let us start by becoming creative in time, we would not only be good at it, it would become easier and very much appreciated by we ourselves.

Thinking of the situation in a perspective point of view, most of us who enters into the UK through being British, immigrants or asylum seekers, immediately forget whatever is happening in our land of origin and our past.

Yet we have and celebrate culture month, and festivals in the UK why can't we find it easy embracing reality, to tolerate and expound within each other about our defects and whatever, could result to progress in and outside Africa as a whole for our own wellbeing? Let us do something to appreciate our lives and respect for each other.

Why should we choose to live a desolate life in despair take the life of a pet in the UK the law protects them you can be sued in a court of law and go to jail for mistreating a creature known as pets. We are humans we do not appreciate ourselves.

They have, their own pet store, with varieties and choice of food of all kinds to choose from infarct, they have their own adverts of commercial on television to imply which pet food is best based on grams for grams, vitamins and cholesterol they even have, their own pet insurance policies. They have their own surgeries to be well looked after if they should become unwell; they have their own DVD Cats&Dog can't we learn.

I appreciate Dr. Pierera, Dr. Mougoud, Cathy, Mr. Kevin Daniel, Mr. Engi, Dupsi, Ms. Mercy Brown and Mr. Akim, Mr. Fidelis from Zimbabwe, Mr. Conrad my carers at the Ferryview mental health team and Ms. Barbera the receptionist at my GP services below the mental health team at the Ferryview health centre are Nurse Kim, Dr. Jane Deacon, Dr. Hughes my personal GP, Dr. Margery, Dr. S. Divall, Dr. Sami Rached.

I might not get on well with all of them but, they have purpose in my life and for good reasons and those at Boot the chemist in Woolwich Mr. Ed, Chu, Bola, and Kyren from New Zealand. Mr. Ed has good resemblance facially, in height and the way he speaks to Mr. Alan Doyle my assistant manager at Iceland Frozen food plc at Lewisham. Mr. Chu is a Chinese.

How long are we going to be like such in our native land, where the most important thing if one should be unwell and needs treatment money has to come first before one is cared for in clinics or in hospitals in Africa.

If this, is the situation in Africa how do doctors, care and social workers from my native Africans feel while working in the UK as doctors and cares? That, they are doing a good job! Far from it not in the condition of caring in your ethnic origin would you be considered as making any progress for which, you should be appreciated working in the UK as a matter of facts, you are nothing but just mere tools while the tools around you, whilst you are working are better off than you. We have a lot to say about racism and prejudice while at the same time, we are found of abusing ourselves we lack respect for each other.

You are a qualified doctor or a psychiatrist from Africa you come into the UK, you want to care for English white race in a hospital theatre? You should go and sit down where, you are most useful! An African woman comes into the UK to seek her stay, she had children when she heard that I have no children she said others, should discriminate against me because, I do not want to have children as she put it 'join them'.

Most of them come into the UK as immigrants the health authority say they need people to care for mentally ill people they rush in to colleges and Universities to study mental health care while certain aspects of our ways of life in Africa have gone beyond insanity.

It would not work, why not when; there are people like Michelle Cook and my late mother in her new reincarnation around who could make it work but are not given the chance! I as an African born British might not be accepted by some people, some Jamaican , Caribbean's would not accept me or each other and we are from the same race while others would us the opportunity in upgrading themselves.

Mr. Dotun Sobowale who had been helping me through my

illness and relapses, filing in my disability leaving allowance, incapacity claim form, and visits me in my flat, whilst he was in Nigeria, he was an employee of Eko Hospital as a manager.

Most professionals after their education or practice in Europe going back to Africa to work in hospitals do suffer from arachnophobia's the only place that could be conducive in health related employment for most of them, is administration or caring for people with disabilities.

My father paid me his last courtesy after all have been said and done with, with him about to go down to his grave. In 2001 my father took me to a night club in central London; just the two of us with Osibisa Ghanaian grand musical band playing for the night, on his last visit to the UK.

Osibisa is a Ghanaian Afro-pop band, founded in London in 1969 by four expatriate African and three Caribbean musicians. Osibisa were one of the first African heritage bands to become widely popular and linked with the world music description. The band spent much of the 1970s touring the world, playing to large audiences in Japan, Australia, India, and Africa. In 1996 Osei reformed the band, and many of their past releases began coming out on CD. The band remains active in 2009.

Mrs. Mary Rodney, Miss. Salina, Mr. Thomas, Mr. Victor and Mr. William, Miss. Elizabeth, Mr. Samuel, Mr. Amos and others are co-workers of mine at the Woolwich Gala club under Initial Rentokil cleaning services. Cathy one of my care at the Ferryview mental health centre told me she is half Ghanaian while at Greenwich hospital in 1995 a fellow patient told me within the hospital ward that Mr. Akim is a Ghanaian.

It was my second time, of watching the Osibisa Ghanaian grand band playing. My first time of watching them play, was during the all West African 1977 FESTAC celebration in Nigeria. I was at the royal festival hall all by myself in Nigeria at the age of 11 years. It was made possible by my sister Oritsegbubemi offering me a ticket she had bought but couldn't attend. It was a last chance of watching the band play since, the festival was about to fold up.

My GP Dr Hughes at one time suggested I give a short version of my name. I was not embarrassed by this and told him, if he can pronounce the word Osibisa, he could easily pronounce my name regardless of its mouthful of 13 letter word or he could use the same word (open-sesame as in the Arabian- night.

After our night out, I and my father come back through a train which stopped us at Lewisham train station just by Iceland Lewisham where I worked with Miss. Michelle Cook, this was the last, I saw of my father after a party without knowing he was going to pass away soon. On our night out when the train stopped on our way back both father and son at Lewisham waited for my brother Mr. Omagbemi to came and pick our father up to his flat in Brockley while I came back to my flat by bus in Woolwich.

I am not happy to see myself as one person in my family who would practice celibacy but the world is an ever changing place choice and chance do not come easy. It is inevitable under certain condition, we need to change.

For an African such is a surprise not only to me but also, to my whole family none of them have come up with an outburst with regards to my being a celibate. While some of them thinks am stupid, or leave him alone they say to themselves let his good luck pass him by. If it were me, I would not let such an opportunity pass me by being British by birth.
Why is it all one can get from those who are not British from their own background in the UK is hat or jealous because one is British? This may be their opinion but there is always a fire burning nearby that needs the fireman's attention in any parts of the world.

How about this? What would you do as a young lady in Nigeria you have had to be a prostitute to see yourself through University education in Nigeria? I have said a lot of prayers about this for several years. I realise, there is always prophesies, an omen of oracles or that God hears our prayers which up-holds each and every one of us in everything we do in life!

As a graduate, to have undergone such an ordeal why not practice celibacy when as a graduate, you can have a job? What is it that could be an ambition of a prostitute if not that others should not suffer the same repercussion as theirs? Salvation is for the taking it never comes to you, you have to go for it. There could be many of your types but few can make it.

Could it be that bad if with your degree you go out with an opposite sex who is below your statues in other to guard him or her, to appreciate you? As a degree holder it's only a little bit of self sacrifices it could lead to some ways of teaching some people better manners. Justice has to come against all injustice. But it never comes about, without some sacrifices.

All origins have their own ways of doing things that is for sure but perceptive are different within origin, culture, tradition, belief, race and creed.

Early 2000 the word celibacy came out loud in America. I had an experience as a young lad when my uncle Mr Temitayo Akinlami came back from America to Nigeria with his family in late 1970s. He died at Abuja Nigeria's federal capital in 2000.

I want people to assess if am suffering from a mental disorder or mental illness. Is my case psychological or is it a behavioural pattern generally associated with subjective distress or disability that occurs in an individual which are not a part of normal development or culture.
The recognition and understanding of mental health conditions have changed over time and across cultures while there are still variations in definition, assessment, and classification of mental disorders. A few mental disorders are diagnosed based on harm to others, a perception in my case would be distress and doing something out of the ordinary feeling it's something I have to do.

• There are different categories of mental disorder or concepts human behavior while personality can become disordered. Such as when Anxiety or fear interferes with normal functioning classified as an anxiety disorder commonly recognized categories include specific ,panic disorder, phobias, generalized anxiety disorder, post-traumatic stress disorder, social anxiety disorder, obsessive-compulsive disorder.

Assess if my patterns of belief and thoughts are disordered or if characteristics over the years have influence my thoughts and behaviours across situations and time could be considered disordered. If judged to be abnormal why a urge to resist certain impulses harmful to myself or others, or if my motion and mood processes has over time and years become disordered through intense and sustained sadness, despair composed of normal or depressed mood.

The use of drugs legal or illegal when it persists despite significant problems related to the use, in some cases are defined as a mental disorder substance use may be due to patterns of compulsive or repetitive use of the drug which could results in tolerance or intolerance to its effects or withdrawal symptoms when its use is reduced or stopped.

Back to the UK in 1989, until 21st century I am still adapting to the new ways of life in Europe, everything is always changing constantly in the UK our ways of life, our environment and much more. One thing about Britain is that as much as you try not to be a stranger; you are still always a stranger as much as you try to embrace the new ways of life. The British strikes me as very sad people.

Paedophiles, lesbians, gay, drug abuse, cloning, now means celibacy would have its way in one person out of every 10 people within a families all around the world, it has now taken a new meaning because of the present row over gay and lesbian clergies with related child abuse. The effect of gay and lesbian clergies having wedlock's at church a place of worship to God have contributed to some people adapting to a new way of life as celibates while the topics of religion is constantly becoming a complicated issue.

I am like something of a living mammy engraved in each hospital or a skeleton. How my father would have wanted to become a skeleton before, he died. But not, when he had wore coral beads as a chief. All that is left of him prior to his going to his grave is his residual image, through which I suffered from personality disorder.

It becomes practically impossible for him becoming a skeleton such is one of the criteria's for members of the Reformed Ogboni fraternity cult in Nigeria would want to pride themselves with.

Since 1966 when I was away from the UK until 1989 the medical history, environment within the European nations have drastically so developed with changes. As a Christian by faith with regards to my survival with my condition of birth, my life in Africa and in the UK, I pride myself and the works of Nuns of the Roman Catholic faith. Earth is finites.

We are all parts and body of the Angelic host of Heaven no matter what race creed, belief or religion. The beginning of wisdom is that fear of God in all living things especially most focused on humans. Let us all pray and hope that when we go to our grave, we would be rapture by the next Angelic bodies coming to earth to undergo their trials to unfold the world and the secrets of the Universe. When am gone, I hope when am gone.

I would go with the wind as to where I belong when my trials are all over. I say fair well and goodbye with the Greenwich Hospital at Vanbrugh road SE18 which had been pulled down. For which I hope there would be no need for me to reincarnate.

Because existence had given me privilege to have established myself as an entity with the trials I have undergone. It's not just me alone; a lot of other individuals also, have under gone their trials! We live in a world, where any new undertaking for better or for worse no matter how small brings in a new order; many would follow, some would not follow because they do not want to change.

Mother, father, brothers, sisters, and friends, I often ask myself when, we would stop living within each other with indifference. For how long would we remain being scotched? If we have been scotched from the sky, for how long, would we continue to scotch ourselves?

There are too many of us crying and dying, we need to embrace ourselves with love with concern for each other, if not love, but with concern for each other. War is not the answer; we need to find ways to bring, happiness and joy into our lives. Our spiritual suffering and heartaches is now far worse than suffering from physical pain.

What I hope to see is changes now and in the future in our lives to reduce suffering. With all that I am going through, without committing suicide I hope many would be happy for me, that I could still be resilient in embracing life regardless of my illness and tribulations. Just as I suffer from side effects of my medication, I suffer the same about life and existence the effect on me is traumatic.

Some parental attitudes leads to worse attributes coming from their children, all children, needs both parents. The effect on children could last for a life time with some children because, they need both parents for example they become socially withdrawn, less confident among their play mates. How would a child being bullied at school feels if he or she receives no support from either their brother or sister at school after being bullied? Why should they care when, they are of mixed parents, or one of the parents live outside their home.

It is wrong to look at any little child as basically a child; some children are grown-ups even before they can walk. They have common sense; they have more to look forward to than any adult. It depends greatly on how much independence allocated to such children for them to grow up in confidence. Do not create any ineradicable situation for any child conflict in all aspects of our life is inevitable it could make them grow up less mature or they could grow up imitating other people's lives.

It is wrong for a parent to instruct a child on following a particular culture, it should be as a matter of, if they could adapt to such a culture invariably you are not forcing them to follow particular culture. He or she is your child; they grow up to know you better just as you their parents get to know them. In good time, they would eventually see reason on whatever, you implied on following any culture.

Since they are your children, they would inevitably follow culture, attributes and characteristics that are akin to yours as their parents. Or why is it common within certain families, were children and their parents, are like a gang in their relationship it boost family morals and close family ties similar to relationships within twins at birth inseparable. I would have loved my family more if we could have been inseparable with created bounds. Why is it, a culture not found in within Africans

I am not one to lives on another person's dreams but I think things are falling apart. The new age is unveiling itself to us whatever we do should be what really matters in this present and difficult times.

I could collapse as a Schizophrenics invariably pull myself out of work, claim benefit, if I loos my flat I could still reside in a hostel if immigration gets worse and since there is an ongoing war. I have lived on meagre amount of income while in Nigeria; I have faced difficult circumstance in my past, as little as I would receive as income in the UK if am unemployed I cannot be left out because I have been built to be ready for some ups and downs.

No one knows this better on how to coup in the UK than people from third world countries who resides in the UK. In their country of origin, were most of them are dependent on themselves for their livelihood. Most children as young as five years of age are thrown out of their family home each day, to fend for themselves on the streets. There is no room for adoption in Africa it is out of consideration. Such children could be picked up from the street and made money out of as slaves in rich peoples home, or to work in farmland with no pay but just food for the day as long as they could work.

Many children born in the UK who have experience glamour unlike the once born in Africa they would do anything to come into the UK even with juju to study and become successful graduates. It's part of African culture it's the African way of doing things, we have taken up politics, education, government ministries making us a recognised part of something similar to the Western hemisphere. But we are still undermining ourselves by not being creative and considerate. If, it becomes an undertaking, it would have to start from the grass root within each African family.

Any individual who has responsibility of upholding equality of other people should accept human diversity such as within family, school staff, care organisations, NHS trusts who they have to interact with; accept diversity of others as part of their daily lives needs to understand the concepts of equality and diversity and enable them to understand peoples' rights and responsibilities in relation to concepts.

To enable understanding of the values and beliefs that underpins human diversity, identify the range of human characteristics that create such diversity. There will be an exploration of how negative views of human diversity can lead to stereotyping, prejudice, harassment and victimisation and the impact it could have within individuals. In some part of the world harassment is a daily occurrences you could be victimised by anyone even within your family.

I often ask myself why should my mother had studied in the UK went back to Africa but could not become a minister in cabinet in Nigeria politics. Not that I could not study in a Nigeria University because my parents could not afford my education or I do not adore being educated in a Nigerian University. It is always something that befalls me even if I choose the easy way out of any given scenario; I am always still faced with difficulty. It's always the case with me and everything I do or that happens in my life because of my background.

Coming back into the UK the issues of education have became questionable in this land of freedom, hope and civilisation yet could one believe that am facing the greatest stereotyping anyone could be faced with in his or her life. I am now a new breed of African born British residing in the UK.

The same way I look at Jamaicans, Caribbean's, Barbados you see we all have a life to live based on preconditions we should stop dwelling on our past, focus on the present then the future. Which could be for the better or for worse things are bound to go wrong but on it, lies a concept if things gets worse, everything needs to be done no matter how difficult for it to get better. This should be the aim and ideology we need to focus on in other to continue to improve our quality of life in time; we would eradicate conflict and diversity to its minimal level. We all need empowerment this can only be achieved if we work together for a common goal rather than being self centred to unit there needs to be cohesion.

I am not saying it should be like the scenario in our past that had led us into more trouble and indifference during a time according the Holy Bible in the book of Genesis regarding the Tower of Babel where all united to speak to God. There is nowhere in this world, were the whole population are united in one voice but there must be a good level of tolerance and unity my family background are too diversified.

With too much indifferences in culture, tradition, history, and heritage in a nation such as Africa where lies the use of the highest number of different dialects it would be when, we begin to focus on ideologies aiming for a better future then and then only, would we be ready to face the outside world. Then we could say to ourselves, welcome to the real world.

I can speak Yoruba, Pigeon English I understand Itsekiri and Ibo dialect but can't speak both dialects fluently. Prime Minister Tony Blair says English should become a common language doing so in my opinion, European nations would understand each other better. I applaud the suggestion since Great Britain in my opinion is a conglomerate of the whole of the Europe nations. I mean, there are much a larger number of people from other European nation residing in the UK. In understanding each other European nation are not all that ahead third world nation with so vast in different languages speak English. For centuries we have been looking for ways to understand each other.

As the tension escalate between Ukraine and Russia over the disputed territory of Crimea as part of human nature conflict is inevitable settling such disrupt one needs to look at the relevant issues. When humans seek peace among themselves want to live happily with each other they need to socialise. Britain and some part of Europe involve themselves with people from all over the world including mostly third world and developing nations they show concern on what goes on out there it has made them very popular all around the world which have not occurred in just one day. Most African parents send their children to school so that apart from their native language they could speak English or French so that they are not isolated from the rest of the world. To have come this far within the European Union am surprise there is language berries among members state. Russia as a super power seems to have isolated itself from developing nations or put input to their development or interest. When members of the European nations seems to have language barriers they need to understand how they sound, how other people from other part of the world including developing nations feel or who doesn't even understand one word in Russia as they try to tag along in relation to the European Union members state commitments to each other and the rest of the world. Men or women from the black communities, Asians seats as members of parliament in Britain, they are doctors who have their own practice or chemist. Some of them are teachers or lectures, weather forecast and currency market and much more across Africa's region and Europe on the news etc. It should all not be a matter of being a superpower through weapon of mass destruction attaining such a position you need to socialise and make other nations understand you through other perspectives not in any way create fear. Good communication is at the heart of happy relationships of all kinds. It's also about understanding others people's need and having our needs heard, connection, focus on exploring different cultures, customs, viewpoints and types of relationships in order to better understand each other.

We all have our own fault, go through dilemmas' I see nothing wrong in having mutual understanding or commitment with each other to make the world a better place, create harmony reduce conflict. Endeavouring to understand other people, if we understand each other we would be kind to each other. Knowing each other well never leads to hate it leads to love and understanding having or keeping commitment with each other that we care.

I started drinking and smoking at the same age my father took up smoking to some extent excessive drinking. I also took-up smoking pipes tobaccos. My father becoming a smoker came to my mother as a surprise immediately after they separated, she told me so at a time when I never dreamt of becoming a smoker.

My mother told me when she become aware my father had become a smoker it took her by surprise and was supposedly the last straw. She told me it was the end of her ever going back to my father after they began living apart from each other. I told her maybe it was because my father had his tonsillitis cut off which made him a smoker.

My mother told me, my father having his tonsillitis taken off was no excuse for him to smoke! I never knew I was going to take up smoking one day until I did. There are two types of craving positive and negative craving. If it is a negative craving one can quit smoking at such a stage, it has not yet become a habit.

Becoming a smoker did not make me sexy, glamorous or more of an adult, it kept my mind and thoughts pre-occupied but never at any time take my mind off my anxiety. I do not enjoy being a smoker, not all smokers like being a smokers anyway. It's not by being irrational about their smoking habits that could make them quite smoking. What could make them quite are what I would call self cognitive therapy as a smoker as in case of all smokers, there are one or two things you do not like about yourself being a smoker that is where the cognitive therapy comes in. It is based on what you do not like about yourself such as being a smoker.

I can't think or conceive the idea of taking marijuana, cocaine or any hard drugs and I don't know what some of them look like. Cigarettes or tobacco I smoke with distaste, it troubles my consciences.

There are several reasons why I could have gone out of my head and mind shouting at my father at the top of my voice to step down and not enter my flat, with me still shouting at the top of my voice told him I was the last child he had with my mother in a polygamous home without his presence in the UK on the 27 of July 1966 when I was born what could be said about all the years I had spent in Africa with him as my parent. All this took place in the presences of my immediate elder brother Mr. Omagbemi standing by my father's side by the corridor of my flat.

I told my father on one of his visit to the UK afterwards that I would not grow up like just anybody in is life or be a façade to him as many of his children are towards him. If he could, in spite of my reaction towards him in front of my flat forgive me, was all I wanted to experience from our father and son relationship. All I ever wanted from him as my father was for him to love me or show concern, even if it's just a little love and understanding was all I had been asking of him!

This was an experience for me contemplating remaining a celibate adding to this, something happened in my youth regarding I and my Uncle Mr. Temitayo Akinlami and my cosine Miss. Layiwola Akinlami for me through the occurrence contributed to the education I received within my family for me making a choice to be celibate there are certain thing parents or adults do not tell children. A child likely grows up to realise them.

There should be distinction between sadness and mental health such as schizophrenia. Through sadness, one could display characteristics of mental illness and it does not necessary mean, they are suffering from mental illness.

Sadness is an <u>emotion</u> characterized by <u>feelings</u> of disadvantage, loss, helplessness, sorrow, and rage it is customary for sad people becoming outspoken, less energetic, and emotional crying and social withdrawals are indication of sadness.

My view of sadness are temporary lowering of mood, whereas depression is characterized by a persistent and intense lowered mood, as well as disruption to one's ability to function in day to day matters as far as the sadness continues without mental disorder.

Mental disorder a psychological or behavioural pattern generally associated with subjective distress or disability which occurs in individuals which are not a part of normal development. There are variations in the definition, assessment, and classification of mental disorders,
Mental health is an expression of our emotions that signifies successful or unsuccessful adaptation to a range of demands related to our cognitive or emotional well-being. I conceptualize it as likely the cause of developing process and experience.

Suffering is an individual's experience of unpleasantness associated with harm or threat of harm. Suffering could be physical, mental or spiritual which comes with certain degree of intensity, from mild to at some point intolerable suffering, which then lead to mental health.
It could be dramatic; all fields of human activities have several bearings related to suffering. Such fields are the nature of suffering, its processes, its origin and causation there meaning and significance is related personal, social, and cultural behaviours.

Mental illnesses affect one in six of us as individuals. At some point in our lives such mental illnesses are depression and manic depression, schizophrenia, anxiety, obsessions, phobias as, as well as alcohol and drug addiction. Such mental health conditions concurrently leave some people confused, isolated or withdrawn. This in turn can lead to profound feelings of despair to even thoughts of suicide. Invariably the magnitude of the sadness, suffering are partly what could lead, to mental illness and presumably, it is my own opinion that suffering, sadness usually leads to issue of mental health illness such as schizophrenic. There are many misconceptions about mental illness, often fuelled by the images that we see on television and the 'scare stories' that we read in the media and the internet.

Whenever I go and see my psychiatrist about my illness, they hardly give me enough time for me voicing out everything in my mind I felt was bordering me in relation to my illness they ought to know. With the little time I spend talking to them, it was until 2009 they stated sending me reports based on their analysis on my progress but not on whatever I had told them during my appointments no wonder 90% of their patients are socially withdrawn from them.
The report covers my mood swing, medication, and relapse but only in small detail. I wish they could go deeper in examining my thoughts. Little or nothing about my hallucinations were ever recorded while I remain traumatic going back to the days when I was a young lad.

Some of the things I would like to tell my psychiatrist about my illness were that I hear voices telling me my father should have been dead long time ago. During those times, he was meant to die many times and even on the very day, he becomes a chief. The voice insight things I have done which to them meant I did certain things spiritually, some philosophically at many different times in my father's life subconsciously which kept my father alive and waxing strong.

The voices tell me I have to suffer from mental illness as a way of insolvent. The thought of my past since I was a young lad continually comes to me; I ask myself and the voices if, there is anything that could intervene and considering I was no longer in Nigeria. For some reason I feel it is partly why I suffer from hallucinations the effects are part of juju inferences whatever parents or our environment cloth themselves with the children and people within its environment cloth themselves with it they are variations to these and how people apply themselves some of us, have no choice.

On my father's first visit to the UK after my arrival I heard voices telling me I should not go and visit my father or set eyes on him. I was at this time in a hostel accommodation but I went to see my father in my brothers flat at Brockley immediately I went into the flat I felt being unwell after he told my brother to give me something to eat rice and stew I ate while my father was seating down watching me. My excuse was that he had built his two family houses while he should have built four houses one. Secondly why should I be living in a hostel if he had so much money?

Thirdly why should I have worked in cement and block making, and loading firm at the very time my father was completing his houses, by this time of my father's visit I was just about to commence my carpentry joinery and office skill course at the Greenwich training centre which meant I had registered myself as the seismograph of my father's house regardless if I wasn't in Nigeria. I have been hearing voices before I was diagnosed as a schizophrenic I hear this voices I apply to what they say in time I realised, the voices just came to me in other to make their own inferences.

On my father's second visit it was the time I just moved into my flat allocated to me through my hostel. He was all dressed up in his chieftaincy attire coral beads' had weight around his neck. I had the premonition something was about to happen if my father comes into my flat with his regalia. That was both of us would die. I had to stop him. When he stopped right in front of my flat he was like a wind and a wave swept through me I heard a voice say accept him in and you die with him decline and the least you can get away with is mental illness caused by the dissatisfaction in your father and the omen he brings with him.

It became eminent that both of us would have died because this was what the oracle wanted for my father to have come into my flat which meant, my father had slipped away again this time, action was to be taken against me. I began suffering from mental illness without my knowing.

I was born and raised in a nation where voodoo known in Nigeria as juju are everyday occurrence rumours of it spread like wild fire day in day out within all communities. They owe their name to god and goddess all family rights, culture and tradition ascribe themselves to one form of juju or another some of them are feared and respected or honoured there are high voodoo priests, and priestesses since I was a little boy all around in my family I sensed the powers involved.

They could create original and unique style of powerful spells with combined ancient and traditional knowledge of juju practice some people say juju help them resolve all kind of problems and could make their wishes come true, help them to find love, bring back lost loves, save marriages, break-up unwanted relationships, protect them from black magic, improve quality of intimacy, to create wealth, to heal souls and bodies envies and evil forces, to improve their luck, help them find new jobs and careers, or to make progress on those jobs and their lives. You need not be told if juju can do all these, it could also do there reverse.

I have not seen Loraine for a very long time. In my mind I thought of celibacy if I should see her again would it cloud my thoughts of interest in remaining a celibate? Over the years with me lonely in my flat, I tend to meditate on the different branches of ontology. Since, If I and Lorain would want to have children, we would have had mixed race or mixed blessing as it is often called in Africans in respect to people such as my grandmother from my father's side. I guess a lot had happened in my life which over the years has weighed down on me for which I have been inclined to meditate on human existence. It's a way of getting out of reverie of mental illness.

Before the 21st century we have heard of priest abusing themselves, children and the churches in many different ways, issues of celibacy came up in many cases through documentaries in USA. I first heard of the word celibacy through my father's third wife Mrs. Aya Megbele through her involvement as a lodge member just about the time I became a freemason.

As at 2002 if I and Miss Loraine O'Connor relationship could not go on any further, it would have to be a case leading to more insight into the study of ontology. If we would achieve our full meaning and potentials as two individuals from two different races, culture and from a different background! We are both one of a kind in some ways we have a slight resemblance and gentle.

If we were ready to permit our relationship to face it's after mouth? I and Loraine had the tendency during our relationship to discuss our likes and dislike which is uncommon in such relationship because. We seem to be two individuals, who wanted to find peace of mind in some of the things we do to find out if we were happy with each other or in whatever we do. I had lived years of my life in West Africa; she had lived years of her's in South Africa. We thought of each other as something from a tail of two cities.

I consider myself to be a mixed race within Eastern and Western origin of Nigeria; I have experienced of what it is like to have emerged from a mixed background relationship. It is a life of two sided coin its either confusion or complaisance's at the end of the day, the compliment is yours.

Though it depends on the individuals, such relationships could be filled with complex issues and questions, with emotion and sociological turmoil, endless search for heaven knows what! Only few mixed race can choose just one side of both coins into the milky-way it is good, to go into such considerations anyway, it is personality that matters when we want to enter into something of a personality difference so.

Before the no smoking policies on all working premises did not border me before the policy it had been done within the privacy of my flat by choice. If I smoke in my flat, it is within my own personal privacy. As a celibate, coupled that am single, with no children around, I felt I made some common sense step towards other people's interest with regards to my being a smoker when I receive visitors I make sure I do not smoke.

We all need to use some common sense in every step we take in our relationship with other people, for example I wish my father had taken more consideration with his relationship with my mother. I never liked the way, he rejected her.

If he had rejected my mother, he had also rejected me. As for other people involved especially members of my mothers family putting her aside, making other people do as they please with her emotions and precondition not from her own choice, to live her life in difficulties, a solitary life filled with embarrassment and unhappiness.

Being a celibate, means the less I do not care for worldly materials things; I would not smoke before any children and I have got none. If smoking is bad for them, I have put consideration on their behalf with regards to my habit of smoking. It's a plausible reason of showing that I care not only for myself but for other people. It's a way of being thoughtful towards other people. I wonder why my father didn't put up with some consideration in his relationship with my mother the situation is no different from a smoke or a smoke screen

Many with similar disability as mine could do paid jobs even better than those who could be considered as having no disabilities. With my present qualifications I could do better and deserve better in the UK but are there any opportunities available for one getting a job if one has a disability and chooses to work through GLLaB, Reed in Partnership or at the job centre? It should be British jobs for British people! Only then can there be value for money and thorough investment in people. In which case, if we make any mess, we can clear up our mess by ourselves.

Many analysts expect unemployment to rise in 2011 because of public sector job cuts UK Economy, Alarm over young jobless numbers , Scottish unemployment rate fells Inflation 'had increase sharply' ,and youth unemployment rose . UK unemployment rose by 44,000 to almost 2.5 million in the three months to the end of December 2011, the Office for National Statistics (ONS) had said.

Youth unemployment rose to fresh record high, with more than one in five 16 to 24-year-olds out of work after a rise of 66,000 to 965,000. The unemployment rate was 7.9%, with youth unemployment running at 20.5%. The number of people claiming Jobseeker's Allowance also increased. Prime Minister David Cameron said unemployment, particularly among the young, was a matter of great regret but stressed it had been a problem for some time.

The number of people in part-time work because they could not find full-time employment rose by 44,000 to 1.19 million, another high since records began in 1992. The latest UK labour market figures provided further evidence job recovery had gone into reverse. Long-term unemployment had also deteriorated, with 17,000 more people out of work for more than a year, to a total of 833,000.

Other data from the ONS showed average earnings rose by 1.8% in the year to December last year, slightly down on the 2.1% growth in the year to November. The figures also showed unemployment fell in Scotland by 13,000, but rose in England, Wales and Northern Ireland.

Employment Minister, Chris Grayling: Said, they would provide more support for young people struggling to get jobs while the government said the latest figures showed that unemployment was starting to stabilise.

'We've got a long way to go and I want to see these figures start to come down, but certainly the evidence is over the past month things have settled down and they are not seeing the increases we saw earlier in the last quarter,' said Employment Minister Chris Grayling.

There were 40,000 more job vacancies in the three months to January than in the previous three months. Which was seen as indicator of the health of the economy and whether companies are creating jobs; the ONS said that most of the new vacancies were temporary jobs, working on the 2011 Census, there were 8,000 more vacancies.

Shadow work and pensions secretary Liam Byrne said it was a sign that the government could not rely on the private sector to create jobs. Because, there were still five people chasing every single job and in about a hundred constituencies, 10 people are chasing every job, he told BBC News.

The Shadow Work and Pensions Secretary Liam Byrne said

there are still five people chasing every single job. Most analysts still expect unemployment to rise in the coming months, largely because of public sector spending cuts implemented by the government, which are designed to bring down the UK's budget deficit.

The labour market data's where disappointingly softer overall and fuel our suspicion that unemployment is likely to trend up gradually in 2011 in the face of below-trend growth and increasing job losses in the public sector,' said Howard Archer at IHS Global Insight. Economists suggest the economy would have to grow at an annual rate of about 2% for unemployment to fall.

In the final three months of last year, the economy shrank by 0.5%, although many analysts expect a return to growth in the current quarter, few expect GDP to top 2% this year. Speaking at a press conference to launch the latest Inflation Report, the governor of the Bank of England said it had lowered its growth forecasts following the weak growth data at the end of the year.

Mervyn King also said the Bank expected inflation to remain high over the next year. Latest figures released showed that the Consumer Prices Index measure of inflation had hit 4%. This was expected to increase pressure on the Monetary Policy Committee to start raising interest rates. The markets expected a series of rate rises. The question for many is how far rates will have to rise.
However, there was still the concern about the possible effect any increases would have on the economic recovery. For this reason, economist James Knightley from ING said unemployment figures supported their view that interest rates may not rise as much as the market anticipated.

I have had a lot of emotional heartaches and pain from my childhood without knowing where I belong, for which reason I just have to grow up putting myself where I belong and to face my reality, because it is more reasonable to do so. Though I have grown up having a total dislike for people taking liberties which I do consider self oriented.

Starting work at my first cleaning job at the royal festival hall at Waterloo while I was residing at the Salvation army hostel at Blackfriars road in 1989 with a question of why, should the 1977 FESTAC town houses in Nigeria been left to deteriorate before I and my mother moved from Lagos state to Ibadan? At my new job at the Royal Festival hall at Waterloo road, I never filled in an application form, money was paid in cash, I filled no application forms, I showed no prove of identity.

The difference when I started with Initial cleaning services at the Woolwich Gala club over some years was very dramatic. I was not paid in cash; it was money in the bank. As far back as 1998, working for Initial cleaning services, one has to fill in an application form, show prove of identity, passport, birth certificate, and bank details.

With my disabilities as a paranoid schizophrenia, I try as much as I could to keep on working, doing so keeps me going as a form of therapy, but do the benefit office see it as a means of therapy for me getting out of my illness?

I had in 2005 applied for another cleaning job to do extra hours apart from the cleaning job I had with Initial cleaning services for the simple reason if I get a job supplementing my present job and income it would reduce my smoking, because I would be preoccupied when am working it would also reduce the amount of cigarettes I smoke a day. In April 2007 smoking in public places was banned. I wished the government had also banned smoking in the streets first before they banned it in all working premises and pubs.

I got a next massage from my step sister Miss. Omawumi Megbele an actress she wanted to communicate with me through the internet so she could inform me about lots of things happening within our family in Nigeria who said this, who did that I knew was all I was going to hear from her. I told my sister Miss. Omawunmi Megbele I considered it would not all be distracting to me in relation to the books I was writing.

I had been with BT open world as my internet provider for

years I had cancelled my contract with BT so that I could spend time writing and word processing my book considering it was expensive for me to be on the internet. I was very happy to hear from her in a family like ours I consider when someone does something out of compulsion that's when it has come from their heart like getting in touch.

I text my sister Omawunmi back told her she should text me and let me know where her mother resides either at Port - Harcourt or at Delta state Warri. She later text me and told me her mother Queen Aya Gogo Megbele resides at number 1 William Oke Street, Off Omoagege Street, Eduegba Warri. This step mother of mine is the mother of Mr. Teddy Oritsejolomi, Ms. Violet Alero, Ms. Brenda Omawunmi and Mr. Moses Oritsetsola Megbele. Their mother moved out of my father's house when my father, got married to his fourth wife Mrs. Tsainomi Ayo Megbele other children are Mr. Oneoritsebawo and Miss. Cecilia Utieyinone Megbele

Mr. Gabriel Awe came into my mother's life to imply he is better off than my father this was, what I expected but it was far from my expectations. My step mother's come into my father's life to imply they are better than my mother and her children, while my step brother's and sister's come into my life as usurpers. If polygamy is right, and not a coincidence of taking advantage, we would be one big happy family rather than live our lives in conflicts.

How would there be unity, peace and togetherness as one big happy family in a polygamous home when; one person, wants to be better off than the next person. Some people say it is culture; how could it be, when it turns our lives into rituals? Culture is a good thing; if it does not strip us from our spiritual freedom, respect for ourselves and other people.

Some people are fond of using other people's mistake or misfortune to make their own cup of tea. Now that is bad in any given situation. It is taking advantage of other people. Doing so, means lack of respect for individuality, our lives becomes a training ground for prejudice. Pretending it is culture the lives of one person within the family could be used in favouring that of another person at the expense of the next person.

When relationships become troubled, they are usually so for predictable reasons. Too much might happen too soon then things might turn out very different from what was expected. The heat becomes disturbed speaking up would still put relationship in jeopardy coming out with it would be a relief. The actions taken are for once safety and well-being. There is nothing wrong in being suspicious when someone who says they love you, wants to speak for you, make decisions for you and give you impression you are not quite capable of being yourself without their benevolent assistance.

You fight about everything when you admit faults, even stupidity, you are at fault or weak for admitting it, when you are right you are wrong for being right or when it becomes clear you are right,

Research shows supportive relationships are good for our mental and physical health. However, dealing with difficult people and maintaining ongoing negative relationships is actually detrimental to our health. Would it be a good or bad idea diminishing or eliminating relationships filled with conflict what do you do if the people in question are family members, co-worker, or someone you otherwise can't easily eliminate from your life?

What else does it mean, when you have a dream or a misfortune with the need to cheer it with other people; and there is nobody around. Such could be the predisposition one could be faced with in a disorientated polygamous family or society. When what you need is a next person who would kiss away you tears, hold you in their harms to keep you worm or dry the tears from your eyes.

My sister in law running to the hospital or Oxleas mental health care waiting for me is far from what I want out of my sister in law Mrs. Nwamaka Megbele. Nobody likes being sick or taken into hospital. It is too close a resort next to death. I am doing all I can to get out of my illness and stay away from hospital with ill health. With the scenario surrounding our relationship why is she calling me or waiting for me in a place I could be faced with death!

Considering in my past I had shied away from studying nursing or work in any job attached to hospitals, care homes, it's kind of something I view with an enigma. As much as I wanted to care for other people, there was always a feeling I do not belong in working in such a place because I have spent half my life in Africa.

Britain and all its social benefits structured; e.g. health care, benefits, housing, environmental policies even politics I gave my views to Ms. Sally Bryden Oxleas head of strategic information in several of my writings to her.

We do not need people going into such places to disengage members of their family and environment from its usual course of procedures, creating favouritism; in some case, enigmas are attached to their presence in such working places especially in relation to people from third world nation residing and working within the UK. A sense of psychology is involved here, it is not just my sister in-law Nwamaka am referring to.

Due to the circumstance surrounding our relationship I would expect my sister in law would have called me by way of understanding each other express why she took up mental health as a course of study in many ways, she could express herself in what she wants to do in life creating a bound within both of us as relatives but when it comes to somebody, who in the future could be caring for me tells me to my very face it is what I carry in my mind is what she considers, is the problem with me came as a shock to me. Its 2011 I have never at any time in our relationship discus any matters contain in any of my books with my sister-in-law how did she know what I carry in my mind and my brother is not very talkative or expressive when he is, he seems to be coming from behind then I asked myself what does my sister-in-law knows about what is in my mind?

We all have different fillings about the thing we do; most

family intervention into their relative care is queries into their personal life. For example how would you feel if your brothers girl friend is pregnant at the same time she was about to give birth, you were in hospital receiving treatment as diagnosed paranoid schizophrenia then the next day he or she is a staff of the NHS in mental health care?

The whole situation is rather queer I do not accept whole heartedly and mind you, my mother became a qualified nurse just about the time I was born in the UK draw me to a conclusion if questions need to be asked on my part as to what is going on, I must conclude because at one point, my sister-in-law told me I am not aware of what was going on in NHS mental health.

To me it's all seems a kind of rituals taking place around me, with questions to be asked, do not make another mans life your pot of tea. Each human endeavours stands to be questioned for example on being aware my mother was a qualified nurse, I would have expected she would had worked as a nurse in any of the hospital in Lagos when we went back to Nigeria from the UK? It wasn't the case her endeavours and careers in lots of ways were partly for my identity becoming transparent as superman to up hold all the stars that falls in Africa and place them, in their archives.

Personally it is all like a ritual one could have experience and very much appreciated if we are in Africa, but happening here in the UK within Africans, here arises a new psychology of some new breed of African born British. In my opinion people from third world nation predominantly feel pleased they are in better hand receiving treatment from Germans', Spanish, Lebanese, Chinese, Japanese or French in the UK.

It is customary in the UK they feel pleased if they receive treatment from them, and that they are in better hands even within Asians. If it were in the UK, I know my sister in law would prefer are children to be treated in any hospital by the white race English.

If Mrs. Nwamaka Megbele is privileged coming into my

family through my brother, she should find something of interest common in relationship with my brother Mr. Omagbemi and not with me. My brother is a better candidate to do it himself if necessary.

This was one reason I would not visit my brother in his home. It is an African terminology that she cannot be making money out of my suffering from mental health if so; I should not eat food or receive gifts from her or from my brother if I should visit them, because she made it her cup of tea. Could such points of view be noted as psychotic, paranoia or arachnophobia or feelings of stereotyping?

Most people feel the same way and they do not suffer from mental illness. I need not be an African to have such temperament; it could come from anybody from any race or creed within the UK. What I felt about the scenarios was inferences where being made to themselves we are African it's our nature, they felt I should be grateful while I felt I was being taking for granted I have never known my brother being supportive to me in anything in my life while we were in Nigeria.

It is a situation even far worse in Africa because superstitions are involved in relation to such issues which often result to the parties throwing jujus and witchcraft at each other through the forces of juju and native priest.

As a result, it's nothing strange it is common among Africans terminology of superstitious believes that in such a situation I should not eat any food from my brothers home and I hear voices telling me to do so as well. Africans need not be within Africa alone to practice juju. If it where in Africa the steps my brother and sister in law have taken in the UK is rationally considered as practicing juju here in the UK we see such activities as not juju but exploiting another member of the family.

I am faced with queries and racing thoughts about my brother and sister in law's motives in relation to my predicament life on earth is considered to be a place where all wrongs stands to be corrected if this could be the case, it was for one of such reason I obliged my sister in law accompanying me to one of my Queen Elizabeth mental health home treatment team appointment.

At some point in 28th February 2001, I wrote to Miss Loraine after several visits later her neighbour told me she was no longer residing at Sara House in Erith in the letter I wrote

Day in, day out, side by side, each day, the work is done, another day, the war is on where are we going, where are we heading to? Is it based on what the future shows? Many would say! A little boy and girl going out each day babies are born day in day out, every day people shout, lies and hat like fumes of fire.

You have been away for a long time yet you are not out of my mind, I miss you I can't wait to see you again my feelings for you have not changed, let's make it right for each other let us just be friends.

When one is in love, your lover needs you, far worse when they spend lonely hours alone. How I long for you, sometimes through the days I reminiscence, thinking of you. I want you to say a prayer for me because at certain point all of a sudden, something made me gaze up to the sky and my heartaches.

Could life be so mean and cruel; I would treasure times I spent with you. There is something I just want to say, please say a prayer for me every man needs a woman. These words are in a letter I had written to Loraine whilst I had spent six months at South Bank University studying at the same time working without seeing her.

I have not seen Miss Loraine for years it is recorded that one baby in every four babies is born to immigrant mothers.

Migrant baby boom is sending the UK's population soaring with one in four children now born to foreign mothers, what is the sense of sheering this one and only life, ending to another lost and lonely lives, count the years, they would be filled with tears, self preservation is what should be going on.

Why should a young heart like mine not run free when love doesn't really love me? It is really difficult to tell when one is really in love in this our complicated world of today.

It's recorded that of the 708,708 births before 2009, 170,089 or 24 per cent were to immigrant's mothers. According to the news, it was the highest number of migrant birth in the UK since record began. The increase is said to worry ministers because it threatens putting more pressure on British public services e.g. jobs, schools and healthcare which have been struggling to coup. Most of the children have been born out of the bounds of marriage.

A question to ask, is did I and Miss Loraine O'Connor given a chance we have along the way, endeavoured to work and attend University may be for some personal reason on my part such as my children could still be confident in me without looking down on my mental health condition and that we are capable of achieving something other people could also aim for by working towards it with efforts to our surprise, student loan had been imposed on us unemployment had reached its peak for decades in the UK.

If we had been faced with such a situation, what would have been my children's future? It was very thoughtful of both of us just being friends. With this turn out of event regardless of my mental health I wanted something my children would look up to in me that was worthwhile.

Could there be anything wrong in giving whatever we want to do thorough consideration first before we embark on them? If one feel neglected is it right to pass it on to others?

Sir Andrew Green of think tank migration watch UK did say the figure of immigrant birth illustrates the impact immigration is recently having within the British communities have laid more pressure on public sector services. 2009 records of migrant's birth is the biggest cause of population growth which outstrips immigration for the first time.

Was my father becoming chief, getting married again,

wearing coral beads, pouring drinks e.g. gin, whisky, brandy on the ground, to pay homage to juju's, culture and tradition customary to his origin, among other things to also prolong his life, was also for the sack of liberating me from some certain aspects of my existence.

It all took place as if during each stage, I was blindfolded or in a dream, it is now all coming back to me. Probably if I had known, things would have been different but I must have known in my conscientiousness' otherwise, why should I have gone into a rage when I was never known to be a radical?

I had to wait until my father's death because of such inclination before I get too involved in a relationship with an opposite sex. To my surprise after my fathers' death, I began suffering from personality disorder of my immediate elder brother facially as if, I am no longer myself but I am my brother.

I suffer long periods of psychotic disorder of my father when he was alive infarct, I suffer from mild personality disorder from all members of my family, in my mind, I seems to have become an archives or gate keeper with their names written all over me.

For these experiences I go through, I would say thanks to whatever had given me religious inclination of being spiritually aware. It is not the strength I want; it is the spiritual part of me that calms me down.

About the age of seven years, I remember touching a live electric wire without feeling anything which I held for one second the only experience I had, was the hair on my head standing out with me just raising my eyebrows I never knew or though it was a live wire with current passing through it before, I touched it is dangerous to touch a life electric wire I was seven years old at the time. It was the first time in my life I experienced what it is to raise an eyebrow. I know only one man who could do this the Saint Simon Templar cast by Roger Moore.

The amplitude I desire to experience is to become like any other human being. Based on the situation I have had to compel myself to be patient, take my stride in things I do and not let emotions rule me. I had to wait each time when things go wrong to divest myself from omens.

At the time my father came for his last visit to the UK, his step sister Mrs. Lanre Charles was in the UK living at Peckham with her children. At this time with these entire event, I was compelled into coming out with what was in my conscience about Michelle.

She is something I would describe as Biblical in reference to our past and present life. In my relationship with Miss. Michelle Cook, the scenario always come about something of a relic from the old testament reading from the Holy Bible relating to the walls of Jericho was pulled down after the twelve sound of the horns blown which pulled the walls of Jericho down or Gideon within the alter of Beal pulled down after which woman began to be recounted as prophets or priests of God.

To my knowledge God, gods, goddesses' architects, Engel's, we exist within all things which came with creation and whatever is beyond creation. We are compelled to exist in other to persist in our trials of life, within everything around us and of cause our faith.

One does not need to wear a priestly robs to be a priest; life on earth is more interesting with spiritual awareness and up-liftment this does not mean am not in favour with religious men and women. I never wonder why it is always customary for both me and Michelle reincarnating to face some life incoherence's, it is always the case; not just with me and Michelle but with lots of other individuals.

Everything on earth had existed within the Heaven before creation on earth we became reality after the conflict in Heaven. No wonder we see visions, we dream, we hallucinate and contemplate. We also feel pain, suffering and lose. Individuality is based on concepts and identity, in relation to what the universe is to them and compels us to be, we have the capability to mediate after Gods creativity, its beauty, its entire meaning and implications.

Except for those who do not believe a creator exist or have humans become all that efficient within their own capacity and creativity to have become recklessly bold to imply that God does not exist? Ethnology ebullient would not so much require we see God face to face it requires we confront our existence in other to see God.

On the other hand the world is a wonderful place, with all kinds of realities through toils and pain humans have ascribe themselves and their names on this planet through abstract perceptions through which we have become very creative only a God fearing minds can be creative.

It is for such reason I hold the opinion God had made man far too sufficient. Through the perception of human creativity I do not see any reason why most of us would not give God the praise for his blessing upon mankind.

The more reason, I would expect them to believe that God exist, they could be creative, some other people would like to be creative but they have no hands, legs, they could be blind while others could be suffering from mental illness. How do we really exist if God does not exist? He exists within us and in things we do.

What is it that prevents us from not relying on the dark side of life? It is the fear of God. God gave dominion of all things on earth to man. No matter how great a man could become he should not loose his salvation.

All things that is good exist within Gods nature; disaster or caters trophies implies nature is beyond human control therefore a God exist. All existence came as a two sided coin for good or for evil. Every human born of woman would face the blame for their good or evil deeds. We all have our enquiries into life and existence. Whether we like it or not, we are already bulls that have been held by our horn before we began to exist.

I do not see Lucifer, the devil and Satan as part and parcel of all human nature. The outcome are instead of emancipating ourselves from their misgiving, we humans partly allow their enforcement into our lives. This is why we suffer from calamities to an extent of suffering from mental illness.

Or why do we destroy each other in conflicts? It is not in my opinion there is a gigantic monster or dinosaur called Lucifer, Satan or the Devil. It is all in our blood through the forbidden fruit that we have and make choice because our eyes became open to good and evil. It is by choice if one wants to be religious based on individuality we have been granted all that we need religion build the mind and soul compelling us to be in good faith and mind when we are down.

Our existence as to whatever we are or would become are already in our sub-consciousness before we are born.

Human creativity is one reason why some people could imply God does not exist can't we all combine our lives in harmony correcting our mistakes and be one big happy family it could not be God who is causing misunderstanding within us he is the author of our existence.

There is a difference within the concepts of God and the concepts of humanity they entwine but how in relation to our going to heaven? What is heaven, what do our religious preachers know about this place called heaven what it would be like or what we would find there. It is not God who has been creating nuclear warheads and missiles or wrestling and boxing championship match it is all human endeavours. In relation to nuclear warheads and missiles this is where my planet Krypton comes in.

There is love and there is hate most people are of the opinion it would be impossible to enforce love, peace and unity all around the world. Where have all these evil came from, that had been attached to human existence after their creation?

One thing is clear man have been given dominion over all things an irony is if man have been granted dominion over all things, in a planet where man have been made sufficient, more than sufficient why should man suffer from mental illness?

There should be concern because it is now possible for this planet of ours, to be completely flushed out forever through human endeavours. The human creativity of nuclear power and weapon of mass destruction coupled with caters trophies and suffering beyond human control leave questions to be asked and answered.

Since our existence is based on trials of life, it is through what we undergo, the steps we take that would decide if we would be granted impunity. On the other hand if we have not been given food for thoughts to consider our ways, left to our own desires we would forever remain indiscipline just as there are reasons for my existence, what has been going on in my life, there are reason for my schizophrenia it could be me just for me to understand and accept certain things about my existence, the existence of other people, God, my environment, the things I am meant to encounter on this planet and about myself and the illness.

For several reasons a human mind is clouded God does not exist because we have been made self sufficient. Our faith or realisation is weak; our entire universe is too vast for us, to comprehend all issues about our existence in one go or in a single life time. We have been pacing on this planet. Who says if you having been lapsing behind in changes and development you cannot start now this, is something third world leaders need to consider entering the 21st century it is never too late to be constructive for third world nations now, reasoning is power learning should come easy.

But not for those who have perceived the existence of God through themselves, with his greatest of all creativity not salvation and a promise of heaven but just you as a human beings. Over centuries humans have been looking into themselves through their own eyes we have become creative to the greatest of achievements if we are not happy there is suffering why should there be madness. Our purpose is to ascertain and implement a vision of God with his authority creating a new civilisation if there is wealth, suffering and madness mental health is just a fraction of madness or why should we have started our existence as primitives.

As it was once in heaven, so it is on earth. It is eminent through our creation heaven have granted us purpose in a world filled with beauty, ugliness and death.

Humans and everything on earth and the entire universe, have come a long way with differences in colour, race, creed, beliefs, religion, custom and tradition through eras of predictable and unpredictable events within centuries that had gone past, with different centuries arising. We have a lot to be grateful for, to appreciate and encapsulate on our existence as entities. Whatever brought about Gods creativity is inevitable. We had all existed before we were created but then, we had no form.

Human creativity began immediately Adam and Eve were ushered out of the Garden of Eden then began human craving for survival. They were both given authority over all things as, they began a new process of evolution to divest the whole occupants of the heavenly host, planets, and the cosmos and stars down to earth to dwell in divesting themselves at the same time, undergo trials of life that we may learn, become authors of our own existence for good or for evil.

This 21st century have existed before we were created blood is thicker than water. One of the enigmas in life is to wonder and be delusions we learn and face realities which can take years, centuries to unfold.

Each day of our existence, we become more defined with lots of different things that make us tick because, we have been granted purpose. For example we are part of a world, we exist as entities whose faith, is in their own hands. Whatever, have granted it to man is obscure but in reality, it exist, which should rightly be obscure because the more it would force we humans and our endeavours to quest and hunger for the true reason for our existence?

Wisdom, reality, purpose and understanding why should our faith been placed in our hands? Yet our purpose and faith remains a mystery. There is a greater force that bends and inclines humans to search even further into life, existence, the mysteries and wonders of the entire universe.

It is therefore not a surprise that humans could suffer from mental illness among several caters trophies and conflicts that besiege human existence each day on earth is a quest; a quest in relation to life, existence, spiritual, physical, mental quest and much more.

It is blood and the human body that holds we humans down; without the human body and blood, humans are spirits with a soul that belongs to God of which if the human have been evil, would face God's contempt.

As it is in heaven so it is on earth. We all need to reach certain stage and dimensions to grasp understanding of what creativity and our existence mean on earth. Our lives and existence shouldn't all be about work, business and marketing. It has a lot more to do about our mind, soul and spiritual awareness, how creation began, what was behind it and to ascertain the reasons, why we are here. Human development including science and technology in all areas would enhance this which we have attained but rather than be jubilation, we are in conflict.

My vision and reality of whatever we accomplish or have e.g. house, children, clothing, business, everything to the last penny we have got, our culture, tradition which, we have earned without ill-gotten wealth and deeds in our trials of existence will remain with us forever after we have quest and attain the fruit of life and immortality. This would be when all our purpose on earth is resolved and is over. This might take a long time probably when the world's astronauts have visited some of the most remote planets or galaxy in our solar system.

All bad and unwarranted things gained through deception would be washed off for ever, so it would be all over the universe. Meaning it is whatever we have gained within all barometer of honesty that would be part of us in heaven.

Coming in terms with the concept of if God exist or not, among those who believe in doing wrong. Among the wicked, the once who reduce themselves becomes the key holder in the field of hell so long for the haughty and boastful because evil also rebels against evil.

The same applies to doing right instead of doing wrong for they would be the forerunners of goodwill and accomplishers for the sake of everything, that would be part and parcels of heaven, with all their works, efforts and accomplishments of their hands on earth, they would live and be called blessed in heaven. This I came about as part of hallucinations I have during the morning or afternoon, when am asleep or half awake. This does occur more often when, there is sunshine in the afternoon may be, probably, there is a snake inside my stomach. It's something I do also experience during full moon and when the stars are out in the night sky.

Isaiah 65:17-25
Therefore for I am about to create new Heavens and a new earth; the former things shall not be remembered or come to mind, but be glad and rejoice forever in what I am creating; for I am about to create Jerusalem as a joy, and its people as a delight.
I will rejoice in Jerusalem, and delight in my people; no more shall the sound of weeping be heard in it, or the cry of distress. No more shall there be in it an infant that lives but a few days, or an old person who does not live out a lifetime; for one who dies at a hundred years will be considered a youth, and one who falls short of a hundred will be considered accused.
They shall build houses and inhabit them; they shall plant vineyards and eat their fruit. They shall not build and another inhabit; they shall not plant and another eat; for like the days of a tree shall the days of my people be, and my chosen shall long enjoy the work of their hands.
They shall not labour in vain or bear children for calamity; or

(sudden terror) for they shall be offspring blessed by the Lord and their descendants as well. Before they call I will answer, while they are yet speaking I will hear. The wolf and the lamb shall feed together, the lion shall eat straw like the ox; but the serpent its food shall be dust! They shall not hurt or destroy on all my holy mountain says the Lord.

Psalm 30: A song for the dedication of Temple of David
I will exalt you O God for you lifted me out of the depths and did not let my enemies gloat over me. O Lord my God, I called to you for help, and you healed me, O Lord, you brought me up from the grave; you speared me from going down into the pit. Sing to the Lord. You Saints of his, praise his holy name for his anger, lasts only a moment but his favour lasts a lifetime; weeping may remain for a night but rejoicing comes in the morning. When I felt secure, I said I shall never be shaken, O Lord when you favour me you made my mountain stand firm but when you hid your face, I was dismayed. To you O Lord, I called to the Lord I cried for mercy, what gain is there in my destruction in my going down into the pit? Will the dust praise you? Will it proclaim your faithfulness? Hear O Lord, and be merciful to me or Lord, be my helper. You turned my wailing into dancing, you removed my sackcloth and clothed me with joy, that my heart may sing to you and not be silent. O Lord My God, I will give you thanks for ever.

Those who have opinion God doesn't exit, are yet to give thorough thoughts about God, his creativity and the wonders of not only our existence on earth but also, the wonders of the Universe. Since it is based on issues that God does not exist, I would consider it rather down- grading of native Europeans who are Christians.

Within such nations those who can literally rejoice that the angel of wisdom and that God is with them as much as they are part of the rest of the would have blessed them with divine thoughts in their mind and ways of dwelling on earth. Which have for years captivated the interest of the rest of the world?

There is something of interest about my father dressing in

his traditional clothing's to parade himself in Europe. Lots of African men and women before, I was born, came into the UK to reside, most of them have been residing in the UK, before, I was born or since when my mother had her first born for my father in Nigeria.

Most of them from various background and culture come into the UK to be educated. I bet most of them most have forgotten their traditional clothing before, they came into the UK. Dose my father need to parade himself it could only result to jealousy from some people who are friends of his or close relatives of his who have for years lived here in the UK over 50 years ago struggling to keep one or two jobs the English pounds is very expensive they hardly have any savings in their bank account after each weeks pay.

White English men I have seen in Africa had been orientated as chiefs with titles; do they come into the UK their native land parading themselves as chiefs? It would be considered as patronising other cultures which is good I was not biased as to the way my father dressed infarct I should be proud culture and tradition are for festivals, carnival and ceremonies.

Does culture only has its relevance's in its place of origin? As much as I wanted to live and enjoy life in African, with culture attached to my father I hoped to be part of it. He had already spelt out his decision since arrangement was made for me to leave West Africa for Europe. He even had to ask me, if I wanted to come back to Europe, which was not necessary I felt hurt moreover, my father had already decided to keep the coral bead for himself.

I do hear voice of my father, in some ways there are feelings, he his inside me, he lives inside me, the food I eat is for him, in my mouth and in my stomach each day. I see reason to continue as a celibate. I believe it's one of the things I have to do, to extricate myself from him this not only involve my father but other members of my family and some friends.

I was already stereotyped to leave Nigeria for the UK. I did not appreciating my father's sidetracked questions of if; I wanted to be in Europe, when it wasn't no longer necessary. When he had used me to serve his juju in Africa to come into Europe to be sick of its ideology of which my father had hoped he would used to prolong his life yet he was asking me if I wanted to come into the UK I had to leave because of my survival.

There comes a time when our existence on earth when all things, including humans and all creatures, and its foundations will have to realise all they need to do, to bring the universe to its circle of completion. The architect of the universe would not induce this world to come to an end for the sake of one soul that would enter his kingdom, who would rip the reward of eternal life. Each day in our existence reveals an open door-way for eternal glory or condemnation.

For one to have such views means that such person holds something tangible about life, nature, super human natural instincts based on the realisation of some inner most consideration of what his or her existence is meant to be. God and the heaven exist; no one needs be told, it should not be taken for granted because God and the heaven's have made humans too sufficient on earth, in my opinion more than sufficient, all too sufficient enough for some people to come out with opinions that God does not exist, is blasphemy.

It's Sunday 9th March 2008 after mother's day Sunday at Saint's Mary's Magdalene church, the gospel reading by Louise van der Valk was John chapter 11 verses 1 to verse 45. We had, the Bishop of Woolwich Right, Reverend Christopher Chessun presiding the worship on this Sunday with Mr Dotun Sobowale's two daughters being christened. My Bible reading in my flat for this Sunday was also a reading from the gospel according to Saint John chapter 5 verses 1 to verse 47.

16th March 2008 Conservative leader, David Cameron called for the needs to increase family ties. From what, I had been word processing over the years about my parental native land; it calls for consideration on what is going in my parental background in the north, the South and the western regions of Nigeria.

I have been word processing the effects of my illness and its relation to my parental background, my feelings and meditation too deeply engrossed in my heart, with me hoping it would call for one thing to redress family issues, ties, conflicts, and misunderstanding. Why should our ways be constantly too involved with conflicts?

Such a loud cry on my part with my illness as a paranoid schizophrenia I feel obliged to come out with my predicaments, with no recall of happy days or happy moments in our family ties. If, there were any moments of happiness, it was all out of compulsion usually a compulsion to gain something e.g. popularity.

David Cameron implied the need to increase family ties I hope, this doesn't only apply within Britain but the rest of Europe in general and the whole world. Britain is such an unhappy and lonely place. People do not seem to be happy. I observe Britain as a rhythmic environment with too much rehearsal and stereotyping.

This is good for some reasons because, it calls for awareness. With my temperament as a quiet sort of person I find happiness in myself, I synchronise and blend into the different changes with considerable ease with wide arrays of opportunities for me to divest myself in, my last trials of life. I have known these parts of the world before in which I was born in this my present life.

Every individual undergo different types of stereotyping, mental health is a condition of stereotyping the same thing applies to religion. It opens the human mind, reality on which their concepts of existence is based on. It has to be so, in order to bring the best out from those who have chosen the milky-way or the worse out of some individuals.

Disadvantage of stereotyping is that it leads to downsizing in my opinion that is when someone is alive. It creates avenues for one to be divested when I mean divested, I mean figuratively most of the blocks we have laid down on earth. Its advantage is that at certain times in a person's life, the individual is forced to face reality.

It is a better approach to life, in Great Britain. America and some parts of EU nations because, there are opportunities, accountability, and not like third world nations. Within all families in Africa and its politics an individual for example the head of a family, wealthy business men and women, the army and the police are all a coalition.

They are related as family members or friends. With such a coalition of politicians, wealthy business men and women they live their lives to do whatever they like, with nobody to query them about their actions. This is not conducive for the development of third world nations.

Though they have the money, the business but nothing has yet condole such men and women and the politician in Africa to stand with a common goal to develop, not only to develop but to care for each other, and appreciate each other. Why should it be after several years in our past in the scramble for Africa by the Europeans, yet we have had our independence.

It should be considered as something in our past we should no longer dwell on anymore while we still us it as excuses. We have had our freedom yet we are still lost in the crowed. If the experience of slavery in Africa have been worthwhile, we would not bother scrambling over Europe it is too obvious and for what reasons?

While the leaders of Africa continually acclaimed themselves with freedom for Africa the nation's wealth go only to them, their families and friends is this what we call freedom and unity? It should have brought peace and unity rather than self centeredness, greed and corruption.

Many of us especially recent resident from all race, creed or culture in British including immigrants and asylum seeker who have lived all their lives in the UK or have grown-up outside the UK, coming back as residents are lost in the crowd to some extent confused while others come and confront us with jealousy, or make us feel inferior to other race.

I rather see my stay in the UK as something from the Holy Bible relating to an incident which took place with The Birth of Esau and Jacob, Esau Sells His Birthright, Jacob Flees from Esau, Jacob's dream of a ladder.

Now Jacob went out from Beersheba and went toward Haran. So he came to a certain place and stayed there all night, because the sun had set. And he took one of the stones of that place and put it at his head, and he lay down in that place to sleep. Then he dreamed, and behold, a ladder was set up on the earth, and its top reached to heaven; and there the angels of God were ascending and descending on it.

I thought our people's lives how our family live in Africa here in Europe they issues of being gay, or being a lesbian has become critical and I see myself as a celibate an in-between its life experience we all have to make choices to wear a crown.

There is too much going on about us within the UK that needs thorough trashing this also involves other race as well. It would be reasonable at this point in time for us to come out with our personal true feelings about ourselves because as it is, we are not getting anywhere; our lives are too self cantered while what some of us do in the UK and Africa, is wait for aids. If we are slaves again, it is our own doing.

I am no longer biased redressing such issues concerning ourselves in our background and within the EU. It's about time we realise each one of us, have one foot in our grave or in slavery. It is not moments, when situations have gone far too difficult to amend we should start taking action. It takes more than efforts to resolve conflicts.

It is about time, it is infarct the right time with President Barack Obama as president of the United State of America. What I have hoped for and made out of his presidency is not forthcoming. Obama's job has just begun because after his presidency, we are going to make him, the president of the whole of Africa.

Or how would we show our appreciation of the efforts and consideration the Americans have taken by not being biased for someone like Barack Obama becoming president of the United State of America. It would be appreciated, if Africans would take a good leaf from the example showed by the entire Americans its implication should be used for a better purpose within the entire communities of Africans and third world countries.

February 2011David Cameron said the Middle East had 'a precious moment of opportunity for momentous changes to take place in the Middle East and North Africa, In a speech to the Kuwaiti Parliament, Mr Cameron said 'history was sweeping' through the region in the wake of the uprisings in Tunisia and Egypt.

He praised the 'brave and peaceful' protests by people 'hungry for political and economic freedom'. He condemned the Libyan regime's violent crackdown against popular protests, describing it as 'appalling'. 'Violence is never an answer to people's legitimate aspirations,' he said, adding that the whole world had been 'shocked' by the actions of the Libyan leadership.

At least 233 people died in Libya, according to Human Rights Watch. Libyan leader Col Muammar Gaddafi is clinging on to power and in an overnight appearance on state TV, criticised 'rumours' he had fled to Venezuela and insisted he was still in the capital, Tripoli.

Attending ceremonies marking the 20th anniversary of the liberation of Kuwait following Iraq's invasion - which sparked the first Gulf War - Mr Cameron said only freedom, justice and the rule of law would allow countries to meet the aspirations of their young populations.

We stand with the people and governments who are on the side of justice, the rule of law and freedom he said In the past, British governments had promoted trade and security links with regimes in the Middle East in the pursuit of stability rather than wider goals - a policy he described as a 'trade-off between interests and values'.

But Mr. Cameron said such approach was no longer justified and that only political and economic reform could ensure long-term stability. He said Great Britain would be ready to help these nations and its people in their aspiration.

There were grounds for 'cautious optimism' in the region because the majority of protesters seeking change have done so 'peacefully and bravely', he said. Although it was not yet clear what the outcome would be in the region, he said he was encouraged by signs of a 'peaceful path' towards wider political participation and an end to the 'false choice between repression and extremism' that countries had sometimes faced in the past.

'This is a precious moment of opportunity for the region,' he said. 'We stand with the people and governments who are on the side of justice, the rule of law and freedom.' During his visit, which was originally planned as a trade-centred tour of the Middle East but was altered to include Egypt, Mr Cameron has also been defending trade between British arms companies and some regimes in the Arab world.

Six of the 20 businessmen who accompanied Prime Minister David Cameron are from defence and aerospace firms and the trip comes just days after the Foreign Office revoked a series of export licences to Bahrain and Libya covering tear gas and gun components following the violence in both countries.

Mr. Cameron said Britain had 'a range of strong defence relationships' with countries in the region. 'I seem to remember we spent a lot of effort and indeed life in defending and helping to defend Kuwait, so the idea that Britain should not have defence relationships with some of these countries I do not understand. It is quite right that we do,' he said.
'We have some of the toughest rules on export licences and exports of arms anywhere in the world. Everything has to meet those rules.'

The BBC's deputy political editor James Landale, who travelled with Mr Cameron, said the prime minister believed it was perfectly legitimate for the UK to have defence contracts with allies such as Kuwait when equipment sold was used to defend that country's borders.

But shadow defence minister Kevan Jones said that while the defence sector was a crucial export industry for the UK, he was concerned about the timing of the trip. 'Many people will be surprised that the prime minister, in that week of all weeks, may be considering bolstering arms sales to the Middle East,' he said. Mr Cameron arrived in Kuwait City from Egypt, where he had met caretaker Prime Minister Ahmed Shafiq and the de facto leader, Field Marshal Hussein Tantawi.

Mr. Cameron walked through Tahrir Square, the centre of the demonstrations that led to the fall of President Mubarak, and met figures from the protest movement.

This is another opportunity Africans should not miss this, is the time to make the change because, we need to change. Or let us stand and look each other in the eyes, and say we hate each other. In relation to Barack Obama becoming the first black African to be elected as president of the United state of America; what I hope for is we should bring what the American people, had done into good use otherwise, some people do change, while some people do not change!

I do not know how the Arab nations want to embrace the rest of the world from what I see, there are lots of conflicts involve. They do not see themselves as the common people in the streets see them. I asked for food, they gave me food, when I asked you for food you kicked me and gave me no food, you told me, I was nothing except going about begging like pigeons.

They have all the knowledge, they have the good manners as great as they are they held no pride in believing in freedom and democracy. In all they do, they do in the name of God and God help them. Love is stronger than pride.

They have had nuclear war heads or missiles, bombs all sorts of sophisticating weapons before any other nations thought of developing theirs. The knowledge was either stolen from them or they gave it willingly. From the little they have or could enhance third world nations are threats to themselves.

If the people of Iraq or Iran are producing weapons of mass destruction or not, not every nation is of the same opinion that they are producing weapons of mass destruction. The way, they present themselves when confronted should show understanding, tolerance or compromise. I can understand there is anger in the air and I wonder if they know what majority of the world think of them especially children who are our future.

From what are going on all around the world most people who are strictly just observers, would imply, God is on their side because they have showed good example of tolerance, good friendship, politics and consideration. We all should be focused on being one big happy family, and ask ourselves why should it be only them, who are friends of the earth.

They have their own place of worship within the UK and other part of Europe, people for example in the UK do not go about their place of worship killing members of their own faith they have an explanation to give why they would wholeheartedly accept people of other religion to worship peacefully in their own land of origin.

Having grown up partly in Africa which would always be part of me regardless if am now here the UK. It happens all over the world, many of us who later through thoughtfulness' choose the milky way often get fed-up too easily on the way of almost all life inherent un-expectancies.

I would rather over the years of watching television on what space 1999, star wars, star trek implies to we humans. We have come to know a lot about child birth, aliens, clones, the cosmos cyclones, sexology etc. Regardless whether they exist or not in my opinion it's all terminology that might describe human existence from other planets, cosmos, and galaxy.

How do we know these things future on our television screen? Authors write them then it is cast showing at cinemas and on our television. Writing is another form of what is in our dreams, thought and minds; they could be true without our knowing I mean, it could become realities.

We have heard of the sun god, Odysseus, Zeus, Aphrodite, Mighty throe the god of thunder, Iron man, Batman, Spider man. Most of these strange encounters written about are not all delusion if they could be part of our subconscious mind, they could be real. They all have a beginning of some strange happening in a planet, galaxy. It could lead to knowledge of how our origin began as a life form.

From these planets and galaxies we are compelled to become humans through divesting ourselves, why do we have dreams or hallucinate. We hear of all kinds of venereal disease e.g. gonorrhoea, we have babies, test tub babies, clone babies through sperm donors; children are born with all sorts of illness and disabilities.

Humans are now experiencing different sexual realisation and tendencies. All these are part of our planet of origin crumbling down to us on planet earth. From which we absorb wisdom, knowledge and strength. Its implications are now what I see as human endeavours that could be resourceful God the architect of the universe.

In Roman mythology, Saturn is the god of agriculture. The associated Greek god, Cronus, was the son of Uranus and Gaia and the father of Zeus (Jupiter). Saturn is the root of the English word 'Saturday'.

Saturn has been known since prehistoric times. Galileo was the first to observe it with a telescope in 1610; he noted its odd appearance but was confused by it. Early observations of Saturn were complicated by the fact that the Earth passes through the plane of Saturn's rings every few years as Saturn moves in its orbit. A low resolution image of Saturn therefore changes drastically.

It was not until 1659 that Christiaan Huygens correctly

inferred the geometry of the rings. Saturn's rings remained unique in the known solar system until 1977 when very faint rings were discovered around <u>Uranus</u> and shortly thereafter around <u>Jupiter</u> and <u>Neptune</u>.

Saturn was first visited by NASA's <u>Pioneer 11</u> in 1979 and later by <u>Voyager 1</u> and <u>Voyager 2</u>. <u>Cassini</u> (a joint NASA / ESA project) arrived on July 1, 2004 and will <u>orbit</u> Saturn for at least four years.

Mars in Greek: Ares is the god of War. The planet probably got this name due to its red colour; Mars is sometimes referred to as the Red Planet. An interesting side note: the Roman god Mars was a god of agriculture before becoming associated with the Greek Ares; those in favour of colonizing and terraforming Mars may prefer this symbolism. The name of the month March derives from Mars.

Mars has been known since prehistoric times. Of course, it has been extensively studied with ground-based observatories. But even very large telescopes find Mars a difficult target, it's just too small. It is still a favourite of science fiction writers as the most favourable place in the Solar System other than Earth for human habitation. But the famous 'canals' 'seen' by Lowell and others were, unfortunately, just as imaginary as Barsoomian Princesses.

The first spacecraft to visit Mars was Mariner 4 in 1965. Several others followed including Mars 2, the first spacecraft to land on Mars and the two Viking landers in 1976. Ending a long 20 year hiatus, Mars Pathfinder landed successfully on Mars on 1997 July 4.

In 2004 the Mars Expedition Rovers 'Spirit' and 'Opportunity' landed on Mars sending back geologic data and many pictures; they are still operating after more than three years on Mars. In 2008, Phoenix landed in the northern plains to search for water. Three Mars orbiters Mars Reconnaissance Orbiter, Mars Odyssey, and Mars Express are also in operation.

<u>Jupiter</u> (a.k.a. Jove; Greek <u>Zeus</u>) was the King of the Gods, the ruler of Olympus and the patron of the Roman state. Zeus was the son of <u>Cronus</u> <u>Saturn</u>.

Jupiter is the fourth underlined brightest object in the sky (after the Sun, the Moon and Venus). It has been known since prehistoric times as a bright 'wandering star'. But in 1610 when Galileo first pointed a telescope at the sky he discovered Jupiter's four large moons Io, Europa, Ganymede and Callisto now known as the Galilean moons and recorded their motions back and forth around Jupiter.

This was the first discovery of a centre of motion not apparently cantered on the Earth. It was a major point in favour of Copernicus's heliocentric theory of the motions of the planets along with other new evidence from his telescope: the phases of Venus and the mountains on the Moon. Galileo's outspoken support of the Copernican theory got him in trouble with the Inquisition. Today anyone can repeat Galileo's observations without fear of retribution using binoculars or an inexpensive telescope but for superman it is just a twinkling of an eye.

Liquid hydrogen LH2 or LH_2 is the liquid state of the element hydrogen. Hydrogen is found naturally in the molecular H_2 form. To exist as a liquid, H_2 must be pressurized above and cooled below hydrogen's Critical point. However, for hydrogen to be in a full liquid state without boiling off, it needs to be cooled to 20.28 K −423.17 °F/−252.87°C while still pressurized.

One common method of obtaining liquid hydrogen involves a compressor resembling a jet engine in both appearance and principle. Liquid hydrogen is typically used as a concentrated form of hydrogen storage. As in any gas, storing it as liquid takes less space than storing it as a gas at normal temperature and pressure, however the liquid density is very low compared to other common fuels once liquefied it can be maintained as a liquid in pressurized and thermally insulated containers.

A gas giant is a massive planet with a thick atmosphere and a dense molten core. The 'traditional' gas giants, Jupiter and Saturn, are composed primarily of hydrogen and helium. Uranus and Neptune are sometimes called ice giants, as they are mostly composed of water, ammonia, and methane molten ices. Among extrasolar planets, Hot Jupiters are gas giants that orbit very close to their stars and thus have a very high surface temperature. Hot Jupiters are currently the most common form of extrasolar planet known, perhaps due to the relative ease of detecting them.

Gas giants are commonly said to lack solid surfaces, but it is closer to the truth to say that they lack surfaces altogether since the gases that make them up simply become thinner and thinner with increasing distance from the planets' centres, eventually becoming indistinguishable from the interstellar medium. Therefore landing on a gas giant may or may not be possible, depending on the size and composition of its core.

A gas giant sometimes also known as a Jovian planet after the planet Jupiter, or giant planet is a large planet that is not primarily composed of rock or other solid matter. There are four gas giants in our Solar System: Jupiter, Saturn, Uranus, and Neptune. Many extrasolar gas giants have been identified orbiting other stars.

Planets above 10 Earth masses are termed giant planets. Below 10 Earth masses they are called super earths or, sometimes probably more accurately for the higher mass examples, 'Gas Dwarfs' e.g. as suggested by MIT Professor Sara Seager for Gliese 581c using a model where that exoplanet was mostly composed of hydrogen and helium. The term 'gas dwarf' was also used previously by others.

Though there was no direct information about Saturn's internal structure, it is thought that its interior is similar to that of <u>Jupiter</u>, having a small rocky <u>core</u> surrounded mostly by <u>hydrogen</u> and <u>helium</u>. The rocky core is similar in composition to the Earth, but denser. This is surrounded by a thicker liquid <u>metallic hydrogen</u> layer, followed by liquid hydrogen, helium layer and a gaseous atmosphere in the outermost 1000 km.

Traces of various <u>volatiles</u> are also present. The core region is estimated to be about 9–22 times the mass of the Earth. Saturn has a very hot interior, reaching 11,700 °C at the core and it radiates 2.5 times more energy into space than it receives from the Sun.

Most of this extra energy is generated by the <u>Kelvin-Helmholtz mechanism</u> slow gravitational compression, but this alone may not be sufficient to explain Saturn's heat production. It is proposed that an additional mechanism might be at play whereby Saturn generates some of its heat through the 'raining out' of droplets of helium deep in its interior, thus releasing heat by <u>friction</u> as they fall down through lighter hydrogen.

These planets are celestial planes hydrogen is part of these planets one would expect oxygen is situated above the solar system while hydrogen comes from below as we know hydrogen and oxygen forms water. Since the eras of astronauts going to our solar system what, they hope to find is water.

We are all individuals assimilating ourselves in different ways on planet earth because such precondition enables us to intervene for our survival. To experiences life on earth as no sugar coated topping, to be creative, to experience what it is to be part of the realm of good and evil with an aim of eternal glory for which reasons we have to undergo trials, to become whole within a new rebirth into eternal life that it those not pay to do wrong or hurt other people's feelings, to unite those who believe in harmony, to reach a better understanding with new bounds as we move towards eternal life.

What do most people make out of people who only want to come up in life living a life of flashy cars, houses, and wealth, and what do people make out of people who live a life with disability e.g. being deaf or blind? There must have been conflicts somewhere before man was created to have embarked on the test and trials of existence.

Suffering cannot continue forever, suffering is a test of life in whatever situation we find ourselves in, is for us to experience something more than impressions I would call it reality. For example you might be a doctor, but what is a doctor without patients to look after? It is through suffering we have purpose.

It is those with ill health that gives purpose to doctors, without them, the science of medicine would not exist. Should we then have the opinion that God those not exist? It is all trials of life. Why should anyone be born into this world in an already arranged table of enjoyment, while others are born into slavery, poverty, illness or degradation? It is for us, to understand the values of beauty, ugliness and death?

Men have not only been to the moon, but to other planets through space missions. A lot of requirements and purpose have been placed on humans before creation to ascertain how we came into existence and the true meaning and reward of our existence? One thing I hope humans in the 21st century would admit is that in the field of science and religion we should be surprised, that we have come this far and everything in doing so, had been a miracle.

As I observe myself and my environments and the universe as a whole, I believe myself, all humans, creatures, plant, the air we breathe in, the earth, the sun, the moon, the stars, and other planet's had been thrown down from the heavens? Have we been programmed to be what we are today in this 21st century as others have been programmed to be what they were in past centuries. We are just assimilating ourselves into something that has been ordained. We have come this far after millions of years to acquired wisdom and knowledge in building a complex and sophistication planet called earth in suffering and in pain, for better or for worse.

The pillars of the universe are held, based on concepts that, all things should go through prepossessions, for me and the entire human race on earth to quest through lots of life inherent traits and inconsistencies. Compelled by nature to either succumb to good or evil in pleasant or difficult situation just to show or experience courage and how decorous we could be to quest, in pain and suffering in good health or in bad health, in fame or in poverty.

Each individual lives have already been ordained depending on whatever; it has been programmed to do or accomplish through stages of different evolution under lots of unforeseeable dispositions. It could be very worrying for some for other; it could lead to disorientation.

It has all ready been presupposed to be what it is, in other for us to encounter the reality of life eternal. Every knee is here on earth to bow even if you do not believe in God. There are a million incoherencies on earth that implies every individuals are faced with, no matter how mighty and great a man or a woman could be, there is always the inclination that every head and knee shall bow if not to God, by nature and mind you God is nature itself.

If some of us hold the opinion God does not exist humans are suffering and that we have been enslaved for the billions of years we have existed on this planet called earth have man stopped man from being slaves to man?

Found among the lowest, the wealthy and famous life on earth is by choice as with a two sided coin. One dose not needs to be wealthy, famous, or popular to really have a life because, the lowest person can possesses, the most important thing a wealthy, popular or powerful person desperately wants or need. Man has always quest for power if God exist what drives human there is beauty, death and ugliness rich or poor in such matters we all stand with the same faith.

Coupled our existence is based on an irony of what all men of power want is more power. Regardless of slavery one can always find something more worthy than being famous, powerful or wealthy, in which case, we are the once who enable interpretations into existence because, we have put ourselves below them it is beauty that stands out most achieving it we say is the problem but we have achieved more than we bargain for its appreciation that we lack it's time we find it in ourselves.

On one side of the coin if the world is not a sugar coated topping, the other side of the coin could be bitter. For example the UK is a sugar coated topping for its citizens because it has pleasant decorous implications on ways of governance and accountability among other nations it cares for its citizens, with state social security benefits and hospital care.

The realisation is that it is just the beginning not until other nations especially third world countries would follow suit and stop being over dependant while the little they get, they fight over.

From a book given to me by my brother's wife Mrs. Nwamaka Megbele titled shared care in schizophrenia making it effective, edited by Tom Burns, department of psychiatrist University of Oxford UK the resultant effects of schizophrenia sufferers are partly because of family problems background, family traits and genetic make-up could also lead to mental illness.

For the past 16 years I have been cared for by psychiatrist, social and care workers there has been failings in my care because, not once had any of them asked me about my family problems, background, or about my youth. Or what I felt in this stage of my life had led to my illness as a paranoid schizophrenia.

The disorder is thought mainly to affect cognition, but it also usually contributes to chronic problems with behaviour and emotion. People with schizophrenia are likely to have additional comorbid conditions, including major depression and anxiety disorders; the lifetime occurrence of substance abuse is almost 45% Social problems, such as long-term unemployment, poverty and homelessness, are common. The average life expectancy of people with the disorder are 10 to 15 years less than those without, the result of increased physical health problems and a higher suicidal rate.

I was never once up to no good in my life, I don't take drugs i.e. ecstasy, cocaine, marijuana infarct; it would destroy my residual genetic nature as superman if I should take such drugs. I was relieved in the month of April 2008 a medication had been manufactured for the cure of bad memories. In my opinion in this my present life has been for me to experience bad memories and the initiatives I have to undergo in becoming more human involving myself in the supernatural and the spiritual.

Isolated lives are too common in the UK where every day is just like any other day but it is peaceful but there is more that meets the eye going on. The Americans needed Superman when they had him. They knew what would be its follow-ups moreover, among them lives the most greatest of rascals.

Before Superman found himself to America, they have started building sophisticated buildings, weapons for combats, guns, rockets, helicopters, airplanes, railway lines and buses for transportation. It was just the right place for him to be.

With the number of rascals in America how many bullets, rockets or caters trophies would Superman be able to catch or correct at one time; it is an open arrays for him to reveal his identity or prune to his enemies.

Not only this, his interaction with villains was also a threat to innocent people. One of the first question the three villains asked when they came into contact with humans was in view of if the weapons' used against them, in their views, were as a result of humans worshiping witchcrafts, magic or sorcery.

It was through these realisations Superman knowingly from his subconscious mind knew he was right to have changed the cause of nature. It would lead him into ways of divesting himself. As a matter of facts could Superman had been able to live a marital life with Lois Lane (Margot Kidder) and have children?

In all the women mention in this book of part one to five who I have been involved with, they are either, my mothers, my sisters or friends in my past life.

They are women who have been powerful in their own rights and privileged what I mean is that they were exceptional women or they were part of my Krypton. Other aspect about my relationships with them is that, I am always short lived. What I mean is that I often die at an early age. At each stage, my strength is spent.

It took little time after the second world war for the Americans to have began building great infrastructure skyscrapers, weapons and the greatest initiators' of the industrial age except for China about to take over in this 21st century. Another reason for supermen's protocol in American was for him to assimilate himself as the seismographs and abyss of American. America is a place where people climb up and down from heavens the same applies to South Africa in my opinion.

The UK is made up of conglomerates of people from all parts of the world. I do not see any reason why people in Britain should not be filled with friendly lively people? They live a life of isolation but in good faith I mean there is conflicts but it could be resolved if you are peaceful, you would like Britain.

The good thing here is that if you are a stranger who had lived part of your life outside the UK for some reason you had come back or you are here for the first time, it is always a good experience to be in the UK. It is customary for them to feel the system is true and fear.

For example with my illness I could still coup, do my writing using a computer, it could be true according to Microsoft director Mr Bill Gate that computers don't bit! I could attend college, community meetings e.g. housing neighbourhood or London safer neighbourhood meetings in my borough.

As a schizophrenic sufferer born premature does not imply I should not have children of cause I should want to have children being British by birth. It has more to offer me and my children medically, socially, life style, freedom of speech, using my own initiatives if, I choose to, and live my life, the way, I choose or I perceive it should be.

If you are asked to choose between a drug addict and a drug trafficker who, would you be against? Such should now be the paradox of our existence. For how many centuries have we been in conflicts? I don't take drugs; in relation to my background as an African it is the worse accusation I could receive from my parents if I were a child of no good.

These you might consider are forces against me the Local council pull down or build new houses and infrastructures each year buildings' each year in the UK are pulled down and rebuilt with more sophisticated infrastructures'. Because they are considered as properties which have outlived its purpose in a way I feel they are regenerating me what I mean is that I like to be exited physically and emotionally.

They have attained some understanding into one of my week points which is why over the years since I return to the UK I have been going down into my grave engrossing myself, into the abyss of Great Britain one of the requirements to do this is not, to move homes. I drink lots of liquid sometimes at least ten cups of tea a day it has implication to my condition of birth.

May 2007, I have not been to work because I suffered a relapse, which had taken me to the month of 17th May 2008. It is not easy for schizophrenia or any one with disability getting employment then not even in 2012. I had a disability and personal adviser Ms Helen Patrick at the Jobcenterplus in Wellington Street Woolwich. They introduced me to Remploy 9 Gunnery House, Cornwallis Road, Royal Arsenal Woolwich SE18 6SW.

I was still unwell at the time but I went for my appointment at Remploy. I had to undergo an induction. I looked at my past in retrospect's over the years since I have been unwell as a schizophrenic, I was working, I had to attend college for my return to learning course and then my 'A' levels and then University with my illness. I was looking for work in administration with training, while my health had not been any better since the month of May 2007.

May 2008 I thought things out. I calm myself down I have been working, I had attained up to date qualification in A level Business studies, advanced HND in Housing management and law and a professional certificate of merit in management relationship and conflict. My aim was that since my health could weigh be down through physical job by this time of my age and illness, I was prepared for a change of job.

I became apprehensive if I do not get a job in administration soon, my qualifications would become outdated my work experience and qualification would be less appreciated by any employer, booking an appointment with Mr. Dotun Sobowale at his working place in Charlton were as a public user I could search the internet for jobs at the same time write my books then, I titled it memoirs of a schizophrenic.

I searched goggle web site for distance learning. The Open University student registration and enquiries services P.O.Box 197, Milton Keynes, MK7 6BJ telephone number 44(0)845 300 6090. I telephoned their office, also the open collage UK limited, 71 Thurleston road, office 2, Longbridge, Birmingham B31 4Q on 01216800141.

The Open University had my intended course of study which was advanced diploma in health care or social care. I would have to speak to my adviser Ms Helen Patrick's at Woolwich Jobcentreplus I told myself.

Studying with distance learning with the open University one had to be on the internet all learning is done through the internet, though they registered me through my telephone conversation with them gave me an identification number A270723 but with me on state benefits I could not afford an internet provider. Though they advised me at the Open University through government help under certain circumstances, I could get a grant. With ICS International Correspondence School, I can do it through the post and the course fee was cheaper by £460.00.

With the Open University it would cost me £650.00 for the advanced diploma in health and social care which is more than half the government set tuition fee at universities of £1,000.00, I have to feed myself, buy books, materials such as internet providers and I might even have to pay for my housing rent. 2015 Open University have taken distance learning to a whole new, incredibly supportive level.

It was all a part of therapy to get me out of my illness which I do not really see as an illness may be it is because of something I feel most people suffer more than dose with mental illness in mind soul and body but they are not diagnosed as mental health sufferers I thought of leisure to make me relax may be, it would reduce my mood swing or going to cinemas or the museum.

Since, I am an African born British I have spent years of my life in Africa, I might be out of my mind and head with mental health issues being in the UK, it induces me to live up to certain expectations or certain conditioning because e.g. past and present experiences. They have lightened my burden. In contrast to my experience in Africa I observe the British environment with interest, it gets me out of the reverie of my mental illness rather than being a sugar coated ice-cream for me.

Cares from my African background who know I suffer from mental illness say, I am doing fine.

It is not surprising that a child can live his or her whole entire life, trying to live up to their parent's expectation without getting anywhere, is there any reason why it should be so? It is for such reasons why; Africans and children from third world countries, do not represent themselves very well abroad.

In Africa, some parents would destroy other people's children for the sake of their own child becoming more successful.

With the wealth my father made, he could have built enough houses to go round his wives and children and even buy my council flat. The two houses my father built did not go round in ownership among is wives. At the moment in my family, it all involves conflict.

I have witness my father having so much money that he would not only had built a house each for his wives but also, build a house personally for me and the rest of his children.

He was the life patron of a Baptism church, a freemason,

and Ogbony cult. As a member of these activities which are mostly founded by him through regular payments as a member. We family members of his hardly get hold of his (dosh) I mean money this is one of the new slangs I have picked whiles living in the UK and my father enjoys sending gifts to friends or assist them financially when they are celebrating.

Only the faithful and the righteous can steel time and use it wisely. Its only time that can complete and fulfil the purpose of our past, our life on earth is a predicament; it's what an individual is capable of conceiving that is in conciliation of disagreement that is worth anything and what he or she can protect, if incoherencies are involved, an alternative could always be to opt-out, bearing in mind that if reincarnation is part of human existence, existence is a race against time.

As long as I remain a celibate my step mothers have some explanation to give before, we could have mutual respect for each other. If we live repeated life through reincarnation whatever could be of our present or next existence if injustice is involved would reflect or be set right in another life time!

It is a common thing for other human setting obstacles in the lives of other individuals. Could it not be said that we could be prey and predators to ourselves in the way we live our lives? it is true with an irony man is a pray and a predators to each other if it is true at this present time in the 21st century's cannibalism is a common occurrence in some parts of the world.

Since these are the case, I conclude that there is no doubt the effect would be the cause of paranoid schizophrenia; other effects could be manic or chronic depression.

This same thing applies to a step mother; my step mother Mrs. Cordelia Megbele paying homage to culture gave me some of Itsekiri Delta state Nigeria pepper soup ingredient. Could this be part of what culture really is? If it is so, I was no longer a young lad at the time, I could see reason if not based on what culture and its effect could have on an individual because of the experience I have undergone?

My step mother Mrs. Cordelia Megbele gave me Itsekiri pepper soup ingredient in a bottle, to create homogenous relationship with herself, my mother, my father, friends and relatives. It should have been given to me by my own mother with no excuses it should not be given to me by any members of my family except my mother or my father. Regardless if at this time my mother lived outside the confines of my father's house she was still lawfully married to my father. They were never divorced or it should not have been given to me at all.

Mrs. Cordelia Megbele, my sister from my mother's side Mrs. Oritsegbubemi Ajagunla and my aunty Mrs. Larne Charles all worked for Pfizer Pharmaceuticals Company at Lagos state Nigeria. Cordelia own and run the canteen of the company, my sister Oritsegbubemi works as secretary to one of the manager, while my aunty worked as an administrator.

I later realise Mrs. Cordelia Megbele gave me the pepper soup ingredient as a predisposition to either keep in touch with her and the rest of the family, or to depute through reincarnation for any of our lost relatives.

By predisposition, I mean Cordelia had given me the pepper soup ingredient to influence me in favour of something; or to make me susceptible to something.

My step mother Cordelia grow up when she was young in Eastern Nigeria among the Ibo's as they are commonly known, so did my father's third wife Mrs. Aya Megbele. Aya Megbele is from Rivers state Nigeria. Just as Delta state was considered to be part of Bendel state of Nigeria, so is Rivers state, considered to be part of the Ibo's in Eastern Nigeria.

My experiences are that their culture and tradition have similarities. Both step mothers' of mine speaks Ibo dialect and their own respective dialect of origin.

Sceptically the relationship of both my step mothers and my mother, my father would be prejudice against in both East and Western Nigeria for the amount of money and influence he had within them.

My father as an Itsekiri from Delta state he would be prejudice against by the Western Nigerians for marrying my mother and neglecting her in the first place, before members of the families of his other wives follow suit to do the same. But where does this leave me if not an individual to be dominated and abandoned.

Even at my father's death the whole scenarios of his life time explicitly became exploitatively for him to create propagandas not only with his death but also, with the episodes' of his life and inherences, the current affairs of Nigeria business and politics, social contrast and norms of Nigerian livelihood. When I scanned the situation my father lived, for himself it would have been different if he wasn't self centred but he had left something of a eureka or bewilderment on my behalf and the rest of his family probably because in Nigeria to become popular you need to apply considerable pressure to be who you are.

Nothing is free in life, if one is fortunate having something of value, use it well, use it wisely it does not customary involve only money experience, within its use, applying wisdom is something of value. There is always a price to pay for everything we do. Or should have done but left undone! One reason for being celibate is for example to reverse inconsistencies that have already occurred that would lead to more causation.

Within culture and religion, which of the two would be more perfect to human existence? Nevertheless the current trend of culture, politics, and fame we feel are now being used to downgrade religion, our spiritual needs and uplifting if only we apply reason, we would feel much better in this approach suffering in itself, is knowledge.

With synergy comes the need for culture linked to attributes perpetrated to please human depression and temperament, activities to interest and unite a group of people. Religion is much more of importance than culture because it chooses to please our souls and conscience, it is a quest. A quest because of the things we do, see and go through in some ways, it is a protest.

Culture in African setting is that from childhood you respect, your parents, you keep close to the influence of culture, you are likely to be offered to the gods and deities for food of which the child's spirit or spirituality is immersed in the act of juju's, most children as they grow up, cannot digest, which in years leads to the child unable to quest for their own spiritual up-liftment.

Moreover some of them are left to fend for themselves and for their livelihoods trading in the streets of Africa and its market place. They can only fend for themselves if they have the courage and resilience if not, they die too early at their youth with no one to bury them.

Could it be said that Britain is being influenced to certain cultures? I do not see people living in Great Britain under a particular culture of any kind all I observe is a system and preludes of historic events and epilogues confronted to changes I do not mean it has not its own culture infarct it comprises of culture from all over the world, of which stereotyping is involved. It is a nation for people who are based on a predetermined life or purpose.

I might have come into the UK to enjoy most of the good things in life most people might think while infarct I have come into the UK in other to prolong my life in some sense I admit this to be true. Just as I have made reference to in African Juju, witchcraft or voodoo applicably being used in Africa for the same purpose. What then, is the comparison of such jujus, witchcrafts or voodoo to the science of medicine it's a big issue because then we can view it from a religious perspective? I leave it to the consideration of atheist who do not believe in the existence of God who science, engineering and technology have always, been their excuse.

What would most people think of men who practice

polygamy with the hope of raising children who would assist them working to till the soil for cultivating crops in their farm? Or raise children up for the sole purpose if they become unwell or old, they would be looked after by their children. This is to predetermine what they want out of their children lives before bearing the children. In the UK it could mean the more state benefits they would have as parents.

Some might have long term illness, they still want to have children who they would be dependent on yet, they have no cure for their illness. This is bending the course of nature. Without considering the faith of their children what kind of solitaire do we call this? Bringing children into this world without defence its taking advantage!

Such as come into the UK to bear children who, in the future, would send money to their parents in Africa. This implies they wanted something out of having children.

If Britain over centuries have been left like a ruined city it would have by now been debilitated the rest would have been history. Britain is always regenerating its self not only this but all so, involve the rest of the world in its own county. Unlike me and my background, I cannot go to delta state, Ibadan, Port Harcourt, Ghana and be happily welcome by them. I have this personal saying about the Americans and the British 'If you should look at yourself in front of a mirror make sure you have judged how you look before, you can tell other people to look at their own reflection'

Even if it is just the British carrying news of events all around the world in some of the world most remote places makes it very interesting as having a purpose. If the whole EU member nations should have come this far as allies such should be akin in all regions of planet earth.

The Americans, British and EU nations seems to be making the world a better place. We all have indifferences which imply we have to compromise not that it would completely resolves the indifference, but it would depict us as tolerant, responsible, a trial of reasoning, being considerate and thoughtful. For example consider the Libyan and Arab unrest, Foreigner evacuation plans, Libya's Profiles and Muammar Gaddafi conflict in March 20011.

As an African born British I see myself as a predicate of Africans and British, I am also a predicate of Western and Eastern Nigeria. If it cannot be generally accepted, Delta state of Nigeria is part of Eastern Nigeria. It would be regarded as part of Western Nigeria for example, my aunty Mrs. Lanre Charles one of my father's step sister from Ondo state, just next to Delta state and former Bendel state of Nigeria, and my aunty is now married to Mr Charles from Bendel state.

This was after both of them, have had a first relationship with children one of the reason I felt might have triggered their relationship is that, we Nigerians are always drifting away from each other or that they were both unhappy, about being an in-between which now condoles them into using body language or self sacrifices that would put right some of the conflicts in Nigeria.

Lots of Nigerians have done the same thing just like my father and mother with such relationship in Nigeria, they and their children never gets anywhere before it leads to more conflicts. Some of which, could disorientate them and their children for life.

Some people in Africa seem to be under laying peace I wonder, why they get nowhere? Nevertheless irrevocably I am a predicate of both East and Western Nigeria. I am a sort of a questionnaire. A questionnaire that I have to give answers to or I would be considered ignorant. Nonetheless within all these factions, I see myself as strictly an observer. The Mid-Western Region was a division of Nigeria from 1963 to 1991, from 1976 being known as the Bendel state. It was formed in June 1963 from Benin and Delta provinces of the Western Region, and its capital was Benin City. It was renamed a province in 1966, and in 1967 when the other provinces were split up into several states, it remained territorially intact, becoming a state.
During the Nigerian Civil War, the Biafran forces invaded the new Mid-Western state, en route to Lagos, in an attempt to

force a quick end to the war. While under Biafran occupation, the state was declared as the 'Republic of Benin' as Nigerian forces were to retake the region. The republic collapsed a day after the declaration as Nigerian troops overtook Benin City.

In 1976 it lost Ughelli to the new Rivers state and was renamed Bendel. This was subdivided into Delta and Edo in 1991.

There is always the need if we are to live happily as one big happy family, to realise or rectifying our wrong doings. Earth is the place, where all our mistakes can be corrected, which is basically one reason for our existence on earth.

I am an African British by birth because of preconditions relating to my existence not because, Britain as many would take it for, is a sugar coated topping. If you have a little in e.g. Africa or Jamaica hold on to it, because you might arrive there later and realise, that your stuff is gone because other people have made a claim to what was yours.

The UK is a setting the British have worked so hard for what they have achieved, over the years for centuries have kept an open door for people from other nations all around the world to come into the UK. They send aid and donations to other nations in need. But do they have enough to feed the whole third world nation? But they can help. Daily mail Monday the 1st of the month of June 2009 page 27 growing queues to die.

800 Britons sign up with suicide clinic as Falconer states bid for the law to change. The number of Britons thinking of travelling to the Dignitas suicide clinic in Switzerland reached 800. What is the realization of using juju, African witchcraft and voodoo implies when they are used in prolonging a person's life span, success or revenge? There is something vague about juju in relation to the science of medicine that needs to be validated.

While at different times in relations to our daily lives we do record omens.

In the DVD Blade starring Wesley Snipes I suffer from

hallucination makes me feel I should question if people with premature birth are denoted as vampires. I think it is the opposite though I do drink a lot of liquid it doesn't make me a vampire.

Considering I suffer from phobias of instrument for use in the human body such as shavers or toothbrush which are battery operated sponge for doing the washing-up in the kitchen; I drink more than ten cups of tea each day. At certain time I had to stock up my flat up with properties things I do not really need in other to hold myself down or my legs would become unsteady. After some time I get rid of them when the feeling comes again I repeat the process.

Before and after the 11th of March 2011 massive earthquake hit the north-east of Japan triggering a tsunami which caused extensive damage. Japan's TV showed cars, ships and even buildings were swept away in the Fukushima prefecture, after the 8.9 magnitude earthquake. I had irrationally changed the batteries of my wristwatch.

If you are waiting as you read this book you are going to read about superman in action flying in the air to save the world forget it! My mention of any such activities would only have occurred through astral experience of which nothing of such nature is in these books.

By the time superman returned Lois Lane was having an affair with someone else. I have been living in the UK for the past 23 years by the time I came back most of my age groups where already spoken for. In some ways I have met Lois Lane in some awkward situation. This book unveils various dimensions on how to understand children of premature birth. I am not overweight but I do experience feeling of being overweight.

The collect for the Pentecost Sunday 31st of May 2009 at Saint Marys Magdalene Woolwich church read together by all its congregation God who as at this time taught the heats of your faithful people by sending to them the light of your Holy Spirit: grant us by the same Spirit to have right judgement in all things and evermore to rejoice in your holy comfort; through the merits of Christ Jesus our saviour, who is alive and reigns with him, in the unity of the Holy Spirit, one God, now and forever. Amen.

The Bible reading from the book of Saint John chapter 15 verse 26 to verse 27 and chapter 16 verse 4 to verses 15 read by Judith Franklin it read. When the Counsellor comes, whom I will send to you from the father, the spirit of truth, who goes out from the father, he will testify about me, and you also must testify, for you have been with me from the beginning.

I have told you this, so that when the time comes you will remember that I warned you, I did not tell you this at first because, I was with you. Now I am going to him who sent me, yet none of you asked me, where are you going? Because I have said these things, you are filled with grief. But I tell you the truth; it is for your good that I am going away.

Unless I go away, the Councillor will not come to you; but if I go, I will send him to you. When he comes he will convict the world of guilt in regards to sin, and righteousness and judgment; in regard to sin because men do not believe in me; in regards to righteousness because am going to the father, where you can see me no longer, and in regard to judgment, because the Prince of this world now stands condemned.

I have much more to say to you, more than you can now bear. But when he the spirit of truth, comes, he will guide you into all truth. He will not speak on his own, he will speak only what he hears, and he will tell you what is yet to come. He will bring glory to me by taking from what is mine and making it known to you. All that belongs to the father is mine. That is why I said the spirit will take from what is mine and make it known to you.

The celebrant on this Pentecost Sunday was Reverend Grahame Stephens whose summons I find always inspirational. The Mayor of Greenwich Allan McCarthy believes the council and groups all around the UK representing our communities should reflect life as it is!

The Mayor of Greenwich was already on the board of governors at both Cherry Orchard primary, Charlton and at Saint Ursula's Convent in Greenwich. For the Mayor, it started with a lifetime of community involvements, the son of two journalists. Not just as one of the last Aldermen, and as a ward councillor for both Kidbrooke and Charlton, but also as a representative on a range of borough art and community group.

It's the second of the month of June 2009 Allan McCarthy become the Mayor of Greenwich at the end of the month before. He believes passionately in getting young people involved in public life in their youth as soon as possible. It could be psychologically true for that children know what they are here on earth to do and the environment in which they choose to be born in, before they are born.

Some of them are born to be inspired on what goes on around them, some of them know what they are here to do and to inspire others, while some them are here on earth to make a dream come true, quarry uncertainties, a move from injustice towards justice.

The Mayor of Greenwich had fond memories, at aged of eight years with his mum taking him to neighbouring mayor's parlour on assignment, the new mayor believes the council and groups who represent the community should reflect life as it is.

Great Britain and the rest of Europe are nations comprising with people who believe that one is free to express whatever it is that affects them with freedom of expression. Both of my parents are dead without my presence to witness their funeral. I would be 43 years of age in 2009; I have since my youth witness a lot about my relatives and friends some of which dramatise themselves again.

I have not introduced any other person except Miss Lorain O'Connor to my brother since we arrived into the UK he has not seen me with anybody introduced to him as my friend,

227

he doesn't not know the name of my general practitioner or any one caring for me after I left hospital in 1995. He had accompanied me for the first time on one of my mental health outpatient appointment at the Farryview mental health centre. All he could say about my job prospect was that his brother was unwell nobody would call him and give him a job and that he works for London underground.

Mr Engi my care worker, whom I have known since 1995, comes into my flat to administer me Dipixsole injection. Engi saw me two days after the appointment in which my brother had accompanied me to the health centre. Mr. Engi was walking towards me at Woolwich Powis Street as I was going for an appointment to seek employment with Reed in partnership part way to work in second floor Royal Sovereign house in Woolwich, after an appointment with my Job centre adviser Ms Helen Patrick at Wellington Street Woolwich.

As Mr. Engi was walking towards me I stopped by about to speak to Mr. Engi in greetings, I had already began to say the word that I was going for a job appointment, Mr Engi just shrugged me with a sign I should give it all I can if it is about looking for work I would describe Mr. Engi as a Chinese. I go through phases I have encounter something about Mr. Engi in a reincarnated life time when I was a *Shaolin* or part of a Monk monastery at Lhasa in Tibet. I experience while I was living at Ibadan in view of advancement regarding my spirituality I was compelled reading most of the books written by Lobsang Rampa the pen name of an author who wrote books with paranormal and occult themes. His best known work is *The Third Eye*, published in Britain in 1956. Some of his books I have read are, *My Visit to Venus*, *Doctor from Lhasa The Rampa Story*, *Living with the Lama*, *You Forever*, *Chapters of Life*, *The Thirteenth Candle*, *Candlelight*, *Twilight* and *The Third Eye*. He most had induced me reading these books because they are beguiled or feel something of an enigma about how West Africans use, consult oracles with powers of the supernatural of juju or how we attain such powers or the mysteries behind our great heritage.

I experienced something peculiar with Mr. Engi at the appointment my brother accompanied me to at the Ferryview mental health centre. The meeting was very brisk As Mr. Engi keyed in words on the computer keyboard I experience phenomena as if a shadow was above my heard I felt movement in my mouth just were one of my Molar tooth was extracted at Kings Hospital and another tooth extracted by my dentist N. Karia and associates at 23 Calderwood Street, Woolwich. Knowing myself for who I am and the experience I went through in Africa my mouth is one avenue I have hidden one of my true self. It is where one of my Ori or Oriki is. My experience was like having a brain, mouth, chest, stomach and pelvic bypass from above the sky. I felt Mr Engi hands are heavy and strong with knuckles just like my earthly father but my father's hands are longer, bigger but light in weight. The experience gave me the feeling the Buddhism penetrate through our African cultural and belief system. A true ninja should be free of all desires, especially greed. Learn to work together for a common goal.

Becoming a monk should be one of the most radical things a man could do with his life, for a monk's constant commitment is to change himself to the very roots of his being. Assumes that when a man comes to a monastery he is still saddled with what he called the 'empirical self,' that is, an illusory idea rather than an existential reality. For some reasons have been built up hiding our true selves far from what God wants us to be or want out of us. A true monk tries to break down that facade and come to terms with his true self declare ruthless war on his false self so that his true self can emerge victorious it's an attribute for mental health sufferers to outlive symptoms of the illness. I know some symptoms of schizophrenia seems like suffering a kind of death, dying to his old self braking down the facade means that the new self might be born.

The first time I experience the tooth in my mouth move involutedly was at Ibadan when two foreign Hare Krishna's spoke to me. They wanted to call me into the movement of Hare Krishna I first thought they wanted a token in other for them to tell what the future holds for me. As they were speaking to me words came out of my mouth as touring words filled with air. First I had no tokens to give was the first thing which came to my mind. I have come across them whilst living at Lagos and have never came that close to them or was aware of what their intentions were but for the way they dress seems religious. When they told me a little about themselves I moved off from them and that was it they also moved off from my direction immediately. It was as if they were moving with the wind all I experience was their legs moving swiftly with their dress moving with the wind as they disappeared into the crowd. My experience was that there might have been two of them speaking to me they said the same words at the same time. The next day in the evening my mother came back from work in apprehension and told me Cocoa House at Ibadan was burning down. Cocoa House was once the tallest building in tropical Africa. It is located in the city of Ibadan in Nigeria. It was built from proceeds from commodities (e.g., Cocoa, Rubber, Timber and so on) of the then Western State of Nigeria. Cocoa House, the 24-storey Cocoa House, Ibadan, is the property of Odu'a Investment Company Limited, Ibadan formerly known as 'Ile Awon Agbe'-translates as the 'House of Farmers' was commissioned for use in August 1965. This building is owned by Wemabod Estates Limited, a subsidiary of O'dua group of companies. The building was gutted by fire on January 9, 1985 and rehabilitated for use in August 1992.

The International Society for Krishna Consciousness (ISKCON), known colloquially as the Hare Krishna movement or Hare Krishnas, is a Gaudiya Vaishnava religious organisation. Founded in 1966 in New York City the distinctive appearance of the movement and its culture come from the Gaudiya Vaishnava tradition, which has had adherents in India since the late 15th century and Western converts since the early 1900s in America, and in England in the 1930s. ISKCON dedicate their thoughts and actions towards pleasing the Supreme Lord, Krishna. ISKCON today is a worldwide confederation some of them aiming for self-sufficiency, In recent decades the movement's most rapid expansions in terms of numbers of membership have been within Eastern Europe since the collapse of the Soviet Union) and India
ISKCON advocates preaching. Members try to spread

Krishna consciousness, primarily by singing the Hare Krishna mantra in public places and by selling books written by Bhaktivedanta Swami. Both of these activities are known within the movement as *Sankirtan*. A study conducted by E. Burke Rochford Jr. at the University of California found that there are four types of contact between those in ISKCON and prospective members. Those include: individually motivated contact, contact made with members in public arenas, contact made through personal connections, and contact with sympathizers of the movement who strongly sway people to join

It is left for those who do right and just to forbear with perseverance, the pain of being let down if there is death, there is a life, to live after death depends on whatever we have done on earth as it is in heaven, so it is on earth.

There are forces on earth beyond human control, in time with perseverance's the after mount is joy, grace, peace, happiness and exhilaration beyond what words or feelings can recite. This is why we have to persevere throughout our trials of life. If you are persevering in life, you will not convert anything that belongs to someone else.

Medication I was on in the month of June 2009 of Olanzapine 15 mg had to be reduced e to 10 mg because I developed over eating.

Why do mental health sufferers become aggressive? If a sufferer had grown-up with some spiritual awareness in their lives they are more able to rehabilitate themselves with religious moral values in other to help them adjust in recovering from their illness. You would know them when, you see them they socially withdrawn or they look depress.

Preachers of hat are being condemned in the UK and the rest of Europe, Police officers want to burnished or punish people with anti-social behaviour. This response by the government is mainly to stop people who seek to put hindrance to other people's quality of life. Such behaviours that risked public lives and safety should be brought into consideration.

This over the years, have led to many private business liaising with officer in the metropolitan police. With respect to Mr David Cameron speech on 15th august 2006, the law provided sub-police officers who are drown from all ethnic background in the UK as officers, with limited powers to answer to real police officers who could then make arrest because of public safety.

The areas, these recommended sub police officers cover are, the sales of DVD piracy, unlawful premises entry, graffiti's, the sales of false cigarettes, tobaccos, drugs, health and safety issues to make everybody including children more alert of our community problems.

A paranoid schizophrenic entering his 40th year on July 2006, disillusioned, living only on housing benefit because he was adamant not to live on benefits regardless of his illness because it is not only therapeutic for him, it was sort of therapy it left room for him to adapt. Yet he did not know what is entitlements are! At some points, he had to pay for his prescription.

Each fortnight by the time I pay my gas and electricity bills I had little left of my wages to live on yet I could manage. I am single with no or children, I am a diagnosed paranoid schizophrenic this, is enough for the sake of moral values for me, if I choose to adapt a life of celibacy who says the heard road doesn't teach us lessons?

It was after I left Iceland frozen food plc, I became determined remaining a celibate, probably because it created a new me, one of my experience was that I could stay in the cold store for as long as I wanted without feeling cold the experience was exhilarating.

A female would do anything to have sex and bear children it is the pride of every woman at some certain point for most women the experience could be a cross road, a roundabout or a traffic light.

Mr Samuel a co-worker of mine at the Woolwich Gala club

communicated the recent death of his mother to all the staff on the 13th of August 2006, after I had in 2004 announced the death of my father Chief Dr Frank Anirejuoritse Megbele the Agbueju of Warri Delta state Nigeria.

Mr Samuel just started working for Rentokil Initial cleaning service with me at the Woolwich Gala club, two month after his announcement of his mother's death.

We talked about several issues and problems that had been foretold would happen in Western Nigeria such as the effects of (Olumo Rock).

At this same time it was foretold the relationship of Orunmila and Orisia would be unfolded its implication with other deities such Oshun the goddess of the flowing stream with a female priestess by its side and those the gods or deities have favoured in one time or another for example Moremi. Problems they always have is calming any entry or outing of Ogun the god of metal in any given situation. Ogun is known to mount people in various aspects of his character, and the people who venerate him are quite familiar with such aspects. Orisia was a very good friend of Orunmila both of them had great powers. They both put the god Shango, the god of thunder and lightning into their privacy. They are known as deities who never die if they die, they would return again in other form.

Shango the god of fire, lightning and thunder is historically a royal ancestor of the Yoruba's. In Johnston's mythological account of racial heroes and kings, contrary to his peaceful brother Ajaka, he was a powerful and violent ruler. He had supernatural forces because he could produce thunder and lightning. He reigned for seven years, the whole of which period was marked by his continuous campaigns and his many battles. The end of his reign resulted from his own inadvertent destruction of his palace by lightning.

According to the palace tradition of Oyo, Shango was a king before he became a thunder god. The religious ritual of Shango was possibly designed in order to help the devotees of Shango gain self-control. Shango's beads tell the story of 'his' essence, the logic of Obatala (white) alternating in balance with the fire of Aganyu (red) in passion towards some goal. Historically, Shango brought prosperity to the Oyo Empire during his reign.

After his deification the initiation ceremony of the cult of his memory dictates that this same prosperity is bestowed upon followers on a personal level. According to Yoruba belief systems, Shango hurls bolts of lightning at the people chosen to be his followers, leaving behind imprints of stone axe blades on the earth's crust. These blades can be seen easily after heavy rains. Veneration of Shango enables according to Yoruba belief a great deal of power and self-control.

Shango altars often contain an often-seen carved figure of a woman holding her bosom as a gift to the god with a single double-blade axe sticking up from her head. The axe symbolizes that this devotee is possessed by Shango. The woman's expression is calm and cool, expressing the qualities she has gained through her faith.

'Shango usurped the duties of an older deity, Jakuta, who hurled fire stones to punish people when they acted against the wishes of Olodumare, the Supreme God'. The name Jakuta, 'Hurler of stones', or 'Fighter with stones' is an allusion to stone implements believed to be his thunderbolts.' Jakuta was 'associated with a fellowship of meteorites'.

Orunmila and Orisia both of whom embraced the deity Obatala in solving problems. If, they find it difficult appealing to Ogun or Obatala; Orunmila and Orisia would deflect with whatever means they have in setting things right in the proper perspectives.

It is human nature when some of us have been granted privileges we misuse it, become arrogant or it leads to self wimp. The deity Obatala later made up his mind up, he would us advice given to him, by Orisia, as she chose. Both Orisia and Orunmila live their lives to divest themselves through which they give purpose in other to avoid conflicts within.

Could this be one of the reasons I initiated myself into the Nigeria defence academy; in other to inscribe and desiccate myself and my Krypton and not to be overweight. I would describe the phenomenon as similar to what superman did when; he tricked the three villains in losing their powers through a switch.

It was for a purpose to ingrain my natural system and Krypton in the military. It is what I have to undergo because I want to be like any other human being. But in another perspective it is an opportunity for me to divest myself.

Other related to Orisha, kings or quest such as Àkàrà-ogun others such as Ogunmola, Moremi Ajasoro. Most of them even within the Orisha's are entwined with conflicts, indifference or disagreement within themselves or they are friends with the trend of events their era's were interrelated which still drags till this century.

Then Africa began to get scotched craving for talisman that would give them strength to undermine each other. Instead of displaying good examples with their powers had to deflect just to be recognised. This for certain reasons was partly what brought Europeans to Africa and not for just slavery our belief system has mystical inference to 'transubstantiation'. The struggles for powers were causing problems within the underworld. At different instance the gods or deities had to unit to set things right.

After each death of these gods or deities, some native doctors, native witch doctors and Juju priest began creating their own interpretation of these deities. Some of them who were given power or ordained could use their gifts whichever way they chose. In these modern times it depends on meeting with the right native doctor or native priest.

This actually was what originated to be known as juju and in Africa and voodoo in Jamaica and the Caribbean's. Orunmila was known to be of good nature. People in Africa as of today still crave for the use of Witch and Juju doctors and native priest giving names to children after birth based on the purpose of past deities.

I visited my great grandmother from my mother's side at Abeokuta in Ogun state in 1979 on a family occasion with celebration going on there was singing, dancing, and hired musicians with the customary (Agbada, Asho-Oke, Damask cloths worn by the Yoruba's).

It was she who encouraged me to re- baptise at Methodist Baptism church at Ibadan. This was when my mother, I and my half brother Mr. Sola Awe moved from Lagos state to Ibadan Oyo state. Our mother had to move from Lagos state to Ibadan to work for Leyland motors within Ibadan and the road to Ile-Ife. Whenever a heavy rain falls in western Nigeria there are always a superstitious beliefs that something is about to occur.

Through history the god Ogun by all means wants to be recognised as more powerful. Compared to Orunmila who was gentle, amicable people loved him.

Children in the UK do not experience such things as a cow or a sheep slaughtered in the UK my father had a job in the UK in a slaughter house taking care of chickens to be sold in supermarkets before he became a postman.

The conflict which came up brought about Orunmila to be recognised as a god's he was, always known to be peaceful and amicable because of his own goodness and consideration in the practices of juju left the practice because he was meek. Rather than being considered as one of the gods Orisia advice him not to take the place of one of the gods because they are always in conflicts.

She described the future for Orunmila he should not worry about them because in the future they would be considered as men who used, their powers to demonstrate it is for their own right and privilege to do as they please; rather than divesting themselves. In doing so they are emphasizing themselves to be like God. It is an issue which has been scotching West Africa for centuries until this 21st century as long as juju's still remains a part of Africa.

One thing about the use of juju in this present day is if a juju priest giving someone juju to make use of, he is sending the person out so the juju would work which means if there is no body to use their juju, the juju priest powers cannot be enforced it is when it is used the juju priest themselves believe the juju works.

Obatala found the god Ogun's agitations were upsetting to that of Orunmila as Orunmila was a meek person, his concepts were running underground within the communities, because Ogun was found to be aggressive though he fought many battle on behalf of his people and won for which they appricated him. After the deity Obatala was given condolence out of consideration by 'she who Orunmila must interact with' condoled Obatala due to power struggled there was a need for refinement. Ogun is mighty, powerful and triumphal, yet is also known to exhibit the rage and destructiveness of the warrior whose strength and violence must not turn against the community he serves. He is believed by his followers to have 'wo ile sun', to have disappeared into the earth's surface instead of dying.

A signing of relationship she who Orunmila should comply with asked of Orunmila was that in any times Orunmila had course to reincarnate for any reason they should liaise with each other.

In the religion of the Yoruba people, Obàtálá is the creator of human bodies, which were supposedly brought to life by Olorun's breath. Obàtálá is also the owner of all ori or heads. Any orisha may lay claim to an individual, but until that individual is initiated into the priesthood of that orisha, Obàtálá still owns that head. This stems from the belief that the soul resides in the head.

Obatala (king of White Cloth) is said to be the Olorun's second son, by others to be merely one of Olorun's favorite Orisha. He is the one authorized by Olorun to create land over the water beneath the sky, and it is he who founds the first Yoruba city, Ife. Obatala is Olorun's representative on earth and shaper of human beings. He is known to some

Yoruba as Orisha-Nla or Olufon.

According to mythical stories Obatala is the eldest of all orisha and was granted authority to create the earth. Before he could return to heaven and report to Olodumare however, his rival Oduduwa (also called Oduwa, Oodua, Odudua or Eleduwa) and younger brother usurped his position by taking the satchel and created in his stead the earth on the Primeval Ocean. A great feud ensued between the two that is re-enacted every year in the Itapa festival in Ile Ife, Nigeria. Ultimately, Oduduwa and his sons were able to rule with Obatala's reluctant consent.

It appears from the cult dramas of the Itapa festival that Obatala was a dying and rising god. He left his Temple in the town on the seventh day of the festival, stayed in his grove outside the town on the eighth day and returned in a great procession to his Temple on the ninth day. The three-day rhythm of descent into the netherworld and subsequent resurrection on the third day shows the closeness of Obatala to the pre-canonical Israelite Yahweh and the figure of Jesus.

In Ifa, Obatala energy is the essence of Clarity. Within the myriad of kaleidoscopic energies that comprise our universe, the energy of Clarity is critically important. It is Clarity that allows us to make the right decisions, to differentiate right from wrong and perhaps most importantly, to see the other energies as they truly are! All the tales, or pataki, of Obatala, are designed to illuminate this reality.

Obatala is always referred to as the Orisa of the white cloth. White, in this sense, forms a perfect background for correctly seeing and identifying that which is around you. White is also viewed as a sign of purity, but, too often, thanks to the pernicious Christian Missionary influence on the Yoruba philosophy, this idea of purity has religious or moral implications. Instead, purity is another aspect of Clarity for this energy is unblemished, pure in its ability to discern.

Moral judgment of Obatala are not based on this sense of Christian purity, but rather on this energies absolute ability to see clearly the total spectrum of energies or issues involved.

Obatala is often seen as the Wise Old Man. Again, age and wisdom are simply representative aspects of increased clarity and judgment. Obatala is seen as the King of the Orisa. Again, this is not a power struggle or ego issue, this is simply a way of pointing out that Clarity of purpose, destiny and behaviour will always take precedence when confusion or disagreement exists.

Obatala is viewed as the Judge. Obatala is said to have been the molder of men. What more important aspect in our creation could be the imparting of clarity into our being? When drinking too much Palm Wine dulled that Clarity, through being drunk of drinking Palm Wine Obatala is said to have created deformed and handicapped people. This is pictured as his 'fall from grace.' That Red Palm oil is never placed on Obatala is another example of this.

The Pure clarity must remain clear and unblemished. That Obatala represents the head is consistent. It is from the mind that Clarity will come forth. Each and every tale is simply a way of expressing Oludumare's creation of this essential energy the energy of Clarity. For the Obatala child the expression and use of this primary energy is complex. The Obatala child will see a world of black and white, no gray. An Obatala child either sees things are either right or wrong there are no middle grounds.

According to mythical stories, Obatala created people with disabilities while drunk on palm wine, making him the patron deity of such people. People born with congenital defects are called eni orisa literally, 'people of Obatala'. He is also referred to as the orisha of the north. He is always dressed in white, hence the meaning of his name, Obatala (King or ruler of the white cloth). His devotees strive to practice moral correctness as unblemished as his robe. They never worship Obatala with palm wine, palm oil or salt. They may eat palm oil and salt, but never taste palm wine.

Lots of the community were friendly with Orunmila because he was meek and peaceful and his proceedings always go in line with she who he must interact with. Orunmila was close to God the architect of the Universe. Power of Orisha was granted to him.

The supernatural is not subject to the laws of nature, or more figuratively, that which is said to exist above and beyond nature. The metaphysical considerations can be difficult to approach as an exercise in philosophy or theology because any dependencies on its antithesis, the natural, will ultimately have to be inverted or rejected. In popular culture and fiction, the supernatural is whimsically associated with the paranormal and the occult.

While the meaning of the term and its antithesis vary, the 'Supernatural Order' is the gratuitous production, by God, of the ensemble of miracles for the elevation of man to a state of grace, including the hypostatic union (Incarnation), the beatific vision, and the ministry of angels. Divine operation, 'spiritual facts' and 'voluntary determinations' are consistently referred to as 'supernatural' by those who specifically preclude the 'extrinsic concurrence' of God or by those espousing a materialist or determinist worldview that excludes immaterial beings or free will.

Sometimes call supernatural the miraculous way in which certain effects, in themselves natural, are produced, or certain endowments (like man's immunity from death, suffering, passion, and ignorance) that bring the lower class up to the higher though always within the limits of the created. Orunmila started from a comprehensive view of the natural order taken, in its amplest acceptation, for the aggregate of all created entities and powers, including the highest natural endowments of which the rational creature is capable, and even such Divine operations as are demanded by the effective carrying out of the cosmic order. The supernatural order is then more than a miraculous way of producing natural effects when, there are problem is a concept of Orunmila

The supernatural order consists in the manifestation of being in perception of reality,

One complicating factor is that there is no universal agreement about the definition of 'natural' or the limits of naturalism. Concepts in the supernatural domain are closely related to concepts in religious spirituality and occultism or spiritualism. Additionally, by definition anything that exists naturally is not supernatural.

The term 'supernatural' is often used interchangeably with paranormal or preternatural the latter typically limited to an adjective for describing abilities which appear to exceed the bounds of possibility. Orunmila stands within the relationship between the supernatural and the natural is indistinct in terms of natural phenomena and what was going on around him and against whatever violates the laws of nature.

Many supporters of supernatural explanations believe that past, present, and future complexities and mysteries of the universe cannot be explained solely by naturalistic means and argue that it is reasonable to assume that a non-natural entity or entities resolve the unexplained.

From a perspective, some events occur according to the laws of nature, and others occur according to a separate set of principles external to known nature.

When I, my mother and younger brother moved from Lagos to Ibadan my mother rented a four bedroom flat owned by an Ibadan man who owns bread making factory. At his time I was just entering my second year at secondary school. I became engrossed in religious activities attending Baptist church and Gospel church e.g. deeper life evangelical ministry and revivals.

Our dwelling at the man who owned several bread making firm, was short lived because on three occasions we were visited by snakes inside the house which was observed by me. My first experience was observing a snake which was already inside the front door of the house. It was moving towards my bed room as the snake saw me; it raised its head as it saw me but moved away and made its way outside the house. As it was moving away I heard a voice radiating around the snake it said in Yoruba Orunmila we came to greet you. I dear not over emphasis this because of its relevance to many people and culture or, may be the interpretation was Orunmila sent us to greet you. Till this very day I do still perceive images of the incidents of each particular snake I experienced had made its way into the house. Never once had it given me unpleasant feelings or paranoia nevertheless it has something of a paranoia. It was not the only time I had such similar experiences.

The second occasion was inside our kitchen by the gas cooker it was on a Saturday afternoon my mother was in the house I told her there was a snake in the kitchen; she went up to the four story building and called for help.

The family who own the house occupied the top floor of the house, which was twice the one we live in. They were a large group of family. Two men came down with my mother to the kitchen and caught the brown snake and took it upstairs to examine it. In some cases a snake caught would defiantly be used for juju, it might be roasted to remove the skin and left it inside houses or taken to a juju priest.

The third occasion was after I came back from school one afternoon. I was having a siestas in my bedroom already asleep, a light shown at me with a voices I heard saying to me wakeup there is a snake inside the house.

I wake up abruptly and looked around my bedroom. I saw nothing but as I went through the door leading from my bedroom to the living room I saw a snake. I dashed bake into my bed room and got hold of some of my shoes. I saw that the snake had turn back towards the entrance of the house it was too late for me taking further action as it made its way out of the house, it was a white snake with green patched making its way out of the house enough said my mother suggesting we have to move home.

My mother made decision we worship at a Aladura church at (Ori-Oke) which is, similar in worship to celestial or Aladura church of worship located on top of a mountain within Ibadan and Ife known as (Ori-oke) It's no way similar to such location is Olumo Rock at Abeokuta in Ogun state which is a tourist attraction. It is known elsewhere oracles are consulted with white women involved.

This was the second time we worshiped at a church similar to Ori-Oke the first place we worshiped, was at Badagry in Lagos state. Something came over me to ask my mother why, weren't they wearing white cloths on our first visit at the church she said, she would explain it to me later. When we moved to Ibadan we began attending Aladura church none as Mercy Church of Jerusalem based on Cherubim and Seraphim fountain with its head of the church as Mr. Alagba Babatunde. I was ordained as a church warden and centurion I wore white rob and a red band tied around my waist for which am known as (Elemi Orun) (having a spirit form heaven). Elemi in Yoruba means a spirited person. This was after our worship at Ori-Oke which is quite a distance from Orita-Challenge where we lived. Elemi means 'the owner of the spirit' to the Yoruba's. God as Elemi gives life to man just before birth he is also believed to control the climatic seasons and movement of heavenly bodies.

Other scenarios of this nature also take place in Abeokuta in Ogun state which did not bother me. White women from Europe could be ordained as priestess some of them make themselves as part of these deities to put checks on the use of jujus. It is an issue that have been scotching West Africa for a very long time. Some of those who practice it could be at times very mean.

This was more reason why I like women curates such as the cruet at Saint John Reverend Christen Bambridge who took over from Reverend April Keech at Saint John's church Lewisham because April Keech received a called from God she should move on.

We all worship one God but in different ways and perspectives to reach deeper levels and meaning relating to our nature, culture, heritage and existence. This was what brought Orunmila and Orisia together for a common goal. As of today in Africa European women most of who are Christian priest have made Africa a part of their lives through the religion of Christianity and understanding of Africa's deities.

God moves in mysteries way he is about to make us all one happy big family after our death and the next stage of our existence. There could be many gods or deities but who ever defies truth would face eternal extinction.

When you say that someone has a wild imagination means that this person has the ability to think and dream about anything; the person has very vivid and colourful thoughts.

Cognitive psychology talks about thoughts but our lives are much more led by what we imagine which is more hypnotic than cognitive.

Depression, anticipatory anxiety even the vivid uncontrolled imaginings of Post traumatic stress disorder and schizophrenia all entail massive firing of uncontrolled imagination. Dreams are processed through powerful imaginings. We don't cognitively decide what to dream we spontaneously imagine vivid dream narratives which sometimes can terrify us or please us.

Learning to gain more control of our imaginations as well as our thoughts and actions which both spring from imagination is an integral part to developing and overcoming psychological difficulties.

Imagination is the ability of forming new images and sensations when they are not perceived through sight, hearing, or other senses. Imagination helps provide meaning to experience and understanding to knowledge; it is a fundamental faculty through which people make sense of the world. It plays key roles in our learning process. It is a whole cycle of image formation or any sensation which may be described as 'hidden' as it takes place without anyone else's knowledge. A person may imagine according to his mood, it may be good or bad depending on the situation. Some people imagine in a state of tension or gloominess in order to calm themselves. It is accepted as the innate ability and process of inventing partial or complete personal realms within the mind from elements derived from sense perceptions of the shared world.

'Imagination is an effort of the mind to develop a discourse that had previously been known, a development of concept of what is already there by the help of reason.

Imagination are linked in the brain, paves the way to better understand one's ability to link significant past experiences with their imagination.

Imagination differs fundamentally from belief because the subject understands what is personally invented by the mind does not necessarily affect the course of action taken in the apparently shared world, while beliefs are part of what one holds as truths about both the shared and personal worlds. It follows that the learned distinction between imagination and belief depends in practice on religion, tradition, and culture.

Medical definition of imagination an act or process of forming a conscious idea or mental image of something never before wholly perceived in reality by the one forming the images as through a synthesis of remembered elements of previous sensory experiences or ideas as modified by unconscious mechanisms; *also* the ability or gift of forming such conscious ideas or mental images especially for the purposes of artistic or intellectual creation.

Field studying the relationships of social, psychological, and behavioural factors on bodily processes and quality of life in humans and animals. The influence that the mind has over physical processes including the manifestations of disabilities that are based on intellectual infirmities, rather than actual injuries or physical limitations is manifested in treatment by phrases such as the power of suggestion, the use of 'positive thinking' and concepts like 'mind over matter'.

However, while it is necessary to identify if an illness has a physical basis, it is recognized more and more that the effort to identify disorders as purely physical or mixed psychosomatic is increasingly obsolete as almost all physical illness have mental factors that determine their onset, presentation, maintenance, susceptibility to treatment, and resolution.

I was having a conversation with a friend on the afternoon of the 23th of August 2006 from my way back to my flat from shopping from boots the chemist, Sainsbury's, toping up my O2 mobile phone it was a pleasant day in Woolwich, it rained with sun shine coming through the sky through my windows, as I word process.

Ten new hospitals would do a great deal for Britain not many see the plight of little children today confused not knowing which way to turn in the right direction, I might be a celibate,

I do a lot of thinking about moral values and what it takes to be a parent. For children to be born in hospitals given all facets to be who they are for what they are worth is what every child hopes for. I mean place like hospitals care homes make a contribution to our quality of life even lifestyles.

On April 2010 honesty is being asked off politicians over hospital cuts a coalition of charities and patient groups said politicians are not being open and honest about the issues of hospital closures. Jeremy Taylor head of National Voices said, the parties were happy talking about the need for savings and moving care into the communities, He said they were shying away from the flip-side-services closing and even a whole hospital shutting down the whole political parties claim they all have clear policies on how to tackle the issues.

What qualifies any one for being a parent? Someone to look up to I guess or someone to do your bidding before and after your dearth it is an opportunity for parents and children to be dedicated, be truthful towards one another and to cherish love and affection.

Places of interest makes me feel wanted, neither rash nor irrational, are my type of place and people. From my youth, I have always wanted people to live among themselves with cohesion. We should no longer be racist against each other. Racism leads to diversity which hinders cohesion.

If relationship gets out of hand, the result would be conflict, probably war. Being a peaceful person does not mean, you would get attention, who cares for the peace makers? The police and lawyers are peace makers so are you and me in our community the police and the court are our; oversees.

I am not in the UK because of my illness feeling sorry for myself; there are others in a far worse condition struggling to make ends meet with all sorts of illness. The UK as a welfare state is always ready to fulfil its obligation as a welfare state even when its economy is in crisis

With my illness, I have studied at two different universities.

Ann Robinson on television weakest-link on certain documentaries involved University students' people from all works of life and most recent students who had studied at more than one University showing their test of knowledge.

I always enjoy Ann's reactions when a contestant is voted off 'you are the weakest-link good by'. The world is at a state of the art, it is survival for the fittest all over the world but whom among them, is drawing the contestant behind?

I at one time said to Loraine, with me and you studying at the same University, your father graduated from in which your mother was also a staff why haven't we met each other long before we met?

Why didn't both of us grow up from our childhood in the UK, you and I are about to enter our 30th years of age, what have you and I, been waiting for Loraine? The same question applies to me what have I been waiting for? If both of us had resided in the UK during our youth, could we have met before now and be friends? Could we have given birth before now to our first child? All Loraine gave me that morning was a shrug and facial expression.

I told her how I very much wanted to study at one of the universities in Nigeria why does it always happen to me, there is no longer absolute free education in the UK. She replied by asking me is it because of the student loan we have to pay back? Yes I replied. Then I said to her am happy the student loans company is based at Scotland from your parents' background so nothing can go wrong if I do not pay it back. She smiled.

Loraine said she knew how African students feel at primary schools if at 11 or 12 years they were not out of primary school' I told her in my time at primary school I was 11 years and there were 15 and 17 years old pupil in my class.

I told her with my illness, there was little point for me to undergo a University degree course. I mean I said to her I am unwell but I needed a change in my job, I wanted to work. Another reason I told her, I enrolled at the universities was with the hope, in doing so, my illness would be overlooked my children would say something right about me; in which case I would be given employment opportunities as anyone else regardless of my illness. It was after these our conversation I felt I was somehow embarrassed about my illness.

We were both working at the same time, while we were at University studying. It got to a point, we hardly see each other, when we saw each other, we are just like friends and not like two people in love it was the way we wanted our relationship to be and I am not forceful by nature, I guess in some way, we were trying to impress or encourage each other.

From February 2007 more young people are out of work, most people working are feeling unrest because of the conflicts in Iraq, Egypt, Libya, Afghanistan and the Middle East. Employment is slowing down; businesses are in economic crisis all over the world.

What can one do without getting hurt? I think, I did the right thing to have plunged myself into education there is nobody too young or too old to be educated. I consider the wealth my father had; my interest depicted I wanted to be educated, in a Nigerian University whilst I was with him at Port-Harcourt.

With my good grades after my secondary school education at Ibadan, I got entry into the University of Port-Harcourt to study geography; my father was known to be careless about his children. This was one reason, why I bragged at my father for the first time in my life on his second visit to the UK, after my arrival. Take a look at the prospects of education in the UK what, has he got to say?

It was when I had a row with him in London 1993 that some consideration was drowned on my father to look into the needs of his children. We all in the family know him as a self centred man, if not for my action, I doubt if two of my step brothers and two of my step younger sisters would have had the opportunity of becoming graduates in Nigeria before our father died at Ibadan in 2004. I would not say actually it's as a result of my own doing its more to do with their own mothers who, had contributed in making me who, I am. In my own opinion as regards to the situation I would have considered myself to be thoughtless. I need not look or hold to heart the way my step mothers had treated me in my youth if I should consider treating them right at least they would look back and do a rethink on how they had treated me. My late parents relationship never went into a divorce it was due to my father's actions several of them which induced my mother into a relationship with someone else through which, I had a step brother for example, he brought his two wives with him and his children from Port Harcourt to live close to her at Lagos. My mother's relationship with someone else indicates my mother understands my late father in view of their relationship, I would not hold it that my father's death at Ibadan Oyo state impresses me because it leaves me an indication that politic is involved on whose sides dose it sounds right in view of their relationship I should take sides because he died at Ibadan I have lived in Nigeria I understand family politics the manner of my father's death would not drive me to such a point. Married to three wives after my mother's relationship with him he became a chieftaincy title holder during which time my mother was not present within his household or at his chieftaincy ceremony after which he got married to his fourth wife just after my mother's death.

There should be calls for honest debate on religion multi-culture in Britain, in tackling extremism, being socially withdrawn, how to facie the community bravely in which we live in. All working environment would be much safer if we all strife to eradicate social segregation.

Other nations in the EU need to make the same contribution as Britain dose, an open door policies, with the greatest amount of people all around the world residing in Britain. Without Britain and the Americans most of us, would not know what is going on around the world.

27th of December 2007 I was at the Queen Elizabeth Hospital regarding my having pains behind my neck. I was told to stay on Ibuprofen Dr Magarey prescribed for me and ibuprofen ointment. 4th January 2008 I mentioned to Dr Jan Deacon I was seven months premature apart from other things we talked about regarding my illness.

She said on our last meeting before this one, I told her I was moving furniture's in my flat and laying new carpet, and my work at the Woolwich Gala club lifting shutters whilst opening up, could have contributed to my having pains behind my neck. She prescribed Diclofenac sodium E/C tablets 50 mg, to be taken three times a day and paracetamol tablets.

Desperate Kate and Garry MaCann lunched a publicity blitz across Morocco in new drive in tracing their missing daughter; more than 11,500 letters and poster have been sent businesses in North African countries after reports that, their four year old daughter Madeleine MaCann had been spotted in the region. On the 7th of May 2009 a new lead came up with a description of someone seen close to Madeleine I hope and pray that Kate and Garry MaCann finds their daughter alive. Its March 2012 Madeleine MaCann is yet to be found.

Heavy snow fall in Northern Island, traffic, road, houses affected, avalanched in Spain hit of-pate area, candidate for American presidency race election and the need for change in America in the present defining moment of history. Kenyan election rigging, cause and mascara at least three hundred people were dead.

It was one of my last initiatives apart from trying to enlist in the Nigeria army; I wanted to join the Nigerian air force this was why I chose geography as a prospect at the University of Port-Harcourt which will at the sometime enhance my chances of being a pilot in the Nigerian airways. It was practically impossible in Western Nigerian because there was no air force base in Western Nigeria apart from Lagos state that I knew of and, I do not know of any in Eastern Nigeria except the Nigerian Naval Base at Port-Harcourt. If I wanted to join the air force, I would have to go to the North.

It meant I would have to go all the way to Northern Nigeria If I had to embark on any of these military careers. For me, it was better than any of the current University at that time. I would have just rush in and out because of its new infrastructure rather than any of the universities in Nigeria which were already crumbled with poor hygiene standards.

Adamawa is a state in north-eastern Nigeria, with its capital at Yola. It was formed in 1991 from part of Gongola State with four administrative divisions namely: Adamawa, Ganye, Mubi and Numan. It is one of the thirty-six (36) States which constitute the Federal Republic of Nigeria.

Following a massive overhaul of the education system in Adamawa State by the Nyako administration, UBEC reportedly adjudged improvements in that sector the best in the country.

The executive chairman of the Adamawa State Universal Basic Education Board, Dr. Salihu Bakali, who spoke to Leadership Weekend, said in the first eight years of democracy, nothing had been put in place to meet up with the growing school population.

He said during a school condition survey, they met schools without classrooms and those that were densely overpopulated.

'The Nyako administration inherited more than 700 schools without a single classroom. Students were sitting on stones and wood. They had schools with about 200 pupils in one classroom, while some schools were running a shift system. They did not know how many teachers they had, or how many students were enrolled in the system,' he revealed which was described as a rotten school.

While assessing the impact they have made on the quality of education so far, he said although they had not yet started recording improved results in the SSCE/WAEC, there was tangible improvement, adding, 'Parents are withdrawing their children from private schools back to public schools because of the reinvigorated confidence in the system.'

He revealed that what got them the recognition as the best in the country was the fact that they had been going by the

UBEC programme, which provides for free tuition, infrastructure to schools, free textbooks as well as working materials.

'UBEC programme is supposed to be adopted by all the states. It is supposed to be implemented in accordance with the national policy on education, which has been bastardised, or even neglected by some states.' The Northwest Des Moines Rotary plans pursue another project in northern Nigeria after helping to improve the lives of residents there by helping to enhance a school. Dr. Diana Reed is a member of the Rotary Club of Northwest Des Moines and past governor of Rotary District 6000. In 2007, she visited Nigeria as part of a team of Rotary members whose mission included vaccinating children against polio. In addition, the team sought humanitarian projects that could be developed between Nigerian Rotary clubs and clubs in Iowa.

As a result of a proposal developed during Reed's visit, the Rotary Club of Northwest Des Moines sponsored some much-needed improvements in the Baban Dodo LEA Primary School in Kaduna, Nigeria. This school of 892 students lacked toilets, so the students could only use the ground outside the school. Faculty members went to their homes for bathroom breaks, which disrupted the school day. Northwest Des Moines Rotary contributed $2,500 toward a grant to correct the situation. The Rotary of North Scott added $1,000. The seed money met the requirement for a Rotary Matching Grant and the project collected $19,670 total. The Rotary Club of Kakuri-Kaduna in Nigeria has subsequently seen to the construction of the toilet facilities.

The money also allowed the purchase of chairs and tables for the school so students no longer have to learn their lessons sitting on the bare floor.

Kaduna state was the successor to the old Northern Region of Nigeria, which had its capital at Kaduna. In 1967 this was split up into six states, one of which was the North-Central State, whose name was changed to Kaduna State in 1976. This was further divided in 1987, losing the area now part of

<u>Katsina State</u>. Under the governance of Kaduna is the ancient city of <u>Zaria</u>.

The Nigerian Defence Academy (NDA) at <u>Kaduna</u> is the only Military <u>University</u> in Nigeria. The NDA was established in January 1964 as a reformation of the British run Royal Military Forces Training College (RMFTC), which had been renamed the Nigerian Military Training College (NMTC) on independence. The military institution trains the officer corps of the Nigerian Army, Navy and Air Force. The initial class was only 62 <u>cadets</u>, and trainers were mostly officers in the <u>Indian Army</u>.

The NDA grew to an all Nigerian training staff only in 1978. In 1981 it began training bilateral training of foreign militaries. In 1985 the academy opened up its doors to the civilian population, offering undergraduate programmers' and post graduate studies both for <u>Msc</u> and <u>Ph.D</u> students both for the military and civilians studies. The central mission remains the five year cadet officer training 'Regular Combatant Course', although from 2002, a four year military programme was also offered. As of 2008, its total cadet class is around 1500.

I was sure two years after leaving Nigeria for the UK; The Nigerian Defence Academy in Northern Nigeria might have been no different from the debilitating states as the rest of the Universities. I was biased about my parental background and the influence of Northern Nigeria; it would also have been unfavourable for me to come out with my best in my military career because of my family background and business affairs.

If I had been left to be whatever I wanted to be in the Nigerian army, by the early 1990'S I would have become a brigadier making my way up to the rank of a major general. Being in the Nigerian Defence Academy for awhile, I had done what, I had to do.

In this case, my intention was instead of me making a switch as superman did with the three exiles from the Planet Krypton to have disrobed them of their powers, he now ran himself underground with the infrastructures of the military base of the Nigerian Defence Academy in Northern Nigeria; in other to emasculate himself.

I wanted to embed myself into the base, and made it my home. Or what do most people know about Prime Minister Tony Blair in his term in office as prime Minster of Great Britain put a motion through for the decommissioning of weapons in Northern Ireland?

My brother, wife and children come over to visit me at my flat. On their visit to my flat on Christmas day 2007 their mother wanted to go into a discussion about my illness in the presences of their children. What she said was (Let us talk about your illness) not within five munities of their arrival in my flat.

I tuned the conversation down immediately; my illness would not be discussed in the presence of the children.

Turning down my sister in laws open discussion during a festive season of Christmas and coming New Year, in the presence of her children and my brother I felt there would have been nothing wrong if my sister in law Nwamaka simply just ask me how I felt instead of let's talk about your illness or can we talk about your illness which she or my brother had never at any time said or asked any question about since 1995. If it was about my illness, I know they talk about me in their home and its obvious the children know am unwell. If there was anything bordering them about my illness, she and my brother can visit me privately then, we could have had a conversation about my illness.

I made a light matter out of my sister in law question about my illness; instead I brought out my late father's hand book of his funeral ceremony looked at it, taking note of their body language reaction.

They were present in my father's burial ceremony, they did not bring me his funeral pamphlet since they were present for the occasion in Nigeria, rather it was my eldest brother Barrister Oritseweyinmi, who brought my father's burial ceremony pamphlet to me in the UK.

All they brought were a cup, an umbrellas and a tray with our father's inscription on them, which they might have made as their own presentation and contribution. While there was cloths for the occasion about, two different types which Barrister Oritseweyinmi brought with him and the pamphlet.

I looked at my brother and his wife and children as if even if I wasn't present in my father's funeral, they cannot deny the fact that they knew my father was using me through the coral bead he gave back to me in their presence and in their flat at Brockley.

Which was too late for it having any meaning, usefulness or significance to me, and why did they bring me cups and trays? Only if they had known, I have work to be done, for the simple reason that my father handed back the coral bead to me, with his intention of using the coral bead in my possession and through me to initiate himself through reincarnation into the UK.

My brother or his wife might also want the coral bead for themselves or to enforce with the rituals inscribed on the coral bead. This is how cultural object of African jujus operate. Meanwhile, they and other people especially within our family would also, want possession of the coral bead for their own use after my father's death, but they cannot have it from me.

For several reasons I was not obliged to pave way for my father's wish but I gave him the opportunity he wanted. It was an opportunity for me to confine and imprison myself in other to expel myself from my krypton because through its concurrencies I chose to be expendable and expedient through human interaction.

At this time I wouldn't want the coral bead any more since it was handed back to me and I would be foolish to give it to my relatives or friend. The thought came to me I should give it to them as a gift not when it had been something in relation to me and my father, knowing what my father had used it for, to prolong his life, the more foolish I would have been, if I should give it to someone else.

Nevertheless I felt I had gone through its theorem inclination, I have been used and I have had the experiences of what culture and African myth could be. I am not only a man of steel; the blood that runs through my veins is of culture while, my Krypton is now, a spent force.

Though my father was dead I had the feelings he knew even in his grave, what I had done with the coral bead. For me it's an experience for the rest of my existence. Is there anything wrong in being a slave? Just as we have good slaves, so do we have bad slaves, such as we could have good masters, so also, do we have bad masters every faith is a two sided coin.

What makes me think the flowing stream of Oshun is related to the Olumo Rock, my late mother's last job was at Nigerian Leyland Motors at Ibadan; her job was imputing data on computer, filing, and check stocks of Leyland motors spear parts. She was given training on her job. It went well for her because; they employed her as a full time employee I visited her twice at her working place before I left Ibadan for Port Harcourt to live and work for my late father this was after, I had completed my secondary education.

This was after my mother's employment at R.T. Briscoe pharmaceutical company as secretary at Lagos within my stay in the UK for over twenty years; I came to experience the reincarnation of my late mothers as a white English young girl. I am not supposed to tell her age.

My late mother is from Abeokuta it is believed when the native people dies they are compelled to wait below Olumo Rock until, the Oshun river comes at certain time, moving them to the centre of the river after cleansing, they are brought back to life again. Olumo sprang from a Rock while the Oshun River sprang from the flowing streams with a goddess known as Oshun she rules the river which sustains life.

At the same time of working at Leyland Nigerian motors Ibadan, my late mother had a business of selling drinks hopping it would enable her build a house on her plot of land at Abeokuta. 'I told her at one time mummy you are educated, you are working. You are not making much profit from your business of selling drinks 'except in my opinion, she turns her business to a bear pallor, which, she was not cut out for.

She was cut out for an administrative job. For the years I spent living with my mother at Ibadan, right from the time we moved into the house of the bread maker until we moved to Mr. Osibowale' house, my mother still carried out her business as a soft drink and bear retailer.

I saw the rebirth of my late mother in the UK   I felt she knew the source from which, she came into life and she had created a sort of life is a circle for herself and her children.

If Miss Loraine O'Connor should come back into my life, we would just have to live a life of just being friends, though, a little more than friends.   Miss Loraine and I have spent our youth growing up in Africa. I grew up in West Africa; she grew up in South Africa.

Considering what I have experienced with my mother's reincarnation Miss Lorain O'Connor could be living in this world in the same disposition should I be adamant to spend a romantic life with Lorain and if the person I saw was my mother in a new reincarnation in the UK how would I feel if in the future in her new reincarnation, she has a relationship with someone from Africa, Jamaica or Caribbean origin considering her trials in Africa now a totally different person in colour and race. A disposition is a habit, a preparation, a state of readiness or a tendency to act in a specified way. Most women are forced into marriages these day, we should not confuse love without reality and disposition. There is certain disposition one could be in, in this world that they would hope to have wings to fly away from it. The present life of my mother disposition cannot be taken for a grey area.

Love is an emotion of a strong affection and personal

attachment. Love is also said to be a virtue representing all of human kindness, compassion, and affection —'the unselfish loyal and benevolent concern for the good of another'. Love may describe compassionate and affectionate actions towards other humans, one's self or animals.

In English, love refers to a variety of different feelings, states, and attitudes, ranging from pleasure ('I loved that meal') to interpersonal attraction ('I love my partner'). 'Love' may refer specifically to the passionate desire and intimacy of romantic love, to the sexual love of eros, to the emotional closeness of familial love, to the platonic love that defines friendship, or to the profound oneness or devotion of religious love, or to a concept of love that encompasses all of those feelings. This diversity of uses and meanings, combined with the complexity of the feelings involved, makes love unusually difficult to consistently define, compared to other emotional states.

Love in its various forms acts as a major facilitator of interpersonal relationships and, owing to its central psychological importance, is one of the most common themes in the creative arts.

Love may be understood as part of the survival instinct, a function to keep human beings together against menaces and to facilitate the continuation of the species.

The terms dispositional belief and occurrent belief refer, in the former case, to a belief that is held in the mind but not currently being considered, and in the latter case, to a belief that is currently being considered by the mind.

Dispositions are the natural tendencies of each individual to take on a certain position in any field. There is no strict determinism through one's dispositions. In fact, the habitués is the choice of positions according to one's dispositions. However, in retrospect a space of possibilities can always be observed.

Entering the 21st century immigration is high in the UK people from third world nation are immigrating into the UK they seems to be giving me something of a replica of who my parents were when I was born in the1960s.

West Africa has changed even those in the streets, are now open eyed they are now more aware of what is going on around the world if they think, they are going back to the same opportunities and welcome my parents had when, they went back to Nigeria they should be doing a rethink of the situation.

When my parents came to the UK then there was a craze and frenzy to be in Europe to be educated. It was like going to the moon and when you get back to Africa, you receive a welcome.

When one is submissive to outside forces; which in the future have to be accountable for the resultant effects are that choices have to be made, faced with the temperaments on which the choice have to be made. Depending on the choices we make, the level, we make the choice depends on if it leads to coherency of making good the situation.

The numbers of children born in the UK each day from African descents are getting higher each year. It is time for Jamaicans, Barbados and the Caribbean's to stop going on about slavery otherwise the more we feel like slaves it's a reverie we and our children have to get out of. We are the once enslaving ourselves the case by now should be, that we have leant a lot.

We have to look into our ethnology it's already spelt out, how long would we go on grumbling let us give the children a chance, just for the sake of peace and development or in darkness shall we remain. What these children from African descent comes into the UK to become are like Jamaican, Caribbean's, Barbados and people from Trinidad we should see ourselves as one and strife towards unity and friendship we cannot learn from each other, if we are divers.

Just one look at my our mother's lives let us make them feel they have used their whole life and efforts bringing us up and working for us let us make them feel they have brought us up to justify something we have always wanted out of life to work through, the most difficult of moments in our trials of life.

My mother's studies in nursing led to her work for R.T Briscoe pharmaceutical company at Apapa Lagos, the very heart of Lagos Port, closed to my father's offices as a joint owner of Star warehouse clearing and forwarding company.

This when we moved from Warri then under Bendel state of Nigeria to Port-Harcourt at this time, my father was working in the shipping business, when he had his third wife Mrs. Aya Megbele.

After which we moved from Port –Harcourt at Rivers state to Lagos the whole family except my mother and his first born son Mr. Olu Megbele all moved to Lagos in 1975 we took resident at number 2 Lawani close Yaba Lagos.

I and my immediate elder brother Mr. Omagbemi Megbele enrolled at Saint Patrick's primary School Yaba Lagos, to continue our primary education. For the second time I saw my mother and got aquatinted with her, while the whole family was at Delta state and Port-Harcourt, my mother was residing at Lagos state.

The first time I saw my mother was at Port-Harcourt when she paid us a visit. She wanted to take me back at the time, my father would not consent it wasn't a good time for my mother to take me back because she had just began to get over the tremor of her chartered relationship with my father.
As for me, this was when my life in Africa actually began. It turned into something of which the after mounts forced me to return to the source I emanated from. Partly because my life had been laid out for me for me to have ventured to intervene into the forces of nature but I would not, my life at each stage starts at the very epicentre of all tribulations and to its end.

When we moved from Port-Harcourt to Lagos state, I and my immediate elder brother Mr. Omagbemi enrolled at Saint Patricks Primary school, for some unknown reasons I chose to be a Mass servant at the Roman Catholic Church within my primary school. You do not just know when one has to be born again it just take hold of the person.

What a huge church it was, always packed full with worshipers. After my baptism at a Methodist church our family was well known with friends and relatives. Both of my father's wives had no job until almost after the end of the all West African FESTAC 1977. Mrs. Aya Megbele had contracts in selling house hold goods e.g. electric fan, Hoovers, carpets while later Mrs. Codelia Megbele had a contract of running the canteen at Pfizer pharmaceutical company. As much as I know my father's wives had to fend for themselves.

By this time, my mother had won a lottery ticket for a two bed room flat under the Nigerian government during the all West African FESTAC 1977 celebration.

At this time the FESTAC 77 was almost over my uncle Tamitayo Akinlami moved in with us on their returned from America, with his daughters born in America and his first wife. If you know Africans very well and the way we live our lives in Africa, it was time for some unscrupulous event to take place. I was about 8 years going to nine years. I was too young to know my father and this uncle of mine had a close relationship or not.

This episode in my life, concerns his second daughter my cosine Miss. Layiwola Akinlami and me, who was 7 or 8 years of age. as a matter of fact, the condition in which I was being brought up as a young lad then could not had given me the time, thoughts or feeling to have fondled my cosine Layiwola though I was traumatised about the experience growing up I felt I was being cautioned in making a choice about my marital life when I get older. Whatever could had brought it up would had been the type of relationship my father and his brother had when they were growing up not all conflicts are bad regardless if there are conflicts, there are situation that arise which makes people draw close relationship likely if it would benefit both parties while other people not involved in the conflict would learn from it. My uncle had reasons to move close to my father since he works in shipping clearing and forwarding. My uncle moving close to my father might contribute in helping him through the procedures of clearing the goods my uncle brought home with him from America if the reason for his coming closer to my father did not seem well, I am not surprised at his reaction the children of both parties should not form a close relationship after my uncle moved out of my father's dwelling to his own dwelling I only saw my uncle and some of his family just twice before I left Nigeria

Though we had several housekeepers if they had to leave I had to wash cloths, fetch water each day; I could not do well at my primary school yet striving to be a mass servant at Saint Patrick primary school Yaba Lagos.

At certain point I felt the world was crumbling down on me. In respect to this, I was not happy within myself but remained resilient but less bubbling a young lad as I used to be when we were at Port-Harcourt. The idea of knowing my true mother that, she was around in Lagos comforted me.

The house we all as a family occupied at Yaba Lagos state, was divided into four blocks of flat, it was a one story building divided into four different dwellings divided into two blocks. Barrister Aronmolarun and his family occupied the ground floor of both blocks of the house while my family occupied the top floor.

At some distance, there was a river we called (Ogbe River) within proximity with the University of Lagos. Children could go through it from behind the Ogbe River, to the University. I was one of those children and we sometimes fetch water from the river; I grow up having something of a secret personality attached to the house we live in and the river as time went by.

This secret personality I suffer from I never realised until after sometime because at its initial stage all I was doing at the river was fetching water or when I had time to play with my play mates.

This went on for some few months until I noticed after years while am asleep, I seems to came out of my body in astral form in which I forth with unseen forces. Sometimes I wake up from my sleep especially in the afternoon sweating and breathing heavily.

It was my first experience of realising I had strength that should be expendable, something of an exorcist. The river had swampy areas with crabs, snakes, bird's e.g. colourful parrots and insect e.g. dragon flies.

The river was also used by celestial worshipers, lighting and burning of different colours of candles, wearing white robs singing clapping their hands in public when they go out to pray or for baptism or to relieve them of evil spirit, juju or African witchcraft. All this was part of my life until my late uncle Mr. Temitayo Akinlami and his family moved in with us, after, we moved in from Port-Harcourt, to Lagos.

My uncle Tamitayo was my father's younger step brother from the same mother. He came back from America and moved in with us at number 2 Lawani Street Yaba Lagos. This was about the time; the all West African FESTAC 1977 was taking place.

He was desperately looking for a business deals, not only this, he needed money to pay custom duties for the properties he brought with him from the United State of America to Nigeria. This included a Mercury car among some high classed furniture. He was very much in need of money after arriving from America this was why; he had to patch up living with his elder brother and his family.

I have frequently, asked myself why it had to be me? I was only a young lad; I had an open mind at my age, I could never have thought of doing such a thing as foundling with my cosine Layiwola! Each day in Nigerian communities, if there is not an outbreak of conflict within one neighbourhood, it would happen in the next neighbourhood unnecessary conflicts my uncle's action I told myself I would not allow to disoriented my life it made me grow up accessing my family background and relationships.

I could not hold a grudge I had no choice nobody asked questions within my family I wondered, what was happening to my life. At such an age and queer moment in my life within that particular environment I needed my earthly mothers' presence in my life more than anything in the world.

It was my mother's eldest son Mr. Oritseweyinmi Megbele and only Sister Miss. Oritsegbubemi Megbele now Mrs. Ajagunla of my mother's children, who showed any concern for me at that time of my life but could do nothing about it. As the day's activities within my family and my environment went on, after the accusation, it wearied me down. My uncle had not spent six month within my father's house before this happened I hardly saw my uncle or had any feeling he knew I exited may be, I was taken for a stranger within the house we were more than ten people living in the house. My father never asked me any questions about it. It was not customary for me approaching my father in relation to the issue rather if he wanted to, he would had called me and we talk about it. My uncle and mother are Yoruba's I took it as a setting in conflict within Yoruba's and Ibo's.

Until this day I still wonder why my uncle laid false accusations on me. He and my father I was later told, were not close brothers since their youth nevertheless, whatever made him lay false accusation on me I would never understand they were two brothers not that I fondled my cosine at the age of nine years, was uncalled for because, it never happened. I was being informed or educated as I was later told by Mrs. Cordelia Megbele that within our family a relationship with children had occurred within family members. Living in Nigeria, house could be crowded with families it is not un-heard of seduction occurs within family members. My uncle may be laying down good example, I had leant one or two things through the occurrence I appreciate his laying down good examples.

What are the causes of aggression within mental health patients? It could be anybody and not just mental health sufferers they are likely to do with life experience being religious at an earlier time before the experience might be helpful in overcoming the effect.

Anger is completely a normal human emotional characteristics natural ways of responding to anger is with aggression to fight or defend ourselves when we come under attack. Certain amount of anger is necessary for our survival. Suppressed anger can lead to depression which could ruin our lives or relationships.

Aggression is a very angry mind sometimes we do not know where our aggression manifests from; at other times it could be someone had upset us one is likely to feel humiliated the only way to go, is to fight back. Our mind could be in turmoil and forever fighting with itself. Ridding my thoughts of the invasive thoughts of my uncle's action made me depress not aggressive if I had done what he accused me of then, I could be aggressive in other to shed the horror of not living with the humiliation. Rather, it made me more focused in life to understand what could be characteristic or uncharacteristic of me.

My eldest brother from my mother's side Mr. Oritseweyinmi after school visits, to our late mothers dwelling once in a while. Before and after, she moved to her two bedrooms flat at FESTAC town on the way to Apapa Lagos Port and Badagry estate.

He was the one who informed my mother of my condition within my father's household. At this time, my immediate elder brother Mr. Omagbemi had completed his primary school education and was sent back to Port-Harcourt to attend boarding school. He had to live with the Uncle of our step mother Mrs. Aya Megbele his name is Mr. Senibo Al-well-brown.

Before leaving Nigeria for the UK, the events made me shy when approaching an opposite sex I was no longer inquisitive I observe other people with queer query without wearing a frown on my face; as time went by I realised it became part of my feature. Though I made friends with some opposite sex such as Miss. Tosin Afolabi from the same origin with my uncle Tamitayo's father from Ondo State when I moved to Ibadan the relationship never gets serious, she had tribal marks on her face and Miss. Koro

Tubonimi at Port Harcourt while working for my father. Honestly every child needs both parents.

It led to prejudice and intimidation in our family. All communities had their own laws and ways of doing things, Mr. Afolabi at Ibadan Tosin father inquired if, I had done such a thing, its outcome was, I never did such a thing, Mr. and Mrs. Afolabi wanted me to have their daughter Miss. Tosin Afolabi as a girl friend. Miss. Tosin Afolabi was the first female child of her parents.

Just after we moved from Port-Hacrout to Lagos state with Ebenezer Obe and Sony Ade notable juju musician band played at Ondo state for our uncle Temitayos eldest sister Miss. Sola Akinlami's marriage to Mr. Tyco's- Lawson.

1980 my mother, I and my step brother Mr. Sola Awe moved to Ibadan. We became not only friends with the Afolabi family. We lived in the same neighbourhood. Tosin and her mother looked after my younger brother Mr Sola Awe whilst my mother was at work and I was at secondary school. Miss. Tosin Afolabi's mother had a business of making and selling (Ogi pap and Moymoy) Ogi is made of ground maize while Moymoy is made of ground beans.

Africans having tribal marks on their face and bodies is not as it uses to be, my eldest sister from my mother's side because of the unique relationship of our parent would have had tribal mark on her face with less intensity, compared to those of Miss. Tosin Afolabi and her mother. In which case my sister Mrs. Oritsegbubemi Ajagunla would have had tribal mark depicting culture within Delta state and Abeokuta how can when my parents intermarriage and are spaced apart within two different cultures in Africa nevertheless my sisters marriage to Mr. Ajagunla who, is Yoruba is somehow a tribal mark within two different culture and origin.

My sisters would have had tribal marks on her face, my father had tribal marks on his back, Miss Tosin Afolabi and her mother had tribal marks on their face and body which they patronise themselves by.

My mother had no tribal marks on her you could ascertain culture in relation to how tribal mark, looks and clothing are worn which interprets personality, culture and tradition in various region of Nigeria. View my situation as premature birth living under such culture some of which could have led, to my emotional content or drive such as stress which could lead to mental health problems.

When such people with tribal marks die, they have children, relative do they really die going back to where their tribal inscription was written? Of cause they are backed by deities could they inscribe when they would die say return to the place of the deity

If yes how long have women been menstruating after, being driven out from the Garden of Eden? Scientist, engineers know about the components of the Abyss African culture through tribal marks confirm to this they believe, they are children of the soil, they have ways of reasoning as archaeologists in their own terms in relation to their environment.

In relation to superman strength and configuration of his molecular structure it is obvious such an individual as superman, had if he had genetic nature it was based on the genetic nature of the planet he came from.

If his molecular dense structure should become expendable for a reason he becomes a spent force through such process, likely for those who have insight into the spiritual to them, his molecular dense structure could be a spectrum.

What can a lighted candle mean to superman structure, if not a spectrum? By just steering at a lighted candle, he could see into the future while the concept of using electricity was to have made superman glow world wide right from below, the Abyss of Africa, where lies, plants and trees of the choicest fruits, wild life and landscape one could find nowhere else in this planet. If not for the presence of the Europeans, there would never have been electricity in Africa existence is a frog jump.

How many children are living in the UK who know what it is to slaughter poultries i.e. chicken, goat, sheep's and, why do the American call cows/cattle herds' and why should another meaning for Cow be described as a disagreeable woman.

The domestics of poultries in Africa is quite different from how, it is done in the UK, I have never come across an African child in the UK asking why there are no large varieties of trees in the UK with edible fruits. All you see are skyscrapers, masterpiece of science and technology.

Computers are an interface in every environment in the UK; no head stands above a computer. This, in my opinion is the creation of another Krypton crystal. Would we go on spilling blood forever? Or would Krypton bring it to an end? Or is it left unto humanity. If superman at such a stage has completely divested himself what greater spectrum can be placed in front of him, than an electrical and microchips generated computer, a television, or a mobile phone?

Filled with knowledge about history, web sites one can obtain any information that has to do with everything to do with humans and their existence infarct comprising the whole solar system. What else could have the same nature as superman's Krypton crystal?

Scientists know most of the gases and molecules which configure the make-up of other planets and our solar system which all have something to do with human biology.

At the age of 45 years, I do not suffer from much allergies; I do not drink milk with my tea at certain times while at other time I drink lots of milk. If, I should feed on anything such as poultry, I most have prepared the meal myself. I feel, if I should drink milk, I would have, to have milked the cow myself.

People suffering from mental illness are a group of people who are suffering from something ethical, that has not yet, been defined or understood.

This is why motions where passed on by a group of cares

and patients with me as one of them that we should also be part of Oxleas NHS trust has governors and representatives.

I would be posting another application form to Oxleas NHS trust at Pinewood house once more to be elected as one of the boards of governors. I also would be posting another word processed document to the Ferryview health centre I realised the content of the document where not really in the right format, to read and understands its content, because I was traumatised, at the time of word processing them.

I was lonely, I had no one to talk to, I felt insecure this was the time I had to really brace myself up on writing about my illness as a schizophrenia and how it was affecting me. It all started after 2002 when I opted out of the University of South Bank by the elephant and castle close to SE.1 which was within a vicinity of social security benefit building when I arrived back to the UK in 1989.

I could have been an engineer, a doctor, a nurse, philosopher, sociologist, economist, geographer, a biologist, an Artist, telecommunication, or religious knowledge graduate in Nigeria. Am a very thoughtful individual, with strong reasoning powers, and abilities.

I still do not mind the idea of being in the UK, entering the 21st century, a schizophrenic sufferer, I am having to pay back a student loan of over £10,000 to student loan company in Glasgow an ancient land of history, relics of old times, solid and firm.

For we students and graduates of this 21st century, I guess what the education policy makers are saying are that lots of development have taken place in the field of science and technology. Not only this, but also that men and women of intelligence have put immersed effort towards these developments. Though we appreciate their works and the values of their products they have been given less recognition.

What others like our lectures are doing is copying, we often hear after a lecture class one or two lectures say they were going to start a business of their own. While potent right are being undervalued or the law enforcement complain of piracy.

They are of the opinion students of the 12st century will contribute less, will become reliant on the works and achievement of other people. It also leaves room and recognition of their potent right. Free education would do less in engineering them to contribute further into their work.

School leavers 'need work skills and knowledge while business leaders have long complained about school leavers' skills with school curriculum revamp outlined and they say curriculum 'is key to behaviour'

I felt I have done well enough for myself and had to persevere regardless of my condition and illness, Some people feel, surprised I can word process with my illness my mother use to have an old typewriter which we took to Ibadan with us from Lagos. I had been practising with my mother's typewriter and it came in handy.

From the moment I knew Miss Loraine O'Connor starting from Charlton Collage I had the feeling she was not a stranger in my life, she is from Scotland, I and Loraine, were a fellow student at Charlton collage in Greenwich. Some of my tutors at Charlton collage were Ms. Margie Knight, Mr. Derek Wilmot, Mr Andy, Ms. Karen Hearne and Mr. Paolo Tomeo.

Bad memories are not good in the life of any individual. It is a point at a person's life to ascertain if one could be good or evil; it is a determining factor of becoming aggressive! A good memory leads to a happy life style while disappointment could make an individual unstable in life.

The level of poverty is now high in the UK, if I and Miss Loraine relationship would had workout, not as in a conversation I over-heard within two couples, just by Sainsbury's food chain store by the Greenwich University.

They were within of 17 and 18 years, with their baby about

one and a half years old, on a push pram, crying out loud in public, while both parents were having an augment, about not having enough money, to buy baby milk for their child, she was almost in tears shouting at her partner.

Their augment gave me something to think about, if I should have rushed into our relationship having children of my own with Miss Loraine. Such epilogue of these two young couples and their child, I witness just by Sainsbury's food chain store in Woolwich, would not have been a tail of the unexpected similar to what I and Loraine's might have encountered in our relationship after some years. 2008, the rate of poverty in the UK have risen drastically.

It was once believed that, the walls of Egypt have ears, so also the walls of all nations would one day have ears. Having witnessing the two couple's ague, the more, I was determined remaining a celibate.

I have some reasons for being a cleaner. I must confess I did look forward coming back into the UK for a better life, I knew of realities I have to face or encounter. I can be in another man's land; it does not stop me from, being what I really am.

Cleaning, mopping, dusting, hovering all day, and much more i.e. my illness, with my meagre earnings as a cleaning, is not enough. My illness as paranoid schizophrenic, the way people look down on people with such illness clouded my personal life and every endeavours and achievements.

I had work experience within my father's company, working for him as account clerk. for some reason it would not do me right and certify my conscience as a working experience in the UK I basically want to from a perspective and reality, face employment with a true conscience of my own knowing what it takes to earn money through my own initiatives working and not by working for my father with loose ends to do as I wish.

No longer had I the same opportunity as when I was working for my father with flexible working hours it was now a new beginning to work and earn my own money and livelihood.

There is no harm starting life anew from the scratch to anchor myself with analogue to something new and strange in dimension that had been waiting for me here in the UK. It was time for anglophile.

The job, I had at the Gala Bingo hall in Woolwich, cleaning, packing papers, rubbish into black bags each day, hovering and opening about twelve shutters a day not by electric but by hands up and sometimes down.

All the way from Nigeria there was nothing wrong in starting all over again. A new experience leads to understanding of difference in perspective it could become handy when our trials of life is hanging on a string. War in Iraqi, now conflict in Iran, the Libyan war with Col Muammar Gaddafi, conditions of living and our environment is always changing, why I shouldn't I change.

Working for the Gala club since 1992 to 2007 at the same time attend college and University, with the hope of ascertaining my bearing with my illness would not dieter me from prospects.

When I was taken in unwell as schizophrenics at the Greenwich hospital in 1995 a psychiatrist Doctor Mourgoud whose care I was under, had body build and facial looks but not in colour had a very good resemblance to Mr Gabriel Awe. Who was this; I asked myself, steering at Dr. Mourgoud head, face, and body build reminded me of Mr Gabriel Awe at the hospital when I was unwell it was as if a shadow of Mr. Gabriel Awe came over the place we were.

Immediately Mr. Gabriel Awe in his own perspectives dumped my mother at Ibadan back at Lagos Mr. Gabriel Awe began driving Mercedes Benz such men do such things to draw inference to themselves.

My father had three different Mercedes Benz after using several other cars. Working at the Gala club, some people have the wrong idea that I was working for Mr. Gabriel Awe probably because the clubs name starts with a G this I considered was not realistic.

After I left Saint Patrick's primary school Lagos I was enrolled into FESTAC Town primary school by my mother.

Within a month of being a pupil at FESTAC primary school, I was out and started my primary school at Apapa Methodist School Logos very close within walking distance to where my father and mother with Mr. Gabriel Awe works, Mr Gabriel Awe was also a staff at the same company my mother works at R.T. Briscoe pharmaceuticals Apapa Lagos. My journey from FESTAC Town to Apapa Methodist primary school was an hour's journey sometimes made on the same kind of bus we now use in London today.
It was where the largest amusement park was built in at Lagos called Apapa amusement park which was where all the kids and their parents' ends up on every weekend, my primary school was just by it.

It had an Army barrack close to it, Mr. Amos Jinodu an Ex military major, working with me at the Woolwich Gala club, told me, he himself had been at the Apapa amusement park several times.

Just imagine a young man born premature in any environment such as in Nigeria imagine what I would have become with dirty roads, houses, people chop firewood each day, cook meals to sell outside, a turbulent environment where people die every day in the streets. In each place I had dwelled I imagine the movements of cars on the road of Nigeria, shipping containers being moved from here to there my life would have been short lived.

I told Mr Samuel I had been at the job just about after Tycoon M.K.O.Abola's death. During the early 1990's at the Woolwich Gala Club by the time one finishes and hours job a day one is tired his days on the job had been made much easier at certain point I had to live the job and return at the job again

When Mr. Samuel started working at the club, something

similar that happened to me when I first took employment at the Club happened in his life, he lost his mother.

I felt like letting him know before he came to work at the Club I had finished packing the M.K.O.Abiola even those of Chief Obafemi Awolowo, Mutaler Mohamed, those of Arisekola Alawo and those of my father these are adage to imply Nigerian currencies. The Itsekiri land is the epicentre of the Abyss of Nigeria. In short few years of my leaving Nigeria for the UK the petroleum wells are now looking forward towards the use of solar energy. The Itsekiri land is also known as anchor in relation to how the word Eko a sign of greeting a gentleman and applause in occasions are used in Itsekiri.

Mr. Amos Jinodu is familiar Mr Paul from Caribbean decent, who was one of my co-workers at Iceland frozen food plc at Lewisham. During my time with victim support I had the premonition if Ms. Karen Dadby had a brother he would in some way have slight resemblance to Mr Paul both of whom, I would describe as originating from the Caribbean.

If an African comes into the UK and they have their stay through immigration in the UK; even me myself we are either classed as Jamaican, a Caribbean or as someone from Barbados.

I was close to my mother Mrs. Tomori Abeni Faneye Megbele, especially at heart I chose her to be the woman who would give birth to me for what she is.

My mother giving birth to me regardless of my condition at birth, amount to something I feel about her she gave birth to me to set me free which is something I appreciate about her.

I have frequently been asked if, I knew my late mother so well why be a celibate, I said I have a life to live in a different perspectives and somehow base on what, she was worthy of by her name (Tomori) which means someone, who had looked after a child before. It has something meaningful about my being her son if she had looked after a child before, she might look after me again. She was from

Abeokuta (Abeokuta) meaning below a rock. This sounds psych but it' logical.

Mr. Amos Jinodu was found of treating me as if, he is bringing up his own son as if, we were in Africa. Mr Amos is about 65 years of age; he is a senior apostle at a Celestial church at Plumstead Common SE 18.

During the Nigerian Biafran War, 6 July 1967–15 January 1970, those in the army of Western Nigeria and defence of the nation involved some people who believed in the gods or, deities among the Yoruba's. All military base or quarters are in locations where something has involved the gods or deities. Either they had died there or had taken actions involving some peculiar incidents.

For example the second resident our family occupied at Port Harcourt was located very close very close to a military base, When we moved back to Delta state Nigeria in 1984, the house we occupied and the second house my father built was very close to a military base, this time the Naval base at Warri.

One of my father's close friend from Itsekiri Mr Brigadier Tuoyo in the Nigerian army stationed at Ibadan Oyo state in 1987 also one of my sponsor for entry into the Nigerian Defence Academy. Brigadier Tuoyo is a relative of my step mother Mrs. Cordelia Megbele mother of Miss. Anita Oritsewarami, Mr. Arnold Ukunoritsemofe, Mr. Richard Oritsetimeyin, and Mr. Donald Omaseyone Megbele.

Mrs. Cordelia Megbele had one daughter with my father and had one daughter, in her first relationship and one daughter in her relationship with my father. My mother had only one female child in her life for my father who is now Mrs. Oritsegbubemi Ajagunla.

Mr. Funso my aunty Lanre's son I accidentally met on a bus on my way to Mr Hurry's resident, He said, he knew I have already received Jesus Christ in my life, I guess his mother might have told him some of the things I went through whilst living under my step mothers while, we were living at Lagos state without my mother's presence in my father's home., a child really needs both parents.

BBC Four with Michael Palin in the Sahara at 20.00pm on the 23rd of July 2008, showing as part of his journeys of discovery on the second leg of his journey, Michael Palin's destination to Timbuktu, Mali, Senegal, gives insight to what a wife could go through under polygamy in Africa. I wish Michael Palin had taken his discovery in much detail concerning jujus in Africa.

Mr. Amos Jinadu being an Apostle in a celestial church in the UK has something to do with Pastor Reverend Babatunde at Ibadan Oyo state. I hope Mr Reverend Pastor Babatunde would come to the UK to express religious views about the conflicts in the Middle East, how it is affecting the lives of people in Western Nigeria relating to intimidation and discrimination within Islam, juju and Christian worshipers.

In 1982 my mother, I and my brother Mr Sola, wore white robs I and my mother wore red band around our waist as ordination represent celestial worship known as (Aladura) to worship God in our mothers green registered LA Toyota car at Ibadan.

Celestial Church of Christ is a spiritual, world-wide, united, indivisible Holy Church which came into the world from heaven by divine order on the 29th of September 1947 in Porto Novo, Republic of Benin through the founder of the Church, the Reverend, Pastor, Prophet, Samuel Bilehou Joseph Oshoffa (1909 - 1985). The Church is well known with Parishes, Dioceses all over the world with its International Headquarters in Nigeria.

Aladura is a religion founded .1922–1930 in West Nigeria by various people, with around 1 million adherents worldwide.'Aladura' means 'Praying People' in Yoruba. Churches known as Aladura churches emphasize the power in praying and believe in faith healing and various elements associated with Pentecostalism. Most of the founders of the churches were associated with Anglicanism some

Methodists joined the movement as well.

The churches despise the power of traditional African religion, because they deem that power to be basically malign in some ways. Therefore they sometimes burn cult images as 'idols' and oppose both polygamy and witchcraft. Unlike Kimbanguism, the churches tend to avoid politics and focus instead on 'holiness movement.'

Aladura Movement started in 1918. It was the movement that later metamorphoshed to Faith Tabernacle and finally to Christ Apostolic Church. Today, although most churches in Western Nigeria can be correctly called 'Aladura'; they can be categorized into Pentecostals and Spiritualists. Popular Aladura Indegenous Churches are, Aladura Pentecostals, Christ Apostolic Church, Redeemed Christian Church of God, Mountain of Fire Ministries, Deeper Life Bible Church, Aladura Spiritualists, Eternal Sacred Order of Cherubim and Seraphim, Church of the Lord (Aladura), Celestial Church of Christ

Not every child born in the UK growing up in Nigeria would want to ascribe his or her self in such religious worship. Such as wearing white robes, beliefs in exorcism, spirit moving humans to see vision of the past and present, speak in tongue, spiritual healing and working against the Devil, Lucifer and Satan it was all part of my life even, when I went back to Port-Hacourt in 1986 to work for my father it is good to worship in other Christian denomination it adds to religious experience and awareness.

I would have loved to go around indulging in my parents and family prestige and wealth, as other children my age group would do. Though, I would have preferred my Catholic church at Yaba Lagos.
I wanted to join the army years later because; I had my own ambitions and opinion of what I wanted out of Africa.

Mr. Amos Jinodu left the Nigerian army as a Major, he come to the UK residing with his wife and family. One of Brigadier Sudelu's sons is the father of Mr. Calvin Sudelu in Mrs. Nwamaka Megbele first relationship. Mr. Calvin is now my immediate elder brother Mr. Omagbemi Megbele step son.

The Nigerian military personnel are partly the organisers of Nigeria's financial administration with the civil services are mainly concerned with paper work. All other paper works of private businesses are under the civil service sector and public utilities board.

Brigadier Sudelu was a close friend of my father; he was one of my referees when I wanted to join the Nigerian Defence Academy.

Coupled as social problems are in Nigeria, we have had too much of polygamy some children are born into polygamy without having anyone to turn to, to feed them, buy clothes for them or a home to live in. There is nothing like adoption in Nigeria if a relative should take one of such children, they are slaves within their homes they have, their own children to look after added to this Nigeria is a place that knows no sympathy. I spoke at a Sunday services with late Ms Florence Mr. O'Je's grandmother about such matters before one of our Sunday service at Saint John's Church Lewisham. We met at Queen Elizabeth hospital one afternoon with her daughter Mr. O'Je's mother. Mr. O'je is a close friend to Mr. Harry Gordon Slade.

In England, anything could happen to you people could seem to do nothing but there are hospitals at least someone would call an ambulance the same thing with accommodation. You can be an asylum seeker with no shelter or food over your head if you are caught hiding without the right papers they will provide you with food, shelter and clothing before they send you back to your country if need be.

Ms Florence who, is one of the children of the (Alake) of Oyo state replied to my question about polygamy was that I should look at her with her sons and daughter, and grandchildren she is trying as best she could to keep them together as one big happy family and she said for those, who would not practice polygamy in Nigeria, God is with them. I though in my mind but being good you don't get attention when I told her this, she said that is our country that is how it is what can be done about it?

On the 22nd of July 2008 as, I was proof reading, correcting, and making my manuscripts readable, after, I came back into my flat, from my outpatient appointment with Mr. Dotun Sobowale, at the Ferryview health centre to see my consultant psychiatrist Dr. B. Bhatnagar. I got a telephone call from Mr Andrew Mayor at Oxleas NHS foundation trust Dartford that they have received my communiqué about the privatisation of the NHS.

Mr Andrew wanted to ask me if I would not mind, if my opinion on the privatisation of the NHS is placed on their web site. I told him why not, they could put it on their data base if they also wish or they could place in on their notice board if they like and thanked them for their politeness for asking me.

Mr. Andrew's call in some ways at that particular time did encourage me to get on with my word processing in writing my books. July 2008 I have been on benefit, for the past one year with my illness and I was unable to work. It's now April 2010 I have not been able to go back to work all I could barely do, was to keep on word processing with efforts.

It had been the third time I had to re-write my manuscripts to be presented to a publisher since 2004. At first it was all in different files of a hundred and ninety-nine documents. I was told to put it all in one file, it turn out to be too large a file of over a thousand pages for which reason I hope to re-write the whole manuscript as several books I hope my health would permits me to fulfil.

Something, I want the NHS to do is to carry out a survey as to how people with mental health issues feel about member of their families working for the NHS under mental health?

My parent's affair with two children born in Africa, two other children born in the UK, where they both got married in a court in London, with both episodes occurring within the Nigerian Biafra war, I cannot believe such togetherness could eventually fall apart. It is quite reasonable and sensible of two people, who choose to be together at such a time what, I would call a measure towards peace in Nigeria, should later be torn apart.

I and my immediate elder brother, were not aged enough getting married in Nigeria, before we came back to the UK, my brother Mr. Omagbemi chose marrying a woman, who was already spoken for was dramatic.

I consider because of our background our relationship should be like jelly and toppings in an ice-cream or groundnuts and pop corns, (In Yoruba it would be described as guguru ati epa) our relationship is far from such why not?

Polygamy results to obscurities within families if one has created a large family they should by all means have very close ties which rarely happens to be the case when polygamy is involved. I and my sister in law Mrs. Nwamaka relationship should be described as groundnuts and bananas which is one of my favourites.

There were obvious reasons for concern why my father had taken so long a time before, building two houses on his land. Which complicated our livelihood after his death? This had also worsened our family relationships and ties.

Men who practise polygamy should be more constructive if it leaves grounds where family members' criticise each other rather than consideration for such constructive intervention to take place it makes life more complicated.

The parentage and family background I was brought up in, I have over the years given much thoughts and consideration into I feel disillusioned having been brought up the way I was brought up of course there was food in the house there were certain things missing a child needs. A parent do no dump his children in Britain or in Europe you can say Britain is better that means my father land do not have much to offer that are conducive to me is there anything wrong for me to ask why not.

It is not unusual for an individual to do thing out of the ordinary preferably, if it has meaning or leads to correction to their personal life.

It is not to justify myself that I remain a celibate it is something I just feel I should do, make it a life experience in an existence were, there is beauty, ugliness and death.

My need for being a celibate I consider on the basis of medical, philosophical, psychological and psychiatrist terms. In spite of these, the strongest emotional factor I suffer from is if I no longer choose to be a celibate and become a parent nothing would stop me from being a good parent but would it be all left to me?

Family and friends knew me to be very obedient to my parents. Some people are of the opinion I was too obedient. Some things do change, but some people do not change its relevance is that they are being opportunist.

I would not say my mother made a mistake having a relationship with Mr Gabriel Awe my father used it as an opportunist but again I suffered the consequences' why? From childhood I was his favourite which, I no longer became as time, went-by.

While my birth condition was swan into Africa to divest myself in its ways of handling money I hope for the day Africa would be organise using the modern Europeanized ways of slaughtering poultries and placing them for sale for customers to buy even if, it is goat head, cow tongue, shaky and abody; .it's all happening in the UK and why, should the Asians do it for us?

I could not have been so unruly; it is not of me, it has never happened in my life towards any of my parents not even with my step mothers or any member of my relatives. That I would not let my father into my flat, in frustration, telling him to step down from my blocks flat shouting at the top of my voice; I was the last child he had with my mother and he never saw me, when I was born in the UK I was brought to him from the UK to Africa it is one way to make him realise who I was or what I was doing then while I was in Nigeria.

Whatever parents do always boils down to their children. Moreover African children don't usually have a choice under their parents, even when they are fully grown ups. Worse if you are considerate it implies you are telling them what to do.

Right before my father's death, I made him realise a lot of things, he had taken for granted. He was a chief at his homeland; he had to travel to my mother's homeland for treatment because he was unwell and died there at Oyo state Nigeria which is the origin of Mr Gabriel Awe of course this had not meant there was no propaganda on my father's part he would not do it without propagandas' the man lived is life with all he owned for himself.

Propaganda is a form of communication that is aimed at influencing the attitude of a community toward some cause or position so as to benefit oneself or one's group.

As opposed to impartially propaganda, in its most basic sense, presents information primarily to influence an audience. Propaganda is often biased, with facts selectively presented thus possibly lying by omission to encourage a particular synthesis, or uses loaded messages to produce an emotional rather than rational response to the information presented. The desired result is a change of the attitude toward the subject in the target audience to further a political, or other type of agenda.

Highly researched area by psychologists our emotions considerably enhance our susceptibility. Fear, for example, either present or created by the propaganda, can be extremely important to our level of susceptibility

Focus on communicative process involved more precisely, on the purpose of the process, allows propaganda to be considered objectively and then interpreted as positive or negative behaviour depending on the perspective of the viewer.

Used to describe the dissemination of information in favour

of any given cause; to be overlooked is the link between propaganda, What sets propaganda apart from other forms of advocacy is the willingness of the propagandist to change people's understanding would it be through deception and confusion rather than persuasion and understanding.

An African country such as Nigeria starting with only three regions under Lord Laggard when Nigeria had its independence later under general Gowon administration was divided into twelve states is now over thirty states. There are further questions to be asked about of the frequent conflicts each day of the countries affairs in relation to business, culture, tradition, history est. While more and more states are being created driving the nation into deeper conflicts.

General Yakubu 'Jack' Dan-Yumma Gowon (born 19 October 1934) was the head of state (Head of the Federal Military Government) of Nigeria from 1966 to 1975. He took power after one military coup d'etat and was overthrown in another. During his rule, the Nigerian government successfully prevented Biafran secession during the 1966–1970 Nigerian Civil War.

Yakubu is an Ngas (Angas) from Lur, a small village in the present Kanke Local Government Area of Plateau State. His parents, Nde Yohanna and Matwok Kurnyang, left for Wusasa, Zaria as Church Missionary Society (CMS) missionaries in the early days of Yakubu's life. His father took pride in the fact that he married the same day as the future Queen Mother Elizabeth married the future King George VI. Yakubu was the fifth of eleven children.
He grew up in Zaria and had his early life and education there. At school Yakubu proved to be a very good athlete: he was the school football goalkeeper, pole vaulter, and long distance runner. He broke the school mile record in his first year. He was also the boxing captain.
Yakubu Gowon joined the Nigerian army in 1954, receiving a commission as a Second Lieutenant on 19 October 1955, his 21st birthday.

He also attended both the Royal Military Academy

Sandhurst, UK (1955–56), Staff College, Camberley, UK (1962) as well as the Joint Staff College, Latimer, 1965. He saw action in the Congo (Zaire) as part of the United Nations Peacekeeping Force, both in 1960-61 and in 1963. He advanced to battalion commander rank by 1966, at which time he was still a Lieutenant Colonel.

Up until that year Gowon remained strictly a career soldier with no involvement whatsoever in politics, until the tumultuous events of the year suddenly thrust him into a leadership role, when his unusual background as a Northerner who was neither of Hausa or Fulani ancestry nor of the Islamic faith made him a particularly safe choice to lead a nation whose population were seething with ethnic tension.

In January 1966, he became Nigeria's youngest military chief of staff at the age of 32, because a military coup d'état by a group of mostly Igbo junior officers under Major Chukwuma Kaduna Nzeogwu led to the overthrow of Nigeria's civilian government. In the course of this coup, mostly northern and western leaders were killed, including Sir Abubakar Tafawa Balewa, Nigeria's Prime Minister; Sir Ahmadu Bello, Sardauna of Sokoto and Premier of the Northern Region; and Samuel Akintola, Premier of the Western Region, as well as several high ranking Northern army officers. My sister in law Mrs. Nuamaka Megbele is from Eastern Nigeria known as the Ibo's from Enugu.

Enugu State is a mainland state in southeastern Nigeria. Its capital is Enugu, from which the state - created in 1991 from the old Anambra State - derives its name. The principal cities in the state are Enugu, Agbani, Awgu, Udi, Oji, and Nsukka.

Enugu State is one of the states in the eastern part of Nigeria. The state shares borders with Abia State and Imo State to the south, Ebonyi State to the east, Benue State to the northeast, Kogi State to the northwest and Anambra State to the west.

Enugu, the capital city of Enugu State, is approximately 2½ driving hours away from Port Harcourt, where coal shipments exited Nigeria. Enugu is also located within an hour's drive from Onitsha, one of the biggest commercial cities in Africa and 2 hours drive from Aba, another very large commercial city, both of which are trading centres in Nigeria.

The then Lieutenant Colonel Gowon returned back from his course at the Joint Staff College, Latimer UK two days before the coup - a late arrival that possibly exempted him from the coup hit list. Success in twentieth century world affairs since 1919 (Murray 1974 and 1983) and the subsequent failure by Major General Johnson Aguiyi-Ironsi (who was the head of state following the January 1966 coup- with Gowon his Chief of Staff) to meet Northern demands for the prosecution of the coup plotters further inflamed Northern anger. It should be noted that there was significant support for the coup plotters from both the Eastern Region as well as the mostly left-wing 'Lagos-Ibadan'.

Then, came Ironsi's Decree Number 34, which proposed the abolition of the federal system of government in favour of a unitary state, a position which had long been championed by the Southern parties - the NCNC and the AG.

This was perhaps wrongly interpreted by Northerners as a Southern (Eastern, Midwestern and Western Regions) attempt at a takeover of all levers of power in the country. The North lagged badly behind the Western and Eastern regions in terms of education due to their religious related unacceptance of western education early, while the mostly-Igbo Easterners were already present in the federal civil service.

On 29 July 1966, while Ironsi was staying at Government House in Ibadan, northern troops led by Major Theophilus Danjuma and Captain Martin Adamu stormed the building, seized Ironsi and his host, Lieutenant Colonel Adekunle Fajuyi, and subsequently had the two men stripped naked, flogged and beaten, and finally shot.

Other northern troops, led by Lieutenant Colonel Murtala Mohammed, the real leader of the counter-coup and who later succeeded Yakubu Gowon as head of state, then seized the Ikeja airport in Lagos. Several Igbo and Eastern minority officers were killed during the counter-coup. All these were happening at the time of my birth even the month's coincides with my month of birth.

The original intention of Murtala Mohammed and his fellow coup-plotters seems to have been to engineer the <u>secession</u> of the Northern region from Nigeria as a whole, but they were subsequently dissuaded of their plans by several advisors, amongst which included a number of high ranking civil servants and judges, and importantly emissaries of the British and American governments who had interests in the Nigerian polity.

The young officers then decided to name Lieutenant Colonel Gowon, who apparently had not been actively involved in events until that point, as Nigerian Head of State. On ascent to power Gowon reversed Ironsi's abrogation of the federal principle.

In the meantime, the July counter-coup had unleashed pogroms against the Igbo throughout the Northern Region. Hundreds of <u>Igbo</u> officers were murdered during the revolt, and in the North, as commanding officers either lost their control of their troops or actively egged them on to violence against Igbo civilians, it did not take long for Northerners from all walks of life to participate. Tens of thousands of Igbos were killed throughout the North.

The persecution precipitated the flight of more than a million Igbo towards their ancestral homelands in eastern Nigeria. Lieutenant Colonel <u>Chukwuemeka Odumegwu Ojukwu</u>, the military governor of the Eastern region who did not allow attempts by Northern soldiers stationed in his region to replicate the massacres of Igbo officers, argued that if Igbo lives could not be preserved by the Nigerian state, then the Igbo reserved the right to establish a state of their own in which their rights would indeed be respected.

There arose tension between the <u>Eastern region</u> and the northern controlled federal government led by Gowon. On 4– 5 January 1967, in line with Ojukwu's demand to meet for talks only on neutral soil, a summit attended by Gowon, Ojukwu and other members of the Supreme Military Council was held at <u>Aburi</u> in Ghana, the stated purpose of which was to resolve all outstanding conflicts and establish Nigeria as a

<u>confederation</u> of regions.

The outcome of this summit was the <u>Aburi Accord</u>. The Aburi Accord did not see the light of the day, as the Gowon led government had huge consideration for the possible revenues, especially oil revenues which were expected to increase given that reserves having been discovered in the area in the mid-1960s. It has been said without confirmation that both Gowon and Ojukwu had knowledge of the huge oil reserves in the Niger Delta area, which today has grown to be the mainstay of the Nigerian economy.

In a move to check the influence of Ojukwu's government in the East, Gowon announced on 5 May 1967 the division of the 3 Nigerian regions into 12 states - North-Western State, North-Eastern state, Kano State, North-Central State, Benue-Plateau State, Kwara State, Western State, Lagos State, Mid-Western State, and, from Ojukwu's Eastern Region, a Rivers State, a South-Eastern State, and an East-Central State. The non-Igbo South-Eastern and Rivers states which had the <u>oil reserves</u> and access to the sea were carved out to isolate the Igbo areas as East-Central state.

One controversial aspect of this move was Gowon's annexing of <u>Port Harcourt</u>, a large city in the Niger Delta, in the South of Nigeria comprising of the Ikwerres, sitting on some of Nigeria's largest reserves, into the new Rivers State, emasculating the migrant Igbo population of traders there. The flight of many of them back to their villages in the 'Igbo heartland' in Eastern Nigeria where they felt safer was alleged to be a contradiction for Gowon's 'no victor, no vanquished' policy, when at the end of the war, the properties they left behind were reclaimed by the rivers state indigenes.

Minority ethnicities of the Eastern Region were rather not sanguine about the prospect of secession, as it would mean living in what they felt would be an Igbo-dominated nation. Some non-Igbos living in the Eastern Region either refrained from offering active support to the Biafran struggle, or actively aided the federal side by enlisting in the Nigerian army and feeding it intelligence about Biafran military activities.

However, some did play active roles in the Biafran government, with N.U. Akpan serving as Secretary to the Government, Lt. Col (later Major-General) Philip Effiong, serving as Biafra's Chief of Defence Staff and others like Chiefs Bassey and Graham-Douglas serving in other significant roles.

I grow up as a young man who never liked the way my mother was treated by her relatives while she was living close to them in the Western region of Nigeria, after she was disserted and neglected by my father.

I wonder when Africans would come in perspective of most of the incoherence's attached to our ways of life in Africa and abroad. Since it all exists as an inseparable part of my life. It drove me into being an observer infused as to what was going on around me. I was socially withdrawn, it might have something to do, as to what drove me into mental illness it is a conditioning it could lead to mental illness.

If applied to my mother it is common for some women in my mother's shoes becoming preys to other men who are not worthy of her, or prey to witchcraft from a jealous wife. More women each day in Africa need deliverance from the hands of Africa men for many of such women; it means life would always be insecure. The question is why care if you do not care.

Africa, Caribbean, Jamaica, Trinidad, and Barbados who have resided within the European Union particularly in the UK and America for centuries before and after the Second World War have to be awaken for a new arisen based on self preservation to extricate themselves from being termed as third world nations the development does not all have to be technology and engineering it could be in our ways of life e.g. living condition.

It surprised me how we could have lived our lives in Europe without making ourselves worthy; or with the inconsistencies attached to our past history should give rise to a sudden surge of becoming self reliant, to initiate changes, call for awareness to extricate ourselves from poverty and so on.

Is it going to be easier now, when the UK is permanently under the same umbrella with the European Union? Life is an achievement, it is always meant to be an achievement, if we are not careful we might be nothing more but past history. Nothing good comes easy in life we just have to try by collaboration the need to enhance ourselves by being more productive.

Africans would have a strong liking for Jamaicans, Caribbean's, and the West Indies if, they have been really realistic facing this part of the world for the better. At least, it would leave us with good memories about Jamaicans or the Caribbean's in the UK at the moment; Africa is desperately in need of help.

We never seem to like each other some people say, it is because of the Europeans; they are not stopping us from being self-reliant they also face problems in the UK as one would find in Nigeria or any third world nation such as this;.

23 January 2012

Business Secretary Vince Cable unveiled plans designed to curb executive pay in a speech to MPs. Shareholders will be given more powers to block excessive pay packages, and companies will be encouraged to increase diversity on their boards. Firms will also have to justify high salaries in their remuneration reports. The proposals had been due but were brought forward following an intervention by Labour, who says they do not go far enough.

Prime Minister David Cameron said he is not opposed to large salaries and bonuses for successful executives, but wants to get rid of what he has called 'rewards for failure'. Mr Cable on consultation on the issue made it clear there was 'disconnect between top pay and company performance'.

He said it was 'not government's role to micro-manage company pay', but there were steps ministers could take 'to address what is a clear market failure'.

Measures proposed include:

Making firms' remuneration reports easier to understand, and requiring them to explain executive salaries in relation to the earnings of other employees
Increasing transparency by requiring the publication of all directors' salaries
Giving shareholders a binding vote on executive pay, notice periods and exit packages
Encouraging a wider range of people onto company boards, including academics, lawyers, public servants and those who have never served on a board before
Requiring all companies to introduce 'claw back' policies, allowing them to recoup bonuses in cases where they are later shown to be unwarranted
Mr. Cable said government hoped to set 'robust framework', but there was 'no magic bullet' to bring about change.

He said progress would depend on shareholders and companies themselves taking more responsibilities.

The government's crackdown on corporate pay was due to be unveiled in a written statement to the House of Commons, ahead of a speech by Mr Cable to the Social Market Foundation in London.

But made his address, after Commons Speaker John Bercow granted Mr Umunna permission to table an urgent question on pay the Labour party says they acted because the business secretary must not be allowed to 'duck' Parliamentary scrutiny of his 'half-baked' proposals.

Following Mr Cable's statement, shadow business secretary Chuka Umunna said he welcomed much of what had been said, the government had not gone far enough.
He said his party would ensure lower level employees were given a position on remuneration boards.

'Employees play this type of role in Europe's strongest economy Germany and on the board of one of their most successful businesses John Lewis,' he said.
He thinks the answer is to empower the shareholders, to have much more transparency'
Mr. Umunna also said Labour would require firms to publish

the ratios between their highest paid employees and the company average.

Mr. Cable said he welcomed 'worker participation', but there were problems around mandating their involvement on boards and it could be done in certain companies but not by government 'prescription'.
He also said pay ratios were 'a good idea', but could be misleading a firm with a large number of low paid workers would compare unfavourably with one which had outsourced all of its low paid work, for example.

At an event in Leeds, Mr. Cameron said he also did not believe that placing employees in the boardroom was 'the right answer'.

He think the answer is to empower the shareholders, to have much more transparency, to have clear votes on pay packages and, particularly, to make sure people can't get these rewards for failure, where some executives who do not perform well get massive pay-offs,' he said.

Such are the things that need to stop and that's the action that will be taken.
24 January 2012.

IMF: Global economy 'in danger zone' over euro crisis Jose Vinals, IMF: 'A failure to address underlying tensions could precipitate a global crisis'

The world's economy is 'deeply into the danger zone' because of risks from the eurozone, the International Monetary Fund (IMF) had said.

The IMF predicts the global economy will grow by 3.25% in 2012, down from an earlier forecast of 4%.

The growth forecast for the UK economy has been cut to 0.6% from 1.6%.

The eurozone is set for a 'mild recession' in 2012, with GDP expected to shrink by 0.5%, compared with a previous forecast of 1.1% growth.

Growth estimates have been reduced for the main eurozone countries, including Germany, which is widely seen as the powerhouse of the region.

Germany is forecast to grow 0.3% in 2012, down from the 1.3% originally predicted in September.

France is expected to show 0.2% growth in 2012, down from 1.4%.
However, the IMF stands by its 1.8% growth prediction for the US, based on recent strong domestic data on jobs and manufacturing.

Emerging markets, such as central and Eastern Europe and Asia, could also be hit by the eurozone crisis.

The IMF said: 'While these markets have been quite resilient to shocks and developments in major economies in the past year, recent indicators have weakened significantly and the general business climate has deteriorated.'

The IMF said Europe's most pressing challenge was to restore confidence and put an end to the crisis in the euro area.
It added that world economies needed 'decisive and consistent policy action' to improve the current financial environment.

'There are three requirements for a more resilient recovery: sustained but gradual adjustment, ample liquidity and easy monetary policy, mainly in advanced economies, and restored confidence in policymakers' ability to act.'

Separately, EU economic affairs commissioner Olli Rehn said he expected a 'moderate recession' across Europe in the first half of this year.

IMF chief Christine Lagarde warned the global economy could fall into an economic spiral reminiscent of the 1930s unless action was taken on the eurozone crisis.

In its update to its September report, the IMF warned that the 'United States and other advanced economies are susceptible to spillovers from a potential intensification of the euro zone crisis'.

20 January 2012
IMF's Lagarde joins in warning on austerity and growth.

The heads of the IMF and World Bank joined other influential figures in calling on countries to implement free trade, reform their economies and protect economic growth.

.
They warned austerity programmes should 'promote rather than reduce prospects for growth'.

The warning came in a 'call to action' in the run-up to the World Economic Forum in the Swiss resort of Davos.

Leaders warned the world faced slowing growth and rising unemployment.

They also called for world leaders to take action to tackle inequality.
The signatories included:
Mark Carney, chairman of the Financial Stability Board,
World Health Organization boss Margaret Chan,
OECD secretary general Angel Gurria,
World Trade Organization director general Pascal Lamy,
International Monetary Fund head Christine Lagarde,
World Bank president Robert Zoellick,
And the leaders of the International Labour Organization World Food Programme and three regional development banks.

Inequality warning: However, the signatories, who sat on the World Economic Forum's Global Issues Group, said their statement did not necessarily reflect the views of their organisations.
In the short term, the statement said, leaders should remove trade barriers, provide capital to the banking system, make government finances more sustainable and focus on youth

and long-term unemployment. However, they warned that 'fiscal consolidation' programmes should be applied in a 'socially responsible' manner, in order to promote growth and employment. In the longer term, the statement called for action on labour market reforms to boost employment, inequality and green growth.

'Rising inequality calls for heightened consideration of more inclusive models of growth. We must deliver tangible improvements in material living standards and greater social cohesion,' it said.

There is lobbying in England but in a different format they use it to initiate proposals all sorts of political and social problems one can find in Nigerian are part of the British way of life but are more into creating a better community lots of people from other part of the world come here to live and are accepted there is indifference but we live together towards harmony regardless of problems associated to humans.

Developments in Nigeria should be initiated into good use how has the social problems of Nigeria become complex? Considering they have taken from other nations knowledge would not be accepted as leading to their problem but what, they have used it for it should rather be easier for third world countries using what they have leant into good use. The situation is money, money, money! It's when you have money in Nigeria or a post of importance that is when people notice you, what do they use the money do develop very little and we are trying to create a better world as it so happens, we are now living in the age of reasoning with all Nigeria could have attained in such a short time what can stop us from making it even better.

Have spent 21 years in Africa and another 21 years in the UK I feel we are in the dark, for how long would we say our tears have been flowing? It is we who are crying we can do something about it. My existence each day in and out is always insecure, it is about time, something is done or my children have no future; for example it is about times black and Asian communities should stop exploiting themselves. Things we do to ourselves should come out in the open because there is a need for change.

Leaning from my parents and my parents learning from me, I would consider being an achievement under an African parentage; this is yet to happen they know everything a child is always bound to do or as they say. More people from third world nation should be given opportunity to at least visit Europe and see for themselves.

I am from a large family with friends and relatives, I always say to myself, O heavens could our tears for ever flow, if it were an enemy who taunted us, we could have bore it but it is our companions, to make sense out of it is we doing things, we should not do to ourselves that is the cause. Why can't we live as one big happy family? All I wanted out of my father was consideration he had grown up to be a man with influences his children would demand more of him.

I had never behave to him, my mother, Mr Gabriel Awe or any of my relatives the way I did it was just by way of expressing myself. It's their lives they can do whatever, they want to do it's their right but it is my life in so doing, they make me what I am the same applies to any child.

Growing up in Africa compelled me to think and give thorough thoughts of what was going on around me. It had contributed into making me a very thoughtful individual. My memories and residual image now lies within my spirituality some of which are lesson and trials that would lead me into negative or positive attributes.

My number 13 Gorman road dwelling is at Woolwich in Greenwich very close to Saint Mary's Magdalene church where I worship each Sunday. Though my illness is a setback I would not let it dither me from helping my soul my thoughts and spirituality.

Dedicated lives based on being wise, truthful, and collaborative is how we should live our lives if not found, we live in conflict. Tradition and culture should not be frog under water. It should be expressed and observed from realistic perspectives. It should make us grow, understand each other and live in unity we already know how rich we are in culture.

Conflicts, and private wars are a stigma in most livelihoods culture and tradition applied in our lives, I would want expression of love, concern and caring and not initiations.

Women of African origin have much to struggle for and to survive; children of African origin find it difficult knowing what it is to be loved. They are always faced with respecting their parents and do as they say that is all; you never know when you have satisfactory paid your dues to your parents or to your origin except you have paid it, to yourself.

Parents should live their lives for their children and children should do the same for their parents but, there are never barometers or scale for this to be measured. When an African child comes out the way I did confronting my father, it is always unusual, I would want my parents and relative not to punish me but, be considerate about my feelings and most important what brought it about.

The effect would be harmony within our family relationship if it is not the case, we need to change

Children growing up in Africa have little to grow up for; we need a light, a touch to guard us through realistic endeavours. We have too much attached to ourselves that is unrealistic, we need to change if we are to change we need to ask more out of our parents. Someone giving you a little bit of love can make a huge difference in your life even if your parents provide you with everything you need, there comes a time you might pack up material things and seek their love, to be close to them or experience you are really wanted.

You are looking after me as your child you provide me with shelter over my head, food and clothing if I would do well at school depends on me that is if I have the chance to be educated. There are other children living in the street without food or shelter, some of them had to fend for themselves you as a parent could tell me when to kneel down or when to stand up the fright of other children living out in the street is enough to compel me to do whatever you as my parent tells me to do.

When it comes to sending me to Europe I am fortunate other children do not have the chance that I have thank you father for giving birth to me in Europe is this what life within God and man or within parents and children entails?

Consider if you do not believe in God by the time we stop believing in God this are the kind of issues we would be faced with it might be chaos.

I still find time to play with my mates, going out of the house, to play with them, at the Ogbe River at Yaba Lagos.

Very close to our dwelling by the river was an uncompleted building in our youth we go there to play as group's as narrated by the popular Nigerian drama (Ologa Village) in village head-master drama.

Accompanied with my friends and me during Christmas and Easter we children of the neighbourhood go to the uncompleted building to change into wearing masquerade in African culture and tradition of singing, beating drums and dancing in the public for some money for our show, with which we spend on buying more decent masquerade clothing's for the coming new year.

At one time during the New Year I was summoned unexpectedly by my friends who I do not spend much time with that it has been decided that I was to wear the masquerade and I had to dance in public.

Why should it be this time and the very first for that matter, my father was just driving into our dwelling from some distance to park by the house and there, was I all dressed up as the masquerade dancing with my mates beating the drums and singing. My father noticed it was me because of my shoes. Adding to one of the things that made it obvious it was me, was that my friends do not wear shoes. I thought my father was going to give me a good telling-off when I got back indoors but he did not query me. I was 8 years of age then could the lives of African children be masquerades because I am going through a life of masquerade.

Africa is meant to have undergone significant growth marked by consumer products businesses that can afford not to ignore capturing opportunities why in Africa has this always been a long and complex journey.

It's the core principle that drives growing up in Africa there should be an essence of being human which is something we can only achieve through interacting with other people. Growing up in Africa there is a realization of a need to stand up for Africa's children a need to consider how difference can be made in their lives on the part of their parents.

A goal to develop aid and support sustainable programs, creating stimulating environments for Africa's children There is nothing more important than education to ensure the advancement of a child's life most important for several reason is the condition in which they are raised and the environment they live.

In realities of everyday life children should be growing up in democratic ways within young people across historically divided communities at home, in the neighbourhoods where they live, and at school.

There is a picture of diversity living on the margins of their daily lives. Although society has changed in many ways material inequalities and poverty continue to shape everyday life; race and class continue to define neighbourhoods integration is a limited experience for the young.

Drawn on varied disciplinary backgrounds to reveal a world in which young people's lives are shaped by both an often adverse environment and the agency that they themselves exercise.

Living out of very harsh conditions and harsh ecosystem with enormous challenges in the part or in the form of corruption, in the form of low income I think it helps them to understand how privilege they are and it gives them a sense of purpose. They have to do something with the privilege there's no better lesson than this. Any of such children comes into Europe they would want to learn but what we grapes from ourselves living in Europe might be taking a turn into some wrong direction are we unstable in ourselves in Europe or is it Europe itself?

Psychologist Abraham Maslow in 1943 posited that humans have a hierarchy of needs, that makes sense to fulfil the basic needs first food, water etc. before higher-order needs are met.

Approach are sought to glimpse the whole person not just the fragmented parts of the personality or cognitive functioning focused on fundamentally and uniquely human issues, such as individual free will, personal growth, self-actualization, self-identity, death, aloneness, freedom, and meaning. The humanistic approach was distinguished by its emphasis on subjective meaning, rejection of determinism, and concern for positive growth rather than pathology.

I see myself as a programmed entity if I should be asked why I would ask is there anything wrong about feeling this way, one has to prove oneself worthy before one can be in heaven or be able to perceive what heaven is like before they die if so why not Paradise first.

An entity is something that exists by itself, although it need not be material existence. In particular, abstractions and legal fictions are usually regarded as entities. In general, there is no presumption that an entity is animate.

An entity could be viewed as a set containing subsets. In philosophy, such sets are said to be abstract objects. Sometimes, the word entity is used in a general sense of a being, whether or not the referent has material existence; e.g., is often referred to as an entity with no corporeal form, such as a language. It is also often used to refer to ghosts and other spirits.

Reincarnation best describes the concept where the soul or spirit, after the death of the body, is believed to return to live in a new human body, or, in some traditions, either as a human being, animal or plant concept of rebirth is also often referred to as reincarnation. It is also found in tribal societies around the world, in places such as Siberia, West Africa, North America, and Australia.

The word 'reincarnation' derives from Latin, literally meaning, 'entering the flesh again'. The Greek equivalent metempsychosis roughly corresponds to the common English phrase 'transmigration of the soul' and also usually connotes reincarnation after death, as either <u>human</u>, <u>animal</u>, though emphasizing the continuity of the soul, not the flesh.

The entire universal process that gives rise to the cycle of death and rebirth, while the state one is born into, the individual process of being born or coming into the world in any way, is referred to simply as 'birth'.

Philosophical and religious beliefs regarding the existence or non-existence of an unchanging '<u>self</u>' have a direct bearing on how reincarnation is viewed within a given tradition. The <u>Buddha</u> lived at a time of great philosophical creativity in India when many conceptions of the nature of life and death were proposed. Some were materialist, holding that there was no existence and that the self is annihilated upon death. Others believed in a form of cyclic existence, where a being is born, lives, dies and then are re-born.

The <u>Buddhist</u> concept of reincarnation differs from others in that there is no eternal 'soul', 'spirit' or <u>self</u> but only a 'stream of consciousness' that links life with life. The actual process of change from one life to the next is called punarbhava while some English-speaking Buddhists prefer the term 'rebirth' or 're-becoming' rendering this term as they take 'reincarnation' to imply a fixed entity that is reborn. Popular <u>Jain cosmology</u> and <u>Buddhist cosmology</u> as well as a number of schools of Hinduism posit rebirth in many worlds and in varied forms. In Buddhist tradition the process occurs across five or six <u>realms of existence</u> including the human, any kind of animal and several types of supernatural being. It is said in Tibetan Buddhism that it is very rare for a person to be reborn in the immediate next life as a human.

Nigerians' connote Ogbanje's as children who die early after birth and are reborn again and might come back to another life. If I had not outlived my mother she would have taken me for an Ogbanje.

I usually have hallucination, breakdowns this is whenever my illness want to occur again with relapse because of the medication am taking, I go into periods of overcoming my relapses.

I don't sleep well sometimes I suffer from loss of memory, my thoughts, mind and head goes blank sometimes losing track of day or night. If am not at work am in my flat or doing the shopping with little task I can manage to do in other to preoccupy myself.

Apart from this, am always in bed sleeping. May be this is the reason for loosing track of day and night. I usually wake-up with a blank mind for this reason; I could be awake but still lying down on my bed for some time to go through a memory recall before starting any activity. Sometimes if I wake up too abruptly I suffer headaches.

2007, there had been a minor earthquake in the UK. Mr Bill gat has done a very good job through Microsoft, e.g. computers don't bit in his published books, and periodicals Mr Bill Gat Microsoft chairman said computers should become part of the world's assets and in every home.

I wonder where the strength and effort, I put into word processing my manuscripts came from, going through emotions, faith, heartaches and pain; I guess it was because I remain resilient, I believe heaven help those who help themselves. One of the good thing that did happen out of my manual job as a cleaner is that it made my hands strong, with good reflex which not only contributed but also enhance my using a computer.

Speaking to Ms Janet Clark on the morning of 6th May 2007, through our conversation, on the telephone, I informed her, I was giving up my afternoon job of one hour a day, I should be left carry out only my mornings two hours job, because I was feeling unwell. The circle job usually done by me would no longer be open for cleaning, as part of my various jobs each morning. The closure of the circle is through the club manager's advice.

The recent outcome of workers union advice about disable people not being given work opportunities as they do before needs a rethink; most employees have become more subtle over people with disabilities getting employments may be because of the recent turn out of events around the world.

Don't we all have equal rights? If our rights were once given to us as people with disability to work, why should it be taken back from us? Yes it is true the world is always changing it should give courage to the week. It is now a common thing for most employment agencies taking less action on behalf of people with disabilities. The NHS says its good exercises for people with disabilities to work, using their own initiatives.

I have been living at my number 13 Gorman road in Woolwich SE18 5SA, for the past 19 years in the south-east of London. My late mother died in May1993. The only close relative I have in the UK is my brother Mr. Omagbemi from the same parents. He lives at Brockley SE 4.

Could we change summer to wither or spring it would mean a great deal to Great Britain and the rest of the EU to stop this entire quarrel about racism, hatred and segregation around us, I do not see it as a religious conflicts rather a cause for change. It is human nature to be selfish and self centred. If certain leaders live for their people and are concern for their welfare things might improve it is time to put consideration into lots of things especially human endeavours; rather than segregate we should unite.

As a result of some of these symptom which are beyond my control in respect of my medication and frequent consultation which I attend at the Ferryview health centre it was my opinion if I just sit down and do nothing my condition might get even worse most mental health sufferers, suffer from restlessness it's a good sign for a patient but it could be a breaking point. I have to keep on working because, I realised it was a form of resuscitation or therapy to keep me going. This was why I continued working until 2007 when I suffered the most devastating relapse since I was diagnosed as a schizophrenic.

I have been put through many social workers and nurses, I could have like to talk with them about a lot of things which might bring about relief because I have sheared out what is bordering me in my mind, but they do not have the time. All they believe in, in relation to mental illness is that a sufferer needs financial help. There are a lot of things I have to get in terms with which is a reason why I had written my books.

It came to me in my sense of reasoning after a stage I began to realise and get in terms with what had happened to me during my period of being hospitalized, starting to put things rightly in perspective. In 2007 I was going through a stage in which I felt I would be unwell for a long time to come probably for the rest of my life.

I manage to reduce the hours I work to three days a week in the afternoon which meant I have to live on less income. It's not that I have the strength to work but from my personal understanding it helps in other to get out of the reverie of my mental illness.

I do not spend time worrying about my health, I suffer less of bad feelings at times, I could stand up to the voices I hear rather than doing the wrong things that comes to my ear or mind; I tend to remain focused to do the right thing but it takes effort. One thing I do not like about hearing voices, is that at certain periods the voices could be very discouraging.

Other things I do to help myself is concentrate on watching television, and I try to eat well, this means the cost for my meals would cost more each fortnight.

I cannot make any use of a computer if it is not very powerful, a computer that cost more than a £1,000, very captivating and sophisticated. It is the sort of computer I need to work with because of my condition at birth I need to be generated to a point that I am my PC.

In 1990 I was at the Greenwich training centre on a course in office skill through which I grasped more skills and knowledge on word processing documents, data base and document handling. I never at this time was aware that in few years time, working with computers would be much more than word processing and data base as it now has to do with word processing, excel, PowerPoint, e-mail and internet.

Most cares would like to know what the voices I hear tells me to do; it covers a wide array of voices from people I know and those I do not know. Most patients could be on the defensive in relation to the voices they hear some may rather, not dwelling on it. As for what they tell me to do I keep it to me and my psychiatrists most people would not want to hear it. It is resuscitating a patient out of it that maters I would like not hearing the voices at all; I have never been given any assurance I would stop hearing the voices.

More is still expected from cares on how mental health sufferers could get over hearing voices. They would always like to know what the voices are saying to us or telling us to do; they need to improve on positive mental attitude towards helping us to overcome our worse predicament and nightmares of hearing voices.

I am on constant medical review with my GP and my physiatrist in my opinion just as there is the need for nurses to study to a degree level, the same thing should apply to carers and social workers the issues' of mental health care might get complicated.

As at 2007 I was desperate for another job I realised if I have to get a job, I would have to lie to my employer about my illness because as much as I tried I could not get a job. These where my circumstances in early 2007; I wrote to my jobcentre plus regarding the Job I had been doing. I informed them I had to leave my job as a deputy cleaning supervisor and key holder. It wasn't because I was not happy with the Job I just have to move on.

I thought of going for similar job like catering or cleaning job in a different environment. Which, would mean I have to work for the same amount of pay? I felt perplexed because it was about time I start working without anxiety on how to live on an income after my expenses have been paid but at least even when am not working I could still get help from social security to afford food, shelter and clothing, collect my prescriptions and medical care free of charge.

I saw my psychiatrist on the 26th of February 2007 hopping I would still be at my job; if I leave my job all of a sudden, I would loose out because, I would not know where I stand in this case not knowing I was in for SSP stator sick pay. The last time I saw my GP was 10th February 2007 prescription given was Erythromycin Stearate tablets.

Mental illness with repeated admission into hospital can lead to the breakdown of a mental health sufferer completely since it's my hope and wish that I should not be put back into hospital again I would appreciate every help I can get.

My conscience would be satisfied, my reality and conscience is my God this is my motor for overcoming my mental illness.

The restoration of the Cutty Sark was given the royal seal of approval on the 16th of March 2011 as work entered a crucial new phase. The Duke of Edinburgh inspected the 19th-century tea clipper as efforts continued to repair damage caused by a fire in 2007. In preparation for its reopening, it would be suspended 10 feet in the air, relieving the 900 tons of pressure put on her keel by sitting in Greenwich dry dock. Richard Doughty, chief executive of the Cutty Sark Trust, called the latest phase of the £50 million project a 'facelift for a grand old lady'.
He said: 'The duke visited the site the day after the fire as an expression of his concern and he personally requested to come today. 'Philip, who is president of the trust, toured the works to examine how the removal of support scaffolding has left it ready for lifting. Mr Doughty said: 'She has been sitting on her keel in dry dock for the past 50 years and was in danger of sagging. 'The renovated Cutty Sark includes a new visitor centre.

I was taken back as a baby from London to Nigeria by sea living in London; I am no different from the restoration of the Cutty Sark. After growing up in different states in Nigeria I became a Freemason in Warri Island Lodge in Delta state in 1989 subconsciously I knew things have to change for the better.

16 March 2011UK unemployment total hits 17-year high while employment Minister Chris Grayling: 'It is a mixed picture'.

UK unemployment rose by 27,000 in the three months to the end of January to 2.53 million, the highest since 1994. The Office for National Statistics (ONS) said the jobless rate was now 8%, the highest since 1996.

However, the ONS figures also showed the number of people claiming jobseeker's allowance fell by 10,200 in February to 1.45 million. Another record high was reached in the unemployment rate for 16-24 year olds, up by 0.8% to 20.6%. This figure, however, does include students who are looking for work. The unemployment rate for 18-24 year olds was also at an all-time high at 18.3%.

The ONS report showed that average earnings in January were 2.3% higher than a year ago, mainly driven by bonus payments in the finance and business services sector. Wage growth, although higher than expected, is well below the level of growth the Bank of England finds concerning and is unlikely to put pressure on the Bank to raise interest rates. Average pay including bonuses was £453 a week.

The jobs data showed that number of people in work increased by 32,000 to 29.16 million, the highest figure since last autumn. A record number of 50-64-year-olds were in work - their numbers rose by 25,000 to 7.3 million. Labour's shadow work and pension secretary Liam Byrne: 'These figures are a matter of deep concern on public sector employment fell by 45,000 in the final quarter of 2010 to 6.2 million, even before the full impact of the government's spending cuts started to take effect. Local government employment fell by 24,000, central government by 9,000 and Civil Service by 8,000, while employment in private firms increased by 77,000 to almost 23 million. There were almost half a million job vacancies in the three months to February, up by 24,000 over the previous quarter.

The Prime Minister, David Cameron, said the youth

unemployment numbers were 'disappointing, once again'. To put it bluntly - it's a good time to be a man, working in the private sector, and/or over 50' But he said it was a 'very mixed picture', pointing to higher number of people in employment and fewer people claiming unemployment benefit.

The Employment Minister, Chris Grayling, said: 'Clearly any increase in unemployment is unwelcome and a disappointment and it underlines the need for a Budget next week which focuses on growth, on creating an environment where businesses are growing and developing and creating jobs.'

He said the data underlined the need to press ahead with policies to stimulate growth in the private sector. However, the shadow work and pensions secretary, Liam Byrne, said that the private sector was not creating jobs fast enough to offset the public sector job cuts that were 'on the way'. 'It doesn't look like the private sector was creating enough jobs to absorb what we know is coming down the tracks, and that's why the government has got to change course on the economy,' he told the BBC. The TUC general secretary, Brendan Barber, called the figures 'shocking'. He said: 'Over a year after the recession technically ended, unemployment is now at its highest level since the mid-1990s, with 2.53 million people out of work.

'While the fall in the numbers claiming the dole is welcome, the number of jobs available in the economy has also fallen and there are over a million people in part-time work seeking permanent jobs.' David Kern, chief economist at the British Chambers of Commerce, described the figures as 'mixed, but not as bad as some had feared'. 'We reiterate our forecast that total unemployment is likely to increase to 2.65 million over the next 12-15 months before it starts declining,' he said.

Graeme Leach, chief economist at the Institute of Directors, said: 'The good news is that there doesn't seem to be any evidence of a wage price spiral developing, with the underlying growth in average earnings (excluding bonuses) actually falling from 2.3% to 2.2%. This clearly helps reduce the upward pressure on interest rates. 'The level of unemployment rose in Wales by 2,000, by 4,000 in Northern Ireland and by 38,000 in England. However, unemployment dropped by 16,000 in Scotland.

10th September 2006 a Sunday morning Janet Clark phoned me that she could not be at work that morning her mum is over retirement age and she was still working. I had to put the rest of the staff in the right form i.e. who is doing what, who wants to do a cover, what area and making certain we all finish in time for me, to lock up and leave the premises when the rest of the staff had left.

Unfortunately on that very Sunday, Mr Joseph Olatunji did not turn up for work I have to do his job. I would have preferred doing the tables simply because I was all ways in charge telling other members of staffs on what to do. I have to do the heavy part of the covers available clearing, racking and vacuuming for Mr Joseph he suffers from asthma and has to be of work once in a while. I have got my own personal job at the circle, padlock all exists back again and set the alarm on.

Initial cleaning services had just won the contract for cleaning all Gala Bingo clubs for another three years. One of the changes was that, we can only work two hours in the mornings no longer two and half hours as from October 2006 with wages loss for each staff of £25.00 a fortnight.

From what, we did experience on this day we acknowledged we can't work on a flow basis meaning everybody ship in and do all the work. We agreed each staff should remain at each of his or her job carrying it out within the two hour period if not problems such as these would follow

Quarrelling about one or two staffs always being lat or absent from work
If such should be the case problem of organising each morning
Favouritism
On member of staff doing most of the work or contributing more than others
Problem of one or two staff feeling they are being used

It could easily lead to ganging.

Mrs. Linda Andrews was on holiday Mr. Asad Gill a new district operation manager was covering on her behalf. A meeting was scheduled for the 15th of September not much could be discussed this Friday since it was Janet's day off work Christen and her Nan where late for we were all given handouts from Linda Andrews which had been brought in by Mr. Asad further discussions would follow on the 18th of the same month I will not be present it would be my day off work. Coming back on Tuesday I was told not much could be discussed further meetings would be held when next Mr. Asad could come in again to see us. The handouts were about health and safety at work.

As I walked back into my flat on this Sunday morning the 10th of September 2006, I had three roll-ups tobacco with coca cola afterwards, I took a good bath hearing voices as instructed by the DVD cats and dogs I should not forget to wash the back of my ears, I included my back, shampoo my head very well with lots of tooth paste for my mouth to brush my teeth, after which I, us flexitol heel balm on my feet and put on my cloths of blue jeans trouser and white polar shirt.

As I walked out the door for Sunday service at saint Mary's church, I had an impulse to walk back into my flat to insert earwax ear drops into my ears because, I don't use any other means of getting reed of ear wax in my ear, I walked out of my flat again on my way to church for Sunday service.

On my way each Sunday when walking to church I do always say my prayers right from the moment I walk out of my flat until I get to church e.g. O God open my ears to your words and do your wish, pardon me for my gilt, show me the way, in thee O' Lord I put my trust, let me not be put to shame, let me not be put into confusion in your righteousness please deliver me etc.

It was on this tent Sunday Pope Benedict was at his home town Munich which was said could be his last. He pointed out that people these days do not care about hearing Gods message or getting close to God they rather want to listen to different frequency.

It was also on the news a Northern Island cathedral would be undergoing refurbishment, Saint Mary's at Woolwich and Saint John at Lewisham are also under going refurbishment; it was said on the news that most people who worship each Sunday do not attend service any more am not surprised because it meant people have different views about the war in Iraq, Libya and Afghanistan, gay and lesbian priest and child abuse while some people are using religion as opportunist.

A conflict is going on within my family; I was the one who told my immediate elder brother he could visit or telephone me in my flat if he wants to as for his wife we hardly see or speak to each other something had been bordering me I need to adjust myself before I could visit them at their home since 2004 at least he had visited me once in a while which has been very good of him. 27th July 2015 which fell on my 49th birthday he visited me with birthday cards from him and the rest of his family wishing me a happy birthday in one of the envelops was £50.00 as a gift I told him, 'I do not want it that I felt he wants to buy my head am not going to let him buy my head' probably I felt it was ritualistic in terms that I was recently in hospital to see a Surgeon who from my observation is the first Asian young man I would describe as having a slight resemblance to Mr. Calvin Sudelu they are both of the same height and age group I had to be at the hospital to see a Surgeon on the month of June 2015 because I was suffering from Cyst on the right side of my neck. He hugged me to take the £50.00 I took it but not before I had told him what was bothering me in certain aspect of our relationship.

Life is always turning around in different ways. I consider, he should know better of what to do after all, he is the eldest. In African culture, the eldest comes first am not the type of person, who is too forward whatever he wants to do or say comes first.

Having a quibble with my father far from it, I could not be having a quarrel with him, there is nothing wrong for an individual to come out openly on how they feel, it improves life and human interaction in this case, we are a family so why not?

I do not expect my brother Mr. Omagbemi taking it to his own hands after all the old man is my father if he feels I have a problem he could collaborate, by voicing out his own feelings in the presence of my father and myself on one of our fathers visit to the UK rather than letting it all die down then taking my father's place on another angle. I am suffering from mental illness; something has to come up on why I am suffering from mental illness.

Though a paranoid schizophrenia I might be I always encourage myself to walk my way each day in the right perspectives. It's difficult but I endeavour my years and experience in Africa had also helped.

Differences between people can be a good thing because, it could makes life and human interaction more interesting; discrimination can result to lack of quality between different people or race. When, there is discrimination some people tend to call other people racist depending on how they feel or express themselves in relation to other groups or sects. Racist and discrimination can also, be found within a family.

Discrimination is not a good thing it leads to more conflicts; it does not bring out the best in a group of people especially, if they are different. Some people are of the opinion conflicts are not all that bad it could bring the best out of a group of people. It could bring about more understanding and close ties.

Discriminating against another person or group is to lower their self esteem rather giving them opportunities to come out with their true feelings which is much more important rather than for it boiling in their hearts and mind which might further deepen relationship.

Where there is discrimination, different groups would have less mutual understanding or consideration for each other disadvantages are it could create exclusion, neglect and avoidance. If racism is noticed within the factions it becomes a difficult problem to interpret or evaluate the opinions and needs of both factions. It could lead to intolerance within the factions.

Once racism is noticed within factions, it becomes a case to be looked into with consideration through management and conflict relationship, if this, is not done at an early stage of the discrimination, the factions would start by avoiding each other, they would not only start avoiding each other, they would display their differences as time goes on, they would not be able to avoid each other and thereby, go into violent conflict. These can take place anywhere to the least even within a home.

Making bad assumptions about other people or label them, criticize each other verbally at certain times with the use abusive words, create conversations which does not value other peoples interest because of their differences.

Some people could be of the opinion a men should not sleep alone or it's not right for any one being a celibate. This world we dwell in is forever changing, at certain point, it could become complicated for some people as humans, we think differently, we act differently, our temperaments are different and we have too many laws and rules. I am not here to say I am right, everyone else is wrong it is just how, I feel in a world where some people could hurt other people's feelings, and get away with it, is not just right!

Some of us have the habit of taking from other people, without giving back to those we have taken from, some of us, will take and give nothing back at all, it is never too late for changes, Life is a long hard road, certain times in our lives could be hard and difficult, so difficult that it could make a man's heart run cold.

Our world is filled with all types of discrimination which entails lot of damaging effects and behaviours which easily leads to diversity and inequality thereby reducing our quality of life. This was why the race relation act of 1976, made it unlawful to discriminate on racial grounds in employment, housing etc. racial grounds means the colour of an individual, his or her race, ethnic origin, backgrounds and nationality.

I am happy about the disability discrimination act of 1995 just after I came out of hospital diagnosed as a paranoid schizophrenic. The design was perfect to prevent discrimination against people with disability in employment, access to education, transport, and housing which was one reason, I went back to my job as a cleaner at the Woolwich Gala Club after I have been diagnosed as a paranoid schizophrenic. If, I were in Africa, would I have such an opportunity?

The act also laid down rules not to discriminate against those with disabilities in obtaining goods and services, including access to health and social care. Employers and landlords are not to treat a person with disability less favourable than a non-disable person. Shops and other services such as collages, new transport should meet the requirements for people with disabilities in all areas of the communities. If this should be the case, what is it that could stop me from working if I want to?

The West African situation calls for conditions that everybody should be housed; nobody should be allowed to sleep on the streets. From this process, all West African countries can then leads to tenancies housing. This was something that has been done before in Nigeria through the FESTAC 1977 celebration. If no other nations in Africa could do this, Nigeria could if they start now. Development should always be a continued process as far as children are being born each day, progress should never stop or our livelihoods' in time would become a dilemma

Where the Act in the UK stipulate, conditions for tenancy agreement such as if a tenant is an individual and occupies the dwelling as his only or principal home, the condition is satisfied. Or if the tenancy is a joint tenancy, each of them as joint tenants occupies the dwelling as their principal home.

Various West African countries should start by providing state benefits for its citizens and wipe out starvation and poverty. If not state benefits at least, food in the stomach and shelter to live in. It is when changes like these begin to take place in Africa that is when we are truly citizens'. We can then carry out census, free and fare elections. We would know the right amount of food crops to cultivate each year or the amount that would feed a whole community there should be homeless legislation imposed on West African nation.

Homelessness reviews should be carried out through all West African countries and its districts, with a homelessness strategy in all its local authority and districts such details into account would be the challenge for any incoming government to pursue.

It is challenges of such nature that should be put forward to African leaders to make them change and be productive. Or they would continually come into power and do whatever they like. They are not to set the goals the people of Africa themselves the common people should set the aim, goals and achievements to be implemented by any government coming into power.

To prevent homelessness in all local government authorities in Nigeria securing accommodations for people who are homeless, arrange for the results to be available at its office for inspection at all reasonable hours without charges from members of the Nigerian public. The least that can hinder these is as a result of not very nation have the ability to comply or would comply people would move freely into other regions they being afraid of some nation who would tarnish such project by bringing their own devastating state or worse scenarios to their own areas if they should carry up such project but should we all go on wallowing and the same time digging graves for ourselves or wait until our own time comes living in such debilitating unhealthy condition while more children are being born each day in all parts of Africa e.g. Nigeria, Ghana. Ivory Coast, Republic of Liberia, Republic of the Gambia, the Republic of Guinea, the Republic of Mali, the Republic of Guinea-Bissau, the Republic of Benin, Burkina Faso etc.

Homelessness in Africa should now be of priority, housing authorities should be formulated to assist each countries development, and caring for the whole people. If we have respect for nature, we should not allow our pregnant women giving birth to babies in unstable living condition or environment.

Things have to change; for our own good, for us to stop being dependant every African woman who comes into the UK immediately wants to give birth to a child, it is an ongoing craze among young men and women even adults.

A criminal offence is an offence against the state e.g. fraud, dangerous driving, theft, burglary, domestic violence, assault and battery. A civil liability is a wrong against an individual or individuals, the objective of the civil trial would be to compensate the defendant rather than jail the person or individual found liable who on the other hand could get a criminal record. Breach of contract, unpaid dept, trespass, and private nuisance are examples of civil wrongs. These have no meaning in Africa or in our livelihoods'.

For someone to be found guilty under criminal law some requirements must be brought to terms: Actus Reus: states that there must be an act or action by the accused for him to be liable e.g. assault or hitting or raping a woman. Mens rea: is intention regarding that a person may not be found liable under criminal law where there was no intention on his or her part to cause the act that he or she had been accused of.

Most African nation have one or two things to say about members of a government embezzling money most of the accuser, are people who are involved in it themselves. Somewhere in the line, they were let down, and then come up with allegation to make names for themselves whereas, they were part of it.

These are money the central government, state government and local authorities have authorized. For an amount of $35 million how could only one man be responsible for so large an amount of money? The bank from which such an amount of money was withdrawn most also be involved.

'I will certainly go back to Nigeria. It's not over. 'This is the sad story of our own country. This is money belonging to the people. 'This is what is supposed to be used to solve the problem that we are facing. Look at how it's being wasted. See what is happening with our people.

Today they use the money to fight for their own survival, they give it to lawyers across the world, and they buy private jets. All a 'Total waste for the nation of Nigeria' We are talking of raw cash how did they get hold of such an amount of money? This is a continued process in Nigeria over the years with each successive government it has to stop.

They are not supposed to keep or have documents it is the central, state and local government who should have and keep such records. In my opinion just one of such embezzlement, should bring down the whole government in power. It is about time the Nigeria people see eye to eye with each other and stop such happenings. The government of Nigeria and its officials should be more accountable. Such an amount of $35 million can wipe out homelessness in Lagos alone within a year.

One thing about such embezzlements is the money are never recovered if it would not be returned to the government and its people? What are the issues of making a loud noise about the money, so that something should be done about it which only the military can do, doing so brings them in power yet Nigeria should be under civilian rule.

Krypton has a hold on Africa. African men get married to European women I experience one of such relationship; he had tribal marks on his face. Jamaicans have been doing it for ages the English women could still contain them.

Medication drain this holds a query we have never heard of medication drain I am born premature I feel, I am a part of a matrix I have no physical disability from birth I feel self contained I was born over 40 years ago cloning of humans is now an issue concerning all parts of the world I am a celibate one reason for this, is to contain medication if I stop being a celibate, my affinity of being self contained is lost the effect could be the closest to epilepsy who say we are not about in years to come, experience medication drain.

I might be a schizophrenia viewed with stigmas it is about time we start knowing in every aspect of our existence who among us are really ready to face this age of reasoning in the 21st century there are all sorts of convictions leading to appeals, there are causation or Mens-rea in a courts of law. We live in different ways some aberrant yet there are different aspect of our lives considered extraordinary or out of the ordinary you do not have to be rich to be poor and you do not have to be poor to be rich this planet is very rich would it be a happy place someday?

Other requirements such as Causation and negligence with regards to negligence though Mens-rea may not be proven, an accused person may still be convicted if he or she was criminally negligent though the prosecution must prove that the accused owed the victim a duty of care, that the duty was broken and that as a result the victim suffered harm.

How long would African people continue to suffer damages from the hands of its government both military and elected? They fail to understand that they are in power because of the African people and the nation as a whole. Some of its people are condition to work for an honest wage just for a day's meal. How could such a condition continue?

The Nigerian ordinary people have no say, How can we live in a nation and be proud of it when somebody is laying on the street dying, with no food or shelter and there is hold to do, as your parents say or you die like them; is this what it takes to be a parent in Africa?

Negligence, Trespass, and Nuisance falls within the law of Tort, they are civil wrongs e.g. an injury done to another person's body, property reputation, cases of such wrong are settled under a civil court where by the person who sue seek remedies in the form of compensation.

Though some of such civil cases may result as a criminal offence because they are considered to be a breach of peace of Society e.g. assault and battery they are tried in criminal court because they are offence against the state. No authority spells these to any African government and its people what is it that might make them change?

Private Nuisance: is an unlawful interference with another person's use or enjoyment of land or some right over or in connection with it. Private nuisance normally affects neighbours, tenants, and landlords or landowners. For such cases of private nuisance to be successful in legal actions, the person who sued must have an interest in the land. I have never come across a case in Nigeria where a civilian sued the Nigerian government and got away with it.

Examples of private nuisance are continuously playing of loud music, emitting noxious gasses, harassment, because they unlawfully interfere with neighbours use or enjoyment of land, which are nuisance. This is how some Europeans or outsiders view the African ways of life and the law as nothing to do with it, even if it is just our ways of living it needs a change there needs to be law and order.

Statutory nuisance is a breach of public law it affects environmental protection and public health.

It should be common for these West African countries to have environmental protection Acts defining circumstance which can then apply statutory nuisance e.g. harmful escapes from premises of smoke, noise, effluent or dust or premises in such state as prejudicial to health or any nuisance within the circle of the Act. The few Acts applied over centuries are public decoration in the central and state government offices no wonder there is no proper law enforcement I want to see the relevance of education.

It is the responsibility of the local authority environment health office to investigate, inspect and a specific duty to investigate complaints made to them by corporate companies members of the public. Where they are satisfied that such a nuisance exists or is likely to occur or reoccurs, the office issue an abatement notice prohibiting or restricting the nuisance.

Contravention of such notices should be made a criminal offence which is subject to a summary trial in a court of law. An individual who was a victim of a statutory nuisance can bring and action in person before a court.

Public nuisance is a nuisance which affect neighbours and the general public e.g. obstruction of a public highway, a hoax bomb alarm, unlawful sleeping in the street and no care for the mentally unwell. Beating other people senselessly, burning of human beings alive because of an offence, it should be left in the hands of the government to legislate and try all cases, and not in the hands of just any individual.

Do African leaders abide by the law and do they implement the laws of their nations? The common people say, they do not abide by the law and they do not implement the laws. It should be made possible for a civil action to be brought against them under statutory laws.

This is where culture, traditional and festive ceremonies are important in every decent communities with different groups and factions, they could in unity bring about a civil action or a breach of statutory nuisance against a central, state, local or district government.

Since, it is such members of government who fund such cultural and traditional ceremonies a civil action or a statutory breach against them is difficult. This is one junction the civilians have to help themselves in other to move towards a better future and progress in their livelihoods and quality of life.

They should by now be aware members of their government are very clever; they know how to manipulate their local government, cultural and traditional groups. With power, they tend to use vice to separate the regions and districts.

They always want to stay in power as long as they want to.

Right from their time in office, they choose the district they want, the people they want. Favour them with opportunities than other groups or districts. While other groups are let down these are the causes of tribal clashes in Africa. This is what has been happening in Africa. It is common for one faction favouring them and other faction want to see them removed from office leading to clashes and segregation which never proves troublesome for the leaders.

Public nuisance is a criminal offence and may result in prosecution. Civil action for damage may be brought by a person who had suffered harm or loss against the perpetrator of public nuisance if you do not have money you cannot take an individual to court for an unlawful wrong can a nation do this for and individual in Africa?

Am not living in a dream world Europe is united they have their disagreement but they are still moving on third world nations should enhance themselves to be met with the right requirement from other nations.

Becoming rich is the aim of every Nigerian we should configure ourselves on its use to create a decent livelihood, environment and policies having money is one thing, what you do with it is another thing it would tell after your death would you want people to sing praises to your name when you die or would you want people to sing of rejection.

Harare, Zimbabwe — Roaming bands of government supporters heckled, harassed or threatened people into voting in a runoff election Friday in which President Robert Mugabe was the only candidate, ensuring he will remain in power despite international condemnation of the balloting as a sham.

Residents said they were forced to vote by threats of violence or arson from the Mugabe supporters, who searched for anyone without an ink-stained finger the telltale sign that they had cast a ballot.
Opposition leader Morgan Tsvangirai, who withdrew from

the runoff after an onslaught of state-sponsored violence against his Democratic Movement for Change, said the results would 'reflect only the fear of the people.'

'What is happening today is not an election. It is an exercise in mass intimidation,' he said at a news conference.

U.N. Security Council rejects vote the U.N. Security Council unanimously 'agreed that the conditions for free and fair elections did not exist and it was a matter of deep regret that elections went ahead,' said U.S. Ambassador Zalmay Khalilzad, who is current council president.

Secretary of State Condoleezza Rice called the vote a 'sham,' and said the United States would use its position as president of the U.N. Security Council to drive international condemnation of Mugabe's regime. 'Operating in Zimbabwe should know that there are those ... who believe that the Security Council should consider sanctions,' she said at a meeting in Japan. 'We intend to bring up the issue of Zimbabwe in the council. We will see what the council decides to do.

Umaru Yar'Adua's presidency of Nigeria was haunted by rumours of his death. In fact, one paper even announced his demise before he was made president. In the middle of the 2007 campaign, he was whisked away to a German hospital for treatment.

His tremulous voice was inaudible under the cheering of the crowd. The reports shocked many Nigerians who considered that, after the selection of the candidate at the ruling People's Democratic Party (PDP) convention, the actual election was going to be just a formality. The question on most people's minds was: why were they being given a sick president by the outgoing leader? President Yar'Adua's record of achievements is not a long one.

The glacial pace of his decision-making virtually locked up all government business for two years. One area where he is said to have made progress is in a peace deal for the oil-producing Niger Delta, where groups of militants had shut down production by about a third, choking off important revenues. In late 2008 and 2009 Nigeria faced a financial crisis, in part caused by the plummeting value of oil during the global economic crash.

The government had made budget assumptions based on a benchmark oil price that was, in the harsh light of the global economic crisis, too high. It struggled to pass a budget on time, realising that unless oil revenue was freed from the grips of militants, government funds - on which much of the economy is reliant - was seriously at risk. The president was left with little choice but to come to an agreement with the militants; they had to be bought off, or 'settled' as it is known euphemistically in Nigeria.

After personal talks with militant leaders in the capital, Abuja, President Yar'Adua got armed groups in the area to come in from their remote bases in the creeks and swamps and hand over their weapons.

But the solution has not lasted. Many of 'the boys', as they are known, were placed in resettlement camps where they sat around waiting to be provided food, clothes, money and jobs. After waiting for a long time, many ex-militants have grown dissatisfied and left the camps. A small number of attacks on pipelines and kidnapping of expatriate workers started all over again. Mr. Yar'Adua has bequeathed one other development to Nigeria.

A dynamic central bank president Sanusi Lamido Sanusi, who has been working to reform the system which was on the brink of collapse just nine months ago the real problem facing Nigeria is a mixture of corruption and the government's inability to enact reforms or even its most basic functions. And the ailing president simply did not have the energy or the capability to push through anything like the reform programme he promised in his inaugural speech what of his successor?

There was much speculation about whether Mr. Yar'Adua's deputy Goodluck Jonathan - now sworn in as president - will actually run for the office.

It was not yet clear if he will. The PDP has a kind of gentlemen's agreement to rotate power between the mainly Muslim north and the majority-Christian south, but it is not impossible that the deal could be changed or altered slightly.

The terms 'north' and 'south' encompass many factions, all representing the interests of a small political elite rather than the needs of a geographic region. This time, there is no large figure on hand to anoint the next president, as Mr Obasanjo did last time, at least not yet.

Mr. Obasanjo is said to be making a play to get the party to accept Mr Jonathan as their next candidate, but he is opposed by other factions in the PDP. To settle the argument, a big political player will have to emerge and placate all the factions in order to find what is called a consensus candidate he will have to have very deep pockets, or make promises which the eventual candidate will have to stick by.

Will Mr Jonathan get the backing he needs to run for president?
One of the tasks Mr Jonathan set himself when he became acting president in was to push through electoral reform that would see elections brought forward.

Life involves more than effective planning, instructional knowledge, and using experience skills it extends dispositions similar to professional beliefs or values, modes of conduct and the ways in which beliefs and attitudes are displayed. More into this are responsibilities to convey, model, and promote positive standards of professional conduct, maintain screening and assessment procedures that assure people with negative dispositions are not permitted to persist in the dark.

In sincerity life dispositions should lead to actions and patterns of professional conduct those we look up to, should be role models and model positive behaviours whatever they do should ascribe to all individuals, reflection combined with experience and undertakings that exercise sound judgment and ethical professional behaviour.

Those whom we look up to should be sensitive to individual differences within this, promote understanding in varied cultural, traditions and needs. They should believe we can learn and should set high, yet realistic goals build our communities to be free from bullying and belittling behaviour they should interact with everybody in the community at all levels thereby promote positive changes a sort of community that benefit the welfare of its people.

Provide affordable services they need with a model for personal and academic integrity by their actions. Role models should be forthright in their interactions with others and uphold high standards of trust, character, and integrity, promote social justice, treat its people equitably, maintain appropriate standards, and exercise fairness.

Nigerians would do anything to tarnish each other's reputations it could be just for recognition this does not only involve those at the top it also involves those at grass root. Leaders should not leave situations until they are at its edge before they do what, they have to do make; progressive changes. The situations there to put pressure to achieve something concrete, define and substantial that benefits everybody in the nation there should be no deception when relevance need to be considered what I see each day in Nigerian politics is another form of privatisation.

Negligence is the most common tort; it's the failure to use necessary care to safeguard others from injury or damage e.g. Construction Company carrying out road works has to make sure pedestrians are safe when using the area or the company will be liable for negligence if a pedestrian should sustain injury in the work area.

Not every act by a person will result in tort of negligence even if it cause damage or injury to another person in order to establish a claim for negligence, the person suing must prove three things, the defendant owes him a duty of care, as a result of the duty being broken, he or she the plaintiff has suffered loss, the duty had been broken

There are a lot of lawyers in Nigeria we ought to see them using the law in practice to safeguard the citizens' of Nigeria and the Nation. It is clear the government of African nations owes the people a duty of care. As a result of the duty of care being broken, the people of African are suffering loss, as a result of the duty of care being broken by any government that comes into power. The citizens should be able to put claims of negligence against any government found irresponsible.

Through contributory negligence a plaintiff may claim damages if the court proves that the defendant was negligent as a result of which he or she the plaintiff suffered injury or loss.

It was obvious through a documentary on the appalling state of some parts of Lagos once the federal capital of Nigeria e.g. Abutemeta the documentary was titled welcome to Lagos on Thursday 22nd of April 2010 at 21.00 to 22.00.

Christians tend to misunderstand the teaching and instruction found in the Bible regarding obeying authority

HEBREW 13:17 obey your leaders and submit to their authority. They keep watch over you as men who must give an account. Obey them so that their work will be a joy, not a burden, for that would be of no advantage to you.

ROMANS 13:1 everyone must submit himself to the governing authorities, for there are no authority except that which God has established. The authorities that exist have been established by God. Consequently, he who rebels against the authority is rebelling against what God has instituted, and those who do so will bring judgment on themselves for rulers hold no terror for those who do right, but for those who do wrong.

Do you want to be free from fear of the one in authority? Then do what is right and he will commend you for he is God's servant to do you good. But if you do wrong, be afraid, for he does not bear the sword for nothing. He is God's servant, an agent of wrath to bring punishment on the wrongdoer. Therefore, it is necessary to submit to the authorities, not only because of possible punishment but also because of conscience.

ROMANS 13:6 this is also why you pay taxes, for the authorities are God's servants, who give their full time to governing. Give everyone what you owe him: If you owe taxes, pay taxes; if revenue, then revenue; if respect, then respect; if honour, then honour. Christians often take the above verses as instruction from God to obey everything anyone in 'authority' attempts to enforce on them. However, there is no such instruction to obey what is wrong or unrighteous. To the contrary the Bible is full of instruction and examples of standing against 'authority' that is in the wrong. What after all, is authority?

If someone in a government position is a law breaker they stand in their position and act without the authority of the law for it is the law which gives the power to authority. And when people make so-called laws that violate the core law, then those so-called laws are lawless, they are void and the person in government attempting to enforce them does so without authority.

The documentary was a two part of three series about people who chose living and working on the waters of Lagos Lagoon with a group of engineers about to start work in developing the area with the hope in some years to come, Lagos would be more attractive.

If the people of Africa do not seek for governments who come into power and improve their quality of life, or make their leaders more responsible and accountable, it would be a case of contributory negligence's we are complaining about the dumping of toxic west, climate change African nations are seeking compensation WHO world health organisation and the UN United Nations.

Each year over 1.4 million tonnes of electrical and electronic waste is thrown into Africa some of them not all are intentionally brought in into Africa they are acquired by Africans themselves. Over 88% of such waste ends up in homes, lagoons, landfill and wastelands leading to toxic waste causing soil and water contamination.

This is ever harmful an effect on the people and natural habitats, wildlife and human health with no answers as to how such waste can be recycled or disposed of.

The developed nations create sound disposal collecting waste electrical and electronic equipments, Africans themselves should do better than encouraging second hand electrical and electronic equipment products into their environment. Think of my condition at birth yet cloning of humans and surrogacy each day is becoming part of our lives.

Manslaughter is an area of criminal law that deals with negligence; the two types of involuntary manslaughter are death of another person either by a negligent or reckless act or omission or by an unlawful and dangerous act. This could be restricted to gross negligence manslaughter.

It's any conduct whether unlawful or not the negligence of the accused went beyond a mere matter of compensation between subjects and showed disregard for the life and safety of another which amount to crime against the state and such conduct deserving punishment e.g. African children sent to waste dump lands collecting electrical or electronic waste to be used as spear-parts it leads to tetanus.

Trespass on land is entering someone's property or land without permission, such person is considered as trespassing. Other cases could still result as trespass even if it was with permission, we are yet to know what made Nigeria more than thirty states It was three regions before later divided into twelve state and now, it's made up of over thirty states.

Nigeria officially the Federal Republic of Nigeria, is a <u>federal constitutional republic</u> comprising <u>36 states</u> and its <u>Federal Capital Territory</u>, <u>Abuja</u>. The country is located in <u>West Africa</u> and shares land <u>borders</u> with the Republic of <u>Benin</u> in the west, <u>Chad</u> and <u>Cameroon</u> in the east, and <u>Niger</u> in the north. Its coast in the south lies on the <u>Gulf of Guinea</u> on the <u>Atlantic Ocean</u>. The three largest and most influential ethnic groups in Nigeria are the Yoruba, <u>Igbo</u> and <u>Yoruba</u>.

Trespass on someone else goods is theft, pilfering, attempt to steal are examples of trespass of goods, they are criminal offences of which a defendant would be prosecuted the same applies to governments who, embezzles its nation's wealth, sing contracts that are never fulfilled in any form.

Trespass on a person requires the plaintiff prove that the defendant's act was direct and physical, it includes, Assault is a criminal offence, Battery which is the physical application of force, False Imprisonment without lawful justification for a claim to be effective, there has to be a total restrain.

These are some welfare benefits of UK citizens and immigrants it solves lots of incoherent issues on how people live their lives if not with ease at least, there is food and shelter. While at the same time, the government can stop anyone who uses fraudulent means against its principles of welfare state.

Homelessness Assistance
Attendance Allowance
Severe Disablement Allowance
Disability Living Allowance
Income Support
Family Tax Credit
Disabled Persons Tax Credit
Social Fund payment
Council Tax Benefit
Income-based Job Seekers Allowance
Housing Benefit
Treatment under the National Health Service
Free or Subsidised Education at the Expense of Tax Payers

In Great Britain

Housing opportunities in the district including those in the private rented sector and housing authority's allocation scheme

Details of landlords and letting agents in the district
Tenants rights and rights of occupation
What to do about harassment and illegal eviction
How to deal with possession proceedings
Rights to benefits
Rent levels
Rent and mortgage arrears.
Tackling debts
Homelessness legislation
Grants on housing repairs
Married couple with family have a need to be re-housed so, they could get on with life and work
The elderly need to be re-housed
The disable, the mentally unwell, those with long time illness need to be re-housed

Employers also, owe employees a duty of care for their health and safety during their employment and working hours in Africa those this applies? There should be relevant code of guidance on health and safety at work. There should be reasonable provisions of practicable health and safety welfare at work for all African employees.

Employers should provide competent staff, adequate materials, proper system of work and adequate supervision at work. We have a good chance by starting right now in pushing such proposal forward only in such avenues can the Nigerian citizen get the best out of its nations, its people and livelihood.

They should provide machinery, equipment and other plant that are safe and sound without risk to health and maintained in good condition.

Risks should be reduced as reasonably practicable e.g. precautions when carrying out hazardous tasks.

Employers should ensure the way materials are used, stored and transported that, they are safe and without risks to health.

They should provide information, instruction, training, and supervision necessary for employee's health and safety at work.

Working environment should be kept safe e.g. buildings, scarf holdings, open air sites, and basic structure of the work place.

Provide, proper an adequate arrangement for the welfare at work for their employees.

They should protect their employees and ensure that they will be safe at work consequences for failure should be immense for employer because, it is negligence.

All these taken into account in the employer and employee relationship an employer is responsible vicariously for the torts committed by an employee in the course of his or her employment. Vicarious liability is a precise liability which means the employer does not have to be at fault for there to be a liability unlike other cases where the employer has a personal duty of care. The plaintiff need only to show the person who committed the tort was in the course of his employment. I am not living in a dream world I know the place has no detail of advocacy the world is changing if it is a matter dragging along fine but be in line as a matter of fact there are no signs of dragging along experience should counts.

In retrospect I do often pray and meditate on having insight to distinguish between right and wrong. It called for awareness within me and my spiritual consciousness in reality of natures misgiving which do occur in every environment because, we fail to do, what we have to do for the good of mankind.

Reality of making a difference is no dream it should be practical in this case, is it nature versus on mankind or is it humans versus humans the importance and clarity lies close to once senses of realities with two distinguish differences e.g. being good or being evil.

Deities; gods passed on traits to present generation, so have Christianity. My writing allows me to demonstrate my idealism of being an African born British. It would do me and most African children good. With more and more of us being born in the UK spreading across Europe, the contents of my books focus on a new generation of the 21st century. Our parental background, leaders and people of our origin should not make us bitter because we are as sad as it is.

Civilisation belongs to every race, colour, creed, and religion in the context of what they are, everything that has existed on this planet dose undergo different phases. Africans were brought as slaves to the Western hemisphere have always been our cries mind you all human race have suffered slavery at one time or another.

After slavery each race starts by implementing moral values which would guard them into civilisation if not civilisation moral wellbeing, implementation of truth and justice for the sake of their cries for freedom. It could be brought about, through efforts it is always worth it and then people sing praises for what you have done especially your children. As time goes on, it is customary for them to develop, no matter how high or low it develops through different level and degrees, over the years, each of them look for ways to become more and more efficient through attributes.

Each individual becomes wise through someone else's stupidity or ignorance infarct each individuals on earth, became wise from the deeds and examples of other individuals or race. We are all meant to learn from each other this, is one reason why we are all humans with difference.

It makes the world a more interesting place we are prone to each others like and dislike and we have ours they are all forms of expression, we are prone to make changes and amends. But from the way Africa is going on and all third world nations; I wonder if we have been scotched from the sky or from beneath. The more reason we should start living up to expectation.

The fear of God is the beginning of wisdom, natural it is for one to become wise, intelligent, clever, and superior through the fear of God which seldom happens. What I hope for is at least an endeavour to raise ourselves up to the challenges before us.

Most achievements are through the expenses of other people most Africans say they are vulnerable. All parts of the world are vulnerable to one thing or the other. Being vulnerable could mean one has been foolish, unaware, ignorant and slow to action. Europeans get oil from Nigeria I see a million things they could do with petroleum yet Nigeria cannot produce kerosene to go round homes.

We are moving into a new phase of using solar energy some oil producing nation feel they have been intimidated. We are all vulnerable to one thing or another with regards to our existence. The world is always a state of the act with the watchful eyes of God and certain architects of the universe watching over us all.

You need not be a doctor, pharmacies, engineer to becoming an architect, each individual most become the architect of his or her lives. God the architect of the universe gave life and purpose to all mankind, he made men and all creation sufficient in doing so, we are all architects of our own lives don't you want to be one of them?

God gave life to man through his own breath; with his own breath, he most have given all that he has got to give, to have made us what we are with the rest of his creativity everything so very good and sufficient.

Man became the holder of the world's adversaries there is none like we humans on earth. In his true wisdom, God and those who have made choice to hold the pillars of the universe with God because they chose from their own initiatives before our creation to do right and abstain from wrong doings.

What is the meaning of caution, causation, mistakes, prayers, an act, or conditions? Are these still mysteries in our lives? Gone are the days when we say, we do not know why certain things happen at least we could try then we would understand.

We have memories of the past, present and future on our mind some, scattered pictures of memories good and bad, happy days that are all behind us, if the way we were in our past was unfavourable, going into the present and feature we would make it simpler regardless if we did not know what struck us in our past. Wouldn't it all be simpler now? Why can't we come into terms of making our destiny a happy one? It is our fault one can understand there are so much evil in the world we say we are making a difference, it is not materializing. Why can't it remain the same if they were all so good, sweet, simple and lovely memories? If we have all the chances we could have why can't we do it right all over again?

Memories could be beautiful, it could make us live a healthy life, live longer and appreciate our existence if they are bad memories the reveres, and it also brings out good qualities and thoughts in our mind cheer good feelings with other people and know, what it is to be said wisdom could be applied regardless of our sorrow. Do schizophrenias have good memories? The illness is always as a result something bad has happened.

As the year 2007 passed by, Christmas come once again, another time for calibration was completely out of my mind, too much set back and unwarranted feeling had come with the year. Decoration as I do all year round? Never crossed my mind, I looked towards solitude. Hoping it passes by with good tidings for the coming year 2008, I prayed over it throughout the month of December in solitude, as we all on earth roles into another new year in this early 21st century.

Over the years, in my Christine faith I have been part of the born again Christian Deeper Life Ministry, for a personal reasons and experiences, I prayed that I should not and hope never to reincarnate to earth again.

I don't know if it's out of my illness as a schizophrenic, I have feelings I have something to do with Zeus, partly while some people give me impressions I have known them in a past life while others seems to be new entrants in my life. Some of whom are Mr Joel manager at Iceland Lewisham and Mr Alan Doyle assistant manager at Iceland Lewisham, Mr Nicolas Walls manager at Iceland Camberwell, Mr Wild district manager, Mr Terry Morley area manager, Mr Knight manager at Iceland Camberwell, Miss Noire working as store supervisor at Iceland Lewisham, Mr Paul and Mr Jeff sales and stock assistant at Iceland Lewisham, Mr Andrew sales and stock assistant at Iceland Camberwell, Miss. Michelle Cook cashier and sales assistant at Lewisham, Mrs. Caroline S deputy manager at Iceland Camberwell, Ms Maureen cashier at Iceland Camberwell, Miss. Julie cashier and sales assistant, Mr. Michael sales and stock assistant, Mr. David James sales and stock assistant Mr. John is car park attendant, Mr. John Molenue worked at Camberwell and Nine Elms, Pamela worked as a cashier and on chill products and Maureen working as a cashier at Camberwell store, Mr. Robin was at New Cross and East Dulwich Iceland as manager, Yvonne worked as Appliance staff at Camberwell store. Msitech, Josephine and Theresa, Nike worked at Camberwell as Cashiers. Some of the sales and stock assistant or cashier who worked at Camberwell store part time were students of Lewisham collage they all know me as Mr Semi and a Mr. Jeffrey from south Africa.

Miss Clara Murphy, Miss Loraine O'Connor from Greenwich University. Mrs. Joanna Tarker, Mrs. Linda Andrews, Ms. Janet Clark her mother Mrs. Joan Clark and daughters Joan Keeble, Carthy, Christine, Jacky and Nucleoli Reid, Mr. Brian Asher, Mr. Green, Mrs. Lee Asher, Mr. Joseph Olatunji, all member of staff of Rentokil Initials cleaning service. Ms. Jane Brieght, Mr. Judge the Woolwich Gala club manager, Mrs. Wendy Loft, Miss. Mary Brieght Jan's younger sister of the Brieght family, Mr. Anthony, Mr. Mark, Mr. Tony, Mr. Trove, and Mr. Ted the handyman all staff's among many others of Woolwich Gala Club they all know me As Mr. Bami.

Dame Dr. Ruth Muldoon Silver, DBE is a British educator principal of Lewisham collage, Reverend April Keech and

Christine Bainbridge both of whom are one time curates of Saint John's Church Lewisham. Ruth Silver retired as Principal of Lewisham College in 2009, a post she held for 17 years.

It's a common thing with employment in the UK to be all work and no play same thing with education because they are progressive towards enhancement in the way they do things, conduct themselves and the way they live their lives. One has to be at the job. Mind you in Africa, the manager can wake up at any time, walk into the office at any time, family members of the business have leisure's, breaks and personal appointments, and they could have fun and relaxation while working. Employees who are not family members are not obliged to the same entitlement while getting on with the job.

Leisure's and breaks quit rare in the UK because, it's all concentrate on the job with work and no play. I like the way it is in the UK, it creates avenues to responsible, good at what you do if you are ready to do the job with all due respect.

It's common among all African families to wage hierarchy or suppress each other, complaint with favouritism. One can complain they do not like somebody and get away with it. No wonder there are a lot bragging and conflicts out there in Africa creating scene of an inferno. How do we get on with live to get a day's work done? It's not that there are no conflicts in the UK there is a sort of responsible approach to deal with conflict and the world, is not getting any better from perspectives except we find a cure for the world. We talk of Lucifer, the Devil and Satan through our faith we haven't even met anyway. They are something else. If you do not keep a tidy home you are likely to be usurped if not by a fellow human being, by disease. Beauty is you and God it is good to keep a happy home.

Where did I get the strength as a schizophrenics being able to do all I have been doing? Having been working since1986 for my father after my secondary school education and several repeated trials, under my mother whilst growing up.

Many times with my experiences as schizophrenic, I would feel, I should just leave in my flat claiming benefit for life. I have to fight against such odds which I have been doing for years; I have a life to live, regardless of my illness I must make myself useful.

My Suffering through my illness at times lead me into a state of not being able to prepare my meals put food in my mouth or cares for myself, sometimes I find it difficult getting out of bed. My condition gets worse any time I eat out or have takeaways.

I have gone into a stage, I feel people are using me to hypo-personalize themselves, yet inside me, I feel like super-human, neutralising myself from negative aspects of my illness and how, it affects me.

If as a sufferer one tries to be in good frame of mind it helps but it comes with lethargy that's why people suffering from mental illness should face less disappointments because it could disturb their temperament or make them feel on edge.

The illness of schizophrenics is getting higher in propulsion in our communities each year, most of us look like people who have no life to live; we are termed as different viewed with stigmas. Stigma is not what the illness schizophrenia should be attached with within our communities issues of mental illness in certain concept describe the state of our environment, the life we live, what we do and how we do things so it is not just the mental health sufferer who, is on the red.

Most people who have knowledge of African background, history, culture and tradition know that African children do not like to eat outside their family home. Even when polygamy is involved the more children always want to eat food prepared by their mother. It would not also seems right for an African in the UK to have ready meals or take-away.

I would rather prepare my meals for myself rather than,

having take-away meals, eating out. I am not looking forward ending my life like Jams Bond live and let die (Kananga).
In another sense it seems I am being suppressed by some evil inside of me. In due course, apart from holding the seal of God inside me, I also feel I have twice the seal of the devil if its goal is to destroy me or wish harm should befall me.

Having another woman who once belong to another man after a first marriage with children is a form of juju, it's a form castration, lower self esteem one is dependent on the wimps of others it is another way of hyper-personalising once self or image yet it is all about love caring and befriending.

Whilst I was taken ill and diagnosed as a paranoid schizophrenics, in hospital I gave my brother my council flat key that he could get me some clean clothes in the presence of his lady friend Nwamaka.

Rather my brother going into my flat and do, as I requested, they took my birth certificate and made photocopies of it which I found not only in my flat but also in my sisters in laws dwelling at Lewisham Just by Saint John's Church.

Was it because I had a recent conflict with my father? From what I observed I considered this to be the case I feel for this reason, they felt I had been hospitalised with mental health problem also think how, did they came about such a conclusion it was for such a reason I had been hospitalised which was not the real issue. And I had never been asked any question by my brother and his wife why I feel I had been hospitalised diagnosed with mental illness or what led to it.

Having given my brother my council flat key to get me some cloths before I came out of hospital diagnosed with schizophrenia I walked into my council flat and found out that it had been painted personally by my brother Omagbemi he painted the wall papers. I found his painting repulsive I never asked him to paint my flat. He never told me, he was painting my flat when he visited me in hospital or if, I wanted it painted. I also found some furniture's from my sister in laws dwelling at Lewisham which she probably might had occupied with Mr. Calvin Sudelu and his father before they parted. I had everything I wanted or needed in my flat, chair, table etc. I never asked anything from them just bring me clothing's from my flat is all I asked for when I gave my council flat keys to my brother whilst I was hospitalised at Greenwich hospital. How dose madness starts there is always something behind it. Such an experience occurring after my being hospitalised not knowing the Greenwich hospital would be knocked down. Not more than two years after our father's death certain words come from my brother to me on a visit to his flat. Because of this I had not visited my brother and his family at Brockley just after Cordelia's daughter Mrs. Oritsewarami Temile heavy with child paid a visit to the UK gave birth and left the UK. She spent some time with them at Brockley during her visit. Just before I became unwell in 2007 my brother announced to me they had bought their number 3 Pulton house at Turnham road SE4 accommodation at Brockley rented it out and have moved to Imorello close Sittingbourne in Kent which I have not visited since I became unwell in 2007.

This was shortly after our father's last visit to the UK and just after his death. The night my father left the UK during which he gave me another box full of Itsekiri pepper soup ingredients, rice, hot pepper etc with a photograph of Mrs. Cordelia Megbele who had aged. I made sue of getting back to my flat from Brockley at about 9.30pm in a Taxi. At a point of asking my sister-in-law to call me a cab I felt like telling my father I felt I go through phase Mr. Calvin Sudelu was his father who had reincarnated at that point I heard a voice say to me do not say a word about it. Hearing the voices I kept quiet and left. Two days later my brother called me on the phone after our father had left the UK informing me I should came to his place to collect a Freemason bible our father had left in his house for me. I went to his place as soon as I could collected the bible and went back home by bus at that time it all seem to me like a ritual.

The next time I went to visit my brother, knocking the door his wife open the door and let me in. I had not sat down she said she wanted a bottle of pink lady wine my brother and his children were out, she could not live me alone inside their house I should go out instead to her nearby corner convenient shop to buy her a bottle of pink lady wine. I went out to the corner shop and bought her a bottle of pink lady wine with the precise and correct amount of money in coins. After a while my brother had not turned up she did not say a word to me I guess at that point I had to live. I felt I was being spoken to in a language I should understand if am not a child. It went further than this.

The next time I visited their house my brother and his children were out again she was the only one in. As I entered their dwelling she asked me abruptly if I would have some pepper soup I said yes. As I sat down in the leaving room she came back with a bowl of pepper soup probably prepared with goat meat which test like what had been prepared by the pepper soup ingredient my father had brought with him to the UK on his last visit. After having it my head went Booyashaka it was as if there was a sudden quietness with a feeling that the leaves on the trees outside where falling down on top of me inside the house from above my head. I have tried buying our Nigerian pepper soup mix several times without being able to have it when I prepare pepper soup. I go through phase as if something about my life based on paranormal or rituals is being extracted from my life. This was after our father's death they had gone to Nigeria for his funeral I hadn't. If you have read other parts of my books about my experience it's imperative I would have considered rather than consuming the home brought box of pepper soup ingredients my father gave to me personally on his last visit to the UK if I did kept them for a long time before consuming them or if I had got rid of them. Two visits I have received from my relatives from Nigeria to the UK I had offered them something to eat in my flat which, they did not eat. This was a visit from Cordelia's daughter Oritsewarami and my elder brother Reverend Barrister Oritseweyinmi's wife Evangelist (Dr) Yvonne Megbele. Both members of my family were heavy with child at the time.

Few occasions I had entered my sister in-laws dwelling Lewisham just at the Vale and Saint John's church I had the feeling it connects to our dwelling at Warri Delta state where my father celebrated his chieftaincy titles and also connects to number one Searles House by Old Kent-road SE 1which also connects to the plot of land my father had build his house at Warri which also connect to Mr Osibowales house at Ibadan. I do still go through such phase living in my Gorman road blocks of flat. I lived at number one Searles house Old Kent road through a Mr. Campton whose office by a Garden at Camberwell Green dealing with private renting of homes with Landlords who are willing to give their homes out for rent. Through Mr. Campton I first lived with Mrs. Millie a Caribbean or Jamaican at Peckham in her case, I had to live with her. Through Mr. Campton I also had the opportunity of living at Clapham Common at a bedsit.

83 New Kent Road is a residence for students at the nearby London South Bank University, with 81 students living in shared flats. In 1878, historian Edward Walford noted that the New Kent Road was formerly named Greenwich Road, and explained that '[it] is a broad and open roadway; it has been lately planted on either side with trees, so that in course of time it will doubtless form a splendid boulevard, of the Parisian type, and one worthy of being copied in many other parts of London. There is a small green space next to Driscoll House, and beyond Searles Road there is a larger one called Paragon Gardens, named after the building erected on the site in 1787 designed by Michael Searles the Surveyor of the Rolls Estate. It was demolished in the 1890s when the road was widened and replaced with more modest housing on Searles Road and a school. The school has since been converted into a residential building and also named The Paragon.

Years later was the time they walked into my flat and wanted to discus about my mental health issues this was after; she had qualified in mental health care. I knew she was at one time when she moved in with my brother, was working in care in home close to Erith and Bexley. All I could tell them later during that period was that I was taken into hospital as unwell by the police.

While I was in hospital rather than for my brother and Nwamaka bringing me my clothes from my flat when I was hospitalised in 1995, they brought me two new shirts. The rest where only two shirts mind you at this time she was pregnant. Why two new shirt and two used shirts which weren't mine. If they were taken from my flat, it would have been part of some used clothing's of my brother which he brought to me in my flat personally two years after I moved into my flat and before my father and he visited my flat on which I told my father not to come into my flat. I was taken aback when my brother brought in the cloths few months before my father's visit we are never known to wear or shear each other's clothing's. During that period my brother brought the clothing's I received a visitor an Itsekiri lady with tribal marks in my flat at Gorman road who I have only met once and a man who is probably her husband for the first time in my brothers flat at Flat No 3, Curlew House Brockley close to when our father first visited the UK after our arrival. I do not know how she got my address. On hearing a knock on my front door when I open the door it was she and her children who were unmistakably very unwell who I met with for the first time in my flat. Since then I have only met her and are children in one of my brother and sister in laws party we sat at the very same table. This was shortly after I had been admitted into hospital and diagnosed with paranoid schizophrenia in several of their parties its friendship they go out to make as for me, I go through experience as if they had put one goat among themselves they would use to make Tête à Tête or as an (Egbe) (Group thing) or play politics with. If this was the case fair enough but it at same time exhume omens within groups. I hope one day the Church would not be like that. The Itsekiri lady did not spend up to five minutes when she visited my flat with her children. I could not ask any question I wanted to offer them orange juice she said I shouldn't bother. I waited for the reason for her call she said she just came to greet me and they left. All I made out of it was body language. What I would add to this is situations in life scenarios do not just occur even stupid mistakes while there is no smoke without fire.

My sister in law told me they bought the clothing's from East Street market. One of London's oldest markets and is as fondly visited now by local people as it was in the 1960's and 70's. It is located off of Walworth Road in <u>South London</u> at which time she was heavy with child. East Street is in the London Borough of Southwark and is between Walworth Road on the western side and the Old Kent Road on the Eastern side. The market runs down East Street from the junction with Walworth Road to Dawes Street, passing East Street Baptist Church and a multitude of shops. The main entrance to the market is from Walworth Road. A bus stop on Walworth road serves the market, with a large number of buses arriving from Elephant and Castle or Camberwell Green

And why didn't he got me my own clothing's from my flat as, I had requested? This wasn't all; before I was discharged from hospital I paid a visit to my brother and his lady friend just by Lewisham collage just for a visit from hospital where I was receiving treatment at this time, my brother was still living in his council flat at Brockley but sheared her accommodation with her at Lewisham while our father stay at my brothers Flat at No 3, Curlew House Brockley on his visited to London.

I have personally made photocopies of my birth certificate but never in colour I was surprised when I saw a photocopy of my birth certificate in colour in my flat after just being discharged from GD psychiatrist ward at Greenwich hospital. On this my visit I found another copy at my sister in laws dwelling at Lewisham which she had probably shared with her first partner. For what reason I asked my brother is my birth certificate been photocopied then, I never knew photocopies could be done in colours because I could had mistaken the original copy from the Photostat copy and what was it doing in her dwelling why had he done such a thing! He gave me no replies for his actions. This was in the presence of his lady friend who was then heavy with child standing nearby steering at us to me in particular. It was not a moment for me to be melodramatic so I kept quite because of the impression I made when I first saw her for the first time in front of my flat.

My birth certificate after all those years in Nigeria I thought to myself good thing my passport was with me when the police officers took me to hospital to identify myself which I gave to a clerk to keep safely for me while I was in hospital. My birth certificate in the UK which is my juju for my cups of tea, water, associated spirit level right from when I was in Nigeria, holy communion and medication in my flat and at church regardless if I had been hospitalised at any time in my life whilst in Nigeria which my father would have used in some ways for any of his own rituals. My birth certificate only came to my mother's presence as far as I knew when, she took it from our father to make arrangement for I and my brother Omagbemi at Ibadan Oyo state to obtain our British passport this meant she had handed them to our father immediately after we arrived back in Nigeria from Great Britain in the mid 1960's. There was a fuss about our passport not being handed over to us at the Oyo state British consulate at Ibadan.

The only time I had seen my birth certificate in another person's hands apart from my own personal parents was with Cordelia I was about getting to my eleventh year of age I had failed my primary school education in my last year a new scheme started pupils had to sit for examinations to get into secondary school which meant, I had to repeat my last year in primary school at Saint Patricks primary school Yaba Lagos. All I knew was to get up one early morning Cordelia was taking me to a primary school to get enrolled for another one year of primary school. On getting there Cordelia showed the principle my papers one of them, was my birth certificate it was the first time I laid eyes on it really. The next thing I heard the school principle said was it was girl's school only. An experience I had while the school principle was speaking to Cordelia was of a flashing image reflecting the face of somebody I never knew or saw in my life until I met the person. I was at the time seating at the principal's office with Cordelia. I recalled the desk, chairs and content on the table of the principals turned into a shrine my whole body became generally alight and I saw a female's reflection flashed across the table not knowing what it meant. Years later when I met with my sister in law Nuamaka in the UK at certain point of my illness and our relationship, I recalled having this strange experience of paranoia and mirage of flashing image was that, of her reflection I saw at the principal's offices. How could it be that of hers! According to

343

what I was told, she had spent part of her life in Northern Nigeria. The first time I saw her, there was something overpowering about her, I cannot explain on the day I first met her for sure in front of my flat, I experience general body weakening. Having met with her for the first time displaying an attitude I cannot really explain my being unwell and admitted in a psychiatrist wards just after I met her personally and few years later, the hospital in which, I was admitted into and diagnosed as a paranoid schizophrenic was shot down, coupled with the experience I am going through about her, leaves me no choice but to recount these experience. It later came back to me in my memory I thought, had come across a customer who looks like my sister in law Nuamaka at Iceland frozen food store at Lewisham whilst I was a staff I remembered the lady steering at me queerly. Within weeks of this experience my brother walked into the same store we greeted each other he told me he came into the store to buy freeze broad beans. He said he had been to Iceland Camberwell and asked of me he was told, I was at Iceland Lewisham. He had just moved into his flat at number 3 Curlew House at Brockley from his hostel at Clapham common which accommodates both male and female. Lancelot Andrews hostel I later accommodated close to Borough high road was for men only. I helped Millie the cook in the kitchen to prepare meals cutting pepper, onions, tomatoes, garbage etc I also helped in cleaning the kitchen and washing up. When I started my training at Greenwich training centre in Woolwich I was let off at the Kitchen only come back after my training to do the washing up sometimes. Some members of staff are Mr David an English man another Mr Brandon. Mr Charles works on admission, Mr. Farie, Ms. Pam working as the hostel cashier, Ms Mavis, and Mr. Ram as the hostel nurse.

Mrs. Cordelia Megbele should have been aware the school was only for girls because it was the same school Patience who is a relative of hers with her elder sister lives with us in the same house at Lawani Street Yaba Lagos attended. The girls school was not far from my former primary school also based at Yaba just immediately after this my experience; my mother took me away from my father house to live with her at FESTAC Town in Lagos why didn't Cordelia and if my father was aware of this, make arrangements for me to enrol at the same Saint Patrick primary school I was attending before, and repeat my last year at primary school. When I went to live with my mother at FESTAC Town I repeated my primary school at FESTAC Town primary school for a month later left to attend Apapa Methodist school; where I completed my primary education and was admitted to Apapa high school just by Apapa Methodist school where I completed my primary education I was one of the first student to attend Apapa high school because it was one of a secondary school recently built at the time to commemorate free education in Lagos state it takes me an hour's drive from FESTAC Town to reach Apapa each morning. FESTAC Town is a federal housing estate located along the Lagos-Badagry Expressway in Lagos State, Nigeria. Its name is derived from the acronym FESTAC which stands for Second World African Festival of Arts and Culture which was held there in 1977. Since my mother had to move from Lagos state to Ibadan, there my mother enrolled me for my second year of my secondary education at Eyinni High school Ibadan it was the same secondary school my brother Omagbemi retook his 'O' Level general certificate of education under WAEC West African Examination Council. After I completed my secondary education at Eyinni High school Ibadan I went to live with my father and immediate elder brother at Port Harcourt Rivers state Nigeria.

In Africa it is customary we eat with our hands in my father's origin it is customary pouring Gin, Whiskey or Brandy on the ground usually the entrance of a house or on slaughtered sheep's and goats as liberation with prayers how does this appeal to you if you were born abroad growing up in a third world nation

When you come to a place like the UK for example with your birth certificate or passport be careful of whose premises you place your belongings or you could find out later your belonging is being used by somebody else as if, it were their own. Everywhere you buy goods there are cash points, you were in an airplane which brought you to the UK you might have travelled through the train taxi or bus you might loos your part of your identity while making your own purchase of African food stuff you might be losing your identity to the person you gave your passport or birth certificate to.

I do wonder what my psychiatrist and care workers think are the causes of Schizophrenia illness. All these happened within short period after my raw with my father in front of my flat. People could be judgmental about schizophrenia sufferers and they never down for the account of what might have gone wrong. In my case what are the precursor that has led to my illness? Schizophrenia finds it difficult to do their toiletries such as wash their mouth in the morning when they wake up, drink too heavily, or prepare meals. They suffer from abnormal thoughts, paranoiac thought and feelings. How do people become powerful in using juju's, voodoo, witchcraft and talisman? They use things which belong to you or have given to somebody things that are dear to your heart.

They should stop and think! The illness is as a result of the problems caused by our background, family members and the community we dwell in. The illness in some ways is caused by the problems created by our societies, such as the government and racial conflicts which lead people into mental illness.

These are two people who had just had a child my nice through a suzerain section, my sister in law already had a son Mr Calvin in her previous relationship with retired Brigadier Sudelu's son who surprisingly, was one of my sponsors into the Nigerian Defence Academy then they look for someone to take it out on why should it be me. At the end of the day, I want to come out openly in relation to what surrounds our family relationship hopping it would not be a case that would be implied why she had my nice as a suzerain because, she was pregnant and I would not let her into my council flat.

If I had not been cultured and well disciplined through these incidents, things might have gone drastically wrong. The Metropolitan police brought in. Everybody wants to live their lives peacefully in the UK it takes a lot for an individual to raise his or her hand against the next person. I want to know from my brother and sister in law what have been the reasons for their actions because even with my step mothers if they believed I actually did it to my father to insult him with bad intention it means I really never had a family.

A month before I was discharged from hospital my father made a visit to the UK I wasn't told he was coming because I simply went to my sister in laws dwelling by Lewisham Vale then I happen to know my father's was in the UK because my brother told me then. Staying with them for a while on my visit my father turned-up immediately we were off to East Street Market because my father had some shopping to do at East Street Market which he wanted me, my brother Omagbemi and Calvin Sudelu to accompany him to in my sister in laws car where he bought himself some few things which included a motionless bicycle for exercise. East Street Market is within walking distance to Searles Road where I once lived and a walking to East Street Market where I sometimes did my shopping.

I spent more years living under my father's step wives than my brother. Not at any time had I gone into conflicts with any of them. They never spoke well about my father. Whatever had happened in London within me and my father, would have been unexpected they would have been very surprise but not heath felt that it happened infarct they wanted something of such nature to happen that my father might change his ways.

I and my brother should be happy for our mother especially and our father bearing us in the UK and then, we returned as young men. Our mother was dead, but her spirit and deeds lives on. She might have taken both of us from the UK to Africa and never came on a visit to the UK until her death. Within the years I have spent in the UK there are things I see, people I meet and their ways of living which has one or two things that reminds me of my mother. More than enough for me to say she was a good mother and I miss her.

Any individual who smuggles had drugs, commit murder are now known to hide under the impression they suffer from mental health.

In every part of the world it is not surprising some people live their lives in fear, anxiety or apprehension such as no friends or anyone to comfort you when you are in need but in the UK you can live without too much of such apprehension.

At certain points I felt like asking my brother what he has to say, if I tell him I and my fathers have so much in common and in resemblance, from what has been happening in our family since I was a young man. For this reason, I and my father could have some indifference; it could be why I was his child.

You know you've been involved in secrecy so much about relationships, and befriending Nonetheless, after making my last post a discussion of the bright side of rebound relationships, I will not yet withdraw myself from the topic, but give it one more go by writing this post about secrecy and secret romantic relationships; which turn out to be positive or negative depending if you could keep your promise.

Few people fully appreciate the psychological cost of secrets, although psychologists for a while now have been able to demonstrate that 'being a keeper of any type of important personal secret is detrimental to well-being'.

One simple reason for this negative effect of secret keeping is that it hinders you from living important parts of who you are. Important secrets also tend to take up an increasing portion of the secret keepers thoughts psychologists know secrets are often harmful, most frequently kept secrets usually surround romantic relationships where secret keeping is mostly motivated by fears of social disapproval. It comes as somewhat of a surprise only recently psychologists have gone into investigating whether secret relationships also exhibit negative effects, and of what nature these might be.

There's no question family secrets are destructive. But it matters mightily when and how you reveal them. Resist the temptation to handle them at transition times except during new beginnings.

From government conspiracies to couples having affairs, secrets permeate every level of society. Secrets have existed throughout time, but the nature of secrets has recently changed in our society. Today's families face special dilemmas about secrecy, privacy, silence, and openness.

We live in a culture whose messages about secrecy are truly confounding. If cultural norms once made shameful secrets out of too many events in human life, we are now struggling with the reverse the assumption of keeping secrets no matter how, when, or to whom is morally superior it is automatically healing. My own experience, however, has shown me that telling secrets in the wrong way or at the wrong time can be remarkably painful and destructive.

The questions we need to concern ourselves with is how do we reveal secret, let the next person do it for you, how do I tell a secret without hurting the next person and how do I know the right time to reveal a secret never except it is crucial. I've learned the answers as I've witnessed sometimes with terror, more often with joy, and always with deep respect families making the courageous journey from secrecy to openness.

Secrets are kept or opened for many complex motives, from self serving abuses of power to altruistic protection of others. Understanding the best ways and situations in which to reveal a family secret can help you decide when and how to do so.

Although we encounter secrets in every area of life, they are perhaps most destructive when kept in the home. Families are support systems; our identity and ability to form close relationships with others depend upon the trust and communication we feel with loved ones. If family members keep secrets from each other or from the outside world the emotional fallout can last a lifetime.

A person who seeks to undo the damage caused by family secrets must accept that revealing a secret is not a betrayal but a necessity.

Not all secrets are destructive. Many are essential to establishing bonds between people or to detach them. Creation of any secret between two people in a family actually forms a triangle it always excludes and therefore involves another.

When family members suspect that important information is being withheld from them, they may pursue the content of the secret in ways that violate privacy.

For the first time after we became Freemason I told my brother what I felt to have been a Freemason and asked him what he thought of himself as a Freemason and for what reason am I still single? Then I reckoned we both have different perspective through the nature of our initiation as freemasons.

I was receiving treatment with Queen Elizabeth home treatment team. On my last appointment I had with the team, my sister in-law Mrs. Nwamaka Megbele accompanied me to Queen Elizabeth hospital before this appointment; I had not seen my sister-in-law Nwamaka for the past two years.

I introduced her to Dr Niangua my psychiatrist at Queen Elizabeth home treatment team and asked my sister-in-law doesn't Dr Niangua looks very much in likeness to my brother Mr. Omagbemi. Yes actually was her reply that Dr Niangua dose has resemblance to my brother Mr. Omagbemi Megbele . In fact what I should have said was that that Dr Niangua have resemblance to Mr. Zack Megbele I had not seen Zach before the appointment It was when I saw Zack it came to me about a strange experience of having felt Mr Zack's presence whilst I was sleeping in our family home at Warri with the rest of my family in which, he had spoken to me in my sleep.

She recently at the time gave birth to Mr Zack for my

brother; during that period she gave me a handout which contains names of several prescriptions for mental health treatment. Then I saw Mr. Zach my nephew after our appointment for the first time he has a slight resemblance to Dr Niangua. The medication Dr Niangua prescribed for me was Olanzapine tablets Olanzapine is structurally similar to Clozapine and Quetiapine which I was put on, on a basis of trial to elect the right prescription for me during that period in 2007 when I become very unwell. I did not do well with Clozapine and Quetiapine. .

I did not do well with the Olanzapine tablets I was frequently having headaches, pains in my joints in my hands and leg, after I had undergone long periods of over eating and weight gain. I was also in the process of having one of my molar teeth extracted because of toothache while Zach was also having tooth problems. I was put on Risperidone tablets in 2008 as at 2014 I was still on Risperidone tablets prescribed by my GP Dr Robert Hughes. After some visit my brother and Mr. Zack made to my flat some years later I noticed my nephew Mr. Zack and I have the same colouration of mouth gum Mrs. Cordelia Megbele was the one in our family who first made me aware I have a unique mouth gum among our family. When my brother told me his sons name I told him I wish he had named him Mr. Daniel Megbele.

I don't know why she quickly told Dr Niangua that I and my brother Mr Omagbemi are from the same parents, she should have also added 'from a polygamous home' then, I wondered why I am the psychiatrist case, I felt at some point she could be making excuse for herself it was left, for me to complete the dialogue in our relationship I had to do it better by writing because I might be feeling she was making implications her giving birth to her daughter as a suzerain had something to do with me. She told Niangua she had just graduated in mental health working at Kent and the procedures they use while steering at me directly which meant she was also informing me as well. But one needs to take a look at the implications and procedures she was making in my life mind you, my late mother was a nursing student in the UK, she worked at Eko hospital in Lagos before I moved in with her at FESTAC Town Lagos by which time, she was a staff of R.T Briscoe pharmaceutical. I have more than two step mothers whom, I have grown up under my sister in law had a son in her first relationship with one of retired Brigadier Sudelu's son before she moved in with my brother and she is two years older than my brother. All my mother's children for my father are two years older than each other I observe it as something of a ritual in my family while my brother's wants to authenticate himself to get a gripe of himself within his relatives based on other related issues which means something to him on his own terms. He was born after the only girl in our parent's relationship. I suffer from a strange paranoia that the man in my sisters in laws first relation whom, she had Calvin Sudelu with is inside my brother sometimes when my brother is speaking to me it is as if, it is the man speaking inside my brother. Being celibate, I also wish to authenticate myself , I reckon, I would have better understanding of my life situation to add something of an enigma about Calvin Sudelu is that I go through stages and flashing images of paranoia and hallucinations he is the reincarnation of my grandfather from my father's side. In our family I have always been told I have good resemblance to our grandfather Mr. Goldpine Megbele in looks, height and body build I and Mr. Calvin Sudelu, have very slight resemblance in such features I often hear his voices how do I know it is his voices because, it has his own tone of voice.

The first time I felt my Goldpine's or rather Calvin presences in the UK, was when I took in the pepper soup ingredients Cordelia gave me from Nigeria in 1990 then, I was living at number one Searles Road within Elephant and Castle and Old Kent road. On the day I took in the pepper soup I had prepared, which I had to get rid of because I felt strange when taking it in such that I felt this overpowering feeling of Goldpine in spirit coming over me and all of a sudden, my head swelled with dizzy sensation. I also felt I was in Mr. Osibowale's house at Ibadan where my mother lived I also saw flashing images of my mother and heard voices telling me not to take in the pepper soup I had prepared and that I should get rid of it I only felt what they said. Both my mother and Goldpine, died in close proximity

I moved in with my travelling bag from Nigeria in which the pepper soup ingredients was flown into Britain on my arrival to the UK, Mr. Kayode Adeneye from an Igebu origin from Ogun state whose father owns a house at Yaba Lagos in close proximity from our dwelling at Lawani Street Lagos his father at Lagos, is a dealer in selling machines for grinding pepper, onions and tomatoes for household use by customers who goes to the actual people who dose the grinding. Mr. Kayode Adeneye picked me and my brother Mr. Omagbemi in his car from New Cross as we had made our way from Heathrow to new cross. We went to his accommodation at New Cross ate rice and strew and he drove use to Mrs. Comfort Iyinboh's resident at number one Chelsea Deacon way at the Elephant and Castle where my brother left me the second day for an hostel at Clapham Common known as Cecile house. I left the second day for a Salvation Army hostel close to Waterloo road.

By this time, Mrs. Comfort Iyinboh whose husband is also a chief her two daughters' Jacky and Alexandra had not arrived back from Nigeria. We met them for the first time in Nigeria as I reckon, they were on a visit to Nigeria with their mother within weeks before I and my brother were to leave Nigeria for the UK we all met at Lagos. When I and Omagbemi arrived in the UK, we both sheared Mrs. Comfort Iyinboh's accommodation with her son Mr. Begho. Mrs. Comfort Iyinboh has a daughter named Gloria I first met at Ibadan she studied at Ife University the same university my brother Barrister Oritseweyinmi and his close friend Mr. Jide are graduates of philosophy.

When my father visited my council flat for the third which was his last visit to the UK during that period, he was accompanied by my brother and his wife I knew he was coming for a visit in my flat. I prepared him a meal and he wanted to have bear instead of gin or Whisky then told me to go and buy him bear my local store had closed, I had to go down to the Greyhound Pub near Kingsman street and buy him a jar of bear after his meal, they left I thought of the implication of my father's visit to my flat in the company of my brother and his wife' did it had anything to do with my not letting him or my sister in law into my flat I contemplate.

If it had, I would have expected any three of them to have implied such was the reason for their visit, and not for me to make up what the implication of their visit was. It should be a father and son discussion they never stayed long the visit was brief there were signs of body language which did not get through to me because at the time, in my mind it was just a visit or was somebody expecting something? This is a family matter there is no way of going forward and backward or backward and forward with it, conflicts are inevitable it should first be avoided in our homes.

I understand it was a wrong thing to do when I started to be myself after my admission to hospital. I should have let them into my flat they are not strangers. Things to be considered are what had led to it, what are relationship and family implications and family matters, was it as a result to my illness at the time, I did not consider having behaved the way I did deliberately or to be rude? Then at least we would know our feelings if they had, had anything to say, and it's what they would have got out of me. According to custom am not permitted having such a say in the presence of my father. If he would not call me privately and speak to me he would not let anyone else interfere in his presence. It was the first time; I had seen my father looking half traumatised.

Just after I left hospital in 1995, my sister in law moved in with my brother in his one bed room flat at number three Curlew house in Brockley SE4 just by Saint Norbert way during our fathers last visit, they had moved from number three Curlew house to number 3 Pulton House at Turnham road also in Brockley where my father sheared their accommodation with them on his visits.

If my sister in law felt bad about it, she could have told me about it or even make a joke of it to let me know her feelings at least I would have preferred one of them to say something coming into my flat and telling me to go out and buy bear was not enough how do I feel about it, traumatised I did not observe it a conflict situation, but it can pump up in the future. I wanted to know how they really felt about it I did not intent to create bad feeling as a matter of fact I was feeling unwell and half traumatised. Could going out to buy him bear meant, I was apologising if they had asked for an apology it would not had come easy from me after the experiences I went through. Before this I had bought my sister in law a purse to figuratively say I was sorry.

After my father's death I told my brother I was going to visit him and his family in their number 3 Pulton house in Brockly at during that period, she was undertaking a course on social care in mental health on getting there knocked on the door she open it told me my brother and his children had gone out I thought of waiting for awhile immediately I got into the living room she told me she wanted a bottle of Pink lady gave me the exact money I should go and get it for her in their nearby convenient store. I went came back after a while left. I remembered one morning my brother walked into my flat unexpectedly handed me a bag and told me his wife told him, he should give then to me. Opening the bag, it contained a jacket that looks like a military top it wasn't really of military clothing just as a way of describing it.

Language is the human capacity for acquiring and using complex systems of communication, and a language is any specific example of such a system. The scientific study of language is called linguistics. Any estimate of the precise number of languages in the world depends on a partly arbitrary distinction between languages and dialects. However, estimates vary between around 6,000 and 7,000 languages in number. Natural languages are spoken or signed, but any language can be encoded into secondary media using auditory, visual or tactile stimuli, for example in graphic writing, braille, or whistling. This is because human language is modality-independent. When used as a general concept, 'language' may refer to the cognitive ability to learn and use systems of complex communication, or to describe the set of rules that makes up these systems, or the set of utterances that can be produced from those rules.

Human language is unique because it has the properties of productivity, recursively, and displacement, and because it relies entirely on social convention and learning. Its complex structure therefore affords a much wider range of possible expressions and uses than any known system of animal communication. Language is thought to have originated when early hominins started gradually changing their primate communication systems, acquiring the ability to form a theory of other minds and a shared intentionality.

When described as a system of symbolic communication, language is traditionally seen as consisting of three parts: signs, meanings and a code connecting signs with their meanings. Languages, understood as the particular set of speech norms of a particular community, are also a part of the larger culture of the community that speaks them. Humans use language as a way of signalling identity with one cultural group and difference from others.

At certain point, my feelings were mixed my brother had somebody else's friend when they already had children my brother became married to her and I had sign their marriage contract on behalf of my brother at a registry did not bother me if they wanted to be together, as long as they are happy it's their choice and I wish them all the happiness they can find but when it becomes a situation as my readers would find out in my next book it becomes something of an enigma or rather puzzling I should say! She is no longer a stranger not in our family as long as she had become my brother's wife if there was need for it, that was if, she had showed her anger to my father my father should had called me, have a good word with me privately I should tell her, I was sorry; fear enough but sorry for what when just weeks after she visited my flat for the first time heavy with a child I was taken ill as unwell into an hospital diagnosed with paranoid schizophrenia in which, I the mother and the child's birthday and my stay in hospital where within a week of her birth. If it were the case, nevertheless I would have done so I had the feeling then she wanted my father to pull me in, in their presence and talk to me but for what? Within years after I was diagnosed as schizophrenia, she was speaking to me and one of my psychiatrists as a carer I would like to know more of what procedures they use at the place she works as a care in mental health. Then I saw reason why our father might have initiated us into freemasons to take up celibacy if we wish and then the more I thought deeper into going through a life of celibacy.

I had the compulsion to ask my brother where in Nigeria did Calvin Sudelu's; father originates from he told me he is from somewhere in Rivers state where our fathers business was based and where he is well known for having lots of young girl friends. I have met his grandfather retired Brigadier Sudelu only once and that's within the UK when our father came for his first visit into the UK after our arrival at this time, I was working at Iceland Frozen food plc and about that time I left the company. Brigadier Sudelu was visiting my father at my brothers new accommodation at number 3 Curlew house in Brockley I only exchanged greetings with him.

I have also met Calvin Sudelu's father then, my nice Lydia had just been given birth to and I had just been discharged from hospital in 1995 I went to see my brother at her place at Lewisham just by Saint John's Church which she and my brother were accommodating at the time before they all moved in to my brothers dwelling at number 3 Curlew house in Brockley at this time, my brother was moving to and fro frequently from Curlew house to Lewisham way where she lived. When I got there I saw a man who had slight resemblance to my brother even in colour of skin, same body build. Who my brother introduced to me, as Calvin's father as I could remember they both throw bald remarks at each other with words with one which came at me. I sensed he wasn't happy he was grudging and news must have come out about Lydia's birth. When I later went to her place at Lewisham after she arrived home from Lewisham hospital where she gave birth to Lydia I had not thought of settling down inside her accommodation at Lewisham Vale just by Saint John's Church when she stretched out a plate containing snails to me and asked me if I would have some with a facial expression. I could not refuse I mean; looking back on the first day we met in front of my flat at number 13 Gorman road later in hospital, her coming to visit me there and when I heard the news about how she gave birth to my niece moreover the need for me to be resilient offering me snails could mean an omen my father ate snails and never offered it to his children except me, my mother offered me snails while I was living with her. Nevertheless for truce and peaceful measures I took the plate of three pieces of fried snails from her and ate them then I thought she had gone native after eating the snails till recently I go through phase of paranoia and hallucinations of something of an omen or voodoo as if I have over the years undergone a ritual with a snake, snail, pigs and humans involved in conflict resolution. All creatures have their own kingdom, rituals, language, abilities and reason for their own creation what brought about the great temptation which is said, led to the rise or downfall of man they might understand it in their own terms since some of them lay down their lives and skin on our table and even, for rituals and sacrifices.

When it comes to being offered snails under such a scenario it's not only a language, gesture, body language or signs. Body language is a form of mental and physical ability of human non-verbal communication, consisting of body posture, gestures, facial expressions, and eye movements. Humans send and interpret such signals almost entirely subconsciously. A gesture is a form of non-verbal communication in which visible bodily actions communicate particular messages, either in place of speech or together and in parallel with words. Gestures include movement of the hands, face, or other parts of the body. Gestures differ from physical non-verbal communication that does not communicate specific messages, such as purely expressive displays, proxemics, or displays of joint attention. Gestures allow individuals to communicate a variety of feelings and thoughts, from contempt and hostility to approval and affection, often together with body language in addition to words when they speak.

A sign language is a language which, instead of acoustically conveyed sound patterns, uses manual communication and body language to convey meaning. This can involve simultaneously combining hand shapes, orientation and movement of the hands, arms or body, and facial expressions to fluidly express a speaker's thoughts. A sign is a representation of an object that implies a connection between itself and its object. A natural sign bears a causal relation to its object for instance; thunder is a sign of storm. A conventional sign signifies by agreement, as a full stop signifies the end of a sentence. (This is in contrast to a symbol which stands for another thing, as a flag may be a symbol of a nation). The way a sign signifies is called semiosis which is a topic of semiotics and philosophy of language. How a sign is perceived depends upon what is intended or expressed in the semiotic relationship of: Signification, Significance (i.e. meaning) and Importance

For example, people may speak of the significance of events, the signification of characters, the meaning of sentences, or the import of a communication. Different ways of relating signs to their objects are called modes of signification. Uses of conventional signs are varied. Usually the goal is to elicit a response or simply inform. That can be achieved by marking something, displaying a message (i.e. a notice), drawing attention or presenting evidence of an underlying cause (for instance, medical symptoms signify a disease), performing a bodily gesture, etc.

I saw my father last at my brothers flat in Brockley after his party as I was about to leave he told my brother to bring out a box full of spices ogbono, dried and ground crayfish and pepper and rice etc of our origin he has done it again I told myself; when I saw the box I steered at my father in the face with a stain voice, told my sister in law to call me a taxi cab which she did his my father making inference to himself or to them I steered at my father again as I was about to leave after he gave me two pictures of himself dressed in freemason a picture of Deaconess Mrs. Cordelia Megbele and a freemason bible I later collected from my brothers dwelling after our father had left the UK. I didn't see frailness of death on my father's face or physic at the time what I experienced was of wedging power or authority what would most people think would had been the effect of me, my brother and the rest of my family relationship?. Before I left one other thing he did that I found quire was my father calling my brother's name with somewhat expression deep in his voice saying 'Omagbemi go and bring that coral bead I gave you'.

It was this time I felt I could not do anything private with my father because the coral bead was the same coral bead I had worn while I paid my respect to the Olu of Warri while he was conferring my father his chieftaincy title. It was one of the same coral bead my father had wore the first time he visited me at my flat when I told him he should not come into my flat now he was handing it back to me but added it was the coral bead he gave my brother what do most sociologist think are the issue that causes discrepancies within children within a family such a thing as the coral bead might hold supernatural omens he did not give the coral bead, pictures or freemason bible to me in my flat as far as am concerned he gave me nothing as for the food he brought to my flat on the first occasion not after I had worked in more than five Iceland frozen food chain store and had worked in a brick making factory in Croydon.

My council flat was not my first accommodation in the UK, it was not brought to me straight from Heathrow and I had met my father on a previous visit. I never informed him I had moved into a council flat. The food was brought from my brother flat where he was spending his visit with his new wife few even before his death, the Asians hold the predominate sale of African food products at least, I ate what he brought but I wouldn't let him in with so much coral beads around his neck he hadn't walked into my flat I was having a fit after I was diagnosed with schizophrenia in my own thoughts I realised I might had suffered from a far more sever fit. I realise on his first visit to my flat something underneath his feet was pining me down from above my head to underneath my feet which might had made me react the way I did. it's when I might had gone in and out of the house he had built in Nigeria that's when I felt I might had done something wrong by not letting him into my flat. Something secret I know about my father within his Ogboni cult is whenever he had been given food from any of his meeting he brings it to his home at Port Harcourt were his wives aware of this sometimes I and my brother ate the food with him within a year of our living Nigeria for the UK. One thing I know is if my mother had fed me with Ejo oka-baba I never knew or heard of our mother feeding my brother Omagbemi with Ejo-oka-baba or any other of her children. At one time at Port Harcourt, I, our father and my brother Omagbemi sat down and ate soup and pounded yam prepared with Alligator which had been prepared by a lady friend of our father quite different from another lady friend who dose his regular cooking for him this lady friend of my father is an Itsekiri living at Port Harcourt. I and my brother Mr. Omagbemi did not see our mother after we had the meal prior to my leaving Nigeria for the UK. As we ate I experienced my father and brother eating through me spiritually, psychologically and emotionally it was an experience that paved a way on my own belief in transubstantiation. At one point as we were eating, I sat up from my chair involuntarily and swore silently inside me. No word came out of my mouth. Our father retorted in a very brisk sudden tone of voice asking me why I stood up from my chair. I told him any word which came into my head which was, I wanted to turn off the air-conditioner. All I remembered my brother doing was steering at me at that point we three finished our meal briskly. The experience left me spiritually drained and a little bit lifeless.

Alligator or Ejo oka-baba I might have eaten in Nigeria was assimilated into our culture it's quite different to feed on snails or Iru in the UK because it's within a different culture and environment. If I were to eat such food here it would have to be, at my own discretion. During his visit I felt like letting him know if he was still upset about what happened in front of my flat why didn't he come with a taxi cab when this incident took place in the early 1990's. My late father was never a man who was upset about anything if he was; he always kept it to himself. At the time I first got to know my sister in law, she drives a car am now taking a taxi to let my father know this, was one of the reason I acted the way, I did in his presence in front of my flat. For what took place in my brothers dwelling on that night at number 3 Pulton House at Turnham road also in Brockley. How I hoped if they are fortunate enough to buy a house, they would not buy number 3 Pulton House. I go through paranoia the effect is that they would have bought something out of the reach of burning coal or fire which epitomise the Greenwich hospital or to have pulled it down. Or the new development at the plot where the Greenwich hospital once stood after it was pulled down. The flats my brother occupied at Brockley and Lancelot Andrews hostel close to Borough high road I lived in before moving to my flat in Woolwich have certain futures similar to the infrastructure of the former Greenwich hospital such as the types of bricks, colour with which they had been constructed quite similar to the types I had worked on in a brick making company in Croydon. I got to work at the brick making company through an employment agency called extra staff located at Waterloo road close to Salvation Army hostel where I once lived during the early years of my returning back into the UK. The types of bricks reminds of Olumo Rock at Abeokuta. Though I and my brother lived in two different hostels we were directed to our blocks of flats by Ms Debbie Whitney.

Borough High Street is a road in <u>Southwark</u>, <u>London</u>, running south-west from <u>London Bridge</u>, forming part of the <u>A3 route</u> which runs from London to <u>Portsmouth</u>, on the south coast of England. By way of reasoning why didn't my father hand me the coral bead in my flat when he visited me? It involves other issues I would only discus with my psychiatrist or psychologist such as he created a vice over me, which he handed over to them because it was through part of that process, he created the broomstick for his own present reincarnation. The last avenue I saw my father last at Lagos before I left Nigeria after he my brother and myself came through from a journey from Warri in his Mercedes-Benz driven by his driver Mr Vincent. We went straight to out aunty Tycos-lawson house where I and my brother ate. Our elder brother later picked us up from our auntie's house to visit our uncle Temitayo who wasn't in at the time. While our father, left us for an appointment. We met our father on the same day at a hotel where we spent the night. Before we met at the hotel on that same day I took an excuse from them during a visit to a friend's house where we met our father after his meeting. On my own I went to Yaba market and bought myself a new travelling suitcase. I told my father of my intention and asked for money I also bought myself some new cloths. The next day we were at Lagos international airport in the company of our father, our elder brother and sister from our mother's side. My story is ironically the opposite difference from that of Eddie Murphy coming to America. Some Jamaicans, Caribbean's, people from Barbados are of the opinion Africans sold them into slavery. Eddie Murphy Coming to America was a movie act mine is reality. I watched at a cinema at the Elephant and

Castle while I was living at number 1 Searles Road house just by old Kent road under a private Landlord through an agency run by a Mr Campton in Camberwell Green it was like a bedsit which I sheared with other tenants.

After the Coral bead was handed back to me I had an overpowering compulsion to take the bead with me to my working place at the Woolwich Gala Club one morning I did not know what made me showed it to Mrs. Joanna Tarker who was the cleaning supervisor and Ms Janet Clark, Brian Archer and Mr Green with a voice coming out of me saying this, is all that I have left of my father, Brian Archer and Mr Green are both Jamaicans. The coral bead was with me in my flat when I lost my father I did not travel to Nigeria for his funeral during his death and funeral whilst working at the Club I felt being pulled with my father's funeral procession from Ibadan to Warri in Delta state. I later had this strange feeling I should quit my job at the Club for some unclear feeling in me which remains to be verified. I remained at the job working until I experience my father's reincarnation. I do not want to imply this because it might be termed as a paranoia that I have experience a relationship with my father and the woman who bore him in his present reincarnation right from when I was at Port Harcourt and Warri It was part of a practice going further to what I might call practising immortality. I also took the coral bean to Saint Mary's Church Woolwich to pray one morning the curate of the church is a vegetarian. I bought a small safe from Argos Woolwich lucked the coral bead with my passport and some jewelleries bought from H.M. Samuel and Argos and lucked it in my flat I have the feeling I had been commissioned my council flat for archaeological reasons.

After our fathers funeral my brother Barister. Oritseweyinmi's wife Yvonne an optician was pregnant was on a visit to the UK she visited me after which her husband came to the UK on his visit, he brought clothing's since I was not present at the funeral made for the whole family for our fathers funeral which is customary of our tradition and culture I left the clothing's for a while in my flat after some months I took photographs with them in my flat with the coral bean my father gave me. Few weeks later I began suffering from swaying, dizzy spells, shaking I mange to call an ambulance which took me to Queen Elizabeth hospital. Any time I had been unwell my sister in law Nwamaka and my brother brought food to me at my flat it was difficult telling them they should not bring me food when I did I felt it caused mixed feelings. These days most people are lacking the affinity to compromise at least things one might view other people would lightly understand. It is not easy for me going out to buy my food and preparing them there some practical things I came to understand such as I wanted to have my driving licence owned a vehicle which did not materials as part of my life's endeavour ironically I felt later it was all for my own good because going to the African Asian store I felt better doing my shopping by hand rather than through my own driving or through a taxi and it was good exercise for me

No man his age dressed the way he did in elegance of our culture with the amount of wealth my father had and the things and shows I had seen my father take part in would my father visit me, bringing a box full of pepper soup ingredients and much more would come to my flat inside a bus he wasn't coming for an occasion.

I would not have written this book or it would have been written in a different format. With no restrain of emotional barriers because, am too emotionally involved they are true events and experience in my life and I reckon if I have not been resilient enough writing my first two books the second one titled memorise of a schizophrenia I would have been more emotionally disturbed or depress. My brother told me he and his wife had lost a child before they had Mr Zach. After giving birth to Zach he told me he and his wife have decided not having any more children. I have not been in a rush to writing my books because of my brother's children at least by now they have reached an age they might understand what could have prompted me to write my books.

During that time in my life at Queen Elizabeth hospital in relation to my care and feelings I suffered a very strong sense of paranoia. I felt I have always wanted to grow up but I had not been given the chance to grow up while other people seem to grow up in one day. I do hear their voices saying things about me, their voices always ringing in my hears; it's as if, they communicate their feelings, thoughts and temperament about everything without actually speaking to me.

At that time I wasn't feeling right. I made a gesture to my sister-in-law with my face twitching with the words slouching out of my mouth. I was fuming from my mouth as the words came out of my mouth 'the medicationone' am taking are 'gooood'.

At this period I felt someone would have an inclination of memories of my past were having effects on me they were partly what was making me go into relapse.

After our appointment my sister-in-law wanted to speak to Dr Niangua privately.

What else could I have done I lost my mother, I should not attend her funeral within the same period my father had a new wife who he brought to the UK close to when he became a chief with other two wives he already had without my mother's presence in his home, he had completed his house it would not accommodate his whole family happily for all he was doing, his money was enough going through all his responsibilities and he wasn't growing any younger he should, had cared very much for his family finances they need not cry out for money before he gives it to them.

There was nothing wrong for me to brace myself up confronting my father for the first time in my life, he did not believed his eye's they way, I reacted it geared him into facing his responsibility about some of his children before he died. I told him he did not see me when I was born in the UK my mother brought me to him in Nigeria by which time, they were separated the way I grow up there were loopholes about my family affairs. It is top of Nigeria to have children born in the UK growing up in Nigeria even if it wasn't then it is now!

Though I had to do it one could ask, I am one of his wives

who should have confronted him if they would not do it themselves and go on winging somebody had to do it and I still ask myself, why should it, be me! While some relatives and friends gained out of it the others would backbite what is it, that can change human nature from wrong to right heaven has made us sufficient, Would it only be through confrontation and irrationality, we are entities of our own with mind body and souls, we have physics and brains to do wonderful things.

Cordelia gave me a bottle of pepper soup ingredient to bring with me to the UK when, there is whisky and brandy if I should catch a cold, working in a cold store few years later, my father brought me more, a box filled with it with rice egusi, smoked prawns, dressed in his traditional attire I would not let him into my flat, he left it by my door step and walked away. Apart from his wives my father was a womanizer.

Moving from Lagos to Delta state, my father rented a whole one story house of five bedrooms, two kitchens his business was based at Port-Harcourt where there are very pretty ladies were he picked and married his third wife Aya who lives with the rest of the family at Warri. She lives at the top floor of the house with her four children with a kitchen and bathroom were my father also occupied one of the bedrooms with a private living room. Cordelia with four children occupies the ground floor were situated the living room a kitchen and bathroom.

Where do I and my brother sleep? At another floor house outside GRA government reserve area with bedroom house rented where lies another bedroom and office my father uses with his girl friend's. Mrs. Cordelia Megbele asked me to shear her bedroom with her because our grandfather had to use my sleeping quarters which is sometimes the living room downstairs? Out of curtsey for my father's wives, I preferred making do with the family parlour as a place to sleep in rather than using a bedroom in my father's office at Warri which he shears with his girl friend's. When a parent provides such amenities for children in Nigeria other people or children your age groups feels one is fortunate only if they know what lies beneath your pride probably not in the best interest of a child or too well un-proportionately perplexingly organised.

Though the incident brought up some family issues but it never changed my father's attitude there is no need to change my family name. He had warned I and my brother before we left Nigeria we should not answer another name. I have leant that humans contribute in making each other what they are. Sometimes it is left for one to use right judgment or consideration in making decision. Why do we have to go into conflicts before we do anything right sometimes certain human nature is difficult to accept or understand?

My father having spent years studying in the UK, back to Africa as a middle class Nigerian, a patron of Freemasons, a grand patron of Rivers State Diocese and grand patron of Holy Trinity Cathedral Choir Port-Harcourt.

During some visits into the UK I had to comply with my father's every wish because I wanted to avoid any tension of bad feelings. My dear reader by the time you read the several books, I hope to write, you would realise I was born into a precondition, to have survived is awesome. There is no reason pretending there is hope when there is no hope if there is reason, there is hope as far, as there is life. I have no idea of what it is to be born premature or even, if I was placed in an incubator but I would hope, born seven month premature in the mid 1960's I was not placed in an incubator through my condition of being born seven month premature.

I have under gone my trials under my mother and father over the years, if there should be reason I am ready to go into further trials as far as there is reason involve.

Crucial family relationship can be devastating, if conflicts are not redressed with consideration, the conflict goes into a deeper level; family relationship is the greatest ties of human relationship it should be a happy relationship while some people feel they could get on well with friends better than their family doing so, you have spilled the beans about your background worst still if you cannot make ends meet or pretend.

My immediate elder brother walks into my flat when the air was with cigarette smoke; he picks a quarrel, because I smoke. Smoking is one of the habits my fathers had, whilst I was growing up, I was the only one in our family who goes out some times about 11pm to buy my father cigarettes while the shops where about to close.

At one time, on one of our all family get together outing, as my father was driving and smoking, ash from his cigarette got cough-up in my eyes because I was seating right behind my father; could I have complained? Do you know what it is for an African child's parent to have a car and the whole family goes out once in a while.

It's always me, my father sends out sometime in the night to buy him cigarettes from my friend Mr Obi's mother's stall of merchandise and household provisions. Mr. Obi originates from Bendel state of Nigeria his father is a police officer they worship at celestial church with Pastor Samuel Bilehou Joseph Oshoffa as their spiritual leader.

Our mother resented our father when, he became a smoker immediately my father dumped her. My brother is only hypo personalizing his own self. Smoking cigarette does not make me feel high, infarct, I hat smoking. It's because, am depressed, giving up the habit of smoking and its treatment, a patient cannot give up such habits through irrational augments, or the patient creates a defence. It is not you, that is dying it is the patient a patient tells you this and you answer back by implying the amount of money the government spends on no smoking campaign, cancer you are being irrational. The problem or issues is why do people continue to smoke even if they know it is bad for their health it cost them money they would rather spend on buying something else that is more special than cigarettes or tobacco the same thing applies to alcohol.

An African individual living in African, each day he or she takes seven different tablets he or she would feel depressed in a place where as sick child is considered as a problem. With my mental health problem, being on medication my brothers and sister in law ought to understand that am depress. As much as I try to stereotyping myself buying things I like, viewing places things of interest I can see and do in the UK why can't I give up such a habit? For a man unable to have his hard on once in a week is a worry to him same thing if a woman misses her period why can't I give up smoking?

I have never been used to taking much medication at certain point I felt upset about it which never occurred while I was in Nigeria.

When I moved in with my mother in 1979 at FESTAC town she was working for Briscoe pharmaceuticals at this time, I never get unwell, or feel unwell, though my mother did put me on some vitamins they where effervescent tablets which dissolves in water, I always enjoy having them.

When I was four to five years my father does provide me with Extra- malt to be taken after meals and the hair on my head each morning is washed thoroughly with curl-out gels put on my hair to coil it and become coyly with waves.

At some stage in my youth, I was taken to see an English medical doctors who advice my father he should, feed me on eggs, pronto chocolate drink, Milo, sausages, bacon and baked beans. With three wives and their own children! Along the line rather for me having such meals my father had them and call me once in a while to put a little bit in my mouth while he is having such meals sometime in the mornings. I had the feeling my father felt it was too much money to spend and under the nose of step mothers with their own children. My father never did what he was told to do by the doctor this was one of the reason my father let go of me to go and live with my mother at FESTAC Town in Lagos.

My father got recognition through my mother in Lagos state Nigerian Ports authority close to my mother's working place at Apapa Lagos, out of it my father got his shipping, clearing and forwarding business. The same scenario happened with my father's third wife and his second wife after his separation from my mother this time my father had moved closer to my mother again since they were still married.

As a schizophrenia I tried at all times to identify myself with my problems, not everybody understands the illness and you cannot just get help from anywhere, more efforts are being put to understand the illness.

From what is contained in this book, consider the situation if I should be speaking to a physiatrist, a care or social worker from my own background or race about these problems I have gone through which have brought a cliché of paranoid schizophrenia attaché to my life would they be effective in helping me overcome my illness as a carer and patient relationship?

I feel they should be more careering and supportive with understanding on what goes on in our background filled with conflict and problems but they cannot represent such course why?; because to them, we are the once who have the British Passport, state benefit entitlement and free health care? I am invariably saying that most care and social health workers are not UK citizens it is not how, to tell me to keep up with awareness the suffering going on in Africa or to be conscious of my background regardless if I am in the UK. This should be left to my own predisposition.

A lot of things happening in our community that warrants alternative approach for example, the NHS and carers to get to know their patients better and develop ways to make them more relax, to talk more of how their illness began this, is very important. In other to really redress such issues related to mental illness including prostitution, lesbian, being gay, taking cocaine, ecstasy, amphetamine, anti -social behaviours etc. Most sufferers are living with the illness at a limbo.

Some of these are quite different from my own jurisdiction on why am suffering from mental illness. All types of mental illness come under different social contrast. What we want is to feel free and calm to talk about our problems with people who are ready to listen and do something towards our care.

My family members have observed me in different way in the past while we were in Africa. There was never a time I was no good a child or a young ending up in no good. In many ways, I am more a different person now, coming into Europe I was faced with a new identity, and a new reality to confront.

I have to explain to my family for them to understand why I become a celibate so that they will come in terms with why I am a celibate for some of them, who cares? Basically it is an issue of fulfilling a purpose partly because I am a schizophrenic with fears for my children to be but with insight to be sincere to them I do not like suffering.

I have fear for my offspring's to be, a feeling of uncertainty that planet earth has not reached its heights for my offspring to survive and display their full potentials or it could be because I would be discovered as being an alien? Why should I feel this way if I do not feel alienated in any environment I have dwelt in considering within good and evil?

The history of the statue of Zeus originates from Europe because of consequence related to my birth in this my present life, I had to be shipped to Africa, It involve all Europe after the second world war, more sophisticated airplanes, sea liners and most considerate American man astronauts on the moon just about when I was born. This became eminent since 1835 in America when the use of incubators to resuscitate children with premature birth was adopted.

Anyway, I felt the most important thing for me to do is to do all I can in retaining the statue of Zeus, which is my whole mass and form as a human being it has a purpose to fulfil in Africa to ascertain the abyss of Africa like a pendulum. It has rightly been the abyss of Africa should be ascertained until it becomes firm for huge constructions and developments. Gold, petroleum diamond the forest and wildlife might make it crumble.

I told my brother on a telephone conversation our fathers should have become the Ologbosere of Delta state second in command after the highest title of Olu of Warri but had only became a chief, which was my father's own doing before my father's death.

Everybody have opinions of who they are or, what other people could be. My father becoming the Ologbosere of Delta state in my opinion is what my father should be I was just telling my brother my opinion I have about our father. Holding the status of Zeus comes with great hopes and aspiration. My handsomeness would not tell my condition of birth not my growing up in Africa or the condition I had lived in before coming back to Europe.

Some misunderstood conceptions about my personality; I do not consider myself suffering from personality disorder I always try to be myself at all times I cannot admit it to myself or to my conscience in any way I am, I might or could be suffering from personality disorder. No matter how queer or genuine it all comes to me that am a child as lovely as a tree it has been so with me, since I was a child. My father cared so much for my hair when my mother took me back to Nigeria and handed me to him because their relationship had collapsed.

Each morning with special hair creams to curl the hair on my head for it to cruel-out, not by any of our house helper but by my father himself or my eldest brothers barrister. Oritseweyinmi. I don't see any other African having such coulee hair as mine.

From my youth my hair cut very too often, it grows out quickly always coyly with a simple body cream as Vaseline. My mother never allows me to see the barber; she cuts my hair for me. In my opinion the hairs on my head right from earth is hanging within the moon and other planet.

At my age of 41 years, it is still very coyly. With lots of different hair creams in Europe, it becomes more curled-up.

My hair has reached its final stage in my point of view I only use or two types of hair cream, it signifies I will no longer be living temporary lives through reincarnation again.

My brother's remark while he accompanied me in 2007 for my outpatient appointment at the Ferryview mental health review for the first time on which I mentioned about getting back to work. My brother's remark on the topic was that I was unwell nobody would call me and give me a job. The appointment I had with Mr. Engi with my brother present I felt my brother probably thought I would go into a craze about how my illness affects me one has to be careful dealing with cares because they might waste no time in sectioning me. I felt by making remarks about going back to work if I get better in the presence of my care and relative, my relative would easily predict, if something unexpected should happen within that period they should be aware of my state of mind at the time the appointment took place. His remarks about my being unwell with me feeling nobody would call me and give me a job really struck me as reality.

Mr. Engi took the place of Dr. Banjac at the Ferryview health centre on this my outpatient appointment because, Dr Banjac was on leave.

I kept calm about my brothers remarks about feeling nobody would call me and give me a job. I mentioned in a philosophical tone in their presence that life is a trial. This was an example of what my cares should observe within their patients and family member.

If family members treat relatives who are unwell with less interest in the presence of their cares, carers do not take caution of what a patient might be going through under their relatives it is negligence on the part of the carer. They are supposed to stand for their patient's interest. It's another avenue for carers to reach deeper level of carers and patient relationship patients will respond to treatment and get on well with their care.

I hope to know, what the NHS, think are the future of Schizophrenics sufferers in our community. NHS and my cares should be aware the illness is also caused by family problems, with related issues that could be very difficult or delicate for some patient's to come out with.

I am aware, I am writing with regards to a kind of illness, which might have over the years ruined most people's lives. 2007, the cause of the illness schizophrenics is yet unknown to its full extent. Because of this since 2004 I had been word processing the manuscripts of this books which I consider to be my project after attending two universities with my illness as a paranoid schizophrenic.

Why not write, I told myself I enjoyed reading since my youth, any book e.g. Mills and booms, Hardly Chase, Harold Wilson, William Shakespeare and the Holy Bible, What I read from news papers or see on television that could captivate me.

As an individual I do try to be very active through this comes my ability for action and to distinguish right from wrong. I do not wish to judge any one or I be judged; every child is born with his or her own capabilities despite if a person is disabled.

If I cannot help doing something I should not do, I do not always feel good about it such as smoking. If causation can lead to more causation how could one avoid an unfortunate disaster if not by being an avoider to restrain from more causation or, I would be scotched? We all have different characteristics, nature, temperaments, and ways of observing ourselves and other people. Life on earth is full of more than conflicts; it could be a happy place to be in some times, but it never last.

Facing my reality with my up-bringing, background and predicament is a confrontation to life's trials. In doing so, it is inevitable I would easily realise and be confronted with lots of alternatives options of things I should do and things I should not do.

I have read many books of Africa authors e.g. Drummer boy, things fall apart. In any case, if I should have children of my own, from my writing, they would understand or at least have a notion of what it is, to be an in-between African and a European mixed race. Then, and then only, can they say a prayer for me.

I have soft feelings for Europeans who visit or have made Africa their home; they must love we African people dearly. Lots of African race in Africa love them as well while they are over there some Africans come into Europe for better life than what it is out there. In some way I consider why not if after a while they could go back to their own land of origin and do some home work now it seem lots of Africans and people from other third world nations would do anything through immigration to have their stay in the UK?

It is not easy to take a serious matter lightly. Doctor who or Frankenstein has caused a serious talk as a TV comedy series documentary in retrospect to the television drama, claimed the world's news head-line.

I could understood, what might have made a man, a doctor for that matter to do what he did. It could be, because of lack of Love and competition from the people of his medical career in the 18th century i.e. His other friends and relatives in the medical field had coursed some un-biased situation, which forced him to do what he had to do in the creation of Frankenstein. One problem about inconsistencies is that it could be wrong but people fail or are too late to have questioned its causation.

It was surprising from my childhood my experience of what my father used to be in the way he treated me, he used to be very fond of me probably he was creating a scenarios based on my mother's absence within the family.

Money is the root of all evil said a friend of mine it could be but it is one small part of the root of all evil they are several causes of the root of evil. I told him money among other causes of evil could mean do the right thing at the right time for money but not solely for the sake of money because money serves other purposes that are not genially for evil.

All am doing was a job to earn my living which didn't reflect on my wages, as a deputy supervisor to have been asked such a question, while my mind was at work; I thought to myself it could have been asked to raise conflict.

As the deputy working within two companies of which one was a subsidiary, one of the subsidiary complained that a particular job had not been properly done. The responsible subsidiary for the job which hasn't been done properly investigated through record, time getting feedback on the job.

In resolving the case, the supervisors thoroughly see the job done properly and took another job to see it properly done with his and his staffs. The job was done to a high slandered. A question is should there be any more compliant so soon for another job not properly done within the same week both companies work as subsidiaries if so one of its staff is not doing his or her job thoroughly.

Should there be another complaint? It should rather be complementary if they had done other jobs well done, next week they would do the rest more thoroughly. Even if there should be another complaint, the subsidiary should reactive a complement before another complaint. For the other job that was well done. Communication and initiative skill is a gift in expressing organisational tool. In such a scenario using abusive word is negligence of duty.

As an illustration I walked into a housing office as an unemployed applicant looking for a job. During the interview, I explained to the interviewer not with regards to all the qualifications I had, but with how, I upgraded my qualification from 'A' level to 'H.N.D he employed me as a housing officer.

My first day at work was on a Monday, all I had in the morning before arriving at work was chickens or fish pies because I was still single, I had to take a lot into detail I could not prepare myself a meal before I left for work.

These is an illustration as an example my first client was a young man who complained one of the water pipe in his kitchen had busted water leaks from it dripping to the floor tiles and in respect that water could sink down-words into the floor bellow.

Why I want to be a qualified housing officer was one aspect taken into account after qualifying, given the post as a housing office, At the reception desk, having skill in his/her own field in counselling, A client walks into the establishment with a problem that needs counselling of a bust pipe licking in the kitchen. Another client walks in and complained water was leaking from the top floor of her accommodation into her kitchen she lives at the same accommodation of my first client.
Would I have to ask what his or her problem has to do with the next person's problem?

The current trend I observed at the Woolwich job centre just entering 2006 was looking for people who would go on a plumbing course. 20% of the job vacancies were for plumbers needed with readiness to pay high wages by employers. The unemployment figures for 2006 have been different from that of 2009 and 2010.

When conflict is not managed properly, it causes friction, ill feelings and wasted time. If differences are not properly dealt with, it leaves emotional scares within working environment. Conflict human activity systems are not easy to predict or model human resources have individual as well as a corporate existence, conflicts can cause problems. These conflicts which prevent organisation from achieving their goal must be prevented even before they occur.

Managers are concerned with efficiency they may want newer, more efficient machinery. This may displace workers as less needed. Conflict may occur between marketing and production managers as their policies and interest often differ. During these, energy is wasted, which could have been used for constructive purposes i.e. productivity, planning and decision making.

It is important unnecessary conflicts should be resolved in

constructive manner. In today's working practice and in our homes, we and managers are better off equipped with conflict resolution skills. Managers regard conflict management of equal or slightly higher importance than planning, communication, motivation, and decision-making.

If we should be able to handle delicate conflicts in a positive and constructive ways, they should be able to determine the causes of conflicts, find ways of diagnosing the type of conflict and developing methods and techniques to cope with differences. This is why it is a creative process, always should be dealt with constructively.

As a result of conflicts one party could feel bad about the other party's reaction which could have been taken lightly with regards that, they were just doing their job. Or the other party may feel, they complain a lot, what am saying is that it could result to a pleasant or unpleasant situation.

In the past, conflict had been overlooked by Managers partly because it was felt conflict was damaging to an organisation and efforts should be concentrated on measures to create harmony.

Conflict is now treated seriously as an important aspect in the proper understanding of organisational behaviour. It has now been realised that not all conflict is harmful and that perhaps a certain level of conflict is inevitable. The present need is to understand the causes of conflict and to develop constructive measures to control and use the energies released by conflicts, since, it is a fact that we are all exposed to conflict on a daily basis.

The definition of conflict is a personal divergence of interest within groups or individuals another definition is that conflict is behaviour intended to obstruct achievement on the goals of another person.
Conflict can increase the motivation and energy available to do tasks, with each party achieving greater understanding of the other parties' needs, wish, expectation, goals and values everyone wants to have a child, a child to create better tomorrow an understanding for love or someone to look up

to in other to express ourselves as e.g. a good parents, even if we don't know how we can learn.

These things happens but we could be there to look behind our backs this is what turns the world around if Interpersonal conflict may arise in this world of today in the business environment it would mean ways of managing intrapersonal conflict more effectively in the working environment. Disadvantages of conflicts

It drains energy that could have been used constructively
Undermines morals
Deepens differences
Creates distrust and suspicion
Decreases productivity
Polarises individuals and groups

With all its advantages and disadvantages, Conflict is inevitable, we find it within ourselves, with others i.e. friends and relatives, in the work place, in our environment, it should be dealt with constructively, and with regards that to each individual, the interpretation which they attach to the word conflict is determined by our perception, expectation and values. As well as the norms of the community in which we live.

In the work place for example an optimal level of conflict enables the employees to strive towards the achievement of goals. We all and employees could, collaborate in order to solve mutual problems. If they are prepared to initiate action and to introduce changes creativity would be enhanced and behavioural changes, such as a high level of flexibility and adaptability, becomes more obvious.

This situation is conducive to higher performance level which is a positive attitude towards conflict. Non-realistic conflict originates from ignorance, misunderstandings, prejudice, rivalry, or unjustified tension. One or both of the parties may be drawn or forced into confrontation.

The situation may arise spontaneously, with no grounds rules and little knowledge of how far the situation could escalate. Most of its outcomes are potentially dysfunctional for at least one of the parties! And in some cases, it's no use getting involved in a conflict resolution e.g. if one of the party is drugged, unfair, irrational or prejudice.

It could create unwarranted tension between people and can cause unnecessary destruction. If efforts are made to resolve it, it will only be prevented or controlled to a significant degree. Action and steps should be taken to prevent needless, unrealistic conflict.

A way to do this in my opinion is to learn to takes some such unrealism lightly. Conflict is inevitable. An example is a customer paying for her shopping, at the pay point the casher said 10 penny more, after she had paid for her merchandise.

The customer replied, I gave you £4.00 exactly and not £3.90, it deed result in a conflict. The customer had to pay her 10p extra, telling the cashier to take more care with her work that her deed was for peaceful measures, if it was for peace, why as she was saying these words.

The cashier replied immediately with aggravation she had been paid her £3.90 and that she had checked, while the customer who had made and over payment of Ten pence was left stunned you know what I mean everybody steering at her and her conscience disturbed.

It results from scarce resources in an organisation, opposing opinions, conflicting needs, mutually exclusive goals or value issues. Realistic conflict occur between two or more people and can be faced and resolved. Extreme cases of conflict in organisation can have very upsetting, or tragic consequences for the employer, an employee or the employees and organisational performance.

Example of conflict situation could be where two managers are in contest with each other to avoid compulsory redundancy, at the same time considering members of staff for promotion. A resolution method would be to help the people with opposing beliefs understand one another better and accept each other's belief. With regards to conflict of value, nothing concrete or tangible is involved so the opposing parties are often forced to resolve the conflict by agreeing to differ.

It can foster intimacy, aid the development of children, encourage personal and intellectual growth, spur technological development, and help create our social, religious, political, and business organisation.

I could be, bring hidden issues to the surface if my book is published, which can result in each party always achieving greater understanding of the other parties needs, wish, expectation, goals and values - a researcher from Harvard said certain degree of dissension in the home is healthy for children. (If disagreement is expressed openly by parents, they raise children who have priceless quality- a high level of self-esteem).

When in conflict, an individual is forced to state their views clearly and bring forth supporting argument. This bring about, an increased understanding of our own position and awareness of our identity.

Disadvantages of conflicts, when conflict is not managed properly it may result in one or more of the following: friction, wasted time, ill feelings, bitter divorces, bickering and back-biting in the work place, within the family and friends including religious groups.

Differences that are not dealt with properly may leave emotional scars. Energy, which could have been used for constructive purposes, is drained. Conflict is perceived as disruptive and unnatural, and represents a form of deviant behaviour which should be controlled and changed. Extreme cases of conflict in an organisation can have upsetting or tragic consequences, and can give rise to excessive emotional or physical stress.

Personality profile could likely be involved, why it is likely that similarity within human personality profiles demonstrating part of human nature reflects conflicts or harmony within their existence.

Something demonstrated about conflict within my family of such nature is my father having, just one step brother from the same mother Mr. Temitayo Akinlami, with three step sisters Mrs. Barrister Sola Tyco's Lawson, Mrs. Deke Majekodunmi, and Mrs. Lanre Charles.

The same may be applied to my mother having just one female child within four male children. Within two different relationships my mother had with two different men, my father and Mr Gabriel Awe. In Africa relationships are mostly conflict related and we quarrel and ague a lot.

Such attributes are demonstrated in the business world when one company is taken over, by another company. A similarity of one kind or another are involved, before such transactions of a takeover is established.

Within every organisation there are various sub-goals of the various groups. Whilst management attempt to manipulate these sub-goals to ensure the survival of the organisation is more readily achieved. It may happen that there is conflict between group norms, individual goals, and organisational goals.

Main problem would be to agree on the various ways of achieving the goals, in doing so; there would be some personality conflict. Conflict is not necessary a bad thing, however, if conflict are properly managed it could have some positive outcomes.

Better ideas produced
People forced to search for new approaches
Long-standing problems brought to the surface and solved
Clarification of individual views
Stimulation of interest and creativity
A chance for people to test their capacity

Out come if we all and mangers do not eliminate climate of mistrust and suspicion develops the distance between workers increases some people would feel demeaned and defeated if individuals and groups concentrate on their own narrow interest resistance develops, instead of teamwork or increase in employee turnovers.

If managers want to resolve conflict effectively, they should develop the proper attitudes towards conflict resolution. Conflict cannot resolve itself they should be there to see themselves as an active communicating agent.

With effective communication, conflict would easily be resolved by managers. They could handle conflict ideally if; they could see it as an opportunity or constructive process for handling emotion-laden disagreement.

They could succeed by changing their attitude and perception of the problem to a win-win or give and I give perspective, it would always increase their chances of dealing with the conflict in the working environment.

They should always extricate themselves from negative reactions. The needs and objectives of the parties involved should be described impersonally. The problem could be impersonalised by listening to both parties' needs and objective. Clarifying the obstacle would then be easy. Conflict should not be repressed; it should rather be channelled to a useful purpose.

The Butter flies, the birds each morning have something to smile about, each day is a new and different experience for them with humour but for each child, it is a time to learn and explore something new and different just as a little child once asked her mother early in the morning why those the Africans live chicken always picks on the ground? Her mother told her, as they steered at each other she would tell her a bed time story.

At 9.30 pm it was time for her story she said long, long time ago, people, in large numbers began doing too many wrong just like as in the time of Noah as recorded in the Holy bible which as you grow older when you began reading your bible you would know.

Then, the chickens came closer to man as men length how

to build and live in houses they go about reminding men that God created all creatures in all things bright and beautiful all creatures great and small all thing wise and wonderful the lord God made them all and that is a reminder that if men don't stop doing bad things the wrath of God would come upon man.

If not, how would it be said the earth is the Lord and its fullness there of then it became true that God had created the chickens, brought it closer to man, lives and feed within men's dwellings to remind us all both young children grown-ups as well as old people e.g. grandma and grandpas that we should not do wrong to others like picking on them if we do, we will be picking our nose instead of cleaning it in the mornings and at the same time picking our nose when people are around us especially in social gatherings.

Picking our nose will tell when we are doing something suspicious because the chickens are around us reminding us not to pick on other people and the mother said sternly remember that we do feed on them before this short story could be completed, the child was fast asleep as all mothers would, she kissed her on the chick and whispered in her ear I would tell you the other part of the story tomorrow morning.

In the early hours the next morning the birds outside were singing there early morning songs, the mother asked her little daughter what are those songs am hearing outside? The birds you mean mummy the little girl replied yes the mother said hastily just to draw the girl's attention to an early morning story of thoughts in another one hour's time prior- to their way to school.

The mother pointed at a butter fly awaking the day's early sun when the girl said to her mother recalling from last night bed time story some birds feed on butter flies mummy yes the mother replied butter flies have beautifully colours they parade it about and we love them but my dear little young girl they don't speak except through phenomenon's.

For the loveliness of butterflies men had realised appreciating for years it's a pity they can't' speak but they do make gestures. Like plants, there sent, colours they try as much as they could blending well in every environment.

Now I know why the birds feed on them so that the birds could chapel and sing beautiful songs to awake the morning of another new day and they are the songs of the butterfly they had eaten while we humans appreciate the early morning songs of the birds. The little girl said and just as they have woken us up this morning so, they would do for another five years time and I pray we, see that day. So do I mummy the little girl replied with acclamation, as they both laughed and walk themselves to school the next day.

What causes worries, anxieties, depression in the UK we have good electricity, gas, supply, good housing and social security, NHS health care, fire brigade and policing service's; we might all have different opinions about this comparing it with the rest of the world, I say Britain and all its work forces, ways of living is well presentable enough for people living in harmony in short with regards to what has being going on around us all over the world such infrastructure are the real gifting of what Britain as today achieved in the real world all nations have theirs as all mothers do have them.

No wonder Britain considers the reality of such gifting and hard work calling for concerns all around the world in relations to each nations polices, ways of life and living I do not want to use the word culture, race creed or tradition but real concern for political leaders all over the world especially developing nations to stop haggling for power, leaders staying too long in politics without doing much for its nation and people in their condition of living while people are suffering. But in the real sense what cases worries, anxiety etc in the UK.

Such infrastructures relating to gas, electricity, good water supplies, fair brigade, education, NHS care and housing relates to worries and anxieties to levels of paranoia's depending on each individuals, background, race or creed and their mental state which could relates to mental faculty and mind in real terms there are less mind and body problems why should it be, man is now frequently going on space missions. Dose Britain really has worries yes they do it takes hard work and caring to control once worries and if you are doing fine some people might think, you have no worries at all. European are in third world countries to work; work in relation to consideration of what is coming to them or related to the third world countries and why, do people from third word under developed countries come to the UK? We have been battling these issues of education for third world nations to develop themselves through free education in the UK for decades and now it has stopped it should be in considering the social. Political significance and the money Britain spends on immigration and all its social services.

The irony is that it's when Britain choose to come out load to what goes on in countries around the world who have been battling with education, dictation, poor water supplies that is when Britain within itself is coming out loud in relation to education students have to pay school fees it might seems an upheaval but it certainly means a lot. A lot more than what is coming out of the bag of what we know about its real significances. As an African born in the UK having lived more than 21 years of my life in Africa I might feel it is wrong or I should say it is wrong but it's not the case I feel it is right. We should move with social and political trend on how it applies to the rest of the world. Education becoming less free in the UK might lead to elite empowerment in West Africa.

Third world nations need to improve their qualities of life and not about bad politics, religion, culture, regional conflicts or tribal conflict and social welfare which, is all reflecting in Britain today from different background, race, creed, religion which are reflecting in our ways of life with the European union and its polices. In my thoughts for people from third world nations and other part of the world who live in Britain especially developing part of the world, it is not about so much of what the reeves are among the European nations and the rest of Europe are debating and politicising about it is for their own mandates for Africans, Jamaican, Asians and the Caribbean it's about how and what move we make from here in Europe back to our native origins of what has been left behind. Most people do talk about leaving behind our past but our past always takes the best part of us.

Lot of people recently have immigrated into the UK recently the UK government and European nations have large pocket of polices to make about immigration Britain, France and Germany are countries who emerge with lots of polices and consideration about immigration to make when it comes to including the Asians, West indies and African nations because of their past relationship with these countries considering as European nations are more at the moment different from what it used to be globalised among themselves it calls for radical shake up of developing nations. It should not be all about people from developing countries with political leaders, background in culture, and ways of living from developing nations immigrating into Britain, France and Germany and later on deeper into Europe. I have my reasons because am one from such background infarct, the livelihood of people from such background within Britain, France, and Germany also, needs a shake up.

They have witchcraft to develop themselves while we have witchcraft to wing ourselves. We are hardly making progress within ourselves while within our leaders back home their feelings about not only the European single currencies or the European union itself is with missed feelings what about those of ourselves while we are abroad sad stories reaches us each day in the presence of modern day civilisation.

European heritage who came to Africa looking for what had played huge roles in African technology, expanded Africa to a huge continent how things have changed over decades with European relationship relating to Jamaica, Caribbean, Barbados and Trinidad after slavery now what they are actually looking for are people from their former origin to live in Europe who would make them understand more of their background. Principles may apply depending on which region of Africa you are from because of our varied background and tradition which have never been considered primitive or it would not have changed at all over decade. In their home land today they want Africans who would come to their country to strengthen relationship.

They are not the once who see our bad side others do because we have become creative through their efforts. If I choose not having children with an European lady my age group it's because, of something I understand about my background, parents transition and our ways of understanding each other if I could endeavour to make them understand this of me, I have the feeling they would like me more for what I am this is what we Africans, Caribbean's, Trinidad and Barbadians should make them understand about us.

It has to be done through my life not based on what they have taken from me or what they have given me but to wish myself a life well spent. Judgment comes before heaven. Our lives are always based on trials, we are visited by omens which we have been for centuries trying to explain or understand the same thing with apocalypse we are frequently going on space mission, some say Jesus is coming look busy are we really going to be judged or are we through our trials to judge ourselves.

There is everything on planet earth enlightening me my life is what I make out of it, other people contribute in making me what I am and we all have choice through certain perspectives or predisposition which might probably be depending on a ratio, why do humans the most intelligent of all living things have legs its people who have seen thing, understand and seen define reality of their native home land of origin who travel to other peoples countries to live who have really survived based on their trials of life which only they could have understood and capable of explaining with sometimes difficulties.

I think the first man who discovered the shape of the earth saw it as a hole not round or flat he most have seen it from above looking downwards. With human endeavours in respect to what we have achieved this world is now one small place if you have faith like a mustard seed you will see and enter the kingdom of heaven. Heaven made us what we are here; we know who we are for what we are.

Now any home computers could be hacked, other people could program themselves into your memory, write their own views based on what your word processing entail, emails could be hacked we are all programmed entities. What about the furniture's you use in your home are they friendly or abusive, do you hear voices, paranoia's about your furniture as if you will live with them in an afterlife or they would be nowhere near you. Do you have feelings you belong to other parts, a part of the world while you are not living there or have not been there before.

Are you suffering from illusions, false beliefs or that you are happy with your life and believes. Do you see yourself as being drawn into another beliefs, awareness or meditation, are you unhappy and want to be happy, do you feel other people have written or sang songs that are relics of your life or for you?

Do you feel other people are telling you how to live your life, do you feel at times a feeling of rejecting yourself?

Are you a peaceful person and sometimes people made you feel aggressive not physical but with a single look at another person do you show signs of not liking them or they do not like you?

Could somebody be walking out his or her front door of a housing blocks of flat you live in as well they are going out the front do while you are inside because of something that has to do with you?

Are running away from your family, feel isolated you feel fear but you are confident of yourselves?

Do people give you any reason, attitude of whatever is wrong with you, is also wrong with them?
October is Black History Month. This national celebration aims to promote and celebrate Black contributions to British society, and to foster an understanding of Black history in general.

As well as the events below across our different museums and galleries, the International Slavery Museum will have a Black achievers picture quiz and Black Pioneers leaflet, available from the Information desk. It's not all about slavery it's about our reality. The meaning of reality itself is about life.

We are always looking at ways to improve Black History Month, and welcome ideas and contributions from the community.

Black history month has been celebrated widely for many years honouring the achievements, culture, and the history of black people.
Black History Month, also known as African-American History Month, is an annual observance in the United States, Canada, and the United Kingdom for remembrance of important people and events in the history of the African diaspora. It is celebrated annually in the United States and Canada in February and the United Kingdom in October.

Black History Month had its beginnings in 1926 in the United States, when historian Carter G. Woodson and the Association for the Study of Negro Life and History announced the second week of February to be 'Negro History Week'. The week was chosen because it marked the birthday of both Abraham Lincoln and Frederick Douglass. Woodson created the holiday with the hope that it eventually be eliminated when black history became fundamental to American history. Negro History Week was met with enthusiastic response; it prompted the creation of black history clubs, an increase in interest among teachers, and interest from progressive whites. Negro History Week grew in popularity throughout the following decades, with mayors across the United States endorsing it as a holiday.

In 1976, the federal government acknowledged the expansion of Black History Week to Black History Month by the leaders of the Black United Students at Kent State University in February of 1969. The first celebration of Black History Month occurred at Kent State in February of 1970. Six years later during the bicentennial, the expansion of

Negro History Week to Black History Month was recognized by the U.S. government. <u>Gerald Ford</u> spoke in regards to this, urging Americans to 'seize the opportunity to honour the too-often neglected accomplishments of black Americans in every area of endeavour throughout our history.'

Or some people from your background feel, your condition is better than theirs because you are born British does it make your feel, worried, anxiety, perceptive of your race its black history month we live the perspective here in the UK as we would if, we were in African people just have to understand this about us. Some people who live in Africa, had not the opportunity to visit Europe feel we Africans, Jamaicans, Caribbean's, Trinidad or Barbados are all the same they really need to visit the UK that's why, the case of adoption is becoming a big issue in countries like Canada, Australia and the UK.

Black History Month (UK) began Monday, 1 October 2012, and ends Wednesday, 31 October 2012

Every October, people across London and the UK come together celebrating black history month, the annual season highlights and celebrate achievements of black communities in London and beyond. There are always a whole programmes of art, culture and entertainment events to enjoy across London with something to appeal the whole family. It is also for reflection and contemplation on our existence and how, we hope to move forward in life. To make people from other communities understand us and accept us for what we are,

My late father Chief Dr. Frank .A. Megbele the Agbueju of Warri Kingdom was born on the 14th of October 1935 which falls on black history month his funeral service took place on the month of October 2004. My father was born into the family of Megbele and Omatseone of blessed memory at Forcados in the then Warri Province of Western Nigeria in Obonteghareda (Dudu Town) in Warri North Local Government Area of Delta State.

He had his primary school education at the following schools:
African Church School Forcados 1943-1945

Ijo Orunmila Primary School Idumagbo Lagos from 1945-1946

Saint David's C.M.S School, Lafiaji Lagos from 1947-1951

After which he got admission into secondary school in Enitonna High school Port Harcourt from 1952-1955 and Hussey collage Warri from 1956-1957 being a brilliant student, he was opportune to study in London and here attended the City of London Collage Moore Gate EC 2 now London Guildhall university from 1962-1965 he obtained qualification as a graduate of the Chartered Institute of Transport London in 1965 he become, a member of the Chartered Institute of transport in 1978.

On living secondary school in 1957 with five credits pass in his general certificate of education (GCE) he was employed by the Nigerian Ports Authority as a Quay staff grade 2 and worked at all sections of the traffic and commercial department both at custom Quay Lagos and Apapa Quay up till 1961 when he resigned to travel to the United Kingdom in February 1962 for further studies.

On his return from the United Kingdom in March 1966 he worked in the capacity of assistant Stevedoring manager and clearing and forwarding manager with Scanship/Alraine Nigeria limited Apapa up till 1968 he returned to the Nigerian Port Authority as management cadet/supervisor traffic. From March 1971 to June 1975 he was the manager of Alhaji. Ramallam and son's limited Port Harcourt and at Lagos.

He established a shipping-Port Operation Consultancy firm in 1975 and was a shipping consultant to Panalpina World Transport Limited up-till 1978. He was also, the executive chairman and managing director of Star Warehousing and Shipping Limited a limited liability company which was established in 1978 with expatriates participation and quota.

My late father was the executive chairman and managing director of Cedar Eagle Limited incorporated since May 1982 his company is registered with the joint Dock Labour Industrial Council Ministry of Transport and the Nigerian Ports Authority as Stevedoring and Cargo handling contractor the company is currently attached to Intel service limited appropriated oilfield supply and transit base at the Federal Lighter Terminal Onne the company had trained personal handling materials and goods for oil companies with permit from the Department of Petroleum Resources of which, I was one of his staff.

During the marking of his first coronation anniversary Ogiame Atuwatse II the Olu of Warri conferred on him the traditional title of Agbueju of Warri on the 12th of November 1988 Due to his impact in the business world the Cornerstone University of the state of Hawaii USA conferred an Honorary Ph.D. Degree in Business Administration (Honours Causa) on him on the 26th of February 1996 at the Abia State Extension Campus of the University. He was a Protestant of First African Church Mission of Nigeria he was also, Grand Patron of Holy Trinity Cathedral Choir Port Harcourt he miraculously gave his life to Jesus Christ before he died.

The word Negro is huge phenomena not really understood in the 21st century about black people all most people consider is the colour of our skin and that we are all the same if you are from a black background because of the influence of other race around the world. In consideration of we black race it is not because of the colour of our skin we are educated in our ways before the Europeans came to the Native Africa understanding our reality until this century now it is about religion, politics, culture we are still being judgmental and prejudiced against even within ourselves and not on the Impact of being a Negro, a Nigeria, Ghanaian, or Caribbean.

Are you from a third world country with every experience you had while you were their some people you meet in the UK give you impression they had the same experiences here, they had knowledge of what happened to you while you where there? Do some people make you bind your relationship with them about something secretive you have experience that has happened to you before you came here in the UK? Do you feel in the UK you are happier than you where before you came to the UK? Do you find the people strange, hard to understand or you do not fit in and want to fit in. Before you came did you family give you reason they want to see you back home safely after some time in the UK. Do you feel other people from your own origin are happy here in the UK or they want to have their way at all cost at anything? Do you feel your relatives here in the UK are using you this is a question I have been asking myself since I came back to the UK?

Realising you are a slave to your self is more important to you than other people calling you a slave do not train up a child from what you see in the eyes of the child but what the child see's himself.

Aesthetics is a branch of <u>philosophy</u> dealing with the nature of <u>art</u>, <u>beauty</u>, and <u>taste</u>, with the creation and appreciation of beauty. It is more scientifically defined as the study of <u>sensory</u> or sensory-emotional values, sometimes called <u>judgments</u> of <u>sentiment</u> and taste. More broadly, scholars in the field define aesthetics as 'critical reflection on art, culture and <u>nature</u>.

<u>African art</u> existed in many forms and styles, and with fairly little influence from outside Africa. Most of it followed traditional forms and the aesthetic norms were handed down orally as well as written. Sculpture and <u>performance art</u> are prominent, and abstract and partially abstracted forms are valued, and were valued long before influence from the Western tradition began in earnest. The <u>Nok culture</u> is testimony to this. The mosque of <u>Timbuktu</u> shows that specific areas of Africa developed unique aesthetics.

Its basic definition is, essentially, 'staging of a story.' It isn't just creating a story but expressing it, presenting it to the audience in an art form. Even if the story is true it has to be presented like a fictional account, such as depicting the exact words spoken in a conversation where no one possess a transcript of it. Performing Arts, Theatre the reconstruction of an event, novel, story, etc. in a form suitable for dramatic presentation

Ali G (born Alistair Leslie Graham) is a <u>satirical</u> <u>fictional</u> <u>character</u> created and performed by English <u>comedian</u> <u>Sacha Baron Cohen</u>. Originally appearing on <u>Channel 4</u>'s <u>The 11 O'Clock Show</u>, as the <u>title character</u> of Channel 4's <u>Da Ali G Show</u> in 2000 and on <u>HBO</u> in 2003–2004, he is also the title character of the film *Ali G Indahouse*. In December 2007, in an interview with *The Daily Telegraph*, Baron Cohen announced that Ali G, along with Borat, had been retired.

Barry White, born Barry Eugene Carter (September 12, 1944 – July 4, 2003), was an American composer and singer-songwriter.

A two-time Grammy Award-winner known for his distinctive bass voice and romantic image, White's greatest success came in the 1970s as a solo singer and with the Love Unlimited Orchestra, crafting many enduring soul, funk, and disco songs such as his two biggest hits, 'You're the First, the Last, My Everything' and 'Can't Get Enough of Your Love, Babe.'
Worldwide, White had many gold and platinum albums and singles, with combined sales of over 100 million, according to critics Ed Hogan and Wade Kergan. His influences include Rev. James Cleveland, Ray Charles, Aretha Franklin plus Motown artists The Supremes, The Four Tops and Marvin Gaye. Along with Isaac Hayes, White is considered by Allmusic.com as the first singer who played disco music before the actual period of the late 1970s.

Ali G is a stereotype of a white suburban male from Staines (now Staines-upon-Thames) who imitates rap culture as well as urban British and Jamaican culture, particularly through hip hop, reggae, drum and bass and jungle music. Ali G was part of a group called Berkshire Massif, and he ran and grew up in an area of Slough called Langley (both actual locations in the UK). He also lived part of his life in Staines. Baron Cohen has stated that BBC Radio 1 DJ Tim Westwood was an influence on the development of his character – Westwood hosts Radio 1's Rap Show and speaks in a faux Multicultural London English and Hip-Hop dialect. Ali G's middle class credentials mirror Westwood's: the latter was brought up in Lowestoft, Suffolk as a bishop's son.

A stereotype is a thought that may be adopted about specific types of individuals or certain ways of doing things, but that belief may or may not accurately reflect reality. However, this is only a fundamental psychological definition of a stereotype. Within and across different psychology disciplines, there are different concepts and theories of stereotyping that provide their own expanded definition. Some of these definitions share commonalities, though each one may also harbour unique aspects that may complement or contradict the other.

Music is a great expression now politics it's taking over our lives so are the cloths and food we eat, where we buy them from.

Prior to his character's appearance on *The 11 O'Clock Show*, Baron Cohen had portrayed a similar character named MC Jocelyn Cheadle-Hume on a show he presented called F2F, which ran on a satellite channel called Talk TV (owned by Granada Television). While chatting to a group of skateboarders, in character, Baron Cohen realised that people could be led to believe his character was real, and filmed a number of segments which were ordered off air by London Weekend Television.

Ali G, a boorish, uneducated, faux-streetwise poseur with a deeply stereotypical view of the world, first came to prominence on Channel 4's *The Eleven O'Clock Show* as the 'voice of da yoof' in 1998. He interviewed various public figures in the United Kingdom, always either embarrassing his interviewee by displaying a mixture of uninformed political incorrectness, or getting the interview 'victim' to agree to some breathtaking inaccuracy or insult. His key saying is 'booyakasha'.

Other examples of his bold interviewing style include getting Lindsay Urwin, the Bishop of Horsham, to admit that God created the Universe, and then asked him, 'And since then, [God]'s just chilled?' Ali G asked the Bishop about God's appearance, to which the Bishop replied, 'Well, he's sort of Jesus-shaped.' During an interview with James Ferman (former director of the British Board of Film Classification), Ali G asks whether his made-up vulgarities would restrict a film to an over-18 audience, and suggests that film censorship be performed by younger persons who understand contemporary slang. In an interview with the Chairman of the Arts Council of England Gerry Robinson Ali G's first question was. Ali G was in a series of ads for the 2005–06 NBA seasons, in which he used his brand of off-kilter journalism to interview various NBA stars. The spots were directed by Spike Lee.

Ali G was also featured in the music video 'Music' by Madonna as her limo driver. Are you from a third world nation living in the UK whilst watching your television or listening to your radio the presenters seems to be talking about you, giving you information's related in actuality what is happening in your country, with impression they are actually giving you information as to how the situation is in the UK with clichés or hidden meaning or reflections or something you have to act on? Sometimes do you feel all they are saying makes you feel tired, the information are unfriendly, thoughtful, something to make reason out of or they are realities of you in movies, entertainment, dreamers they show on their TV channels? Britain now has over a hundred TV channels when I came to the UK they were only four when I did settle down to really enjoy watching television.

Most of Barry White songs I interpret has having meaning within me and my father as men talk I like his baritone voice he and my father died within close proximity of the same time I wanted to be a musician at one point in my life what gives the paranoia it has something to do with my father having his tonsillitis removed in the UK around the time when I was born I often have this feeling I and my father have mutual understanding to our existence moreover, we have acute resemblance to each other. I seems to stand as the only person within his wives who connected his relationship within he and my mother even if, they lived apart he knows when am standing in the rain. Sometimes it's all about me since I call for awareness of why my mother doesn't live within his family.

Since you came back to the UK do some of your relatives, friends or people from your own background make you feel they are just expressing their foolishness?

If you are a schizophrenic or bipolar since you came back to the UK do you hear voices of members of your family, friends or people from your own background wanting to rule your life, show their aggression in your relationship with them, through the voices you hear?

Do their voices or presence make you paranoid at times if so why? While you are just trying to make a living in a land that is not your origin, why feel this way?
Do some of them make you have feelings they want to be friendlier or in favour of other race in the UK at work, home or within the people you associate yourself with. Do you feel or have a general opinion of yourself, appearance or attitude that people from other race have a liking for you just because of your appearance as an individual.

Have you came to the UK with no close relatives lived with private landlords in several accommodation, in one of the accommodation you experienced the furniture's in the house did not meet your liking, meet your requirement or gave you a sense of paranoia and reflected in you working life you were becoming unwell or when you go out to visit friends and relatives they seems to find you unwelcome in their home for no reason, do you believe or have experience voodoo, witchcraft in your life and is it likely in your life you had bought or used talisman or juju?

Do you sometimes find you are doing some abnormal things, or feel like pressing the stop button more than once even when a police officer vehicle was in sight to stop moving vehicles a traffic pedestrian stopping signals for you to cross the road bear in mind there are duplicate signals, known as secondary signals that could be located on the opposite sides of junctions if, the primary signals is not working vehicle users obey the secondary signals as if it were the primary singes.

How did you feel about the introduction of British citizenship test I wonder why I bought a book on the essential study guide for life in the UK test it was a comprehensive study guide containing official materials, study advice and samples questions. The publication was a study guide for candidate intending to take life in the UK test.

Are you a UK citizen you have, lived part of your life in your native land under your parents sometimes you suffer from paranoia some people in the UK from you native land or from other parts of Europe are in the UK under sponsorship to do things you like or do not like, felt some of them infringe in your human right here and from your native land some of which, make you act for not doing things not in your own impulse. Some of this people you know them, have not met them before they are from your native origin or from abroad who you consider out of your jurisdiction because they are not from your own race.

How do you feel, about how the Asians demonstrate their affinity for Africans who come into the UK through immigration do I feel history is repeating itself about the relationship of Asians, Ghanaians, Nigerians in relationship to Caribbean's, Trinidadians and Jamaicans.

Do you, or anyone you know who have children who are from third world nations in the UK who, want to show, imply, and exaggerate their livelihood within friends, relatives they had signed in with Sky TV HD in other to show off. Sky or any other TV channels providers are hi-tech technology do we really appreciate such providers in reality in the UK for what they provide? Considering how children live these days in the UK because of the educational shack up in GCSE and at graduate level. Do children really like schools these days? All sorts of household furniture's and goods come from all over the world of all nature into third world countries into the hands of reach people when those looking for stay from third world countries are from poor background how, would they manage with the educational system running in the UK some of us might be going back into the hands of making our children clever or intelligence in the hands of native witch and native medicine and voodoo priest here in the UK. Food is now being declared at Heathrow why did we have enough information why food are being declared. It's a ding in our lives and culture, tradition and creed why food is being declared and we are ready to keep silent as to why Britain to my knowledge is the most multi cultured country in the world having people from all parts of the world and background living in the UK is this not worries and anxiety to the British people yet not much noise is being made about it because the brightest among us try to live in harmony in the UK.

The family is a group of people who care about each other or depend on each other and consider themselves as such. It may be a nuclear family of parents, step-parents and children but may also include grandparents, step-children and half-siblings.

Family life can be a place of refuge and security but for some it is a source of pain and disappointment. Our families absorb many of the stresses and strains from the outside world pressures can boil over. Sometimes a personal problem, particularly in an adolescent, can overwhelm a family and there seems to be no clear way forward. At other times changes within the family leave other members confused and angry or hurt. When a crisis or disappointment happens for one member the family group absorbs the impact, sometimes helping and sometimes hindering. Sometimes the help comes at a high price to one or more members.

A family is a 'system' or an organisation but the rules and expectations of each one are different and unique and often seen differently by each member. It is through examining what the explicit and hidden 'rules' might be in each family and how they are seen and interpreted by each member that creates harmony.

- Disruption after separation or divorce or a new partner moving in
- Problems with step-family life
- Debt
- Alcoholism
- On drugs
- Mental health problems
- self-harm
- Inappropriate sexual behaviour in young people
- Aggression
- Intimidation
- Problems with adolescents or older children
- Children leaving home
- Unwanted pregnancy

- Family's complex and unspoken rules can cause confusion and misunderstanding
- Particularly when there are changes. When someone joins a family or when someone leaves or changes their position in it the structure is altered for other members
- Changes within the group members, from child to adult or from wage-earner to unemployed, are felt by the others in different ways.

Private family therapists are increasing in number and some charitable and voluntary agencies now offer family counselling. They usually work with Systemic theories or in a cognitive way looking at thoughts to clarify what the problems are and then focus on solutions rather than delving into the origins of the problems. This can help with self-reflection for the individuals and increase self-awareness of their family's stage in its life cycle.

Issues which might be explored may relate to one incident or a repeated pattern. They can include exploration and understanding of

- the current problem
- how it is seen differently by different members
- successful ways of dealing with past problems
- parenting issues
- characters of each member
- communication
- alliances and hostilities within the group
- how the group functions emotionally - who is close and who is distant
- who expresses anger or sadness and who comforts

A family counsellor maintains neutrality at all times to establish a platform free from blame and prejudice to allow members to explore the problem and then express their concerns for the family's ability to change. Each family is unique, even within its own culture, and a non-judgemental view about the family's beliefs and values; ethnicity, sexuality, religion, ability, age and class is essential to allow a new, better 'system' or set of rules to be formed.

If so why should the police want to carry guns in public in the UK? Taking a real view of the cultural disposition in the UK when there is problem or worries it is sometimes not good to over react. Britain is a peaceful place and has been considered so by people all over the world if the police start carrying guns in public, it means it's no longer a peaceful place. While there should be a distinction if they are to carry guns for their own protection or is it for the public? Here people do things in constrain carrying guns may lead to worse situation I thought the government decommissioning weapons even knives from the public was to demonstrate a peaceful culture within Britain.

Not all countries in the world operate pension social services regardless of how hard you work. We come from all parts of the world to reside in the UK Britain is pull and tear mind my saying so, homes facility being pulled down and rebuild creating better, more advance infrastructures in all areas of our lives nobody seems to complement them enough. How do we know a man or woman who, is an angel in the UK while it seems everyone is an angel who in my cases would I hold as an angel from what I have experience in life? In short why do you know people? Anyone can use a Church hall rent it to throw a party why should food not be declared on entering any country are they experiencing witchcraft, juju and voodoo in our homes after Church services and in halls rented for parties. What is this paranoia I go through that in Britain in reality, you only exist in yourself.

Worry is thoughts, images and emotions of a negative nature in which mental attempts are made to avoid anticipated potential threats. As an emotion it is experienced as anxiety or concern about a real or imagined issue, usually personal issues such as health or finances or broader ones such as environmental pollution and social or technological change. Most people experience short-lived periods of worry in their lives without incident; indeed, a moderate amount of worrying may even have positive effects, if it prompts people to take precautions (e.g., fastening their seat belt or buying fire insurance) or avoid risky behaviours (e.g., angering dangerous animals, or binge drinking).

Anxiety consists of two components; worry and emotionality. Emotionality refers to physiological symptoms such as sweating, increased heartbeat and raised blood pressure. Worry refers to negative self-talk that often distracts the mind from focusing on solutions to the problem at hand. Is this what worries entail in the real world in relation to mind and body problem it is what you make out of it if you have done your home work you would only act upon you consciences a man who understands worries is a man who has got a hart. The problem is huge and psychological in relation to race, creed and belied in relation to our mental state considering and our ways of life, the world situation worries have become more complex how are you confronting yours?

Do you know what it is having your stay in the UK, working as a housing officer in any of the London Borough to let or supervise housing need of a client putting them in any infrastructure to live with their family what do you always come about easy and pleasant job how many of us come into the UK from third world nations and become a builder, engineer or pharmacist if you, you are really privilege how does it spell not you, but your background. You can't come into the UK experience more people each day suffering from mental illness and you feel, you can talk how dose mental health depict your culture in your own background and your stay in the UK regardless if you are here and not there.

You go to their homes give them medication, social care, they come to you, you give them advice people from all backgrounds, race how would you feel if someone says you look like a distant uncle of mine or his relatives because your cousins, cousins nephew from you country in let say Ghana is married to one of my aunties who, is from Nigeria. In Britain almost everything change each year now Britain and the rest of Europe is reaching out to the rest of the world especially developing nations and its leaders and all of a sudden, I am surprise to experience in my stay in the UK that white parent do what African parent do to their children in all areas of life. They treat their children in the UK and do things as for example African parents do to their children in Africa here in the UK. while we Africans living in the UK behave here as we do in Africa in manners, language and culture, the British environment makes us think of changes we want to see in our lives.

Basically the culture here in Britain doesn't change us from being Africans or Jamaicans, Caribbean's or from Barbados.

The problems are about some people who are just prejudice against African living at home and abroad they continually want to makes us feel inferior to say they are better. Yet they are not Europeans and they, in their home land are not all that developed they do not see us in reality for what we are .They just make talk of our lives. We the British and Europeans should have our say about third world nations in what we hope to see as a transformation that would also help those who are here e.g. doctors, engineers, and pharmacist infarct in all works of life. As much as we want to see part of our lives transformed into something you also find in a place in your mind we all should be a developed nation, civilise as the seat of the eyes of civilization no different from a galaxy call they eyes of God. We act and do things in relics you can only understand Africans if you have got a mind Africa should no longer be an expression other race should look down on. Since after slavery we were the once who seems to be gradually corroding after every apocalypse that comes into planet earth and they have always been ever ready working at their best to do what they have to do. In some ways we contributed in appealing for everyone who has got a hart to do anything they can to stop the apocalypse. Its only in suffering you can really appeal to those, who have got loving heart.

The educational system in the UK entering the 21st century is moving into huge shake up for women all over the world the latest news on the free Royal Greenwich times of September 2012 produced by the Royal Borough of Greenwich for the community for over 25 years just as its feet for the 21st century rebuilt girls school opens its doors for brighter future.
1st September 2012 a brand new school is opening in Eltham Town Centre
Along with other secondary schools in Eltham, Eltham Hill School has been completely rebuilt to make it fit for the 21st Century. The new building opens soon. The School has seen year on year improvement in exam results and this year 88% of students achieved 5+ A* to C grades. They have open days during September and October 2012. A new school is always a good addition to a Town centre as it brings a high level of footfall which benefits both business

and social life in the area. To have a rebuilt school which already has a good reputation is a double bonus. The school promises to provide local girls a modern curriculum which is exciting, challenging and creative, enabling students to excel in all areas. The school will provide an environment where ambitious targets can be set, so as to ensure that every student achieves results beyond national expectations. This year 88% of students achieved 5+ A* to C grades. A new forward thinking 6th form, opening in Autumn 2013 will have a good range of courses, including the International Baccalaureate.

Femmes Fatale jazz singer Sarah Moule tells Peter Cordwell about her new show show Serah Moules your scars and she'll show you hers. She performs Femmes Fatales songs for the fallen, wild and wicked at Charlton House on Friday 21 2012 but a few minutes on YouTube.

On the Royal Greenwich times it says don't be ashamed if you're covered with scares, on this planet of ours, that's the way we keep scores Sarah Moule sang how show is about what we know and what we don't, about some of Sarahs favourite femmes from Cleopatra to Mata Hari, from Salome to Judith who cut off Holoferns head (he should never have taken that penalty) but she emphasized that while she'll have to do the introduction, it will be the music that really matters.

'I wanted to find a place for my show about powerful and very famous women who are not always what, they seems' said Sarah 'the organizer, Louisa Le Marchand, liked the idea and booked it although to be honest, they're not a particular peaceful bunch. The idea is that the songs might be songs that they might have sung or thoughts they might have had' Sarah headlines the Global Fusion Music and Art International Day of Peace event from 7.30-10pm Sarah not far away in Dulwich was snapped up after wowing all and sundry as late sub at GFMA's International Women's Day gig last year. The subject matter was enough to give Lee lad the sweats but Sarah insisted it's not anti-men but a celebration of what people think these women were or what they really were 'Those two things, don't always mean the same thing she said with a twinkle in her eyes (we were on the phone, but you can picture these things)

They were all rule breaking women but the show was not anti-men in any way. Men are really attracted to very strong women but at the same time the same time there are things they fear about them.

Sarah's inspiration are her composer husband and pianist Simon Wallace and legendry American lyrics Fran Landsman who fought her last feisty fight last summer aged 83 'I've been recording her songs for the last 10 years and made three albums with them' Said Sarah.
Lots of people sing Simon and Fran's songs they got together once a week to argue their way to a conclusion. We do miss Fran, She was 80 going on 18 she could be difficult but she was an extraordinary woman ' their songs are about things that are important to all of us, not just about love, and Fran was a proper wordsmith

My late father was a jazz fan and as a youth I wondered at his amazing jazz collections of LP's my sister in law Mrs. Nwamaka Megbele told me my nice Lydia Omagbuse Megbele plays a violin I, prefer to play the piano. I have a Yamaha key board in my flat bought from Woolwich Argos and a Gear 4 music MP8820 digital piano but why, is my kitchen blender bought from a local Asian stores in Powis street Woolwich pots, plates, microwave cover, are sold in the stores, the Asians are also our Butchers are they also some of Jamaicans or Caribbean's? American Musicians say Have some fun. Recently my brother told me Lydia is very good at chemistry. He told me he wish is son Mr. Zach would be good at drawing.

What about white men and women who have had children in Africa, how do they treat their children growing up in Nigeria they educate them to behave in Africa as thorough English men and women aristocrats in this regards, culture has entwine then, I mean then in Nigeria you get to know African parents and children who live in Africa their native land having respect through their behaviours for Europeans living in Africa. After graduating in the UK you seek employment in

Nigeria for example it's not only about the business life you will encounter whilst you take a trip to and fro each year within the UK and Nigeria as I had experience my late father's colleagues do. After your education going to Africa to work I understand you seek progress to the developing world that's why you are there, what would you life and career be like in the 21st century? You hardly are aware of it if you do not work your way into their culture and real aspects of their lives. The UK is a place where we more than cherish love it's a place we cherish reality in some ways hidden reality which makes us and the place we live in feel special.

When you become terminal with an illness you see things twice,, kids laughs,,, trees birds and all the beautiful things the world offers, you cry over all the trivial things that don't mean much that people will kill someone for,,, our words to all the people here in this world is this,,, cherish all of the things in life,,, like Kool and the gang says,, cherishthe love,,, cherish the life,,,,,,

This reminds me of the music group called Cool and the Gang and a saying this reminds me of my first concert in the '70's. The bands were Frankie Beverly and the Emotions. I will never forget my first sight of thousands of beautiful, happy Black people grooving together. My heart was full. There were a few white couples in the audience but nobody bothered them. What the hell happened? One thing I pray for is May my soul rest in peace, and May we all ever be forever remain blessed and cherish the love as song by Cool and the Gang. This is what I love about America. That was when Black music was cool and fun. No other country in the world could have produced a groove like that.

Agreed, The UK had some excellent 1970s Soul Bands like Delegation / The Real Thing, Linx, Imagination, High Tension, Second Image and Central Line back then. How about 5 Star, Soul to Soul and Loose ends in the late 80s, Or the multitude of 1990s UK soul acts like Mark Morrison, Omar, Jamiroquai, and the Brand New Heavies of the UK based Acid Jazz 70s Funk revival movement, where does Leona Lewis come from ?..And Black British 70s/80s Reggae is Legendary to those who truly know their music.

That's not the point. You said no other country went international with their black music and I have just demonstrated to you that the Black Brits for example have been laying down the Funk since the early 1970s, even topping the US soul charts. You're the one that needs to 'go figure'....

Earth, Wind & Fire are one of the most dynamic and creative funk bands to come out of the seventies and also one of the most successful. The group was led by Maurice White and this new DVD & CD release captures them on stage in Japan in1990 during the last tour that Maurice made with the group following the release of the 'Heritage' album spectacularly staged, the concert features all their best loved songs. The DVD is out now and includes the hits 'Let's Groove.

Their music is a collection of African, Latin, funk, soul, pop, rock, jazz, world, and other music genres that perfectly blend together. Many of the songs are either highly rhythmic featuring horns to sensual ballads with two of the band members lending their tenor and falsetto vocals on a number of album tracks. 1975 was the breakthrough year for Earth, Wind & Fire even though they began their musical career in Chicago back in 1969. Slowly, but surely they kept building onto their success until it reached pinnacle fame. There's been no letting go of that since.

They are considered the first black crossover arena band with their progressive sounds and slick stage productions that included magic acts. Earth, Wind and Fire have also changed the sound of black pop music. The group has sold over 90 million albums worldwide. They are ranked as the seventh best-selling American band of all time. You've probably grown up with their music while roller skating to their powerful sounds during the 70's and 80's. Maybe you've just become familiar with their songs recently when they were featured on a TV commercial for Target during the Christmas holidays. Whatever is the case, once you hear an Earth, Wind & Fire song you never forget them. They truly get your attention like no other musical group. Here are the top ten songs of Earth, Wind, & Fire based on chart position, personal preference, and critical acclaim.

<u>Let's Groove</u> (1981) - The music video for this song was the first to be played on BET (Black Entertainment Television). It also used auto-tuning and the vocoder in the opening as well as in other parts throughout it. This is a classic EWF funky dance song. 'Let's Groove' peaked at #3 on the Billboard Hot 100 Pop and #3 on the Billboard Hot Dance Club Play charts. The single sold over a million copies making it a Gold certification by the RIAA.

<u>Getaway</u> (1976) - Here is one of many of their intense rhythmic songs with an upbeat tempo and a great horn section. It reached #1 on the Billboard Hot Soul Singles, but only peaked at #12 on both the pop and dance charts for Billboard. Once again this single was certified gold when it sold over a million copies. 'Getaway' is one of my favourite EWF songs.

<u>That's the Way of the World</u> (1975) - Now to slow things down a bit this is one of their mellow songs. There are some beautiful harmonies and a nice keyboard in the opening. One thing about Earth, Wind & Fire is they are unique with their instrumentations, but also with vocal talent. Maurice White sings tenor and Philip Bailey provides the falsetto. 'That's the Way of the World' has been covered by many artists and featured in episodic television. It made Rolling Stone's list of the 500 Greatest Songs of All Time.

<u>After the Love Has Gone</u> (1979) - Another slow ballad of theirs that has also been covered and sampled by a number of artists the song has been featured in episodic television. It won a Grammy for Best R&B Vocal Performance by a Duo or Group. 'After the Love Has Gone' fared nicely on the pop, adult contemporary, and R&B charts peaking at #2 & #3 respectively. One of the writers of this song is David Foster who was responsible in discovering Celine Dion, Josh Groban, and Michael Buble.

<u>Sing a Song</u> (1975) - It's been considered one of their more popular songs and another favorite of mine. This infectious song has a catchy hook with the title in the verse. You can't help but actually sing along to it. Many have reported it is used in music class for chorus a la 'Glee', the hit TV show

about a glee club or extra-curricular singing club. 'Sing a Song' has been featured in films, covered by a gospel band, reached certified gold status, and peaked at 1 on the soul charts as well as #5 on the pop and dance charts.

Reasons (1975) - One of Earth, Wind & Fire's most romantic song, yet it was never officially released as a single though the song gets airplay on oldies and adult contemporary radio stations to this day. Back in 1975 it received airplay on both the R&B and pop charts. 'Reasons' is popular as a wedding song. Philip Bailey's falsetto is heard very prominently giving it emotional depth.

Fantasy (1978) - Maurice White, the singer/songwriter of the group, saw the film 'Close Encounters of the Third Kind' and got needed inspiration from it. 'Fantasy' has been covered and sampled by other artists. The falsetto voice of Philip Bailey is heard. It's nice soft opening gets right into their signature funky groove sound. Once again you hear great harmonies, intense guitar riffs, and brilliant instrumental breaks. The song reached the Top 40 for pop and at #12 on the R&B charts.

September (1978) - A great musical intro with its brilliant disco and funky rhythms, awesome horn section, and catchy lyrics, especially about a month in the calendar year. Another certified gold single that was also one of three of their most famous songs in the UK. It was used during Al Gore's 2000 Presidential campaign. 'September' reached #1 on the R&B charts.

Shining Star (1975) - Finally a song of theirs that reached both #1 on the Pop & Soul charts it has a catchy intro, infectious guitar work, horns blasting, a funky groove going on, and soft voices in the chorus. It's got a killer ending that is sung entirely in acapella. I really miss hearing so much going on with real musical instruments in recordings nowadays. It won a Grammy for Best R&B Vocal Performance by a Duo or Group and has been certified Gold.

Boogie Wonderland (1979) - You've heard this song featured

in the animation film 'Happy Feet' and on TV for Target during the holidays. It is regarded as a classic during the disco age and features the singing trio, The Emotions. 'Boogie Wonderland' was covered by the late Brittany Murphy in the film, which increased the popularity of the song for a new generation. It is high-energy with intense rhythms, an infectious dance beat, and catchy lyrics and hooks. Someone recently told me they played this song all the time at her roller skating rink many years ago. A few notable music critics have stated it is one of the best singles ever made. I agree, I can never sit still whenever I hear this song.

• Now that you've read, watched, and listened to all of these Earth, Wind & Fire songs you no doubt want to get their music. Simply head on over to Amazon for either the CD or download it digitally. Also, iTunes is another source for downloading music. As you can see Earth, Wind & Fire took traditional R&B and the progressive sound of funk by merging them together. Then they took it to an even greater level by making it mainstream for all music listeners. No wonder other music luminaries such as Miles Davis and Quincy Jones are huge fans of their music from the beginning. Barack Obama is also a fan of Earth, Wind & Fire. Not a bad place to be for a music group.

• How Deep is Your Love from the Bee Gees, originally made up of three brothers: Barry Gibb, Robin Gibb (died 2012), and Maurice Gibb (died 2003), have been successful for most of their 40-plus years of recording music. They had two distinct periods of exceptional success: as a pop act in the late 1960s and early 1970s, and as a foremost act of the disco music era in the late 1970s.

I had an appointment with Dr Georgina Deighton about feeling dizzy, sensation of floating below my legs sometimes while walking and swaying which is normally consistent with my illness of paranoid schizophrenia. She is one of my GPs at Ferryview health centre.

I told Dr Georgina about pain in my left abdomen and top of abdomen no fever or change to my medications was recorded she asked I replied no. My eating was not ok for a long time I customary eat three particular kind of food and nothing else except drinking tea which were rice, meat and chicken no vegetables Georgina advised me to drink tea with decaffeinated eat vegetables, add other kinds of food to my diet which she discussed with me. I had to go for ECG test at the Cardiac Department at Queen Elizabeth hospital. She also booked me an appointment to see Ms. Debra Morris a nurse at Francis Street health centre in Woolwich to take my blood pressure again.

Monday morning which was on the 24th of September I was at Francis Street health centre Pam the receptionist took note of my arrival. I met with Debra she took my blood pressure and asked me if I had collected the ECG form Dr Georgina Dighton left for me at the receptionist at the Ferryview health centre I told her I had collected the form, she asked me if I had gone for the ECG I told Debra I was going straight to Queen Elizabeth Hospital immediately our appointment is over to get the ECG done. I feared my case would far worse but my situation wasn't anything close to that. Few days I was feeling much better after some dosage of Senecot tablets.

After our appointment I made my way to the bus stop by the former Woolwich Gala Club. I took the 161 bus going to Chislehurst War Memorial. I made my stop at Queen Elizabeth Hospital. I did not wait long at the Cardiac Department, on sight of the young nurse who had my ECG done I remembered Miss. Michelle Cook they look alike. She was a nice person; she spoke straight from her heart just like Michelle.

One thing about schizophrenia is one is likely to suffer from certain symptoms as a result you need to see a GP regularly or it makes one feel insecure. It feels good when you meet with nice people who care for you and make you feel welcome and you are in good hands it removes the feeling of insecurity.

Dr. Robert Kieron Frederic Hughes, Dr. Sarah Elizabeth Divall, Dr. Sami Toufic Rached, Dr. Kara Rosemary Mckenna Tanega, Dr. William Morgan, Dr. Andrew Paul Brown, Dr. Ijeoma Nina Anozie, Dr. Georgina Louise Deighton, Dr. Ngozi Nwanosike, Dr. Rebecca Celia Rosen, Dr. Shabina Siddiqi, Dr. Celestine Trawin, Dr. Tuan Quoc

Tran, Dr. S Pillai are my GPs at the Ferryview health centre at John Wilson Street they are all nice people.

- *Others are Practice nursing team Mrs. Aileen Palanisamy* Practice Nurse, *Mrs. Paula Butler* Practice Nurse, *Mrs. Fiona Hammond* Administrator, *Mrs. Phyllis Iwowo* Practice Nurse, *Miss. Gwen Harley* Practice Nurse, *Mrs. Debbie Morris* Practice Nurse, *Mrs. Briget Lawrence* Practice Nurse, *Mrs. Kim Hanney* Practice Nurse, *Ms. Kathy Steedman* Practice Nurse, *Mr. Tye Reeves* Community Nurse.

Others handling my care at Greenwich hospital and Ferryview mental health are:

My consultant psychiatrists: Dr. Banjac, Dr. Mougoud, Dr. Pereira, Dr. Patel, Dr. Mazaroli, Dr. Padamolis and Dr. Bhatnagar, Dr. Palademis.

Care and social workers are: Ms. Barbra receptionist, Ms. Shirley receptionist, Ms. Cathy, Mr. Engi, Mr. Fedelis, Mr. Kevin Daniel, Ms. Dupsi, Mr. Akim,

When you care that means that you take interest in something or someone and you make sure that they are taken good care of because it means a lot to you

Feeling and exhibiting concern and empathy for others: it helps in forming new generations united to argue for a caring society.

Health care is the diagnosis, treatment, and prevention of disease, illness, injury, and other physical and mental impairments in humans. Health care is delivered by practitioners in medicine, chiropractic, dentistry, nursing, pharmacy, allied health, and other care providers. It refers to the work done in providing primary care, secondary care and tertiary care, as well as in public health.

Access to health care varies across countries, groups and individuals, largely influenced by social and economic conditions as well as the health policies in place. Countries and jurisdictions have different policies and plans in relation to the personal and population-based health care goals within their societies. Health care systems are organizations established to meet the health needs of target populations.

Their exact configuration varies from country to country. In some countries and jurisdictions, health care planning is distributed among market participants, whereas in others planning is made more centrally among governments or other coordinating bodies. In all cases, according to the World Health Organization (WHO), a well-functioning health care system requires a robust financing mechanism; a well-trained and adequately-paid workforce; reliable information on which to base decisions and policies; and well maintained facilities and logistics to deliver quality medicines and technologies.

Health care can form a significant part of a country's economy. In 2008, the health care industry consumed an average of 9.0 percent of the gross domestic product (GDP) across the most developed countries. Health care is conventionally regarded as an important determinant in promoting the general health and well-being of people around the world.

The delivery of modern health care depends on groups of trained professionals and paraprofessionals coming together as interdisciplinary teams. This includes professionals in medicine, nursing, dentistry and allied health, plus many others such as public health practitioners, community health workers and assistive personnel, who systematically provide personal and population-based preventive, curative and rehabilitative care services.

While the definitions of the various types of health care vary depending on the different cultural, political, organizational and disciplinary perspectives, there appears to be some consensus that primary care constitutes the first element of a continuing health care process, that may also include the provision of secondary and tertiary levels of care. Healthcare can be defined as either public or private healthcare

Primary care is the term for the health care services which play a role in the local community. It refers to the work of health care professionals who act as a first point of consultation for all patients within the health care system. Such a professional would usually be a primary care physician, such as a general practitioner or family physician, or a non-physician primary care provider, such as a physician assistant or nurse practitioner. Depending on the locality, health system organization, and sometimes at the patient's discretion, they may see another health care professional first, such as a pharmacist, a nurse such as in the United Kingdom, a clinical officer such as in parts of Africa. Depending on the nature of the health condition, patients may then be referred for secondary or tertiary care.

Primary care involves the widest scope of health care, including all ages of patients, patients of all socioeconomic and geographic origins, patients seeking to maintain optimal health, and patients with all manner of acute and chronic physical, mental and social health issues, including multiple chronic diseases. Consequently, a primary care practitioner must possess a wide breadth of knowledge in many areas. Continuity is a key characteristic of primary care, as patients usually prefer to consult the same practitioner for routine check-ups and preventive care, health education, and every time they require an initial consultation about a new health problem. The International Classification of Primary Care (ICPC) is a standardized tool for understanding and analyzing information on interventions in primary care by the reason for the patient visit.

Common chronic illnesses usually treated in primary care may include, for example: hypertension, diabetes, asthma, COPD, depression and anxiety, back pain, arthritis or thyroid dysfunction. Primary care also includes many basic maternal and child health care services, such as family planning services and vaccinations.

In context of global population aging, with increasing numbers of older adults at greater risk of chronic non-communicable diseases, rapidly increasing demand for primary care services is expected around the world, in both developed and developing countries. The World Health Organization attributes the provision of essential primary care as an integral component of an inclusive primary health care strategy.

Secondary care is the health care services provided by medical specialists and other health professionals who generally do not have first contact with patients, for example, cardiologists, urologists and dermatologists.

It includes acute care: necessary treatment for a short period of time for a brief but serious illness, injury or other health condition, such as in a hospital emergency department. It also includes skilled attendance during childbirth, intensive care, and medical imaging services.

The 'secondary care' is sometimes used synonymously with

'hospital care'. However many secondary care providers do not necessarily work in hospitals, such as psychiatrists, clinical psychologists, occupational therapists or physiotherapists, and some primary care services are delivered within hospitals. Depending on the organization and policies of the national health system, patients may be required to see a primary care provider for a referral before they can access secondary care.

For example in the United States, which operates under a mixed market health care system, some physicians might voluntarily limit their practice to secondary care by requiring patients to see a primary care provider first, or this restriction may be imposed under the terms of the payment agreements in private/group health insurance plans. In other cases medical specialists may see patients without a referral, and patients may decide whether self-referral is preferred.

In the United Kingdom and Canada, patient self-referral to a medical specialist for secondary care is rare as prior referral from another physician (either a primary care physician or another specialist) is considered necessary, regardless of whether the funding is from private insurance schemes or national health insurance.

Social work is a professional and academic discipline that seeks to improve the quality of life and wellbeing of an individual, group, or community by intervening through research, policy, community organizing, direct practice, and teaching on behalf of those afflicted with poverty or any real or perceived social injustices and violations of their human rights. Research is often focused on areas such as human development, social policy, public administration, psychotherapy, program evaluation, and international and community development. Social workers are organized into local, national, continental and international professional bodies. Social work, an interdisciplinary field, includes theories from economics, education, sociology, medicine, philosophy, politics, anthropology and psychology. In many jurisdictions, clinical social workers are licensed mental health professionals.

The concept of charity goes back to ancient times, and the practice of providing for the poor has roots in many major ancient civilizations and world religions.

Social work has its roots in the social and economic upheaval wrought by the Industrial Revolution, in particular the struggle of society to deal with poverty and its resultant problems. Because dealing with poverty was the main focus of early social work, it is intricately linked with the idea of charity work, but it must now be understood in much broader terms. For instance it is not uncommon for modern social workers to find themselves dealing with the consequences arising from many other 'social problems' such as racism, sexism, homophobia, and discrimination based on age or on physical or mental ability. Modern social workers can be found helping to deal with the consequences of these and many other social maladies in all areas of the human services and in many other fields besides.

Whereas social work started on a more scientific footing aimed at controlling and reforming individuals (at one stage supporting the notion that poverty was a disease), it has in more recent times adopted a more critical and holistic approach to understanding and intervening in social problems. This has led, for example, to the re-conceptualization of poverty as more a problem of the haves versus the have-nots rather than its former status as a disease, illness, or moral defect in need of treatment. This also points to another historical development in the evolution of social work: once a profession engaged more in social control, it has become one more directed at social empowerment. That is not to say that modern social workers do not engage in social control (consider for example statutory child protection workers), and many if not most social workers would likely agree that this is an ongoing tension and debate.

Social determinants of health are the economic and social conditions – and their distribution among the population – that influence individual and group differences in health status. They are risk factors found in one's living and working conditions (such as the distribution of income, wealth, influence, and power), rather than individual factors (such as behavioural risk factors or genetics) that influence the risk for a disease, injury, or vulnerability to disease or injury. According to some viewpoints, these distributions of social determinants are shaped by public policies that reflect the influence of prevailing political ideologies of those governing a jurisdiction. The World Health Organization says that 'This unequal distribution of health-damaging experiences is not in any sense a 'natural' phenomenon but is the result of a toxic combination of poor social policies, unfair economic arrangements [where the already well-off and healthy become even richer and the poor who are already more likely to be ill become even poorer], and bad politics.

Profound differences in overall health status exist between developed and developing nations. Much of this has to do with the lack of the basic necessities of life (food, water, sanitation, primary health care, etc.) common to developing nations. Yet among developed nations such as Canada, less profound but still highly significant differences in health status indicators such as life expectancy, infant mortality, incidence of disease, and death from injuries exist. An excellent example is comparison of health status differences and the hypothesized social determinants of these health status differences among Canada, the United States, and Sweden.

People in rich countries live dramatically longer, healthier lives than people in poorer countries. It can be argued that it is the huge wealth inequalities between rich and poor countries that is acting as a fundamental driver of poor global health.

Traditional approaches to health and disease prevention have a distinctly non-historical here-and-now emphasis. Usually adults, and increasingly adolescents and youth are urged to adopt 'healthy lifestyles' as a means of preventing the development of chronic diseases such as heart disease and diabetes, among others. In contrast to these approaches, life-course approaches emphasize the accumulated effects of experience across the life span in understanding the maintenance of health and the onset of disease

Reducing the health gap in a generation requires that governments build systems that allow a healthy standard of living where no one should fall below due to circumstances beyond his or her control. Social protection schemes can be instrumental in realizing developmental goals rather than being dependent on achieving those goals. They can be effective ways to reduce poverty and local economies can benefit.

Policies to reduce child poverty need to be enacted as an investment in the future of all countries. As a child, when stress levels go up and stay up as a result of constantly having to worry about shelter and food, high hormone levels interfere with the development of brain circuitry and connection causing long term chemical damage.

Policies to reduce child poverty need to be enacted as an investment in the future of all countries. It would involve providing resources such as quality education, decent housing, access to affordable health care, access to healthy food, and safe places to exercise for everyone despite gaps in affluence.

Much social determinants of health research simply focuses on determining the relationship between a social determinant of health and health status. So a researcher may document that lower income is associated with adverse health outcomes among parents and their children. Or a researcher may demonstrate that food insecurity is related to poor health status among parents and children as is living in crowded housing, and so on. This is what is termed a depoliticized approach in that it says little about how these poor-quality social determinants of health come about.

Social determinants of health do not exist in a vacuum. Their quality and availability to the population are usually a result of public policy decisions made by governing authorities. As one example, consider the social determinant of health of early life. Early life is shaped by availability of sufficient material resources that assure adequate educational opportunities, food and housing among others. Much of this has to do with the employment security and the quality of working conditions and wages. The availability of quality, regulated childcare is an especially important policy option in support of early life. These are not issues that usually come under individual control. A policy-oriented approach places such findings within a broader policy context.

Yet it is not uncommon to see governmental and other authorities individualize these issues. Governments may choose to understand early life as being primarily about parental behaviours towards their children. They then focus upon promoting better parenting, assist in having parents read to their children, or urge schools to foster exercise among children rather than raising the amount of financial or housing resources available to families. Indeed, for every social determinant of health, an individualized manifestation of each is available. There is little evidence to suggest the efficacy of such approaches in improving the health status of those most vulnerable to illness in the absence of efforts to modify their adverse living conditions.

Free health check for all as people are being invited to have a pre-winter health MOT check on Wednesday September 2012 within 10an to 3pm. The health and wellbeing day was being held at the Greenwich Heritage Centre in Woolwich, opposite the Firepower museum everyone can go along absolutely free.

The event was packed with stands and workshops giving handy tips and information, you can get your blood pressure checked, learn more about diabetes or get advice on how to quit smoking or cut down on your drinking.

You would have also had talk to a nutritionist, a nurse or a health trainer for free advice as well as get free massage to help you de-stress while healthy refreshments were available. The day was organized by the Irish community services charity which supports thousands of residents within the Royal Greenwich and neighbouring borough director Ellen Stafford said young and old, are all warmly invited down to Woolwich Riverside come and get checked out for free and have a good time.

Tuesday 25 September 2012 Sky news says more than half of all Britons risk their lives and ignore the first signs of potentially serious illness, hoping they will simply go away.

According to the YouGov survey commissioned by private healthcare provider Bupa, two in five delays visiting their GP, even when they believe their symptoms could be an indication of serious illness.

One in three put off having such symptoms looked at because they do not wish to waste their GP's time. Department of Health figures demonstrate that early diagnosis is hugely important. Dr Marie Tyrell told Sky News they are used to seeing and talking to people about everything and they would be listened to. They are quite happy to be seen. 'Anything that's worrying you and lasts for more than three or four weeks and is persistent - come and ask us about it.'

The research also found three in 10 delayed calling the doctor because it was difficult to make an appointment and more than half would not make an urgent appointment if they suffered a persistent cough for more than a few weeks.

Dr Annabel Bentley, Medical Director at Bupa Health and Wellbeing, said: 'It is worrying that people put off seeing their doctor for worrying symptoms. 'It may turn out to be nothing, but seeing your doctor can help give you peace of mind. 'And, if the symptoms could be due to a serious problem, this allows you to discuss this with your doctor and work out the best plan of action together. 'Early stage diagnosis can be really important with some illness. In Britain people have behavioural patterns about their health because, they have choice in other parts of the world, it's a worrying aspects of their lives. Some government does not really see to how people receive proper care.

Health care provision in Nigeria is a concurrent responsibility of the three tiers of government in the country. Because Nigeria operates a mixed economy, private providers of health care have a visible role to play in health care delivery. The federal government's role is mostly limited to coordinating the affairs of the university teaching hospitals, Federal Medical Centres (tertiary health care) while the state government manages the various general hospitals (secondary health care) and the local government focus on dispensaries (primary health care), (which are regulated by the federal government through NPHCDA). The total expenditure on health care as % of GDP is 4.6, while the percentage of federal government expenditure on health care is about 1.5%. A long run indicator of the ability of the country to provide food sustenance and avoid malnutrition is the rate of growth of per capita food production; from 1970–1990, the rate for Nigeria was 0.25%. Though small, the positive rate of per capita may be due to Nigeria's importation of food products.

Historically, health insurance in Nigeria can be applied to a few instances: free health care provided and financed for all citizens, health care provided by government through a special health insurance scheme for government employees and private firms entering contracts with private health care providers. However, there are few people who fall within the three instances.

In May 1999, the government created the National Health Insurance Scheme, the scheme encompasses government employees, the organized private sector and the informal sector. Legislative wise, the scheme also covers children under five, permanently disabled persons and prison inmates. In 2004, the administration of Obasanjo further gave more legislative powers to the scheme with positive amendments to the original 1999 legislative act.

The majority of mental health services is provided by 8 regional psychiatric centres and psychiatric departments and medical schools of 12 major universities. A few general hospitals also provide mental health services. The formal centres often face competition from native herbalists and faith healing centres.

The ratio of psychologists and social workers is 0.02 to 100,000.

In 1989 legislation made effective a list of essential drugs. The regulation was also meant to limit the manufacture and import of fake or sub-standard drugs and to curtail false advertising. However, the section on essential drugs was later amended.

Drug quality is primarily controlled by the National Agency for Food and Drug Administration and Control (NAFDAC). Several major regulatory failures have produced international scandals:

In 1993, adulterated paracetamol syrup entered into the health care system in Oyo and Benue State, the end result of was the death of 100 children. A year after the disaster, batches containing poisonous ethylene glycol, the major cause of the deaths, could still be purchased.

In 1996, about 11 children died of contamination from an experimental trial of the drug Trovafloxacin.

In 2008-2009, at least 84 children died from a brand of contaminated teething medication.

Health care in Nigeria is influenced by different local and regional factors that impact the quality or quantity present in one location. Due to the aforementioned, the health care system in Nigeria has shown spatial variation in terms of availability and quality of facilities in relation to need. However, this is largely as a result of the level of state and local government involvement and investment in health care programs and education. Also, the Nigerian ministry of health usually spends about 70% of its budget in urban areas where 30% of the population resides. It is assumed by some scholars that the health care service is inversely related to the need of patients.

Retaining health care professionals is an important objective Migration of health care personnel to other countries is a taxing and relevant issue in the health care system of the country. From a supply push factor, a resulting rise in exodus of health care nurses may be due to dramatic factors that make the work unbearable and knowing and presenting changes to arrest the factors may stem a tide. However, because a large number of nurses and doctors migrating abroad benefited from government funds for education, it poses a challenge to the patriotic identity of citizens and also the rate of return of federal funding of health care education. The state of health care in Nigeria has been worsened by a physician shortage as a consequence of severe 'brain drain'. Many Nigerian doctors have emigrated to North America and Europe. In 2005, 2,392 Nigeria doctors were practicing in the US alone, in UK number was 1,529. Retaining these expensively trained professionals has been identified as an urgent goal.

A new bone marrow donor program, the second in Africa, opened in 2012. In cooperation with the University of Nigeria, it collects DNA swabs from people who might want to help a person with leukemia, lymphoma, or sickle cell disease to find a compatible donor for a life-saving bone marrow transplant. It hopes to expand to include cord blood donations in the future.

The 2000 WHO report on the performance of health care systems rank the country 187 out of 191.

The life expectancy of the country is low and about 20% of children die before the age of 5.

Traffic congestion in Lagos, environmental pollution and noise pollution are major health issues.

In 1985, an incidence of yellow fever devastated a town in Nigeria, leading to the death of 1000 people. In a span of 5 years, the epidemic grew, with a resulting rise in mortality. The vaccine for yellow fever has been in existence since the 1930s.

In June 2011, the United Nations Population Fund released a report on The State of the World's Midwifery. It contained new data on the midwifery workforce and policies relating to newborn and maternal mortality for 58 countries. The 2010 maternal mortality rate per 100,000 births for Nigeria is 840. This is compared with 608.3 in 2008 and 473.4 in 1990. The under 5 mortality rate, per 1,000 births is 143 and the neonatal mortality as a percentage of under 5's mortality is 28. The aim of the report was to highlight ways in which the Millennium Development Goals can be achieved.

A health system, also sometimes referred to as health care system or healthcare system is the organization of people, institutions, and resources to deliver health care services to meet the health needs of target populations.

There is a wide variety of health systems around the world, with as many histories and organizational structures as there are nations. In some countries, health system planning is distributed among market participants. In others, there is a concerted effort among governments, trade unions, charities, religious, or other co-ordinate bodies to deliver planned health care services targeted to the populations they serve. However, health care planning has been described as often evolutionary rather than revolutionary.

The goals for health systems, according to the World Health Organization, are good health, responsiveness to the expectations of the population, and fair financial contribution. Progress towards them depends on how systems carry out four vital functions: provision of health care services, resource generation, financing, and stewardship. Other dimensions for the evaluation of health systems include quality, efficiency, acceptability, and equity. They have also been described in the United States as 'the five C's': Cost, Coverage, Consistency, Complexity, and Chronic Illness. Also, continuity of health care is a major goal.

Since 2000, more and more initiatives have been taken at the international and national levels in order to strengthen national health systems as the core components of the global health system. Having this scope in mind, it is essential to have a clear, and unrestricted, vision of national health systems that might generate further progresses in global health. The elaboration and the selection of performance indicators are indeed both highly dependent on the conceptual framework adopted for the evaluation of the health systems performances Like most social systems, health systems are complex adaptive systems where change does not necessarily follow rigid epidemiological models. In complex systems path dependency, emergent properties and other non-linear patterns are under-explored and unmeasured, which can lead to the development of inappropriate guidelines for developing responsive health systems.

Healthy Cities is a term used in public health and urban design to stress the impact of policy on human health. Its modern form derives from a World Health Organization (WHO) initiative on Healthy Cities and Villages in 1986, but has a history dating back to the mid 19th century. The term was developed in conjunction with the European Union, but rapidly became international as a way of establishing healthy public policy at the local level through health promotion.
Many jurisdictions have healthy community programme, cities can apply to become a WHO-designated 'Healthy City'. WHO defines the Healthy City as 'one that is continually creating and improving those physical and social environments and expanding those community resources which enable people to mutually support each other in performing all the functions of life and in developing to their maximum potential.'

Measuring the indices required, establishing standards and determining the impact of each component on health is difficult. In some regions, such as Europe, a health impact assessment is a required piece of public policy development. There are many networks of healthy cities, including in Europe and internationally, such as the Alliance for Healthy Cities. A key feature is ensuring that the social determinants of health are taken into consideration in urban design and urban governance. For example, 'urbanization and health' was the theme of the 2010 Day. One tool in developing healthy cities is social entrepreneurship.
The philosophy of healthcare is study of the ethics, processes, and people which constitute the maintenance of health for human beings. (Although veterinary concerns are worthy to note, the body of thought regarding their methodologies and practices is not addressed in this article.)

For the most part, however, the philosophy of healthcare is best approached as an indelible component of human social structures.

That is, the societal institution of healthcare can be seen as a necessary phenomenon of human civilization whereby an individual continually seeks to improve, mend, and alter the overall nature and quality of his or her life.

The philosophy of healthcare is primarily concerned with the following elemental questions. Who requires and/or deserves healthcare? Is healthcare a fundamental right of all people? What should be the basis for calculating the cost of treatments, hospital stays, drugs, etc.? How can healthcare best be administered to the greatest number of people? What are the necessary parameters for clinical trials and quality assurance? Who, if anybody, can decide when a patient is in need of 'comfort measures' (euthanasia)?

However, the most important question of all is 'what is health?' Unless this question is addressed any debate about healthcare will be vague and unbounded. For example, what exactly is a health care intervention? What differentiates healthcare from engineering or teaching, for example? Is health care about 'creating autonomy' or acting in people's best interests? Or is it always both? Ultimately, the purpose, objective, and meaning of healthcare philosophy is to consolidate the abundance of information regarding the ever-changing fields of medicine, and nursing.

And seeing that healthcare typically ranks as one of the largest spending areas of governmental budgets, it becomes important to gain a greater understanding of healthcare as not only a social institution, but also as a political one.

Being diagnosed with schizophrenia may seem like the end of the world, but it doesn't have to be that way. Yes, it is bad news and yes, the illness is difficult to manage at least, there is some cure and it shouldn't stop you from moving on and living your life.

Of course, going about your daily routine will be much more difficult than ever, but the good news is that there are many ways to manage your symptoms to a point wherein they don't cause a major disturbance in your life and if they do how do you coup try and live a healthy and normal life.

Having enough rest and sleep is a solution against schizophrenia in itself. Sleep allows you to restore your body's internal batteries, allowing your body to heal and regain strength it's important to remember that the more rest you have, the stronger your immune system is, which puts you at less risk to develop depression. It is difficult to sleep sometimes try and put your mind at rest think of beautiful things, meditate do not let your mind wonder about in thoughts and hallucination.

Getting enough exercise also builds your immune system and release endorphins, giving you that feel good sensation I do not mean strenuous exercise you can seat down stretch your hands and legs forward and backward at least there are some few easy exercise you can do it takes your mind off hallucination, emotion try as much as you can to feel good in yourself.

If your diet consists of fried fatty foods, you'll need to change things especially if you are on drugs. Increasing your intake of healthy food such fresh vegetables and fruits I have had eating problems for a while, I cannot seem to eat the right food at certain times but it's good being aware when things aren't right or done properly at least one can easily change rather than getting to a stage one cannot help doing the right things

One of your best defences against schizophrenia in my own experience is being on sound medication plan for suppressing symptoms. Your doctor will emphasize the importance of taking your medicine, so be sure to listen to the advice you're given and I hope that may the forces be with you. We go through many different episode with the illness new once each day might unfold cares should lay emphasis on our trying to outlive the illness. One thing about the illness is that it is through the amount of effort we put in as sufferers to outlive the illness that triggers us to show certain concern about being supportive to ourselves. It could make us frequently ask or remind ourselves to take our medication they are often worried about the behaviour of sufferers but they are not all the same if you are trying to outlive the illness and they are not supportive it could be worrying leading to changes in behavioural patterns among sufferers. Such as being withdrawn from them, not speaking up when you have appointments with them.

Having schizophrenia does not necessarily mean the end of a normal life. At the beginning, it will take some time to learn how to manage your condition so that you can lead a normal life, but consistent medical and emotional support and a lot of deep breaths help. Soon you'll be back to your fulfilling, productive, and creative life.

There has been international condemnation of North Korea's long-range rocket launch, as Pyongyang admits the mission failed to put a weather satellite into orbit.

Britain's Foreign Secretary William Hague condemned the launch and said North Korea's ambassador in the UK would be summoned to the Foreign Office.

The launch programme has drawn international criticism due to concerns it could further the reclusive state's ability to deliver a nuclear warhead.

Mr Hague said: '(North Korea) can expect a strong response from the international community if it continues to develop its missile and nuclear capabilities.

'I strongly urge (it) to suspend all missile and nuclear-related activity and to commit to re-engaging with the international community.'

The UN Security Council is meeting later to discuss a possible response to the rocket launch, diplomats had confirmed.

The North American Aerospace Defense Command (Norad) said it tracked the Taepo Dong-2 missile after its launch.

The launch control centre looked rudimentary compared to Western equivalents

The first stage fell into the sea 103 miles west of the South Korea capital Seoul, and the remainder of the satellite-carrying missile was deemed to have failed.

Norad said no debris fell on land and at no time was the missile or debris deemed a threat.

Officials in Seoul had earlier announced that the rocket broke into pieces and crashed a few minutes after take-off.

Japan's defence minister also said a 'flying object' fell into the ocean after a short flight.

'The flying object is believed to have flown for more than one minute and fallen into the ocean. This does not affect our country's territory at all,' defence minister Naoki Tanaka said.

Sky's Holly Williams, reporting 30 miles from the launch site in China, said: 'The three-stage rocket was supposed to carry a weather satellite into space.

'There is a lot of speculation this whole launch is about the young North Korean leader, Kim Jong-un.'

The White House slammed the launch attempt and said North Korea's leaders should be providing for the nation's impoverished people instead of wasting resources.

US ambassador to the United Nations Susan Rice sought international support and said the 15-nation Security Council should 'respond credibly' to the launch.

A North Korean soldier has defected to the South across the two countries' heavily armed border, South Korean officials have said.

The soldier said he shot dead two officers before crossing over just after noon.

More than 20,000 North Koreans have gone to the South in the last 60 years, mostly via China and SE Asia.

The two countries are still technically at war after the 1950-53 conflict, which ended in a ceasefire not a peace treaty.

The soldier was quoted as saying that he killed his platoon and squad commanders while on guard duty.

A defence ministry official said six gunshots were heard and guards saw the soldier cross the demarcation line on a western section of the tightly guarded border.

They used loudspeakers to establish that he wanted to defect and guide him to safety, they added.

The official said he was in protective custody and was still being interrogated.

There has been no confirmation of the North Korean casualties and no unusual activity observed on the North Korean side of the border.

The BBC's Lucy Williamson in Seoul says that about a million soldiers and a million land mines line the Demilitarised Zone, and only a handful of people have

crossed from North to South by land in the past few years.
Most make their way to the South by a long and dangerous
land route, she says.
This takes them through China and on to countries such as
Thailand or Mongolia.

North Korea's next step after rattling the world by putting a
satellite into orbit for the first time will likely be a nuclear test.
A nuclear test would be the logical follow-up to a successful
rocket launch, analysts said.
The costs of the rocket program and its allied nuclear
weapons efforts estimated by South Korea's government at
$2.8-$3.2 billion since 1998 and the risk of additional U.N. or
unilateral sanctions are simply not part of the calculation.
'North Korea will insist any sanctions are unjust, and if
sanctions get toughened, the likelihood of North Korea
carrying out a nuclear test is high. The United Nations
Security Council is to discuss how to respond to the launch,
which it says is a breach of sanctions imposed in 2006 and
2009 that banned the isolated and impoverished state from
missile and nuclear developments in the wake of its two
nuclear weapons tests. It is true that both satellite carrier
rocket and a missile with warhead use similar technology,'
its Foreign Ministry said in an eight-page statement carried
by state news agency.

The end-game for the North is a formal peace treaty with
Washington, diplomatic recognition and bundles of cash to
help bolster its moribund economy. They might hope that the
U.S. will finally face the unpleasant reality and will start
negotiations aimed at slowing down or freezing, but not
reversing, their nuclear and missile programs. If such a deal
is possible, mere cognition is not enough. The U.S. will have
to pay, will have to provide generous 'aid' as a reward for
North Koreans' willingness to slow down or stop for a while.

Friendship is a relationship between two people who hold
mutual affection for each other. Friendships and
acquaintanceship are thought of as spanning across the
same continuum. The study of friendship is included in the
fields of sociology, social psychology, anthropology,
philosophy, and zoology. Various academic theories of

friendship have been proposed, including social exchange theory, equity theory, relational dialectics, and attachment styles.

The value of friendship is often the result of friends consistently demonstrating the following:

- The tendency to desire what is best for the other
- Sympathy and empathy
- Honesty, even in situations where it may be difficult for others to speak the truth
- Mutual understanding and compassion; ability to go to each other for emotional support
- Enjoyment of each other's company
- Trust in one another
- Positively strong, deep, close reciprocity, mutuality equal give-and-take between the two parties
- The ability to be oneself, express one's feelings and make mistakes without fear of judgment

There has been a large rise in the number of migrants living in England and Wales, according to the results of the 2011 census.

Data from the Office for National Statistics shows that the population of England and Wales now stands at 56.1 million people a rise of 3.7 million since 2001. Some 55% of the growth - around 2.1 million people was due to migration from outside the country. The number of foreign-born residents has increased to 13%, from 4.6 million to 7.5 million. In London one person in three was born abroad, compared to the North East where the figure is one in 20. The majority of those from abroad come from India, Poland and Pakistan. Poland is a new addition to the top ten of where people came from and did not feature at all in the last census in 2001.

Dr Scott Blinder, deputy director of the Migration Observatory at the University of Oxford, said there had been 'a very noticeable change in the population of England and Wales' over the last decade. It is the second major tranche of information to be revealed from the 2011 census, covering topics including ethnicity, country of birth, religion, health and housing. The census shows the makeup of the population is changing the census also showed 86% of people recorded their ethnicity as white, a fall on 2001. It remains the majority ethnic group in all areas apart from London. All other ethnic groups grew over the 10 years since 2001.

Two million respondents listed their partners or fellow household members as being of different ethnic groups - 47% more than in 2001. The number of people claiming to have mixed ethnicity almost doubled, up by 563,000. Some 91% of respondents to the 2011 census claimed to speak English. Just 4% of households had no English speaking residents. The statistics also offer a snapshot of how people live.

Since 2001, the proportion of people owning properties through a mortgage or loan has decreased from 39% to 33% but the number of people who own homes outright increased from 29% to 31%. Ownership of cars and vans has also gone up - increasing by 3.4 million to 27.3 million, a rise of 14%. Last year there was an average of 12 cars for every 10 households - up on 11 cars per 10 households in 2001. London was the only region where the number of vehicles was lower than the number of households. Four out of five people claimed to be in good health. The questionnaire was sent to around 26 million households in England and Wales on March 27 last year.

The population of England and Wales has increased by more than 7% during the last 10 years the biggest increase since records began. There were 56.1 million people living in England and Wales on the day of last year's Census an increase of 3.7 million since 2001, the Office for National Statistics (ONS) said.

This marks the largest growth in population in any 10-year period since the first Census in 1801, and a rise of approximately 50% since 1911. The number of households in England and Wales increased by 8% to 23.4 million - although the average size remained unchanged at 2.4 people. The once-a-decade survey from 2011 illustrated an aging population, with one in six people in England and Wales aged 65 or over. There were also 430,000 people aged 90 or over compared with just 13,000 when the Census was carried out 100 years earlier.

The number of women to reach this age was more than three times higher than the number of men. But the amount of children under the age of five was also up, with 400,000 more last year than in 2001. London experienced the largest population boost - surging by 12% to a total of more than eight million - although the figures showed an increase in every region in England and Wales over the decade. In total, England's population hit 53 million, Wales' reached 3.06 million and Northern Ireland's increased to 1.8 million. Figures for Scotland will be released later in the year.

The ONS estimates that around 55% of the increase in population between 2001 and 2011 was the result of net migration. National Statistician Jil Matheson described the 2011 Census as a 'resounding success'. 'Across England and Wales around 19 out of 20 people responded and we have excellent statistical methods for ensuring we have a complete estimate of the whole population,' she said. 'These statistics will provide valuable information for planners, policy-makers and the public for years to come.'

• UK 'More Open To Mixed Marriage'

The British have become far more comfortable than they used to be with interracial marriage, according to a report. Research by British Future estimates that more than a million people in Britain are now of mixed parentage it came as census data from the Office for National Statistics (ONS) showed a significant increase in the number of mixed race people living in the UK. There was also a huge rise in the number of migrants.

The think-tank's report, The Melting Pot Generation - How Britain Became More Relaxed About Race, says 'mixed Britain is fast becoming the new normal'. At that time, a British Social Attitudes survey showed 50% of the public were against marriage across ethnic lines. The figure dropped to 40% in the 1990s and now stands at 15%. Sunder Katwala, director of British Future, said under-30s were Britain's most tolerant generation. 'One in four of the over-65s still say that they would be uncomfortable about a child or grandchild marrying somebody from a different race, but that falls to one in 20 of those under 25.

'It ranked last out of 10 as a possible source of concern, with even worries about the idea of marrying somebody much richer being slightly stronger among the youngest group.' 'Over a million Britons will have ticked the census box as mixed race and that is only half the story of the rapid growth of mixed Britain,' he said. 'Twice as many people have ethnically mixed parentage but over half of them choose other census categories, such as black or white.'

The think-tank believes that Britain has a greater claim to 'melting pot' status than the US. The number of foreign-born residents in England and Wales has risen by nearly three million since 2001 to 7.5 million people, the 2011 census shows. That means about one in eight - 13% - of residents were born outside the UK. The most common birthplaces outside the UK for residents are India, Poland and Pakistan. The number of ethnic white British people is down to 80%. London has become the first region where white British people have become a minority. Some 45% (3.7 million) of people in the capital described themselves as white British, down from 58% (4.3 million) in 2001. The Office for National Statistics said the findings showed a 'diverse' and 'changing' picture. 'The question of do you want this to happen or don't you want this to happen implies that you've got a choice and you could say 'let's not have any diversity',' Guy Goodwin, from the Office of National Statistics, told BBC News: 'It's a really changing picture so the 2011 census population will go down as a diverse population compared with 2001.' The census also shows that, while fewer people own their own home, more people own it outright.

Just fewer than 15 million households owned their own home in 2011, either with a mortgage or loan, or outright down 4%. The 2011 census shows beyond any doubt that the UK is now in the midst of an astonishing era of demographic change due to globalisation.

Parts of the country are witnessing such rapid flows and movements of people that they are becoming super-diverse

- home to many different people from many different backgrounds. If you want just a snapshot of that rapid change - look at Boston in Lincolnshire. In 2001, it was home to fewer than 1,500 people born abroad - and because of a statistical quirk many of those are thought to have been people born to parents once stationed with the British Army in Germany. Today, almost 10,000 people born abroad call Boston home - and it has more Polish residents than any other local authority outside of the South East. The 2011 census confirms what people see around them. However, those who owned their home outright increased two percentage points from 29% (6.4 million) to 31% (7.2 million). The group that rented from a private landlord or letting agency increased by six percentage points from 9% (1.9 million) in 2001 to 15% (3.6 million) in 2011. Campbell Robb, chief executive of housing charity Shelter, said the figures 'confirm that home ownership is slipping further and further out of reach, no matter how hard people work or save'.

Back in 2005, the BBC ran a project to map the modern face of the UK, so we could explain to our audiences the role immigration was playing in modern Britain. The figures in the eventual Born Abroad report showed an unprecedented transformation that confirmed everything that we saw around us as we travelled around the country gathering stories of migration and change. What the census shows beyond any doubt is that the UK is in the midst of an astonishing era of demographic shift - and like the experience of many of its international peers, it is being driven by globalisation. Ten years ago, there were some 4.3 million people in the UK who told the census that they had been born abroad. Almost all areas had been touched by changes from immigration - although in some areas the numbers were so small that it clearly amounted to little more than a family moving in or out - the phenomenon of a single Indian restaurant in a village, for instance.

In 2011, there were 7.5 million people born abroad living in England and Wales up almost three million and taking their proportion of the population to 13%. The UK is experiencing such rapid flows and movements of people from so many parts of the world, that parts of it can lay claim to being 'super-diverse' the idea that an area is home to so many people it's almost impossible to describe it in simple terms, such as home to one community or another.

The 2011 census used three measures to understand migration - it asked people where they were born, when they came to the UK and what passport they held. The Census also tried to capture who was a long-term migrant and who was only in the UK temporarily. But even with these kinds of understandable limitations, we have a very good idea of what is going on. In 2001, the top three places where people were born abroad (excluding the Republic of Ireland) were India, Pakistan and Germany. Poland lay 18th on the list - but over a decade numbers increased nine-fold as its workers came to the UK once the country joined the European Union. The change has been so rapid that almost half of those born abroad arrived in the decade leading up to the 2011 census. All regions witnessed an increase - although the changes varied greatly from area to area. London, already a global city in 2001, became more so, with its boroughs holding all the places in the diversity top 10.
EU workers

One of the key drivers of the change was the expansion of the EU and the arrival of Polish workers. If you want just a snapshot of that change - look at Boston in Lincolnshire. In 2001, it was home to fewer than 1,500 people born abroad - and because of the statistical quirk I've already mentioned, some of those were Brits born in Germany. Today, almost 10,000 people born abroad call Boston home - 3,000 of them from Poland, more than any other local authority outside of the South East. The greatest numerical change has however been in London. In 2001, almost two million people in the capital were born abroad. Today it is almost three million. If anyone doubted that London was now a world city, rather than just the capital of the UK, the figures say different. Only 44% of people in London now describe themselves as white British. In the east London borough of Newham, fewer than a fifth of the population described themselves so.

Four out of every 10 people in London in 2011 were foreign-born - up from three in 10 in 2001. Overall, four London boroughs - Newham, Brent, Westminster and Kensington and Chelsea are now home to a majority who were born outside of the UK. Three other parts of the capital are not far off. The history of migration was once the story of cities: We had very distinct communities in specific places - an African-Caribbean community in London or Birmingham, for instance, and Indian or East African Asian people in Leicester. Large historic communities remain but there is also greater geographic spread among newcomers. For instance, some 90% of the Poles in the UK are spread across England and Wales in community after community. So overall, increasing change, rapid change and increasing diversity. Is this something happening to the UK alone? It lies 12th in the list of EU nations when you look at the proportion of people in each nation who were born abroad.

But England and Wales comes top in this category when you rank it alongside France, Germany and Italy - the other states with populations of over 50 million. The 2001 census confirmed the change in the face of Britain the 2011 census confirms that the change continues yet Britain is still a peaceful place to live in.

Each friend represents a world in us, a world possibly not born until they arrive, and it is only by this meeting that a new world is born.' Though some natural loners are happy without them, most of us depend greatly on the company of true friends. As with any relationship, friendships bring support and joy and occasionally strife. Here in Europe and America there are many ways to make friends, understand friendship better, and be a great confidante to others. They help those from third world countries fight poverty and disease, make corrupt leaders change their ways for the betterment of their people. Some of them are allowed into Europe made welcome and not made felt as if, they are strangers. We all need friendship, to be a developed nation it must come with having friends. Friend who are not made to be afraid because of your atomic warfare or nuclear missiles, Nuclear warhead some nations had used hundred years in attaining for consideration they try to reduce their nuclear warhead to imply they are not a treat to the rest of the world while some nation aren't that friendly nuclear warheads taken hundred year in attaining within ten years some nation wants to attain the same military capabilities its unfriendly. Third world nation are trying to attain lasting peace, they need to develop to meat required standard of care for the people in those nation this is what we are aiming for we feel with some nations we have friends because they care. It is not the number of nuclear warheads a nation has, which makes it a nation of super power. The implication of race, background, ethnicity and culture, constructivism, they way they shape their lives with freedom or democracy, each individual life is respected and given attention to their basic needs, how they came this far, as super power nation of planet earth should be respected in view of their values or morals. Within some of them most race or other nations of the world do not feel alienated infarct they are doing something in relation to globalising the world, create awareness I would not be surprise if one day Britain becomes the capital of the European Union.

Globalization is the process of international integration arising from the interchange of world views, products, ideas, and other aspects of culture. Put in simple terms, globalization refers to processes that promote world-wide exchanges of national and cultural resources. Advances in transportation and telecommunications infrastructure, including the rise of the Internet, are major factors in globalization, generating further interdependence of economic and cultural activities.

In 2000, the International Monetary Fund (IMF) identified four basic aspects of globalization: trade and transactions, capital and investment movements, migration and movement of people and the dissemination of knowledge. Further, environmental challenges such as climate change, cross-boundary water and air pollution, and over-fishing of the ocean are linked with globalization.

Though several scholars place the origins of globalization in modern times, others trace its history long before the European age of discovery and voyages to the New World.

Some even trace the origins to the third millennium BCE. Globalizing processes affect and are affected by business and work organization, economics, socio-cultural resources, and the natural environment. Understanding ethnicity, diversity and segregation is one thing practicing it and obtaining result is another thing.

Different approaches to understanding ethnicity have been used by different social scientists when trying to understand the nature of ethnicity as a factor in human life and society. Examples of such approaches are primordialism, essentialism, perennialism, and constructivism. Modernising, using initiatives and socializing while at the same time, paying a huge price in using such approach by bringing people from diverse ethnic group, race and culture from all over the world together.

Blessed are the peacemakers those who strive to prevent contention, strife, and war; that use their influence to reconcile opposing parties, and to prevent lawsuits and hostilities in families and neighbourhoods

Peacemaking is a divine work for peace means reconciliation and God is the author of peace and of reconciliation it is hardly surprising, therefore, that the particular blessing which attaches to peacemakers is that 'they shall be called sons and daughters of God for they are seeking to do what their father has done, loving people with his love blessed are the merciful, for they shall obtain mercy.

There are two ways of thinking about ethics the good and the right. The good has to do with achievement of goals; the right, with laws and rules. The goodness recognizes that people have desires and aspirations, and frames values in terms of what enables a being to achieve its ends. Rightness recognizes that people live in groups that require organization and regulations, and frames values in terms of duty and conformance to rules. The primary task of morality is to guide one's actions. Focus on qualities of character and motives for action. One should cultivate answers on the basis either of what is good or of what is right.

- Whatever is good for a thing enables that thing to serve its purpose. From a third world nation you live in Europe or are on a visit your generation from your background have had a standing relationship with European countries and their culture, what does it seems to you, understand or feel if you encounter an English white young lad or man spit on the street even close to where you are standing? What kind of manners would you consider it to be and how would you address such a white person if he asks you for a lighter to light up his cigarettes what, do you make out of what other people from his race think of him? Considering your background see the English race as very thorough and tidy people. There exists something absolutely good, that is, something alleged to be good without reference to its effects. Whatever that is right has to do with conformance to rules or regulations.

- An action is justified on the basis of a quality or characteristic of the act itself, the characteristic is its conformance to a rule. Morality is concerned with identifying and obeying moral rules. It is right to obey the rules while wrong disobey them. Any particular act can be judged right or wrong according to weather and to what extent it conforms to the moral rules. A central concern, then, is to identify the rules so one can make sure one is acting in accordance with them. Once the rules are established, all one needs to do in order to be moral is to do one's duty, which is to act in accordance with the rules.

- Making the distinction between good and right is important because it promotes clarity of thought.

- It is not impossible to make a choice, however. It makes more sense to adopt goodness and rightness.

- We find ourselves with a sense of duty and wonder who or what imposes that duty. Many believe that God defines the moral rules and imposes the duty to obey. God is thus a surrogate parent, and by obeying God's commands we gain divine reward and (we hope) avoid divine punishment. Others postulate an unseen world of values.

- From the Goodness point of view, the answer to why one should pursue what is good is straightforward. If you do, you will feel better and function better than if you don't. If you don't, you will feel and function worse.

- At Church every Sunday, do the white members of the congregation give you impression they know you right from your native origin, dose a particular white man looks at you with understanding you tend to understand things if you have lived in two different parts of the world where do I stand when my origin is missed with Yoruba's and Ibos from Nigeria and the Northerners are in between.

- If you have visited Britain from a third world nation within the 1970's came back from Nigeria or Ghana to stay later in the years what would you say was your experience then about churches in the UK from what it is now. I mean did you find out that most British do not attend church services as you experienced when you first had opportunity visiting the UK in the 1970's

- The fact that it is easy to justify adherence to moral rules on the basis of consequences, and easy to justify concern with goodness on the basis of consequences, but difficult to justify concern with consequences on the basis of moral rules, leads me to believe that a concern with goodness has logical priority over a concern with moral rules.

- What do you hold as an opinion of what people from your race holds as their religious rights now that you are in the UK?

- Focusing on being right promotes emotional distress, but seeking to increase benefits and reduce harms promotes emotional health.

- While you were in Nigeria there are all kinds of Christine denominations different in ways of worship through culture, tradition and lifestyles now that you are in Europe's getting to know the people do feel religious is about who you are as to material needs or is a hidden concept you have to discover if you have been good or bad in times of your life or let's say when you realise acceptances of your reality which is an individual aspect of each lives

- There is, of course, no way to compare one person's emotional state to another's. But one can compare, via memory, one's own emotional states at different times. This requires some degree of self-observation and consequent self-knowledge. If you put in the effort to do so, I think you will find out that focusing on how to obtain good outcomes is a much more pleasant way to live than focusing on who is right and who is wrong and feeling resentful and blaming toward those you think are wrong.

• Goodness is closer to reality in that it promotes recognition of the unity and connectedness of all things.

• Focusing on goods, one looks at the health of the whole and of each part of the whole. One seeks to include the parts in the whole. This approach is more conducive to recognition of Oneness and is thus more aligned with reality.

• For all these reasons, it makes more sense to frame ethical considerations in terms of good and bad, beneficial and harmful, or effective and ineffective, than in terms of right and wrong, proper and improper, or correct and incorrect. When asking any ethical question as to what should one do in a given situation, what kind of person one should strive to be, how to resolve conflict among persons or nations – frame the question in terms of goodness and badness, what is beneficial or harmful, to yourself and those around you.

• Self-realization is an expression used in psychology, spirituality and Eastern religions. The basic premise of self-realization is that there exists an authentic self which has to be discovered by psychological or spiritual self-striving. Self-realization can be gradual or instantaneous phenomena depending on the school of thought but in all cases it involves extensive preparation of mind and emotions to recognize self-realization when it occurs.

• Self-realization is a maturing of the ego or personality to accept its own evanescence and thus allow space for the true Self to reveal itself. The moon veiled by clouds is an apt metaphor for the Self's apparent absence in our everyday lives. The dissolution of the ego's obsessive, internal pre-occupations with its psycho-somatic complexes frees the psyche's energy to directly experience Reality of the world as it is, free of any assumptions.

• For the Hindu religion self-realization is knowledge of the true self beyond both delusion and identification with material phenomena.

• A branch should develop such concept of perfect existence, consciousness, bliss. Whereas the manifest universe which is a play of energy is temporal, the immutable principle or reality is beyond time. God is not exactly a being - because in order for there to be a being there has to be non-being - and it is said that such dualism within the differentiated reality does not exist in that state. It cannot be described, quantified, reasoned, or explained all of which exist on a differentiated basis only directly experienced as itself. Energy as an abstraction is eternal but its manifestations are continually changing. Therefore God represented himself in all things while being omnipresent and immanent in reality, if the universe ceases to exist at one point, it will eventually be reborn, in an immaterial form also eternal.

• The yearnings or desires cause the soul to seek out new manifestations. At death, though the gross body and senses die, the causality of those desires does not die. It seeks out a new corporeal existence. If the motive force is good, then the bound soul will go to any number of heavens, and if the motive force bad, it will go into any number of hells. The place where it goes is precisely motivated by its own nature. Hell is a place where there is suffering and ignorance. Heaven where there is adventure.

• But neither the heaven nor hell in that state for the bound soul is permanent. The soul while working off its previous karma also continually acquires new karma. Like a metal is hammered with new impressions, in the course of a life, the actions we reinforce shape the quality of the mind and the subtlest part of the mind is the soul. Therefore it is conceivable that if someone continually acquired bad karma by reinforcing bad actions they would remain in hell for a very long time. However, the soul always can be redeemed because there is a power of free will or independence from causality that originates from God himself.

• Good and bad is equivalent to knowledge and ignorance. Knowledge is good. Ignorance is bad. Ignorance leads to suffering and bondage. Knowledge leads to happiness and liberation. The highest heaven is said to be self realization because that state is eternal, pure, perfect, and rapturous. Therefore it is considered to be better than any sensual heaven such as those in the realms of the gods.

• In the western world 'self-realization' has gained great popularity. Influential in this popularity were psycho-analysis, humanistic psychology, the growing acquaintance with eastern religions, and the growing popularity of western esotericism.

• Though Sigmund Freud was sceptical of religion and esotericism, his theories have had a lasting influence on western thought and self-understanding. His notion of repressed memories has become part of western mainstream thinking.

• Freud's ideas were further developed by his students and neo-psycho-analysts. Especially Carl Jung, Erik Erikson and Winnicott have been important in the western understanding of the self. But also other alternatives have been developed.

• Jung developed the notion of individuation, the lifelong process in which the centre of psychological life shifts from the ego to the self.

• Erikson described human development throughout the life-span in his theory of psychosocial development.

• Winnicott developed the notion of the true self.

• Roberto Assagioli developed his approach of Psychosynthesis, an original approach to psychology.

• Humanistic psychology

• Abraham Maslow and Carl Rogers, leaders in the Humanistic Psychology movement, developed the concept of self-actualization.

• Based on Maslow, the most common meaning given to self-realization is that of psychological growth. It represents the awakening and manifestation of latent potentialities of the human being -for example, ethical, aesthetic, and religious experiences and activities.

• Maslow

• Maslow defined self-actualization as:

• The impulse to convert once self into what one is capable of being.

• Rogers

• According to Rogers, self-actualization involves the notion of self as process, instead of self as a 'thing'.

Spirituality is belief in an ultimate or an alleged immaterial reality; an inner path enabling a person to discover the essence of his/her being; or the 'deepest values and meanings by which people live.' Spiritual practices, including meditation, prayer and contemplation, are intended to develop an individual's inner life. Spiritual experiences can include being connected to a larger reality, yielding a more comprehensive self; joining with other individuals or the human community; with nature or the cosmos; or with the divine realm. Spirituality is often experienced as a source of inspiration or orientation in life. It can encompass belief in immaterial realities or experiences of the immanent or transcendent nature of the world.

Traditionally, many religions have regarded spirituality as an integral aspect of religious experience. Among other factors, declining membership of organized religions and the growth of secularism in the western world have given rise to a broader view of spirituality. The term 'spiritual' is now frequently used in contexts in which the term 'religious' was formerly employed.

That's if we believe cultism, false spirituality, juju, witchcraft, voodoo and rituals and the use of talismans still exist in the 21st century

Secular spirituality emphasizes humanistic ideas on qualities such as love, compassion, patience, tolerance, forgiveness, contentment, responsibility, harmony, and a concern for others, aspects of life and human experience which go beyond a purely materialist view of the world, necessarily accepting belief in a supernatural reality or divine being. Spiritual practices such as mindfulness and meditation can be experienced as beneficial or even necessary for human fulfillment without any supernatural interpretation or explanation. Spirituality in this context may be a matter of nurturing thoughts, emotions, words and actions that are in harmony with a belief that everything in the universe is mutually dependent; this stance has much in common with some versions of Buddhist spirituality. A modern definition is as follows:

'Spirituality exists wherever we struggle with the issues of how our lives fit into the greater scheme of things. This is true when our questions never give way to specific answers or give rise to specific practices such as prayer or meditation. We encounter spiritual issues every time we wonder where the universe comes from, why we are here, or what happens when we die. We also become spiritual when we become moved by values such as beauty, love, or creativity that seem to reveal a meaning or power beyond our visible world. An idea or practice is 'spiritual' when it reveals our personal desire to establish a felt-relationship with the deepest meanings or powers governing life.'

In a wide variety of traditions, spirituality is seen as a path toward one or more of the following: a higher state of awareness, perfection of one's own being, wisdom, or communion with God or with creation. Plato's Allegory of the Cave, which appears in book VII of The Republic, is a description of such a journey, as are the writings of Teresa of Avila. The Vedas and Upanishads also describe such a path of transformation.

Disciplines such a path entail may include meditation, prayer, and the contemplation of sacred texts; ethical development through the world social interactions. Love and/or compassion are often described as the mainstay of spiritual development if you love, you will be kind to others.

Religion
Whilst the terms *spirituality* and *religion* both relate to a search for an Absolute or God, and thus have much overlap, there are also characteristic differences in their usage. Religion implies a particular faith tradition that includes acceptance of a metaphysical or supernatural reality, whereas spirituality is not necessarily bound to any particular religious tradition. Thus William Irwin Thompson suggests that 'religion is the form spirituality takes in a civilization.'

Those who speak of spirituality outside of religion often define themselves as 'spiritual but not religious' and generally believe in the existence of different 'spiritual paths,' emphasizing the importance of finding one's own individual path to spirituality. According to one poll, about 24% of the United States population identifies itself as spiritual but not religious.

Since the scientific revolution, the relationship of science to religion and spirituality has developed in complex ways. Historian John Hedley Brooke describes wide variations: 'the natural sciences have been invested with religious meaning, with antireligious implications and, in many contexts, with no religious significance at all.' The popular notion of antagonisms between science and religion has historically originated with 'thinkers with a social or political ax to grind' rather than with the natural philosophers themselves. Though physical and biological scientists today avoid supernatural explanations to describe reality in consideration with naturalism in keeping with a general increase in interest in spirituality and complementary and alternative treatments, prayer has garnered attention among some behavioural scientists. Masters and Spielmans have conducted a meta-analysis of the effects of distant intercessory prayer, but detected no discernible effects.

Spirituality has played a central role in self-help movements such as Alcoholics Anonymous: '...if an alcoholic failed to perfect and enlarge his spiritual life through work and self-sacrifice for others, he could not survive the certain trials and low spots ahead....'
Philosophers across many traditions, from Stoicism to Buddhism, have suggested that a spiritual practice is essential for personal well being. Such practices do not necessarily include a belief in supernatural beings. Contemporary authors, too, suggest that spirituality develops inner peace and forms a foundation for happiness. Meditation and similar practices may help any practitioner cultivate his or her inner life and character.

If consciousness exists apart from the body, which includes the brain, one is attached not only to the material world, but to a non-temporal (spiritual) world as well. This thesis is considered to be analyzed by testing the reports from people who have experienced death.
Social scientists have defined spirituality as the search for 'the sacred,' where 'the sacred' is broadly defined as that which is set apart from the ordinary and worthy of veneration. Spirituality can be sought not only through traditional organized religions, but also through movements such as the feminist theology and ecological spirituality. Spirituality is associated with mental health, managing substance abuse, marital functioning, parenting, and coping. It has been suggested that spirituality also leads to finding

purpose and meaning in life.

Words translatable as 'spirituality' first began to arise in the 5th century and only entered common use toward the end of the Middle Ages. Spiritual innovators who operated within the context of a religious tradition often became marginalized or suppressed as heretics or separated out as schismatics. In these circumstances, anthropologists generally treat so-called 'spiritual' practices such as shamanism in the sphere of the religious, and class even non-traditional activities such as those of Robespierre's Cult of the Supreme Being in the province of religion.

Eighteenth-century Enlightenment thinkers, often opposed to clericalism and sceptical of religion, sometimes came to express their more emotional responses to the world under the rubric of 'the Sublime' rather than discussing 'spirituality'. The spread of the ideas of modernity began to diminish the role of religion in society and in popular thought. Ralph Waldo Emerson (1803–1882) was a pioneer of the idea of spirituality as a distinct field. Important early 20th century writers, who studied the phenomenon of spirituality, and their works, include William James, *The Varieties of Religious Experience* (1902), and Rudolph Otto, especially *The Idea of the Holy* (1917). The distinction between the spiritual and the religious became more common in the popular mind during the late 20th century with the rise of secularism and the advent of the New Age movement. Authors such as Chris Griscom and Shirley MacLaine explored it in numerous ways in their books. Paul Heelas noted the development within New Age circles of what he called 'seminar spirituality' structured offerings complementing consumer choice with spiritual options.

Study:
In the late 19th century a Pakistani scholar Khwaja Shamsuddin Azeemi wrote of and taught about the science of Islamic spirituality, of which the best known form remains the Sufi tradition (famous through Rumi and Hafiz) in which a spiritual master or *pir* transmits spiritual discipline to students.

Building on both the Western esoteric tradition and theosophy, Rudolf Steiner and others in the anthroposophic tradition have attempted to apply systematic methodology to the study of spiritual phenomena, building upon ontological and epistemological questions that arose out of transcendental philosophy. This enterprise does not attempt to redefine natural science, but to explore inner experience – especially our thinking – with the same rigor that we apply to outer (sensory) experience.

Spirituality Portals

- Afterlife
- Deities
- Parapsychology
- Quantum mysticism
- Reason
- Religion
- Scepticism
- Spiritual But Not Religious
- Supernatural
- Superstition
- Awareness

The supernatural (Medieval Latin: *supernātūrālis*: *supra* 'above' *naturalis* 'nature', first used: 1520–30 AD) is that which is not subject to the laws of nature, or more figuratively, that which is said to exist above and beyond nature. With neoplatonic and medieval scholastic origins, the metaphysical considerations can be difficult to approach as an exercise in philosophy or theology because any dependencies on its antithesis, the natural, will ultimately have to be inverted or rejected. In popular culture and fiction, the supernatural is whimsically associated with the paranormal and the occult, this differs from traditional concepts in some religions, such as Catholicism, where divine miracles are considered supernatural.

I often suffer with paronomasia in my capabilities including my writing skills, things am able to do, feel regardless of my past experience if am 'not Orunmila, I would not have been able withstand my life to write this book for example alone. I mean consider my background, upbringing, they way I am living my life, there is a strong unknown spirituality, resilience to live my life in certain expectations. What could have led to my strength, knowledge or willingness to search myself, my life and my whole existence? Regardless of my health and what people say or do about schizophrenia.

In Catholicism, while the meaning of the term and its antithesis vary, the 'Supernatural Order' is the gratuitous production, by God, of the ensemble of miracles for the elevation of man to a state of grace, including the hypostatic union (Incarnation), the beatific vision, and the ministry of angels. Divine operation, 'spiritual facts' and 'voluntary determinations' are consistently referred to as 'supernatural' by those who specifically preclude the 'extrinsic concurrence' of God or by those espousing a materialist or determinist worldview that excludes immaterial beings or free will. Barring disingenuous intent, there is no objection to this manner of speaking.

Catholic theologians sometimes call supernatural the miraculous way in which certain effects, in themselves natural, are produced, or certain endowments (like man's immunity from death, suffering, passion, and ignorance) that bring the lower class up to the higher though always within the limits of the created, but they are careful in qualifying the former as accidentally supernatural (*supernaturale per accidens*) and the latter as relatively supernatural (*prœternaturale*). For a concept of the substantially and absolutely supernatural, they start from a comprehensive view of the natural order taken, in its amplest acceptation, for the aggregate of all created entities and powers, including the highest natural endowments of which the rational creature is capable, and even such Divine operations as are demanded by the effective carrying out of the cosmic order. The supernatural order is then more than a miraculous way of producing natural effects, or a notion of relative superiority within the created world, or the necessary concurrence of God in the universe; it is an effect or series of effects substantially and absolutely above all nature and, as such, calls for an exceptional intervention and gratuitous bestowal of God and rises in a manner to the Divine order, the only one that transcends the whole created world... It is obvious also that this uplifting of the rational creature to the supernatural order cannot be by way of absorption of the created into the Divine or of fusion of both into a sort of monistic identity, but only by way of union or participation, the two terms remaining perfectly distinct.

Divine revelation of the supernatural order is considered to be a matter of fact, contingent upon proper evidence of such, (miracle, prophecy etc.). 'The revelation and its evidences are called extrinsic and auxiliary supernatural, the elevation itself retaining the name of intrinsic or, according to some theological supernatural.' The supernatural order was analyzed primarily by scholastic and post-Tridentine theologians. Theories denying or belittling the supernatural order are historically classified into three groups:

1. present *de facto* condition (Pelagianism, Beghards, Stoic influence),
2. the original status of man (Reformers such as Baius, Protestant and the Jansenist School),
3. possibility and evidence (Rationalist School, from Socinus to the present Modernists).

Rosmini … unwittingly, [may] have paved the way for them in the following vaguely Subjectivist proposition: 'The supernatural order consists in the manifestation of Being in the plenitude of its reality, and the effect of that manifestation is a God-like sentiment, inchoate in this life through the light of faith and grace, consummate in the next through the light of glory' (36th Rosminian proposition condemned by the Holy Office, 14 Dec., 1887). Preserving the dogmatic formulæ while voiding them of their contents, the Modernists constantly speak of the supernatural, but they understand thereby the advanced stages of an evolutive process of the religious sentiment. There is no room in their system for the objective and revealed supernatural: their Agnosticism declares it unknowable, their Immanentism derives it from our own vitality, their symbolism explains it in term of subjective experience and their criticism declares non-authentic the documents used to prove it. 'There is no question now,' says Pius X, in his Encyclical 'Pascendi' of 8 Sept., 1907, 'of the old error by which a sort of right to the supernatural was claimed for human nature. We have gone far beyond that. We have reached the point where it is affirmed that our most holy religion, in the man Christ as in us, emanated from nature spontaneously and entirely than this, there is surely nothing more destructive of the whole supernatural order.

From the commonly received axiom that 'grace does not destroy but only perfects nature' they establish between the two orders a parallelism that is not mutual confusion or reciprocal exclusion, but distinction and subordination. The Schoolmen spoke freely of nature's possibilities (*potentia obedientialis*) and even conations (*appetitus naturalis*) towards the supernatural. To those traditional methods and views some Christian writers have, of late, endeavoured to add and even substitute another theory which, they claim, will bring the supernatural home to the modern mind and give it unquestionable credentials. The novel theory consists in making nature postulate the supernatural. Whatever be the legitimity of the purpose, the method is ambiguous and full of pitfalls. Between the Schoolmen's *potentia obedientialis* and *appetitus moralis* and the Modernist tenet according to which the supernatural 'emanates from nature spontaneously and entirely' there is space and distance; at the same time, the Catholic apologist who would attempt to fill some of the space and cover some of the distance should keep in mind the admonition of Pius X to those 'Catholics who, while rejecting immanence as a doctrine, employ it as a method of apologetics, and who do this so imprudently that they seem to admit that there is in human nature a true and rigorous necessity with regard to the supernatural order and not merely a capacity and suitability for the supernatural such as has at all times been emphasized by Catholic apologists'

Process theology or *process thought* is a school of thought influenced by the metaphysical process philosophy of Alfred North Whitehead (1861–1947) and further developed by Charles Hartshorne (1897–2000).

It is not possible, in process metaphysics, to conceive divine activity as a 'supernatural' intervention into the 'natural' order of events. Process theists usually regard the distinction between the supernatural and the natural as a by-product of the doctrine of creation *ex nihilo*. In process thought, there is no such thing as a realm of the natural in contrast to that which is supernatural. On the other hand, if 'the natural' is defined more neutrally as 'what is in the nature of things,' then process metaphysics characterizes the natural as the creative activity of actual entities. In Whitehead's words, 'It lies in the nature of things that the many enter into complex unity' (Whitehead 1978, 21). It is tempting to emphasize process theism's denial of the supernatural and thereby highlight what the process God cannot do in comparison to what the traditional God can do (that is, to bring something from nothing). In fairness, however, equal stress should be placed on process theism's denial of the natural (as traditionally conceived) so that one may highlight what the creatures cannot do, in traditional theism, in comparison to what they can do in process metaphysics (that is, to be part creators of the world with God).

One complicating factor is that there is no universal agreement about the definition of 'natural' or the limits of naturalism. Concepts in the supernatural domain are closely related to concepts in religious spirituality and occultism or spiritualism. Additionally, by definition anything that exists naturally is not supernatural.

For sometimes we use the word *nature* for that *Author of nature* whom the schoolmen, harshly enough, call *natura naturans*, as when it is said that *nature* hath made man partly corporeal and partly immaterial. Sometimes we mean by the *nature* of a thing the *essence*, or that which the schoolmen scruple not to call the *quiddity* of a thing, namely, the *attribute* or *attributes* on whose score it is what it is, whether the thing be corporeal or not, as when we attempt to define the *nature* of an *angel*, or of a *triangle*, or of a *fluid* body, as such. Sometimes we take *nature* for an internal principle of motion, as when we say that a stone let fall in the air is by *nature* carried towards the centre of the earth, and, on the contrary, that fire or flame does *naturally* move upwards toward heaven.

Sometimes we understand by *nature* the established course of things, as when we say that *nature* makes the night succeed the day, *nature* hath made respiration necessary to the life of men. Sometimes we take *nature* for an aggregate of powers belonging to a body, especially a living one, as when physicians say that *nature* is strong or weak or spent, or that in such or such diseases *nature* left to herself will do the cure. Sometimes we take nature for the universe, or system of the corporeal works of God, as when it is said of a phoenix, or a chimera, that there is no such thing in *nature*, i.e. in the world.

And sometimes too, and that most commonly, we would express by *nature* a semi-deity or other strange kind of being, such as this discourse examines the notion of! And besides these more absolute acceptations, if I may so call them, of the word *nature*, it has divers others (more relative), as *nature* is wont to be set or in opposition or contradistinction to other things, as when we say of a stone when it falls downwards that it does it by a *natural motion*, but that if it be thrown upwards its motion that way is *violent*. So chemists distinguish vitriol into *natural* and *fictitious*, or made by art, i.e. by the intervention of human power or skill; so it is said that water, kept suspended in a sucking pump, is not in its *natural* place, as that is which is stagnant in the well. We say also that wicked men are still in the state of *nature*, but the regenerate in a state of *grace*; that cures wrought by medicines are natural operations; but the miraculous ones wrought by Christ and his apostles were *supernatural*.

The term 'supernatural' is often used interchangeably with paranormal or preternatural — the latter typically limited to an adjective for describing abilities which appear to exceed the bounds of possibility. Epistemologically, the relationship between the supernatural and the natural is indistinct in terms of natural phenomena that, *ex hypothesi,* violate the laws of nature, in so far as such laws are realistically accountable. Africa and America have uncovered more in the paranormals it's not everything you see on television that applies it's what you have seen and experience and confronted with, with criticisms.

Many supporters of supernatural explanations believe that past, present, and future complexities and mysteries of the universe cannot be explained solely by naturalistic means and argue that it is reasonable to assume that a non-natural entity or entities resolve the unexplained. Proponents of supernaturalism regard their belief system as more flexible, allowing more diversity in terms of intuition and epistemology.

Views on the 'supernatural' see it, for example, as:

- Indistinct from nature. From this perspective, some events occur according to the laws of nature, and others occur according to a separate set of principles external to known nature. For example, in Scholasticism, it was believed that God was capable of performing any miracle so long as it didn't lead to a logical contradiction. As a pedagogical exercise, a physics university instructor might ask what the aftermath would be, as nature returns to normal, following a hypothetical miraculous intervention by God, similar to a modern thought experiment. Some religions posit immanent deities, however, and do not have a tradition analogous to the supernatural; some believe that everything anyone experiences occurs by the will (occasionalism), in the mind (neoplatonism), or as a part (nondualism) of a more fundamental divine reality (platonism).

- Incorrectly attributed to nature. Others believe that all events have natural and only natural causes. They believe that human beings ascribe supernatural attributes to purely natural events, such as lightning, rainbows, floods, and the origin of life

Self-actualization is a term that has been used in various psychology theories, often in slightly different ways. The term was originally introduced by the organismic theorist Kurt Goldstein for the motive to realize one's full potential. In his view, it is the organism's master motive, the only real motive: 'the tendency to actualize itself as fully as possible is the basic drive...the drive of self-actualization.' Carl Rogers similarly wrote of 'the curative force in psychotherapy - man's tendency to actualize himself, to become his potentialities...to express and activate all the capacities of the organism.' However, the concept was brought most fully to prominence in Abraham Maslow's hierarchy of needs theory as the final level of psychological development that can be achieved when all basic and mental needs are fulfilled and the 'actualization' of the full personal potential takes place.

Kurt Goldstein's book *The Organism: A Holistic Approach to Biology Derived from Pathological Data in Man* (1939), presented self-actualization as 'the tendency to actualize, as much as possible, [the organism's] individual capacities' in the world. The tendency toward self-actualization is 'the only drive by which the life of an organism is determined'. However, for Goldstein self-actualization cannot be understood as a kind of goal to be reached sometime in the future. At any moment the organism has the fundamental tendency to actualize all its capacities, its whole potential, as it is present in exactly that moment in exactly that situation in contact with the world under the given circumstances.

Maslow's hierarchy of needs
The term was later used by Abraham Maslow in his article, *A Theory of Human Motivation*; Maslow explicitly defines self-actualization to be 'the desire for self-fulfillment, namely the tendency for him [the individual] to become actualized in what he is potentially. This tendency might be phrased as the desire to become more and more what one is, to become everything that one is capable of becoming.' Maslow used the term self-actualization to describe a desire, not a driving force that could lead to realizing one's capabilities. Maslow did not feel that self-actualization determined one's life; rather, he felt that it gave the individual a desire, or motivation to achieve budding ambitions. Maslow's usage of the term is now popular in modern psychology when discussing personality from humanistic approach.

A basic definition from a typical college textbook defines self-actualization according to Maslow simply as 'the full realization of one's potential'.

A more explicit definition of self-actualization according to Maslow is 'intrinsic growth of what is already in the organism, or more accurately of what is the organism itself...self-actualization is growth-motivated rather than deficiency-motivated.' This explanation emphasizes the fact that self-actualization cannot normally be reached until other lower order necessities of Maslow's hierarchy of needs are satisfied. While Goldstein defined self-actualization as a driving force, Maslow uses the term to describe personal growth that takes place once lower order needs have been met, one corollary being that, in his opinion, 'self-actualisation...rarely happens...certainly in less than 1% of the adult population.' The fact that 'most of us function most of the time on a level lower than that of self-actualization' he called the *psychopathology of normality*.

Maslow considered self-actualizing people to possess 'an unusual ability to detect the spurious, the fake, and the dishonest in personality, and in general to judge the people correctly and efficiently.'

Maslow based his theory partially on his own assumptions about human potential and partially on his case studies of historical figures that he believed to be self-actualized, including Albert Einstein and Henry David Thoreau. Maslow examined the lives of each of these people in order to assess the common qualities that led each to be to become self-actualized. In general he found that these individuals were very accepting of themselves and of their life circumstances; were focused on finding solutions to cultural problems rather than to personal problems; were open to others' opinions and ideas; had strong senses of privacy, autonomy, human values and appreciation of life; and a few intimate friendships rather than many superficial ones.

Maslow's Characteristics of Self-Actualization
A self-actualizer is a person who is living creatively and fully using his or her potentials. In his studies, Maslow found that self-actualizers share similarities. Whether famous or unknown, educated or not, rich or poor, self-actualizers tend to fit the following profile.

- *Efficient perceptions of reality.* Self-actualizers are able to judge situations correctly and honestly. They are very sensitive to the fake and dishonest.
- *Comfortable acceptance of self, others, nature.* Self-actualizers accept their own human nature with all

its flaws. The shortcomings of others and the contradictions of the human condition are accepted with humour and tolerance.

- *Spontaneity.* Maslow's subjects extended their creativity into everyday activities. Actualizes tend to be unusually alive, engaged, and spontaneous.
- *Task cantering.* Most of Maslow's subjects had a mission to fulfil in life or some task or problem outside of themselves to pursue. Humanitarians such as Albert Schweitzer and Mother Teresa represent this quality.
- *Autonomy.* Self-actualizers are free from reliance on external authorities or other people. They tend to be resourceful and independent.
- *Continued freshness of appreciation.* The self-actualizer seems to constantly renew appreciation of life's basic goods. A sunset or a flower will be experienced as intensely time after time as it was at first. There is an 'innocence of vision', like that of an artist or child.
- *Fellowship with humanity.* Maslow's subjects felt a deep identification with others and the human situation in general.
- *Profound interpersonal relationships.* The interpersonal relationships of self-actualizers are marked by deep loving bonds.
- *Comfort with solitude.* Despite their satisfying relationships with others, self-actualizing persons value solitude and are comfortable being alone.
- *Non-hostile sense of humour.* This refers to the wonderful capacity to laugh at oneself. It also describes the kind of humour a man like Abraham Lincoln had. Lincoln probably never made a joke that hurt anybody. His wry comments were gentle prodding's of human shortcomings.
- *Peak experiences.* All of Maslow's subjects reported the frequent occurrence of peak experiences (temporary moments of self-actualization). These occasions were marked by feelings of ecstasy, harmony, and deep meaning. Self-actualizers reported feeling at one with the universe, stronger

and calmer than ever before, filled with light, beautiful and good, and so forth.

In summary, self-actualizers feel safe, not anxious, accepted, loved, loving, and alive. Additionally, Schott discussed in connection with transpersonal business studies.

Psychology

Self actualization is at the top of Maslow's hierarchy of needs - becoming "fully human'...maturity or self-actualization' and is considered a part of the humanistic approach to personality. Humanistic psychology is one of several methods used in psychology for studying, understanding, and evaluating personality. The humanistic approach was developed because other approaches, such as the psychodynamic approach made famous by Sigmund Freud, focused on unhealthy individuals that exhibited disturbed behavior; whereas the humanistic approach focuses on healthy, motivated people and tries to determine how they define the self while maximizing their potential.

Stemming from this branch of psychology is Maslow's hierarchy of needs. According to Maslow, people have lower order needs that in general must be fulfilled before high order needs can be satisfied: 'five sets of needs - physiological, safety, belongingness, esteem, and self-actualization'.

As a person moves up Maslow's hierarchy of needs, eventually they may reach the summit — self actualization. Maslow's hierarchy of needs begins with the most basic necessities deemed 'the physiological needs' in which the individual will seek out items like food and water, and must be able to perform basic functions such as breathing and sleeping. While with an illness of schizophrenia today entering the 21st century one can feel that their breath is being stolen. Once these needs have been met, a person can move on to fulfilling 'the safety needs', where they will attempt to obtain a sense of security, physical comforts and shelter, employment, and property. The next level is 'the belongingness and love needs', where people will strive for social acceptance, affiliations, a sense of belongingness and being welcome, sexual intimacy, and perhaps a family. Next are 'the esteem needs', where the individual will desire a sense of competence, recognition of achievement by peers, and respect from others.

Some argue that once these needs are met, an individual is primed for self actualization. Others maintain that there are two more phases an individual must progress through before self actualization can take place. These include 'the cognitive needs', where a person will desire knowledge and an understanding of the world around them, and 'the aesthetic needs' which include a need for 'symmetry, order, and beauty'. Once all these needs have been satisfied, the final stage of Maslow's hierarchy—self actualization—can take place.

Classical Adlerian psychotherapy promotes this level of psychological development, utilizing the foundation of a 12-stage therapeutic model to realistically satisfy the basic needs, leading to an advanced stage of 'meta-therapy,' creative living, and self/other/task-actualization. Gestalt therapy, acknowledging that 'Kurt Goldstein first introduced the concept of the *organism as a whole* ', built on the assumption that 'every individual, every plant, every animal has only one inborn goal - to actualize itself as it is.'

Maslow's writings are used as inspirational resources. The key to Maslow's writings is understanding that there are no keys. Self Actualization is predicated on the individual having their lower deficiency needs met. Once a person has moved through feeling and believing that they are deficient, they naturally seek to grow into who they are, that is self-actualize.

Do you live and feel sometimes you are living with your last breath or you seem to take in breath into your lounges it encapsulate everything you own, fear, panic, anxiety? You feel fatigue but you are resilient in your work, at school hoping for the better of many things you have to do that are not in your power but only thinking of what you can do right in helping yourself in good or bad health. You can't eat, can't sleep the world is a state of the art it realize on you to be self actualized. How do you feel in a situation where health, suffering and expectations you seems helpless while other people can do almost anything you can't do? Yet you have to look forward this could happen within you, you and your family, friends, co-worker or school mates.

Criticism
Maslow early noted his impression that 'impulsivity, the unrestrained expression of any whim, the direct seeking for 'kicks' and for non-social and purely private pleasures...is often mislabelled self-actualization.' In this sense, 'self-actualization' is little more than what Eric Berne described as the game of "Self-Expression'...based on the dogma 'Feelings are Good".

Broader criticism from within humanistic psychology of the concept of self actualization includes the danger that emphasis on the actualizing tendency can lead to high positive views of the human being but one which is strangely non-relational. According to Fritz Perls there is also the risk of confusing self-actualizing and the self image actualizing the curse of the ideal by conflating the virtue of self-actualization and the reality of self actualizing. The latter becomes merely another measuring rod for the 'topgog'- the nagging conscience.

Maslow's hierarchy of needs, Outline of self, Humanism, Perfectionism (philosophy)
Power process, Self-esteem, Nirvana.

The self is the individual person, from his or her own perspective. To you, self is you. To a different person, self is that person. In relation to: Body, Brain / Mind / Intelligence, Character, Experience, Gender, Human, Human condition, Identity, Person, Personality, Skill, Virtue, Wisdom
Self constructs: Individual, Personal identity, Personality, Self-awareness, Self-concealment, Self-concept, Self-consciousness, Self-control, Self-identity, Self-image, Self-ownership, Self-perception, Self-realization, Self-esteem, Self-knowledge, Self-serving, Life stages/events.

Stages of life:, Infancy, Childhood, Adolescence, Adulthood,

Middle age, Old age.

Major life events: Birth, Education, Graduation, Coming of age, Employment, Marriage, Parenthood, Retirement, Death.

Much of the western world values the concept of individual rights. These rights vary from culture to culture, and by very definition, from person to person, and appear mainly in individualist societies. In considering the self, the most intimate legal relation would be what is codified as 'sui juris', or what laws have a purposed place so far as they are derived of the self.

In such cultures, it is generally considered that each and every individual has the following rights:

- *security rights* – protect people against crimes such as murder, massacre, torture and rape
- *bodily and property rights* – encompass 'ownership' of your own body and choosing what to do with it, as well as the fruits of the labour that spring forth from using your own body. ('Every man has a property in his own person. This nobody has a right to, but himself,' per John Locke, *Second Treatise on Civil Government*)
- *liberty rights of the Classical era* – protect freedoms in areas such as belief and religion, association, assembling, movement, and other self-determination (as an individual person), privacy from government and others, and freedoms from other paternalist meddling generally, whether by governments or others; also encompasses security, bodily and property, political, and due process rights, many group rights, some welfare rights, and (especially outside of the USA in the Classical era) equality rights, as all of those categories appear in this list
- *political rights* – protect the liberty to participate in politics by expressing themselves, protesting, voting and serving in public office
- *due process rights* – protect against abuses of the legal system such as imprisonment without trial, secret trials and excessive punishments; often overlaps with the bodily rights, listed above

- *equality rights* – guarantee equal citizenship, equality before the law and non-discrimination in regards to one's eligibility for all of the other rights in this list
- *welfare rights* (also known as economic or social rights) – require the provision of education and protections against severe poverty and starvation; generally an expansion of positive liberties
- *group rights* – provide protection for groups against ethnic genocide, and self-determination (as a group) and the ownership by countries of their national territories and resources; may overlap with the bodily and property rights, and Social equality rights, listed above

Personality traits: Extraversion and introversion, Agreeableness, Conscientiousness, Neuroticism / Emotional stability, Openness to experience.
Vices: Seven Deadly Sins, Pride, Vanity, Avarice, Greed, Lust, Wrath, Anger, Gluttony, Envy, Jealousy, Sloth, Laziness

Self-actualization: Action, Competence, Effectiveness, Efficacy, Success

Self management: Autodidacticism (self-education), Goal, Goal setting, Personal budget, Personal development, Personal finance, Problem solving, Self-actualization, Self-assessment
Self-awareness, Self-compassion, Self-consciousness, Self control, Self-defence, Self-discipline, Self-development, Self-disclosure, Self-efficacy, Self-enhancement, Self-esteem, Self-gratification, Self-help, Self-interest (disambiguation), Self-justification, Self-knowledge, Self-love, Self-monitoring, Self-motivation, Self-policing, Self-reflection, Self-regulated learning, Self-respect, Self-sufficiency, Self-verification, Stress management, Time management, The role of Hope and Personal Faith

Self-preservation and self-maintenance: Enlightened self-interest, Health, Housekeeping, Life extension, Personal hygiene, Personal safety, Physical fitness, Self-care, Self-preservation

Personal concepts: Adolescence, Adulthood, Aptitude, Birth, Infancy, Childhood, Competence (human resources), Death, Diary, Duty, Evil, Failure, Good, Freedom (philosophy), Freedom (political), Hobby, Home, Individualism, Individuality, Individuation, Influence, Intrapersonal communication, Liberty, Lifestyle (List), Meaning of life, Parenthood, Personal boundaries, Personal homepage, Personal income, Personal life, Personal property, Personal space, Personal time, Possession, Privacy, Reputation, Self-talk, Self-schema, Self-worth, Sex, Sexuality, Success, Taste (aesthetics), Taste (sociology), Thought, Virtue.

Harmful traits and practices: Abjection, Crime, Self-abasement, self-absorbed, Self-abuse, Self-blame, Self-criticism, Self-deception, Self-deprecation, Self-envy, Self-handicapping, Self-harm, Self-hatred, Self-immolation, Self-loathing, Self-pity, Self-propaganda, Self-punishment, Self-righteousness, Self-sacrifice, Self-serving, Self-victimization, Sexual self-objectification, Stress, Suicide.

Morality is the differentiation of intentions, decisions, and actions between those that are 'good' (or right) and those that are 'bad' (or wrong). The philosophy of morality is ethics. A moral code is a system of morality (according to a particular philosophy, religion, culture, etc.) and a moral is any one practice or teaching within a moral code. Morality may also be specifically synonymous with 'goodness' or 'rightness.' Immorality is the active opposition to morality (i.e. opposition to that which is good or right), while amorality is variously defined as an unawareness of, indifference toward, or disbelief in any set of moral standards or principles. An example of a moral code is the Golden Rule which states that, 'One should treat others as one would like others to treat oneself.'

All these in our modern lives have erased the impact of juju, voodoo and witchcraft they are knowledge based encapsulating them in our procedures in life makes more meaning than the relevance of witchcraft. They are more in the way of grooming ourselves religiously in relationship to mind and body problem, our souls, mind and in view of who and what we are. If Pagans could accept them as set rules and guidelines they are very powerful tools to achieve self actualization.

The development of modern morality is a process closely tied to the Sociocultural evolution of different peoples of humanity. Some evolutionary biologists, particularly sociobiologists, believe that morality is a product of evolutionary forces acting at an individual level and also at the group level through group selection (though to what degree this actually occurs is a controversial topic in evolutionary theory). Some sociobiologists contend that the set of behaviours that constitute morality evolved largely because they provided possible survival and/or reproductive benefits (i.e. increased evolutionary success). Humans consequently evolved 'pro-social' emotions, such as feelings of empathy or guilt, in response to these moral behaviours.

On this understanding, moralities are sets of self-perpetuating and ideologically-driven behaviours which encourage human cooperation. Biologists contend that all social animals, from ants to elephants, have modified their behaviours, by restraining immediate selfishness in order to improve their evolutionary fitness. Human morality though sophisticated and complex relative to other animals, is essentially a natural phenomenon that evolved to restrict excessive individualism that could undermine a group's cohesion and thereby reducing the individuals' fitness.

What moral virtue is entwined in Juju is juju a form of slavery? Juju is a word of either West African or French origin used previously by Europeans to describe the traditional West African religions. Today it refers specifically to objects, such as amulets, and spells used superstitiously as part of witchcraft in West Africa.

Juju is sometimes used to enforce a contract or ensure compliance. In a typical scenario, a juju spell will be placed on a Nigerian woman before she is trafficked into Europe for prostitution, to ensure that she will pay back her traffickers and won't escape. The witch doctor casting the spell requires a payment for this service. Juju is also commonly used in an attempt to affect the outcome of soccer games.

The term juju, and the practices associated with it, travelled to the Americas from West Africa with the influx of <u>slaves</u> and still survives in some areas, particularly among the various groups, who have tended to preserve their African traditions.

Contrary to common belief, voodoo (known as <u>Vodun</u> in West Africa) is not related to juju, despite the linguistic and spiritual similarities. Juju has acquired some karmic attributes in more recent times. Good juju can stem from almost any good deed: saving a kitten, or returning a lost book. Bad juju can be spread just as easily. These ideas revolve around the luck and fortune portions of juju. The use of juju to describe an object usually involves small items worn or carried; these generally contain medicines produced by witch doctors

In a country as deeply religious as West Africa, there is still great belief in juju acclaimed with supernatural forces regardless West Africa seems to have a two-tier belief system. On the one hand they believe in God/Allah, and attend church/mosque.

Yet they still believe in the power of non-Biblical or Koranic spirits to cause harm, misfortune, and death or heal sickness, with the same conviction that they believe in God/Allah.

The hunt for the fabled 'God particle' that lends mass to matter and holds the universe together could soon be over.

Scientists giving a progress report on the search later are expected to say they are almost at the point of confirming the existence of the Higgs boson.

Scientists at the Large Hadron Collider (LHC) - the 'Big Bang' particle accelerator which recreates conditions a billionth of a second after the birth of the universe - revealed they had caught a first tantalising glimpse of the Higgs.

Since then they have sifted through vast quantities of data from innumerable high energy collisions in an effort to reduce the odds of being wrong.

A statistical standard of proof known as 'five sigma' would be the ultimate confirmation of a discovery. In this case, the chances of a mistake are one in a million.

The scientists at Cern, the European Organisation for Nuclear Research in Geneva, are likely to announce a significant step further towards the five sigma goal.

They might even be at 'four sigma', a hair's-breadth away from having the Higgs in their grasp. In that case the final 'discovery' of the Higgs particle will be virtually a foregone conclusion.

Cern's director for research and computing, Sergio Bertolucci, said: 'We now have more than double the data we had last year.
'That should be enough to see whether the trends we were seeing in the 2011 data are still there, or whether they have gone away. It's a very exciting time.'

At the LHC, scientists shoot two beams of protons - the 'hearts' of atoms - at each other round 27km of circular tunnels at almost the speed of light.
When the protons smash together the enormous energies involved cause them to decay into an array of more fundamental particles. These may then decay further into yet more particles.

By following the decay patterns, scientists hope to see the 'fingerprint' of the Higgs boson.

Physicists need the Higgs to plug a gaping hole in the 'Standard Model', the theory that explains all the particles, forces and interactions making up the universe.

So far nothing has been observed to account for mass, and the fact that some particles weigh more than others.

Scientists at the Large Hadron Collider in Switzerland claim to have narrowed the search for the 'Higgs Boson', known as the elusive 'God particle'.

Two independent teams of researchers working at the <u>Cern physics research centre</u> in Switzerland say the particle is more likely to be found in lower mass or energy ranges. Fabiola Gianotti, an Italian physicist who heads the team running what's called the ATLAS experiment, said 'the hottest region' is in lower energy ranges of the collider. She said there are indications of the Higgs' existence and that with enough data it could be unambiguously discovered or ruled out next year. Several mass or energy ranges within the atom smasher are now excluded to a '95% confidence level,' she told other physicists at Cern.

Guido Tonelli, lead physicist for the team running what is called the CMS experiment, outlined similar findings, saying that the particle is most likely found 'in the low mass region' of the collider. The Higgs particle, or boson, is a key missing piece in the most widely accepted theory of physics - called the Standard Model - which describes how particles and forces interact. 'I am feeling quite a level of excitement,' said Oliver Buchmueller, one of the senior scientists seeking the particle following the latest developments. For more than a year, scientists at Cern have been firing particles in opposite directions around a 27km long ring-shaped tunnel 100 metres below ground. When the particles have accelerated to almost the speed of light, they are encouraged to collide. Sensitive detectors are then used to examine the debris for new particles.

There is still a possibility that the findings are down to chance disturbances, rather than a real observation. Further tests are planned. 'We are moving very close to a conclusion in the first few months of next year,' said Dr Buchmueller. The £6bn experiment is an attempt to replicate the conditions shortly after the universe was created 13.7 billion years ago in the Big Bang. The Standard Model of physics predicts that sub-atomic particles should have no mass. But, according to the theory proposed by some scientists, an invisible Higgs force field and an associated boson were created soon after the Big Bang. These create a drag on other particles, giving them mass.

If the Cern experiments confirm the Higgs boson exists, it would fix the biggest hole in the Standard Model - and give credence to what has been a largely mathematical model of how the universe works. But, if they showed it does not exist, it would shake the foundations of modern physics and force a massive rethink on the forces that glue the universe together. Scientists are to make an announcement that could bring us closer to discovering the mysteries of the universe. Clue To The Universe? Q&A On The Higgs Boson.

Scientists have revealed tantalising evidence of a mysterious force that binds the universe together – the Higgs Boson.

What is a Higgs Boson?
Physicists have tried to explain how the universe works in mathematical equations. But the sums just do not add up. According to the maths, the building blocks, or particles, that make up the universe should be whizzing around at the speed of light. In that scenario the planets, people and objects around us simply couldn't exist so, British physicist Peter Higgs proposed that there was an invisible force field that permeates the universe glues together the particles, giving them mass.

This is the Higgs field and it has an associated 'boson', a go-between that governs how sub-atomic particles react to the force field. Together they are called the Higgs Boson - and they make the maths work. So is that the 'God' particle?

The Higgs boson is popularly known as the God particle because it is invisible; its effects can be felt everywhere and it gives substance to everything in the universe. Most physicists cringe at the name, though. So they've found it? Not quite. But they think they've caught a glimpse.

Two parallel teams of scientists working at the Large Hadron Collider in Switzerland have both found 'bumps' on the graph that suggest the particle is real. But it could be a chance quirk, so the teams need to do more experiments - and they hope to confirm whether or not it exists next year. How do they do that? Scientists use the £6bn Large Hadron Collider, a 27km-long doughnut-shaped tunnel buried deep underground. They fire proton beams (hadrons) at almost the speed of light in opposite directions around the tunnel until they collide. These are conditions similar to the Big Bang theory of how the universe was created. And in the debris of the explosion they look for evidence for the Higgs Boson. So this is all about the Big Bang?

This so called God particles should not be mistaken from hidden Ogbanje Ochie's the Born-to-die, in African American Literature beware of kindred new spirits that end childhood lurking in sprouting new religions that reinvent the power of witches and wizards selling, suspicion and superstition to unsuspecting slumbering followers, to superficially bewitch emasculated by fear, minds entrapped or to be empowered while on earth.

All the particles in the universe would have been created in the aftermath of the Big Bang. But so far scientists have only been able to get a handle on 4% of the universe. The rest is made of dark matter and dark energy, which scientists can't see. They know it exists, though, from its effects on other celestial bodies. If the Higgs Boson does exist it could be the gateway to understanding how the Universe works. What if the Higgs Boson doesn't exist? Scientists say that if experiments find evidence that it doesn't exist, that would be just as interesting. It would mean physicists would have to go back to the drawing board and come up with a new mathematical explanation of how the universe works.

It would also mean astrophysicist Stephen Hawking wins his $100 bet that the Higgs Boson only exists in the heads of some scientists.

Prime Minister Stephen Harper went to New York, but he couldn't bother to walk a flew blocks and address the UN General Assembly, where leaders of other countries, including U.S. President Barack Obama, gave keynote speeches.

Then, Foreign Affairs Minister John Baird stood in the front of the world body and dismissed it as a useless debating society that was preoccupied with 'procedure and process.' The Conservatives, Baird lectured, want 'substance and results.'

Well, welcome to the club. It's hard to find any country that believes the UN is doing the job for which it was established after the Second World War. There's no question it needs reform, particularly the Security Council, but so far no one has proposed a formula that would be accepted by the world's nations.

Despite its problems, the United Nations is still a useful forum for multilateral engagement, even if some of its members are considered anathema to Canadian and western interests. And if it is unable to project force into troubled areas, such as Syria today, it's because there is wide disagreement among the world's nations on how to solve the problems that have emerged in the last 25 years.

Harper's snub, followed by Baird's lecture, were both undiplomatic, but at least the Conservatives did not threaten to quit the UN or abandon multilateral engagement.

Both are necessary, even if they do not always provide solutions to the problems facing the world.

Pharaoh advised his son do not let ambition cut off you princely lucks when Moses spoke to God in the Wilderness of fires I have no voice the voices say take your brother with you he would speak for you.

Most kids plug into the world of television long before they enter school. According to the Kaiser Family Foundation (KFF):

Two-thirds of infants and toddlers watch a screen an average of 2 hours a day kids under age 6 watch an average of about 2 hours of screen media a day, primarily TV and videos or DVDs kids and teens 8 to 18 years spend nearly 4 hours a day in front of a TV screen and almost 2 additional hours on the computer (outside of schoolwork) and playing video games.

The American Academy of Pediatrics (AAP) recommends that kids under 2 years old not watch *any* TV and that those older than 2 watch no more than 1 to 2 hours a day of quality programming.

The first 2 years of life are considered a critical time for brain development. TV and other electronic media can get in the way of exploring, playing, and interacting with parents and others, which encourages learning and healthy physical and social development.
As kids get older, too much screen time can interfere with activities such as being physically active, reading, doing homework, playing with friends, and spending time with family.

TV in moderation can be a good thing children get help learning the alphabet on television, wildlife on nature shows, and parents can keep up with current events on the evening news TV is an excellent educator and entertainer.

Despite its advantages, could too much television be detrimental Kids who view violent acts they say are more likely to show aggressive behaviour but also fear that the world is scary and that something bad will happen to them.

TV characters often depict risky behaviours, such as smoking and drinking, and also reinforce gender-role and racial stereotypes.
That's why they say, it's important to monitor the content of TV programming and set viewing limits to ensure that your kids don't spend too much time parked in front of the TV. There needs to be consideration on why some children do not like school. It also, depends on what types of programme the children watch I find out that watching and listening to news about how the GCSE battle goes on is a bit scary for some pupils.

If we watch TV with discretion it reflects on our personality sense of reasoning, common sense that sort of thing it could also reflect if you are a good listener, have sensible conversation with other people inversely TV is good to watch but the content, is at parental discretion if, they should complain, only use caution. If such qualities do not represents itself with pupils when they are young, parents could sort out other activities such as reading or writing. I have in my youth years lots of book it has in some ways helped me manage my illness of paranoid schizophrenia though process e.g. of thinking, using my own faculties, going through emotions, thoughts, mannerisms and feelings.

Heads have been protesting since the GCSE results were published

Head teachers say they remain committed to legal action in the unresolved dispute over GCSE English grades.

A summit of heads and teachers' unions met in Leeds to discuss the GCSE controversy - in which schools have protested that grades were unfairly manipulated downwards.

Head teachers' union leader Russell Hobby said the regulator Ofqual had 'lost credibility'.

Ofqual has rejected calls to regrade this summer's English exams.
'There was a great deal of anger expressed about Ofqual's retreat to statistical arguments,' said Mr Hobby, general secretary of the National Association of Head Teachers, after a meeting at Leeds Town Hall.

'The alliance remains committed to legal action as the current best way to ensure fairness for this year's GCSE students.

'Most delegates clearly felt Ofqual had lost credibility and expressed a desire to build a rigorous, profession-led examination system rather one that becomes the playground of politicians and business interests.'

The meeting in Leeds brought together representatives of the NAHT, the National Union of Teachers, the Schools Network and Leeds City Council.

Months after the results were issued dispute over the summer's results continues to rumble on - with the threat of legal action from an alliance of schools and local authorities.

Head teachers had argued that exam grade boundaries were shifted unfairly in an attempt to prevent exam results rising - meaning that C grades were pushed down to D grades.

Ofqual has rejected such claims and refused suggestions that the exam papers should be regraded.

The regulator said that examiners had acted properly and had set the boundaries correctly and that pupils had received the proper grades.

But further complicating the dispute, the Welsh government has ordered a regrading for its own pupils - many of whom were taking the same exam papers as their English counterparts.

The leaders of independent schools added their voices to the disquiet, publishing a report that claimed that the exam system had become unreliable and unfair.

Speaking ahead of a meeting, Councillor Judith Blake, Leeds City Council's executive member for children's services said: 'Here in Leeds we are determined to get a fair decision for our young people, which is why we are leading the national consortium calling for a judicial review.'
Pupils in England who took the disputed GCSE English exam could end up with a lower grade for exactly the same work as their counterparts in Wales.

This follows an order from the Welsh government to regrade GCSEs in Wales.

The WJEC exam board says it is being told to raise GCSE

grades in Wales while keeping them down in England.

The exam board says it wants conflicting regulators, Ofqual and the Welsh government, to find a more 'coherent and rational way forward'.

Head teachers earlier told the education select committee that many schools had been angered by what they thought had been unfair GCSE English results.

But Glenys Stacey, head of Ofqual, told the education select committee that she rejected claims of any unfair manipulation of results or suggestion of political interference.

'We played our proper part,' she told the investigation into this summer's controversial GCSE exam grades - and ruled out any further change in grades in England.

But the Welsh exam board, WJEC, has been ordered by the education minister in Wales to regrade the results in the disputed English exam - a requirement that would only apply to pupils in exam centres in Wales.

GCSE GRADING ROW

Issues with GCSE English grading emerged as results reached schools the month before.

Heads suggested the exams had been marked over-harshly after Ofqual told exam boards to keep an eye on grade inflation

Exam boards told reporter's grade boundaries had changed significantly mid-way through the year

Alterations were as much as 10 marks

Heads complained pupils who sat GCSE English in the winter might have got a lower mark had they sat it in the summer
Their unions called for an investigation and some mentioned legal action

Ofqual held a short inquiry but refused to order regarding.

Welsh Education Minister Leighton Andrews said that pupils should not have to 'live with the consequences of having been awarded what, in all likelihood, is the wrong GCSE grade' - and promised 'swift resolution of injustice'.

This places the exam board - which has more candidates in England than Wales - in what it calls a 'difficult and unexpected position'.

'We now find one regulator confirming that the decision made was correct, and another asking us to re-grade, reversing the previous joint decision,' says a spokesman for the WJEC exam board - which is believed to be the second biggest provider in the UK for this exam.

This would mean that within the common currency of the GCSE, there could be different levels of awards for the same piece of work from the same exam board, depending on whether the exam was taken in Wales or England.

The select committee had also been told by Ofqual that there had been concerns that pupils in Wales were performing at a lower level than in England - and that this had caused difficulties in setting grades with the WJEC exam board.

This confusion over the value of GCSEs comes against a background in which Education Secretary Michael Gove is preparing to overhaul the GCSE system for pupils in England.

On Tuesday morning, MPs on the education select committee had heard accusations from head teachers' leader Brian Lightman that there had been 'major flaws' in this year's GCSE English grades.

Mike Griffiths, head of Northampton School for Boys, told the select committee that the unreliability of the results in his school showed that 'Ofqual failed to maintain standards'.

Pupils who were given a D grade rather than the expected C grade could mean that difference between staying on at school or dropping out and becoming a Neet, said Kenny Fredericks, head of George Green's School in east London.

Mr Lightman, leader of the Association of School and College Leaders, told MPs that he believed that the exam grades for pupils taking the English GCSE in the summer had been been forced downwards in an attempt to balance an 'over-generous' marking in January - in a way that was unfair for individual students.

But Ms Stacey defended Ofqual's role in ensuring that the grades awarded for exams accurately reflected the level of achievement.

She said there had been many 'significant unknowns' in changes to modules of the GCSE English exam, which had to be resolved in the final awarding of grades.

Ofqual says that the June grade boundaries were set at the right level, but has acknowledged there was a problem with the January boundaries - and it has continued to refuse to order exam boards to regrade this year's exams.

Before the committee took evidence, the Times Educational Supplement published letters revealing the pressure put on one of England's largest exam boards, Edexcel to change its grade boundaries - in a way that prevented a rise in grades.

Ms Stacey told the select committee that if the exam board had not complied, she would have used her powers to force them to change the grades.

Shadow education secretary Steven Twigg called on Mr Gove to make all correspondence between Ofqual and the Department for Education 'publicly available at the earliest opportunity'.

Teaching unions are 'holding back' children by taking industrial action, the education secretary has said.

Michael Gove attacked members of the National Union of Teachers and NASUWT, who recently voted to take action short of going on strike.

The dispute is over pay, pensions and conditions.
Speaking at the Conservative Party conference in Birmingham, Mr Gove said union leaders shouldn't let their 'ideology hold back our children'.

In a speech to activists he said he had friends in the teaching unions and that being a teacher was 'the highest calling any of us can be called for'.
But he singled out union general secretaries who he said warned him not to identify successful schools because it made teachers from other schools 'feel uncomfortable'.

'How can we succeed as a country when every time we find success and celebrate it there are those who say 'no, someone might feel uncomfortable'?' the education secretary asked the Conservative conference.

'What I feel uncomfortable about is the soft bigotry of low expectations.'
Sean Coughlan BBC News education correspondent

Alongside a traditional conference season swipe at the teachers' unions - 'don't let your ideology hold back our children' - Michael Gove's speech had a much less traditional underlying message.

He talked of the 'dark secret' at the heart of English education - that it wrote off far too many children far too early, with the poorest most likely to be left behind.

He referred to a recent OECD report that the UK has among the most socially segregated education systems in the developed world.

The education secretary said that a system in which only an elite progressed was 'economic madness'.

The most successful international education systems made

sure that few failed to make the grade.

The education secretary borrowed an old phrase from George Bush - the 'soft bigotry of low expectations' - but his message revealed a subtle shift towards a new education system which could compete in a fast-changing, skill-hungry global economy.

NASUWT and the NUT represent nine out of 10 teachers in England and Wales.

Members from both unions have voted to work only to what it says in their contracts. This involves action such as refusing to cover for absent staff members and not invigilating exams.

In his speech Mr Gove accused union general secretaries of telling teachers not to 'devote themselves to children'.

'I have a simple message to those union general secretaries. Don't let your ideology hold back our children,' he said.

'At the moment the general secretaries of some of their unions are making it very difficult. The general secretaries are ordering - ordering - their members not to cover classes where another teacher might be ill or away at a relative's funeral,' he added.

The two unions recently launched joint action because of their 'serious concerns... about the way the present government is undermining the education system'.

In a joint statement the general secretaries of both unions listed unacceptable and excessive workload pressures, changes to pensions, pay freezes and the 'privatisation and academisation of schools' as the reasons for taking industrial action.

Responding to the education secretary's speech, Christine Blower, general secretary of the National Union of Teachers, said: 'Michael Gove does not have a monopoly of concern that all children and young people should have high aspiration and the very best teaching and support to achieve. In the NUT we believe this is best done in schools which are well supported by local authorities.

'The secretary of state continues to be obsessed with school structures despite there being no evidence to show that academies in themselves improve educational achievement.'

Chris Keates, general secretary of the NASUWT teachers' union, said: 'This attack on teachers taking lawful industrial action in defence of their statutory contractual rights and entitlements will be greeted with deep concern by the profession.

'Michael Gove appears to want to return schools to a past where teachers spent their days standing at photocopiers or undertaking bureaucratic form filling, rather than concentrating on teaching and learning.'

History meaning 'inquiry, knowledge acquired by investigation it's the discovery, collection, organization, and presentation of information about past events. History can also mean the period of time after writing was invented. Scholars who write about history are called historians. It is a field of research which uses a narrative to examine and analyze the sequence of events, and it sometimes attempts to investigate objectively the patterns of cause and effect that determine events. Historians debate the nature of history and its usefulness. This includes discussing the study of the discipline as an end in itself and as a way of providing 'perspective' on the problems of the present. The stories common to a particular culture, but not supported by external sources (such as the legends surrounding King Arthur) are usually classified as cultural heritage rather than the 'disinterested investigation' needed by the discipline of history. Events of the past prior to written record are considered prehistory.

Amongst scholars, the 5th-century BC Greek historian Herodotus is considered to be the 'father of history', and, along with his contemporary Thucydides, forms the foundations for the modern study of history. Their influence along with other historical traditions in other parts of their world, have spawned many different interpretations of the nature of history which has evolved over the centuries and are continuing to change. The modern study of history has many different fields including those that focus on certain regions and those which focus on certain topical or thematical elements of historical investigation. Often history is taught as part of primary and secondary education, and the academic study of history is a major discipline in University studies.

Historians write in the context of their own time, and with due regard to the current dominant ideas of how to interpret the past, and sometimes write to provide lessons for their own society. In the words of <u>Benedetto Croce</u>, 'All history is contemporary history'. History is facilitated by the formation of a 'true discourse of past' through the production of narrative and analysis of past events relating to the human race. The modern discipline of history is dedicated to the institutional production of this discourse.

All events that are remembered and preserved in some authentic form constitute the historical record. The task of historical discourse is to identify the sources which can most usefully contribute to the production of accurate accounts of past. Therefore, the constitution of the historian's archive is a result of circumscribing a more general archive by invalidating the usage of certain texts and documents (by falsifying their claims to represent the 'true past').

The study of history has sometimes been classified as part of the <u>humanities</u> and at other times as part of the <u>social sciences</u>. It can also be seen as a bridge between those two broad areas, incorporating methodologies from both. Some individual historians strongly support one or the other classification. In the 20th century, French <u>historian</u> <u>Fernand Braudel</u> revolutionized the study of history, by using such outside disciplines as <u>economics</u>, <u>anthropology</u>, and <u>geography</u> in the study of global history.

Traditionally, historians have recorded events of the past, either in writing or by passing on an <u>oral tradition</u>, and have attempted to answer historical questions through the study of written documents and oral accounts. For the beginning, historians have also used such sources as monuments, inscriptions, and pictures. In general, the sources of historical knowledge can be separated into three categories: what is written, what is said, and what is physically preserved, and historians often consult all three. But writing is the marker that separates history from what comes before.

Archaeology is a discipline that is especially helpful in dealing with buried sites and objects, which, once unearthed, contribute to the study of history. But archaeology rarely stands alone. It uses narrative sources to complement its discoveries. However, archaeology is constituted by a range of methodologies and approaches which are independent from history; that is to say, archaeology does not 'fill the gaps' within textual sources. Indeed, Historical Archaeology is a specific branch of archaeology, often contrasting its conclusions against those of contemporary textual sources. For example, Mark Leone, the excavator and interpreter of historical Annapolis, Maryland, USA has sought to understand the contradiction between textual documents and the material record, demonstrating the possession of slaves and the inequalities of wealth apparent via the study of the total historical environment, despite the ideology of 'liberty' inherent in written documents at this time.

There are varieties of ways in which history can be organized, including chronologically, culturally, territorially, and thematically. These divisions are not mutually exclusive, and significant overlaps are often present, as in 'The International Women's Movement in an Age of Transition, 1830–1975.' It is possible for historians to concern themselves with both the very specific and the very general, although the modern trend has been toward specialization. The area called Big History resists this specialization, and searches for universal patterns or trends. History has often been studied with some practical or theoretical aim, but also may be studied out of simple intellectual curiosity.

Black British are British people of black African descent, especially those of African-Caribbean background. The term has been used from the 1950s to refer to Black people from former British colonies in the West Indies (i.e., the New Commonwealth) and Africa, who are residents of the United Kingdom and consider themselves British. Others are also from former French-speaking colonies in Africa such as Senegal and the Democratic Republic of the Congo (which was Belgian), and many of the Black Africans in Britain still speak French as well as their own native languages.

The term 'black' has historically had a number of applications as a racial and political label, and may be used in a wider socio-political context to encompass a broader range of non European ethnic minority populations in Britain, though this is a controversial and non standard definition.

Black British is primarily used as an official category in UK national statistics ethnicity classifications, where it is sub-divided into 'Caribbean', 'African', and 'Other Black' groups.

The black population has increased from 1.1 million to over 1.5 million from 2001 to 2009, a growth of 40%. The UK has the second-largest black population in Europe, after France.

Historically, the term has most commonly been used to refer to Black people of New Commonwealth origin. For example, Southall Black Sisters was established in 1979 'to meet the needs of black (Asian and Afro-Caribbean) women'. 'Asian' in the British context means from South Asia only. 'Black' was used in this inclusive political sense to mean 'non-white British' the main groups in the 1970s were from the British West Indies and the Indian subcontinent, but solidarity against racism extended the term to the Irish population of Britain as well. Several organizations continue to use the term inclusively, such as the Black Arts Alliance, who extended their use of the term to Latin America and all refugees, and the National Black Police Association. This is unlike the official British Census definition which adheres to the clear distinction between 'British South Asians' and 'British Blacks'. It is to be noted that as a result of the Indian diaspora. Many British Asians are from families that have spent several generations in the British West Indies or East Africa. Consequently, not everyone born in, or with roots in, the Caribbean or Africa can be assumed to be 'black' in the exclusive sense.

Black British was also an identity of Black people in Sierra Leone known as the Krio who considered themselves British. They are generally the descendants of black people who lived in England in the 18th century and freed Black American slaves who fought for the Crown in the American Revolutionary War. In 1787, hundreds of London's Black poor a category which included the East Indian seamen known as lascars agreed to go to this West African country on the condition that they would retain the status of British subjects, to live in freedom under the protection of the British Crown and be defended by the Royal Navy. Making this fresh start with them were many white people, including lovers, wives, and widows of the black men.

African-American history is the portion of American history that specifically discusses the African American or Black American ethnic group in the United States. Most African Americans are the descendants of captive Africans held in the United States from 1619 to 1865. Blacks from the Caribbean whose ancestors immigrated, or who immigrated to the U.S., also traditionally have been considered African American, as they share a common history of predominantly West African or Central African roots, the Middle Passage and slavery.

It is these peoples, who in the past were referred to and self-identified collectively as the American Negro, who now generally consider themselves African Americans. Their history is celebrated and highlighted annually in the United States during February, designated as Black History Month, and it is their history that is the focus of attention in black history month.

Others who sometimes are referred to as African Americans, and who may self-identify as such in US government censuses, include relatively recent Black immigrants from Africa, South America and elsewhere who self-identify as being of African descent.

Africa is in a disposition to thrive people need certain qualities to thrive and contribute according to their potential in the new world of work:

- Adaptability: Openness to new ideas and experiences
- Achievement orientation: A need for continuous growth and the motivation to take ownership of own development, pushing oneself to achieve,
- Self-efficacy: Confidence in own ability to succeed and handle challenges

Expected outcomes
- Have greater levels of emotional maturity
- Be more self-aware and able to more effectively manage their own emotions
- Have the skills to build and maintain positive, constructive relationships, and more effectively deal with diverse people
- Experience greater work/life balance
- Experience greater levels of productivity and success

The organization will experience:
- A work environment where people thrive and grow
- Increased commitment and spontaneous contributions
- Accelerated development of high potential candidates or people with leadership potential.

The history of Africa begins with the prehistory of Africa and the emergence of Homo sapiens in East Africa, continuing into the present as a patchwork of diverse and politically developing nation states. Some early evidence of agriculture in Africa dates from 16,000 BCE, and metallurgy from about 4000 BCE. The recorded history of early civilization arose in Egypt, and later in Nubia, the Maghreb and the Horn of Africa. During the Middle Ages, Islam spread through the regions. Crossing the Maghreb and the Sahel, a major centre of Muslim culture was Timbuktu. Some notable pre-colonial states and societies in Africa include the Nok culture, Mali Empire, Ashanti Empire, Kingdom of Mapungubwe, Kingdom of Sine, Kingdom of Saloum, Kingdom of Baol, Kingdom of Zimbabwe, Kingdom of Kongo,

Ancient Carthage, Numidia, Mauretania, the Aksumite Empire, the Ajuuraan State and the Adal Sultanate.

From the late 15th century, Europeans and Arabs took slaves from West, Central and Southeast Africa overseas in the African slave trade. European colonization of Africa developed rapidly in the Scramble for Africa of the late 19th and early 20th centuries. Following struggles for independence in many parts of the continent, as well as a weakened Europe after the Second World War; decolonization took place.

Africa's history has been challenging for researchers in the field of African studies because of the scarcity of written sources in large parts of sub-Saharan Africa. Scholarly techniques such as the recording of oral history, historical linguistics, archaeology and genetics have been crucial.

In the western Sahel, the rise of settled communities was largely the result of domestication of millet and sorghum. Archaeology points to sizable urban populations in West Africa beginning in the 2nd millennium BCE. Symbiotic trade relations developed before the trans-Saharan trade, in response to the opportunities afforded by north-south diversity in ecosystems across deserts, grasslands, and forests. The agriculturists received salt from the desert nomads. The desert nomads acquired meat and other foods from pastoralists and farmers of the grasslands and from fishermen on the Niger River. The forest dwellers provided furs and meat.

Tichit (Dhar Tichitt) and Oualata were prominent among the early urban centres, dated to 2000 BCE, in present day Mauritania. About 500 stone settlements litter the region in the former savannah of the Sahara. Its inhabitants fished and grew millet. It has been found that the Soninke of the Mandé peoples were responsible for constructing such settlements. Around 300 BCE, the region became more desiccated and the settlements began to decline, most likely relocating to Koumbi Saleh. From the type of architecture and pottery, it is believed that Tichit was related to the subsequent Ghana Empire. Old Jenne (Djenne) began to be settled around 300 BCE, producing iron and with sizable population, evidenced in crowded cemeteries. Living structures were made of sun-dried mud. By 250 BCE, Jenne was a large, thriving market town.

Farther south, in central Nigeria, around 1000 BCE, the Nok culture developed on the Jos Plateau. It was a highly centralized community. The Nok people produced miniature lifelike representations in terracotta, including human heads, elephants, and other animals. By 500 BCE, they were smelting iron. By 200 CE, the Nok culture had vanished. Based on stylistic similarities with Nok terracottas, the bronze figurines of Ife and Benin are believed to be continuation of the tradition.

Traditionally, the Yoruba people viewed themselves as the inhabitants of a united empire, in contrast to the situation today, in which 'Yoruba' is the cultural-linguistic designation for speakers of a language in the Niger–Congo family. The name comes from a Hausa word to refer to the Oyo Empire. The first Yoruba state was Ile-Ife, said to have been founded around 1000 CE by a supernatural figure, the first oni Oduduwa. Oduduwa's sons would be the founders of the different city-states of the Yoruba, and his daughters would become the mothers of the various Yoruba obas, or kings. Yoruba city-states were usually governed by an oba and a iwarefa, a council of chiefs who advised the oba. By the 18th century, the Yoruba city-states formed a loose confederation, with the Oni of Ife as the head and Ife as the capital. As time went on, the individual city-states became more powerful with their obas assuming more powerful spiritual positions and diluting the authority of the Oni of Ife. Rivalry became intense among the city-states.

The ongoing debate about the need for social, economic and political reforms in Africa centres on issues of peace, security and development. Peace. Security and development are viewed as necessary conditions for social stability and the promotion of human security.

Conflict in a significant number of African countries has often resulted in severe disruption of social and economic development. Consequently, efforts to reduce poverty and sustain basic human rights have been severely constrained; leading to recurrence of violence where peace agreements have been sealed and the escalation of violence where conflicts have hitherto been latent.

Another significant problem faced by Africans is the understanding of the fundamental causes and conditions of violence and approaches to peace in Africa with all its peculiarities can only be achieved when Africans and others engage in the critical exploration of the African realities. It is in view of this, the aim is peered to review process to rigorously seeks to encourage the building of the field, combining the disciplines of peace and conflict studies, development, and human and social security.

The Oyo Empire rose in the 16th century. The Oyo state had been conquered in 1550 by the kingdom of Nupe, which was in possession of cavalry, an important tactical advantage. The alafin (king) of Oyo was sent into exile. After returning, Alafin Orompoto (c. 1560–1580) built up an army based on heavily armed cavalry and long-service troops. This made them invincible in combat on the northern grasslands and in the thinly wooded forests. By the end of the 16th century, Oyo had added the western region of the Niger to the hills of Togo, the Yoruba of Ketu, Dahomey, and the Fon nation.

A governing council served the empire, with clear executive divisions. Each acquired region was assigned a local administrator. Families served in king-making capacities. Oyo, as a northern Yoruba kingdom, served as middle-man in the north-south trade and connecting the eastern forest of Guinea with the western and central Sudan, the Sahara, and North Africa. The Yoruba manufactured cloth, ironware, and pottery, which were exchanged for salt, leather, and most importantly horses from the Sudan to maintain the cavalry. Oyo remained strong for two hundred years. It became a protectorate of Great Britain in 1888, before further fragmenting into warring factions. The Oyo state ceased to exist as any sort of power in 1896.

The Kwa Niger–Congo speaking Edo people. By the mid-15th century, the Benin Empire was engaged in political expansion and consolidation. Under Oba (king) Ewuare (c. 1450–1480 CE), the state was organized for conquest. He solidified central authority and initiated 30 years of war with his neighbors. At his death, the Benin Empire extended to Dahomey in the west, to the Niger Delta in the east, along the West African coast, and to the Yoruba towns in the north.

Ewuare's grandson Oba Esigie (1504–1550) eroded the power of the uzama (state council) and increase contact and trade with Europeans, especially with the Portuguese who provided a new source of copper for court art. The oba ruled with the advice from the uzama, a council consisting of chiefs of powerful families and town chiefs of different guilds. Later its authority was diminished by the establishment of administrative dignitaries. Women wielded power. The queen mother who produced the future oba wielded immense influence.

Benin was never a significant exporter of slaves, as Alan Ryder's book Benin and the Europeans showed. By the early 1700s, it was wrecked with dynastic disputes and civil wars. However, it regained much of its former power in the reigns of Oba Eresoyen and Oba Akengbuda. After the 16th century, Benin mainly exported pepper, ivory, gum, and cotton cloth to the Portuguese and Dutch who resold it to other African societies on the coast. In 1897, the British sacked the city.

The Niger Delta comprised numerous city-states with numerous forms of government. These city-states were protected by the waterways and thick vegetation of the delta. The region was transformed by trade in the 17th century CE. The delta's city-states were comparable to those of the Swahili people in East Africa. Some, like Bonny, Kalabari, and Warri, had kings. Others, like Brass, were republics with small senates, and those at Cross River and Old Calabar were ruled by merchants of the ekpe society. The ekpe society regulated trade and made rules for members known as house systems. Some of these houses, like the Pepples of Bonny, were well known in the Americas and Europe.

The Igbo lived east of the delta (but with the Anioma on the west of the Niger River). The Kingdom of Nri rose in the 9th century CE, with the Eze Nri being its leader. It was a political entity composed of villages, and each village was autonomous and independent with its own territory and name, each recognized by its neighbors. Villages were democratic with all males and sometimes females a part of the decision-making process. Graves at Igbo-Ukwu (800 CE) contained brass artifacts of local manufacture and glass beads from Egypt or India, indicative of extraregional trade.

Historical study often focuses on events and developments that occur in particular blocks of time. Historians give these periods of time names in order to allow 'organising ideas and classificatory generalisations' to be used by historians. The names given to a period can vary with geographical location, as can the dates of the start and end of a particular period. Centuries and decades are commonly used periods and the time they represent depends on the dating system used. Most periods are constructed retrospectively and so reflect value judgments made about the past. The way periods are constructed and the names given to them can affect the way they are viewed and studied.

Africans should:

- Build coalitions of institutions, interest groups and individuals with the common aim of seeking solutions to Africa's developmental and governance challenges;
- Promote peaceful civic action as a response to the threats of war and human rights abuses;
- Support dialogue, debate, and the free exchange of ideas across the African continent, especially focusing on the promotion of innovative and constructive approaches to the resolution of conflicts in Africa;
- Enhance democracy in Africa at local, sub-regional, regional, national and international levels, thereby increasing the legitimacy and accountability of African states and Africa-wide institutions;

- Support the creation and development of robust and principled civil society groups across Africa;
- Forge partnerships with a network of organisation to initiate and support civil society activities promoting justice, human rights, democracy and peace in Africa;

The <u>Ghana Empire</u> may have been an established kingdom as early as the 4th century CE, founded among the <u>Soninke</u> by Dinge Cisse. Ghana was first mentioned by Arab geographer <u>Al-Farazi</u> in the late 8th century. Ghana was inhabited by urban dwellers and rural farmers. The urban dwellers were administrators of the empire, who were Muslims, and the Ghana king, who practiced traditional religion. Two towns existed, one where the Muslim administrators and Berber-Arabs lived, which was connected by a stone-paved road to the king's residence. The rural dwellers lived in villages, which joined together into broader polities that pledged loyalty to the Ghana. The Ghana was viewed as divine, and his physical well-being reflected on the whole society. Ghana converted to Islam around 1050, after conquering <u>Aoudaghost</u>.

The Ghana Empire grew wealthy by taxing the <u>trans-Saharan trade</u> that linked <u>Tiaret</u> and <u>Sijilmasa</u> to Aoudaghost. Ghana controlled access to the goldfields of <u>Bambouk</u>, southeast of <u>Koumbi Saleh</u>. A percentage of salt and gold going through its territory was taken. The empire was not involved in production.

By the 11th century, Ghana was in decline. It was once thought that the sacking of Koumbi Saleh by Berbers under the <u>Almoravid dynasty</u> in 1076 was the cause. This is no longer accepted. Several alternative explanations are cited. One important reason is the transfer of the gold trade east to the <u>Niger River</u> and the <u>Taghaza</u> Trail, and Ghana's consequent economic decline. Another reason cited is political instability through rivalry among the different hereditary polities. The empire came to an end in 1230, when <u>Takrur</u> in northern <u>Senegal</u> took over the capital.

The Mali Empire began in the 13th century CE, when a Mande (Mandingo) leader, Sundiata (Lord Lion) of the Keita clan, defeated Soumaoro Kanté, king of the Sosso or southern Soninke, at the Battle of Kirina in c. 1235. Sundiata continued his conquest from the fertile forests and Niger Valley, east to the Niger Bend, north into the Sahara, and west to the Atlantic Ocean, absorbing the remains of the Ghana Empire. Sundiata took on the title of mansa. He established the capital of his empire at Niani.

Although the salt and gold trade continued to be important to the Mali Empire, agriculture and pastoralism was also critical. The growing of sorghum, millet, and rice was a vital function. On the northern borders of the Sahel, grazing cattle, sheep, goats, and camels were major activities. Mande society was organize around the village and land. A cluster of villages was called a kafu, ruled by a farma. The farma paid tribute to the mansa. A dedicated army of elite cavalry and infantry maintained order, commanded by the royal court. A formidable force could be raised from tributary regions, if necessary.

Conversion to Islam was a gradual process. The power of the mansa depended on upholding traditional beliefs and a spiritual foundation of power. Sundiata initially kept Islam at bay. Later mansas were devout Muslims but still acknowledged traditional deities and took part in traditional rituals and festivals, which were important to the Mande. Islam became a court religion under Sundiata's son Uli I (1225–1270). Mansa Uli made a pilgrimage to Mecca, becoming recognized within the Muslim world. The court was staffed with literate Muslims as secretaries and accountants. Muslim traveller Ibn Battuta left vivid descriptions of the empire.

Mali reached the peak of its power and extent in the 14th century, when Mansa Musa (1312–1337) made his famous hajj to Mecca with 500 slaves, each holding a bar of gold worth 500 mitqals. Mansa Musa's hajj devalued gold in Mamluk Egypt for a decade. He made a great impression on the minds of the Muslim and European world. He invited

scholars and architects like Ishal al-Tuedjin (al-Sahili) to further integrate Mali into the Islamic world.
The Mali Empire saw an expansion of learning and literacy. In 1285, Sakura, a freed slave, usurped the throne. This mansa drove the Tuareg out of Timbuktu and established it as a centre of learning and commerce. The book trade increased, and book copying became a very respectable and profitable profession. Timbuktu and Djenné became important centres of learning within the Muslim world.

After the reign of Mansa Suleyman (1341–1360), Mali began its spiral downward. Mossi cavalry raided the exposed southern border. Tuareg harassed the northern border in order to retake Timbuktu. Fulani (Fulbe) eroded Mali's authority in the west by establing the independent Kingdom of Fouta Tooro, a successor to the kingdom of Takrur. Serer and Wolof alliances were broken. In 1545 to 1546, the Songhai Empire took Niani. After 1599, the empire lost the Bambouk goldfields and disintegrated into petty polities.

The Songhai people are descended from fishermen on the Middle Niger River. They established their capital at Kukiya in the 9th century CE and at Gao in 12th century. The Songhai speaks a Nilo-Saharan language.

Sonni Ali, a Songhai, began his conquest by capturing Timbuktu in 1468 from the Tuareg. He extended the empire to the north, deep into the desert, pushed the Mossi further south of the Niger, and expanded southwest to Djenne. His army consisted of cavalry and a fleet of canoes. Sonni Ali was not a Muslim, and he was portrayed negatively by Berber-Arab scholars, especially for attacking Muslim Timbuktu. After his death in 1492, his heirs were deposed by General Muhammad Ture, a Muslim of Soninke origin.

Muhammad Ture (1493–1528) founded the Askiya Dynasty, askiya being the title of the king. He consolidated the conquests of Sonni Ali. Islam was used to extend his authority by declaring jihad on the Mossi, reviving the trans-Saharan trade, and having the Abbasid 'shadow' caliph in Cairo declare him as caliph of Sudan. He established Timbuktu as a great centre of Islamic learning. Muhammad

Ture expanded the empire by pushing the Tuareg north, capturing Aïr in the east, and capturing salt-producing Taghaza. He brought the Hausa states into the Songhay trading network. He further centralized the administration of the empire by selecting administrators from loyal servants and families and assigning them to conquered territories. They were responsible for raising local militias. Centralization made Songhay very stable, even during dynastic disputes. Leo Africanus left vivid descriptions of the empire under Askiya Muhammad. Askiya Muhammad was deposed by his son in 1528. After much rivalry, Muhammad Ture's last son Askiya Daoud (1529–1582) assumed the throne.

In 1591, Morocco invaded the Songhai Empire under Ahmad al-Mansur of the Saadi Dynasty in order to secure the goldfields of the Sahel. At the Battle of Tondibi, the Songhai army was defeated. The Moroccans captured Djenne, Gao, and Timbuktu, but they were unable to secure the whole region. Askiya Nuhu and the Songhay army regrouped at Dendi in the heart of Songhai territory where a spirited guerrilla resistance sapped the resources of the Moroccans, who were dependent upon constant resupply from Morocco. Songhai split into several states during the 17th century.
Morocco found its venture unprofitable. The gold trade had been diverted to Europeans on the coast. Most of the trans-Saharan trade was now diverted east to Bornu. Expensive equipment purchased with gold had to be sent across the Sahara, an unsustainable scenario. The Moroccans who remained married into the population and were referred to as Arma or Ruma. They established themselves at Timbuktu as a military caste with various fiefs, independent from Morocco. Amid the chaos, other groups began to assert themselves, including the Fulani of Futa Tooro who encroached from the west. The Bambara Empire, one of the states that broke from Songhai, sacked Gao. In 1737, the Tuareg massacred the Arma.

Around the 9th century CE, the central Sudanic Empire of Kanem, with its capital at Njimi, was founded by the Kanuri-speaking nomads. Kanem arose by engaging in the trans-Saharan trade. It exchanged slaves captured by raiding the south for horses from <u>North Africa</u>, which in turn aided in the acquisition of slaves. By the late 11th century, the Islamic <u>Sayfawa (Saifawa) dynasty</u> was founded by <u>Humai (Hummay) ibn Salamna</u>. The Sayfawa Dynasty ruled for 771 years, making it one of the longest-lasting dynasties in human history. In addition to trade, taxation of local farms around Kanem became a source of state income. Kanem reached its peak under Mai (king) <u>Dunama Dibalemi ibn Salma</u> (1210–1248). The empire reportedly was able to field 40,000 cavalry, and it extended from <u>Fezzan</u> in the north to the <u>Sao</u> state in the south. Islam became firmly entrenched in the empire. Pilgrimages to <u>Mecca</u> were common; <u>Cairo</u> had hostels set aside specifically for pilgrims from Kanem.

Around 1400, the Sayfawa Dynasty moved its capital to <u>Bornu</u>, a tributary state southwest of <u>Lake Chad</u> with a new capital <u>Birni Ngarzagamu</u>. Overgrazing had caused the pastures of Kanem to become too dry. In addition, political rivalry from the <u>Bilala</u> clan was becoming intense. Moving to Bornu better situated the empire to exploit the trans-Saharan trade and to widen its network in that trade. Links to the <u>Hausa</u> states were also established, providing horses and salt from <u>Bilma</u> for <u>Akan</u> gold. Mai <u>Ali Gazi ibn Dunama</u> (c. 1475–1503) defeated the Bilala, reestablishing complete control of Kanem.

During the early 16th century, the <u>Sayfawa Dynasty</u> solidified its hold on the Bornu population after much rebellion. In the latter half of the 16th century, Mai <u>Idris Alooma</u> modernized its military, in contrast to the <u>Songhai Empire</u>. Turkish mercenaries were used to train the military. The Sayfawa Dynasty were the first monarchs south of the Sahara to import firearms. The empire controlled all of the Sahel from the borders of Darfur in the east to Hausaland to the west. Friendly relationship was established with the <u>Ottoman Empire</u> via <u>Tripoli</u>. The Mai exchanged gifts with the Ottoman sultan.

During the 17th and 18th centuries, not much is known about Bornu. During the 18th century, it became a centre of Islamic learning. However, Bornu's army became outdated by not importing new arms, and Kamembu had also begun its decline. The power of the mai was undermined by droughts and famine that were becoming more intense, internal rebellion in the pastoralist north, growing Hausa power, and the importation of firearms which made warfare more bloody. By 1841, the last mai was deposed, bringing to an end the long-lived Sayfawa Dynasty.

The Fulani were migratory people. They moved from Mauritania and settled in Futa Tooro, Futa Djallon, and subsequently throughout the rest of West Africa. By the 14th century CE, they had converted to Islam. During the 16th century, they established themselves at Macina in southern Mali. During the 1670s, they declared jihads on non-Muslims. Several states were formed from these jihadist wars, at Futa Toro, Futa Djallon, Macina, Oualia, and Bundu. The most important of these states was the Sokoto Caliphate or Fulani Empire.

In the city of Gobir, Usman dan Fodio (1754–1817) accused the Hausa leadership of practicing an impure version of Islam and of being morally corrupt. In 1804, he launched the Fulani War as a jihad among a population that was restless about high taxes and discontented with its leaders. Jihad fever swept northern Nigeria, with strong support among both the Fulani and the Hausa. Usman created an empire that included parts of northern Nigeria, Benin, and Cameroon, with Sokoto as its capital. He retired to teach and write and handed the empire to his son Muhammed Bello. The Sokoto Caliphate lasted until 1903 when the British conquered northern Nigeria.

The Akan speak a Kwa Language. The speakers of Kwa languages are believed to have come from East and Central Africa, before settling in the Sahel. By the 12th century, the Akan Kingdom of Bonoman(Bono State) was established. During the 13th century, when the gold mines in modern day Mali started to dry up, Bonoman and later other Akan states began to rise to promince as the major players in the Gold trade. It was Bonoman and other Akan kingdoms like Denkyira, Akyem, Akwamu which were the predecessors to what became the all-powerful Empire of Ashanti. When and how the Ashante got to their present location is debatable.

What is known is that by the 17th century an Akan people were identified as living in a state called Kwaaman. The location of the state was north of Lake Bosomtwe. The state's revenue was mainly derived from trading in gold and kola nuts and clearing forest to plant yams. They built towns between the Pra and Ofin rivers. They formed alliances for defense and paid tribute to Denkyira one of the more powerful Akan states at that time along with Adansi and Akwamu. During the 16th century, Ashante society experienced sudden changes, including population growth because of cultivation of New World plants such as cassava and maize and an increase in the gold trade between the coast and the north.

By the 17th century, Osei Kofi Tutu I (c. 1695–1717), with help of Okomfo Anokye, unified what became the Ashante into a confederation with the Golden Stool as a symbol of their unity and spirit. Osei Tutu engaged in a massive territorial expansion. He built up the Ashante army based on the Akan state of Akwamu, introducing new organization and turning a disciplined militia into an effective fighting machine. In 1701, the Ashante conquered Denkyira, giving them access to the coastal trade with Europeans, especially the Dutch. Opoku Ware I (1720–1745) engaged in further expansion, adding other southern Akan states to the growing empire. He turned north adding Techiman, Banda, Gyaaman, and Gonja, states on the Black Volta. Between 1744 and 1745, Asantehene Opoku attacked the powerful northern state of Dagomba, gaining control of the important middle Niger trade routes. Kusi Obodom (1750–1764) succeeded Opoku. He solidified all the newly won territories. Osei Kwadwo (1777–1803) imposed administrative reforms that allowed the empire to be governed effectively and to continue its military expansion. Osei Kwame Panyin (1777–1803), Osei Tutu Kwame (1804–1807), and Osei Bonsu (1807–1824) continued territorial comsolidation and expansion. The Ashante Empire included all of present-day Ghana and large parts of Côte d'Ivoire.

The ashantehene inherited his position from his mother. He was assisted at the capital, Kumasi, by a civil service of men talented in trade, diplomacy, and the military, with a head called the Gyaasehene. Men from Arabia, Sudan, and Europe were employed in the civil service, all of them appointed by the ashantehene. At the capital and in other towns, the ankobia or special police were used as bodyguards to the ashantehene, as sources of intelligence, and to suppress rebellion. Communication throughout the empire was maintained via a network of well-kept roads from the coast to the middle Niger and linking together other trade cities.

For most of the 19th century, the Ashante Empire remained powerful. It was later destroyed in 1900 by British superior weaponry and organization following the four <u>Anglo-Ashanti wars</u>.
During this era a sense of local patriotism or nationalism took deeper root among African intellectuals and politicians. Some of the inspiration for this movement came from the First World War in which European countries had relied on colonial troops for their own defence. Many in Africa realized their own strength with regard to the colonizer for the first time. At the same time, some of the mystique of the 'invincible' European was shattered by the barbarities of the war. However, in most areas European control remained relatively strong during this period.

Social history, sometimes called the new social history, is the field that includes history of ordinary people and their strategies and institutions for coping with life. In its 'golden age' it was a major growth field in the 1960s and 1970s among scholars, and still is well represented in history departments. In two decades from 1975 to 1995, the proportion of professors of history in American universities identifying with social history rose from 31% to 41%, while the proportion of political historians fell from 40% to 30%.

In the history departments of British universities in 2007, of the 5723 faculty members, 1644 (29%) identified themselves with social history while <u>political history</u> came next with 1425 (25%). The 'old' social history before the 1960s was a hodgepodge of topics without a central theme, and it often included political movements, like Populism, that were 'social' in the sense of being outside the elite system. Social history was contrasted with political history, intellectual history and the history of great men. English historian G. M. Trevelyan saw it as the bridging point between economic and political history, reflecting that, 'Without social history, economic history is barren and political history unintelligible.' While the field has often been viewed negatively as history with the politics left out, it has also been defended as 'history with the people put back in.'

After World War I the formerly German colonies in Africa were taken over by France, Belgium, and the United Kingdom. Italy, under the government of Benito Mussolini, invaded Ethiopia, the last independent African nation, in 1935 and occupied the country until 1941.

The decolonization of Africa started with Libya in 1951 although Liberia, South Africa, Egypt and Ethiopia were already independent. Many countries followed in the 1950s and 1960s, with a peak in 1960 with independence of a large part of French West Africa. Most of the remaining countries gained independence throughout the 1960s, although some colonizers (Portugal in particular) were reluctant to relinquish sovereignty, resulting in bitter wars of independence which lasted for a decade or more. The last African countries to gain formal independence were Guinea-Bissau (1974), Mozambique (1975) and Angola (1975) from Portugal; Djibouti from France in 1977; Zimbabwe from United Kingdom in 1980; and Namibia from South Africa in 1990. Eritrea later split off from Ethiopia in 1993. Because many cities were founded, enlarged and renamed by the Europeans, after independence many place names were renamed.

World peace is an ideal of freedom, peace, and happiness among and within all nations and/or people. World peace is an idea of planetary non-violence by which nations willingly cooperate, either voluntarily or by virtue of a system of governance that prevents warfare. The term is sometimes used to refer to a cessation of all hostility among all individuals. For example, World Peace could be crossing boundaries via human rights, animal rights technology, education, engineering, medicine, diplomats and/or an end to all forms of fighting. Since 1945 the United Nations and the 5 permanent members of the Security Council (the US, Russia, China, France, and the UK) have worked to resolve conflicts without declarations of war. However, the United States and other nations have entered several military conflicts since that time.

Even without a declaration of war, the use of military force prevents the realization of World Peace. Many interpretations of peace and conflict in Africa are too simplistic while infarct, it is wrecking African nation like a disease it is affecting some parts of the world. I came to Europe to find peace and make friends we Africans should not give ourselves the craps here as we do to ourselves in Africa here if one has problem, there are people to talk to who can help over there in Africa, and we do not give ourselves help out of concern.

Families are facing disruption and breakdown each day their wealth, property and livelihood taken from them by people who want by drastic means to take over within African this is moving into Britain offsetting our livelihood here even here in Britain a Jamaican treats an African with indifference so dose a Caribbean if so, what would the Indians or Asians make out of us?

Ghanaians' want to imply in Britain they come first because they come first in having their independence Nigeria which should have become more democratic, with the three regions South, East and North uniting for common goals still remains something to achieve leaders should understand their importance on the basis of uniting Africa at home and abroad. Other African nations should do the same regardless of conflict call for peace within the countries make leaders understand enslaving their nation is bad for the countries welfare try as much as possible to give clear and sound advice and undertaking towards a united Africa some of the countries recourses are being squandered by leaders themselves it should stop. The turn up of events entering the 21st centuries should lead to greater peace measure not an excuse to create further conflicts. Our faith, belief religion and culture enable us to live in peace, love one another not diversify us or being self centred towards one another. Religion is politics how to get richer quickly make fixation among one another that is not what they do here in Britain or America can we please understand that in certain ways we are offsetting their lives, they are making amends calling for peace an aim to unite the world towards common goal that we need not be diversified our leaders should start thinking. There situations in third world countries that are similar to what we have here in Europe one can still live in it with tolerance this is something I hope within developing nations conflict is not a solution in our divers ways of life relating to our religion, beliefs, creed, origin, culture or tradition why not condole ourselves to live in harmony to make the world a better place for some people it seems as if the world is coming to an end why wouldn't our leaders rise and give us hope what more can people ask of their leaders.

Following World War II, nationalist movements arose across West Africa, most notably in Ghana under Kwame Nkrumah. In 1957, Ghana became the first sub-Saharan colony to achieve its independence, followed the next year by France's colonies; by 1974, West Africa's nations were entirely autonomous. Since independence, many West African nations have been plagued by corruption and instability, with notable civil wars in Nigeria, Sierra Leone, Liberia, and Côte d'Ivoire, and a succession of military coups in Ghana and Burkina Faso. Many states have failed to develop their economies despite enviable natural resources, and political instability is often accompanied by undemocratic government.

In 1948 the apartheid laws were started in South Africa by the dominant National Party. These were largely a continuation of existing policies; the difference was the policy of 'separate development.' Where previous policies had only been disparate efforts to economically exploit the African majority, apartheid represented an entire philosophy of separate racial goals, leading to both the divisive laws of 'petty apartheid,' and the grander scheme of African homelands.

In 1994, the South African government abolished apartheid. South Africans elected <u>Nelson Mandela</u> of the <u>African National Congress</u> in the country's first multiracial presidential election.

Philosophy of history is a branch of philosophy concerning the eventual significance, if any, of human history. Furthermore, it speculates as to a possible teleological end to its development that is, it asks if there is a design, purpose, directive principle, or finality in the processes of human history.

Aretha Louise Franklin (born March 25, 1942) is an American <u>musician</u>, <u>singer</u>, <u>songwriter</u>, and <u>pianist</u>. In a recording career that has spanned over half a century, Franklin's repertoire has included <u>gospel</u>, <u>jazz</u>, <u>blues</u>, <u>R&B</u>, <u>pop</u>, <u>rock</u> and <u>funk</u>.

Franklin is known as one of the most important popularisers' of the <u>soul</u> music genre and is referred to as the <u>Queen of Soul</u>, a title she was given early in her career. Franklin, the daughter of prominent <u>Baptist</u> <u>minister</u> and <u>activist</u> <u>C. L. Franklin</u>, began her singing career singing in her father's church at the age of ten and started recording four years later. After several years in the gospel circuit and with her father's blessing, she formed a secular pop music career at the age of eighteen, signing with <u>Columbia Records</u>, where she was branded by its CEO <u>John Hammond</u> as his most important act since <u>Billie Holiday</u>. Aretha Franklin is one of my favourite artist all her songs means something to me one of her songs which inspires me is if ever a love there was featuring the four Tops and Kenny G: I saw your face as I hurried past the café and the rain felt like long lost tears as it trickled

Love is an <u>emotion</u> of a strong <u>affection</u> and personal <u>attachment</u>. Love is also said to be a <u>virtue</u> representing all of human <u>kindness</u>, <u>compassion</u>, and affection —'the unselfish loyal and benevolent concern for the good of another'. Love may describe compassionate and affectionate actions towards other humans, one's self or animals.

In English, love refers to a variety of different feelings, states, and attitudes, ranging from pleasure to <u>interpersonal attraction</u> 'Love' may refer specifically to the passionate desire and intimacy of <u>romantic love</u>, to emotional closeness of <u>familial</u> love, to the <u>platonic love</u> that defines <u>friendship</u>, or to the profound <u>oneness</u> or devotion of <u>religious love</u>, or to a concept of love that encompasses all of those feelings. This diversity of uses and meanings, combined with the complexity of the feelings involved, makes love unusually difficult to consistently define, compared to other emotional states. Music gladdens the human heart and mind we have made more music to last us a life time and to contemplate on in this era the age of reasoning each life should contemplate and make reason out of their existence as it is, the age of reasoning, it is also the age for action to better human existence at least understand, where we are heading for.

These are times for positive psychology human functioning to build, give and understand scientific understanding and effective interventions to build thriving individuals, families, and communities.' Positive psychologists seek 'to find and nurture genius and talent', and 'to make normal life more fulfilling', rather than merely treating <u>mental illness</u>.

To complement and focus, not to replace or ignore the rest of psychology but seek to understand why and how things go wrong. To emphasize the importance of using <u>method</u>s to determine and understand how things would go right. This field brings attention to the possibility that focusing only on the disorder itself would result in only a partial understanding of a patient's condition.

<u>Researchers in the field</u> analyze things like states of <u>pleasure</u> or <u>flow</u>, values, strengths, virtues, talents, as well as the ways that they can be promoted by social systems and institutions. Positive psychologists are concerned with four topics positive experiences, enduring psychological traits, positive relationships and positive institutions. Psychology has seen various practical applications such as emotional wellbeing.

Love in its various forms acts as a major facilitator of interpersonal relationships and, owing to its central psychological importance, is one of the most common themes in the creative arts.

Love may be understood as part of the survival instinct, a function to keep human beings together against menaces and to facilitate the continuation of all species.

Peace, happiness and unity should be all human universal goal based on idea of moral duty. Good will is the only intrinsically good thing an action is only good if performed out of duty, Humanity as an end in itself ensures the motivation behind every action must be the good of humanity. Rationalism is appealing to reason as a source of knowledge or justification in more technical terms, it is a method or a theory 'in which the criterion of the truth is not sensory but intellectual and deductive.

Peace is a state of harmony characterized by the lack of violent conflict and the freedom from fear of violence. Commonly understood as the absence of hostility, peace also suggests the existence of healthy or newly healed interpersonal or international relationships, prosperity in matters of social or economic welfare, the establishment of equality, and a working political order that serves the true interests of all. In international relations, peacetime is not only the absence of war or violent conflict, but also the presence of positive and respectful cultural and economic relationships.

The shadows our lives cast or conveys remarkable and incredible legacy creating amazing touch on someone else's journey, producing a ripple effect in each life, and having an incredible adventure in the process. We are born to be in relationships to one another, and make impact in each other's lives as we customary would do for ourselves it leads to one thing that is to better our existence leaning on each other, walking in love, and praying faithfully, we let go of the weights we are not meant to carry. We should be counting more on our achievements' and blessings and paving ways to move forwards.

Positive psychology finds its roots in the humanistic psychology of the 20th century focusing heavily on happiness and fulfillment. Earlier influences on positive psychology came primarily from philosophical and religious sources, as scientific psychology did not take its modern form until the late 19th century. Judaism promotes a Divine command theory of happiness: happiness and rewards follow from following the commands of the divine.

The ancient Greeks had many schools of thought. Socrates advocated self-knowledge as the path to happiness. Plato's allegory of the cave influenced western thinkers who believe that happiness is found by finding deeper meaning. Aristotle believed that happiness, or eudaimonia is constituted by rational activity in accordance with virtue over a complete life.

The Epicureans believed in reaching happiness through the enjoyment of simple pleasures. The Stoics believed they could remain happy by being objective and reasonable, and they ascribe to many spiritual exercises.

Christianity continued to follow the Divine command theory of happiness. In the middle Ages, Christianity taught that true happiness would not be found until the afterlife. The seven deadly sins are about earthly self-indulgence and narcissism. On the other hand, the Four Cardinal Virtues and Three Theological Virtues were supposed to keep one from sin.

During the Renaissance and Age of Enlightenment, individualism came to be valued. Simultaneously, creative individuals gained prestige, as they were now considered to be artists, not just craftsmen. Some philosophers believed moral actions are actions that maximize happiness for the most number of people, suggesting an empirical science of happiness should be used to determine which actions are moral a science of morality. Life, liberty and the pursuit of happiness' are inalienable rights.

The Romantics valued individual emotional expression and sought their emotional 'true selves,' which were unhindered by social norms. At the same time, love and intimacy became the main motivations for people to have a relationship. Happiness encompasses many different emotional and mental phenomena so dose beauty, ugliness and death. But when a person experiences an unexplained sudden decline in functioning, health, or disposition, it may be caused by a syndrome known as 'Failure to Thrive'.

Read part two of this book titled Memories of Schizophrenia.

www.ingramcontent.com/pod-product-compliance
Lightning Source LLC
Chambersburg PA
CBHW020652270326
41928CB00005B/78